Chris Evans

June 1987

A proletarian science
Marxism in Britain 1917–1933

D1615274

A proletarian science

Marxism in Britain 1917–1933

STUART MACINTYRE

Formerly Research Fellow, St John's College, Cambridge

LAWRENCE AND WISHART

LONDON

First published by
Cambridge University Press 1980

© Cambridge University Press 1980

First paperback edition,
with corrections,
published by
Lawrence and Wishart 1986

Set by Western Printing Services
Printed and bound in Great Britain at
Oxford University Press

Nae simple rhymes for silly folk
But the haill art, as Lenin gied
Nae Marx-without-tears to workin' men
But the fu' course insteed.

Hugh MacDiarmid
Second Hymn to Lenin

Contents

Tables and figures

Preface

This book originated as a doctoral thesis. Much of the published version is new, and a good part of the remainder has been extensively re-written, so that I hope it does not betray too many of the characteristics commonly associated with that genre. If I have retained a high proportion of the quotations and citations that sometimes displace argument from the dissertation, it is no longer in order to persuade an examiner of my industry, but rather because I feel that they are best able to convey a sense of my subject. Contrary to the experience of some, the period I spent researching and writing my doctoral thesis was fruitful and enjoyable – under what other circumstances is one enabled to spend three uninterrupted years on a research project?

In the preparation of the thesis I received valuable suggestions from Professor Alan McBriar and the late Dr Maurice Dobb. I am indebted to my examiners, Professors Royden Harrison and Eric Hobsbawm, who made fundamental and challenging criticism seem almost painless. Above all, I am grateful to Dr Henry Pelling who indulged my errant enthusiasms, encouraged me in periods of self-doubt and helped me in many other ways far beyond the course of a supervisor's duties.

I have been fortunate to have worked on the manuscript of the book while a research fellow of St John's College, Cambridge and I thank the Master and Fellows of the College both for this and for other forms of assistance. During the process of revision I benefited in particular from the comments of Alastair Reid, who read the penultimate draft and enabled me to see the central problems afresh. Mrs Elizabeth Wetton and Mr Eric Van Tassel guided the manuscript through the press, and I am grateful for their assistance. I have a long-standing debt to Hywel Francis and his collaborators in the creation of the South Wales Miners' Library, which stands as a reminder of what it is possible to do in the preservation and use of the materials of labour history. John Foster has striven to collect oral history in the Clyde area, and I thank him for making it available to me. Mr J. P. M. Millar allowed me to use the archives of the National Council of Labour Colleges. Vivien Morton let me read the unpublished part of her father's autobiography in the most pleasant of surroundings. With her husband she recalled for me many of the individuals who appear in this book, as too did Bill and Frances Moore of Sheffield. It would be invidious to single out others who participated in the events with which this study is concerned and who have been able to recall those events with clarity, critical awareness and pride. Neither they nor any of the others mentioned here are responsible for my interpretation; but I would like to dedicate the book to the memory of all those who struggled and sacrificed to create the Marxism of the 1920s.

August 1978   S.F.M.

Abbreviations

B.S.P.	British Socialist Party
C.P.B.S.T.I.	Communist Party, British Section of the Third International
C.P.G.B.	Communist Party of Great Britain
I.L.P.	Independent Labour Party
L.R.D.	Labour Research Department
N.C.L.C.	National Council of Labour Colleges
N.U.R.	National Union of Railwaymen
N.U.W.C.	National Unemployed Workers Committee
S.D.F.	Social Democratic Federation
S.L.P.	Socialist Labour Party
S.P.G.B.	Socialist Party of Great Britain
S.W.M.F.	South Wales Miners Federation
T.U.C.	Trades Union Congress
U.D.C.	Union of Democratic Control
W.E.A.	Workers Educational Association
W.E.T.U.C.	Workers Educational Trade Union Committee
W.S.F.	Workers' Socialist Federation

Introduction

From its title this study may seem a storm in a teacup. With pleasure or regret, various commentators have remarked on the nonrevolutionary character of the British working class, its lack of interest in doctrine and its persistent attachment to orderly and peaceful improvement of its position. 'We are a solid people,' wrote Keir Hardie to Frederick Engels, 'very practical and not given to chasing bubbles.'[1] Ever since the failure of Chartism in the middle of the last century, it is claimed, Britain has escaped those social convulsions which from time to time wracked every other capitalist state. This social peace has been punctuated by outbreaks of unrest: union 'outrages' in the 1860s, acute discontent among the poor in the 1880s, the Featherstone incident, Tonypandy and widespread industrial militancy before and after the First World War, the General Strike of 1926 and further confrontations over the past few years. Yet in every case the grievances did not constitute a revolutionary objective, and on each occasion the tide turned, carrying with it a certain quantity of capitalist detritus but always leaving the essential structure of the existing order intact.

As for Marxism, has it not always languished in this uncongenial environment? The Social Democratic Federation, itself the creation of an English gentleman and the despair of Engels, failed to attract the British working class. Various offshoots and doctrinaire sects had even less impact. The Communist Party formed after the First World War proved unable to compete with the Labour Party and remained alien to the mainstream of the labour movement; and the alternative Marxist groups which have emerged since the Second World War are isolated and ineffective to a corresponding degree.

This historical evaluation of British Marxism is linked to certain political evaluations, and while it would be rewarding to study the linkages, such a task falls outside the scope of this study. I am concerned only with their historiographical effects. In common with the overwhelming corpus of labour history, the history of Marxism in

Britain suffers from a preoccupation with the successful – successful organisations, leaderships and ideologies. The concern for success is registered in the genetic character of most labour history, which traces the evolution of enduring and significant practices and institutions. The class itself has been persistently identified with the organisations and leadership of that class for, despite the intent of such works as Cole and Postgate's *The Common People*, social history of real substance has only recently begun to appear. Furthermore, most studies of these industrial and political organisations have been insensitive to regional variations and local practice. And insofar as the ideology of the move-ment has received serious attention, it is nearly always in the form of ideas espoused by an articulate elite, so that ideology practised in a material form within working-class communities remains largely un-explored. All this is not to press the claims of a populist antiquarianism, for this merely displaces the essential task of analysis. We are not interested in the neglected past merely for its own sake, nor in this particular context am I asserting that certain pockets of unsuccessful radicals should be paid the hollow honour of admission to Clio's sanctuary. Rather, I am rejecting the widespread notion of a linear historical process with a mainstream, which belongs to the victors, and various backwaters, on which the vanquished lie shipwrecked or becalmed. The labour movement as we know it today should rather be seen as the outcome of a highly uneven historical process, involving the ebb and flow of various currents.

Following in the footsteps of Edward Thompson's *Making of the English Working Class*, there is now a significant corpus of historical writing dealing with movements of social protest during the first half of the nineteenth century, and it is no longer possible to view that past in terms of the present. Other historians, notably Gareth Stedman Jones, have also shown the survival of certain forms of craft production and a continuing artisan culture well into the second half of the nineteenth century. Yet 1850 remains the great divide. Prior to the final failure of Chartism we have a variety of forms of popular protest, organisation and ideology; afterwards the dominant motif is a unitary Whig chronology which can be suggested by a list of its terms: the 'new model' unionism, Lib–Lab, L.R.C., Labour Party, *Labour and the New Social Order*, Transport House. The final outcome of that history, the modern trade unions and Labour Party, are read back over the preceding century, thereby fixing these phenomena into a mislead-ing perspective and suppressing other phenomena to a greater or lesser degree. This Whig interpretation of labour history can be found in the literature of the Labour Party and trade unions themselves – for instance in MacDonald's *Socialism: Critical and Constructive*, Francis Williams's *Magnificent Journey* or either edition of the *Book of the Labour Party* compiled by Herbert Tracy in 1925 and (under a new title) in 1948 – as well as in much academic writing.

My study of Marxism over a limited period is intended to call attention to one neglected episode of labour history. It is presented not as an isolated or aberrant episode but as part of a more general militant and anti-capitalist tradition that runs from the demise of Chartism to the present day. This is an almost subterranean tradition which cannot be defined institutionally and finds organised expression only fleetingly in periods of special stress, but is nevertheless rooted in different sections of the British working class. Indeed the tradition might almost seem to define itself against the respectable lineage, the 'moral force' Chartists, the top-hatted leaders of the early T.U.C., the Lib–Lab M.P.s, the men who organised, lobbied, waited on Royal Commissions and finally were admitted to office. The hallmark of our tradition is a certain stubborn intransigence, a rejection of both the mores and the institutions of the existing social order combined with a deep suspicion of the respectable path to social reform. We should be careful not to imply that we are dealing with a single stream of social protest, for this would merely revive a new genetic reading of labour history as a radical counterpart to the conventional one rejected earlier. Anyone studying the organised labour movement in the early part of the twentieth century must be struck by its untidiness, not just the considerable degree of regional and sectoral differentiation but the co-existence of quite separate strands of social thought. It was, for example, characteristic of popular socialism at the turn of the century that it combined moral criticism of laissez-faire economics drawn from writers such as Carlyle, Kingsley and Ruskin with utilitarian and Social Darwinist notions taken from Mill and Spencer, who accepted the necessity of political economy. While this eclecticism is revealing in itself, it is part of the task of the historian to disentangle and analyse these components of working-class ideology.

Finally, a brief explanation of the arrangement of this study. I have chosen a thematic method of presentation rather than a chronological one, because it allows a more adequate consideration of the actual content of British Marxism. This arrangement requires a moderate degree of familiarity with the period. To assist the reader who lacks it

I endeavour to provide a summary of the main features in the remainder of this introduction; if a full-length history of the period is
required, then the most useful and evocative is probably Allen Hutt's
Post-War History of the British Working Class.[2] Chapter 1 provides
a general account of Marxist organisations and the influence of
Marxism within the mainstream of the labour movement. Chapter 2
attempts a general comparison of Marxism with other strands of
working-class ideology, with particular reference to the socialism of
the Labour Party. Chapters 3 and 4 investigate the cultural conditions of British Marxism by reference to the availability of texts and
the provision of Marxist education. Then chapters 5 to 9 take up
particular aspects of Marxism, trace their understanding in this country
and assess their impact. The first two of these, which deal with
historical materialism and the dialectic, may strike the reader as more
specialised, for these were topics on which Marxist enthusiasts talked to
each other and which were largely ignored by the rest of the left. The
reason for treating them first is that as the philosophical foundations of
Marxism they reveal its intellectual tone with particular clarity. A final
chapter considers the problem of the applicability of Marxism to Britain.

There is no consensus among economic historians about the interwar
period. The old staple industries – coal, cotton, iron and steel, ship-
building and engineering – all experienced various degrees of difficulty,
and this was expressed in severe long-term unemployment in the areas
in which these industries were concentrated. South Wales, the North
and the industrial belt of central Scotland all experienced particular
hardship. On the other hand, the period registered an acceleration in
the rate of growth over the preceding Edwardian period; the standard
of living as measured by all conventional indices rose, and it is possible
to discern a partial adjustment of the British economy to new forms of
enterprise. It is easy enough to identify these different trends from a
long-term perspective, and we may expect future work to illuminate
the present debate over the precise form of their combination. What
needs to be emphasised for our purposes is the degree of regional
variation within the national economy and the violent character of the
short-term fluctuations.

In 1919 and the first half of 1920 there was a brief and feverish
inflationary boom. Wages and prices both rose to new levels but there
was no corresponding increase in output, and too much of the invest-
ment that was not purely speculative was nevertheless directed towards

unsuitable or unnecessary forms of capital equipment. The boom ended in the summer of 1920, and by the next year the number of unemployed passed one million, a mark below which it would not fall for the remainder of our period. The staple industries were already experiencing grave difficulties in winning back pre-war export markets, and even in maintaining those they still enjoyed, and they responded with an attempt to reduce costs. The trade unions resisted wage cuts, and in 1921 more than 85 million working days were lost in industrial disputes (a figure that doubled any previous annual aggregate); but by the end of the year wages had fallen more than 20 per cent on those obtaining twelve months earlier and two million men and women were out of work.[3] Between 1923 and 1929 there was a partial recovery based on some technological advances and the emergence of new industries, but the old industries still languished. At the end of 1929 that limited improvement was swept away by a world economic crisis of unprecedented severity, one which did not show any sign of lifting until the end of our period. The actual financial crisis occurred in the third quarter of 1931, and the industrial depression was at its worst a year later, but the numbers of unemployed did not begin to decline until 1933 and had not returned to the still considerable level of the 1920s until the end of 1936.[4]

This national overview conceals the gravity of the problems that affected the old staple industries and their regions. Coal was the largest single industry. In 1913 the total output was 287 million tons and the industry employed 1 128 000 workers. During the war the pressing need for maximum production meant that the easier seams were worked out and there was insufficient long-term improvement of the pits; then in the immediate post-war period the miners won large wage increases and shorter hours. Demand remained high despite the decline in productivity and in 1923 1 160 000 workers produced 276 million tons. Thereafter a number of overseas markets were lost, and the owners and workers were locked in a protracted conflict principally over wage reductions. By 1928 only 922 000 workers remained in the industry and produced 237 million tons; and by 1933 the number had fallen further to 772 000 who produced 207 million tons. Thus in the decade ending in 1933 the industry shed nearly 400 000 workers.[5]

Experience in the cotton industry was not dissimilar. Cotton had contributed some 40 per cent of Britain's pre-war exports and was more vulnerable than coal to the loss of overseas markets. The brief post-war boom handicapped the industry with watered stock and much unsuitable machinery, and there was inadequate reorganisation to meet the new patterns of demand. Various indices suggest the drop in production: consumption of raw cotton in 1913 was 2174 million pounds, in 1923 1357 million pounds, in 1933 1487 million pounds; exports of piece goods, thread and twist yarn declined to a corresponding degree. The wage-earners employed in the industry had totalled well over half a million before the war; in 1923 there were 479 000 and in 1933 377 000.[6] The experience of the iron and steel industry was equally gloomy. The war created a large surplus capacity of an uncompetitive character: 'steelworks were antiquated, the furnaces too small, mechanised aids insufficient, and the layout of the works dictated by history rather than technical needs'.[7] During the 1920s British producers lost foreign customers and the domestic market was flooded with foreign products. Total production of iron and steel declined from 10 260 million tons in 1913 to 7441 million tons in 1923 and 4136 million tons in 1933 – the pre-war level was not reattained until 1937. There had been half a million wage-earners before the war; in 1923 there were 310 000 and in 1933 239 000.[8]

Shipbuilding suffered to an even greater degree. Replacements of war losses kept the yards busy until 1920, when the industry employed 259 000 wage-earners, but once again the British makers were slow to adapt to newer types of ships, and demand collapsed. By 1933 launchings from British yards had fallen to 7 per cent of the pre-war figure. Meanwhile the number of wage-earners fell to 126 000 in 1923, and to a mere 56 000 in 1933.[9] It is more difficult to summarise the fate of the engineering industry because some sectors, such as electrical engineering, were expanding rapidly, while others, such as those involved in the building of locomotives and textile machinery, languished. At the beginning of our period the Ministry of Labour grouped approximately one and a half million workers in this portmanteau category. In 1920 it is possible to distinguish 784 000 wage-earners engaged in mechanical engineering and 139 000 in electrical engineering. The former fell to 413 000 in 1923 and to 320 000 in 1933; in contrast, the electrical engineering wage-earners totalled 130 000 in 1923 and 170 000 in 1933.[10]

The crucial feature underlying this decline in production and employment in the staple industries is their high degree of regional concentration and the dependence of these regions on their prosperity. We can best illustrate this dependence by taking each region in turn and examining the occupation categories of the 1911 Census. South

Wales was absolutely dependent on its coalfields, which contributed approximately a fifth of national output and were particularly sensitive to overseas demand. On the eve of the war no less than 119 per thousand of population were occupied in mining; metals, which employed 39 per thousand, was the only other significant industrial occupation. Northumberland and Durham also contained important coalfields and supported iron and steel works, engineering and ship-building; 98 per thousand of population were occupied in mining, 40 in metals and 21 in ship- and coachbuilding. Lancashire, Cheshire and the West Riding relied heavily on textiles, with mining, iron and steel and engineering also significant: 73 per thousand of population were occupied in cotton, 24 in wool, 43 in metals, 29 in mining. The industrial belt of central Scotland also produced a significant quantity of coal but was heavily dependent on engineering, textiles and ship-building: 46 per thousand of population were occupied in mining, 49 in metals, 17 in cotton, 15 in ship- and coachbuilding.[11] We should, however, be careful not to lay too great an emphasis on the region as a unit of analysis. In this study we are more directly concerned with areas and communities within them, which were dominated by one or a few major industries to a far greater degree than these numbers suggest: the pit-village, mill-town or industrial city whose everyday life was inseparable from a particular staple or staples. Thus various parts of the Midlands were also dominated by coal-mining, and the economy of Belfast leaned heavily on flax, another declining industry, and ship-building. But the regions examined above were the areas of greatest unemployment – the 'distressed areas' as they were designated later – and they suffered not just from the stricken state of major industries but from repercussions on subsidiary economic activity. The cumulative effect of their economic decline is indicated in Table 1, which shows percentage rates of unemployment on a regional basis. It will be seen that in 1922 there is a less marked regional variation as all parts of the country felt the effect of the slump. By 1927 London, the South, and to a lesser degree the Midlands had recovered; Scotland and the North had recovered to a perceptibly lesser degree, and in Wales (which was still suffering the effects of the General Strike and its bitter aftermath) the employment situation had deteriorated. The effects of the depression at the end of the decade were national in scope, but more severe and protracted in the old industrial regions. And these statistics under-state the disparities since in the old industrial regions many of the unemployed were not on the main register.

Table 1   *Percentage rates of unemployment by regions, 1922–32*

Region	August 1922	1927	1932
London	13	5.8	13.5
South-East	12	5.0	14.3
South-West	15	7.3	17.1
Midlands	18	8.4	20.1
North-East	18	13.7	28.5
North-West	16	10.6	25.8
Scotland	21	10.6	26.1
Wales	12	19.5	34.6

Source: col. 1 is from *The Third Winter of Unemployment* (London, 1923), p. 16;
cols. 2 and 3 from Lord Beveridge, *Full Employment in a Free Society*, 2nd edn
(London, 1960), p. 61.

The comparative success of the Midlands and South of England is
related to the emergence of what are known as the 'new' industries –
notably motor vehicles, electrical goods, artificial fibres and chemicals.
The distinction between the 'old' and 'new' industries has been
criticised on various grounds: it encourages a concentration on technology at the expense of relations of production and distribution; many
of the so-called new industries developed out of established ones; and
in any case there is no absolute regional contrast.[12] Yet it remains clear
that the majority of new enterprises were established in the Midlands,
in London, or elsewhere in the South, and the growth of such new
industry stimulated building and other forms of employment in these
regions. The expansion of the distributive and service sectors of the
economy, which was a marked feature of the period, is also relevant.
Even though many of the unemployed refused to move, there was
movement of population out of the old industrial regions, especially
South Wales, into new ones; and it has been estimated that between
1920 and 1935 the South-East made a net gain of about one million
workers as the result of migration from other regions.[13] The new
industries were less dependent on old forms of power and transport,
they used less brawny or skilled male labour and more adaptable but
essentially unskilled labour, much of it female. The workforce also
enjoyed a new mobility so that the older communities made up of
workers in one or more staple industry increasingly gave way to more
heterogeneous social groups in new suburbs and housing estates.

Among the conjunction of factors that produced the Labour Party
at the end of the nineteenth century is one of particular significance, the

emergence of an independent working-class political consciousness. The invaluable analysis provided by Henry Pelling in his *Social Geography of British Elections 1885–1910* (1967) suggests that with two exceptions the working-class transition from Liberal to Labour was based on these old industrial regions – the two exceptions are London, which falls outside the category and requires separate analysis, and Lancashire, which belongs to it but where working-class Liberalism had never developed to the same degree. Without wishing to advance any oversimple generalisation, it seems that this independent working-class consciousness emerged with particular strength and clarity in those areas where distinct working-class communities existed and were united in a few large-scale industries. Already in 1892 these regions contained a far higher degree of trade union organisation and membership than in most other parts of Britain.[14] At the turn of the century the gospel of Labour took root in various forms in the mill towns of the Pennines, and in the industrial areas of Scotland; it began to displace Liberalism in the northern mining areas; some time after the turn of the century it swept into the South Wales valleys. The forms of this working-class consciousness vary widely – all the way from socialism in its various forms (whether the ethical socialism of Keir Hardie's I.L.P., the less moralistic doctrines of the *Clarion*, the dour message of the Lancastrian S.D.F., or perhaps most typically a combination of these and other influences) to the Lib–Lab consciousness which prevailed in many mining areas right up to and beyond the First World War. The Labour Party inherited these various traditions and carried them into the post-war period with new emphases; but the old industrial regions remained for a time the home territory of the Labour Party. It is not too much to assert that the inter-war shift from the old industrial regions to the new ones changed the character of the working class and ultimately transformed the Labour Party and trade union movement. Of course many of the centres of growth contained older industries and more traditional working-class communities: London, Bristol, Derby, Nottingham and Leicester had not been sluggards in the pre-war labour movement. But their working classes lacked the same degree of homogeneity and organic solidarity as existed in pit-villages, mill-towns and heavy industrial centres elsewhere; and these looser urban working classes were in any case undergoing a transformation with the development of the new industries. In 1917 the T.U.C. was unmistakably controlled by the giant industrial unions and the Labour Party was a working-class party. By 1933 the dominant industrial figure was Ernest

Bevin, whose vast conglomerate Transport and General Workers' Union continued to swallow smaller unions, and the class character of the Labour Party had been considerably eroded in leadership and appeal.

What held for organised labour in general held with particular force for the Marxist sections of the labour movement. It is difficult to measure the significance of Marxism in different parts of the country, for British Marxism cannot be equated with its principal organisations. But if we take the Communist Party, the labour colleges and militant sections of certain trade unions as a limited index of a Marxist presence, we are driven back to the working-class communities of these old industrial regions. Marxism was most influential in central Scotland and South Wales; it exercised a distinct influence in the North-East and can be detected to a lesser degree and more fitfully in parts of Lancashire and Yorkshire – Manchester and Sheffield are perhaps the most important centres. Elsewhere there were handfuls of enthusiasts but they remained peripheral at best to the politics of the working class. The vagaries of Marxism in Britain between 1917 and 1933 are thus bound up with the history of the old industrial working class.

The dominant image of these communities in the inter-war era comes from such popular writing as *The Road to Wigan Pier*, *Love on the Dole* and *The Town that was Murdered*. They do not exaggerate the debilitating effect of mass unemployment. A committee was set up in 1933 to investigate unemployment in six towns; among them were Blackburn, the Lancastrian cotton town; Crook, a mining town in County Durham; and the Rhondda, a mining valley in South Wales. In September 1936 the percentage of recorded unemployed in these three localities was 30, 34 and 45 per cent respectively (and a considerable number of other workers did not bother to register). In each there was a high proportion of 'long' unemployment, a significant minority were in poor health, and a large number of the young had left the region in search of work. A third of the unemployed were below a poverty line which made no allowance for recreation, insurance, medical fees, furniture or newspapers. The report records with chilling clinical detail the physical and psychological effects on those who suffered such deprivation, but what emerges with particular force is the actual dismemberment of the community itself – one young Welsh miner writes from London: 'I am sitting in Hyde Park. There are thousands of people all round me and not a single one has spoken to me.'[15]

This is the destination of our history, yet we are more immediately concerned with an earlier period, not of resignation but of struggle. There was significant long-term unemployment in the old industrial areas from 1920 onwards, but the political atmosphere was quite different from that of the 1930s: growing war-time unrest, an upsurge in 1919–21, militant defence of living standards in 1926, and a final weaker resistance between 1929 and 1932. Here we shall briefly sketch an historical outline which will be of primary interest to those who lack familiarity with the period.[16] Taking the trade unions first, there was marked growth during the First World War (see Table 2), and yet the war-time regulation of certain key industries opened a wide gap between the union leadership and sections of their membership.

Table 2   *Trade union statistics, 1914–33*

Year	Total number of trade union members	Total affiliated to T.U.C.	Aggregate working days in stoppages
1914	4 145 000	2 682 357	9 880 000
1915	4 359 000	2 850 457	2 950 000
1916	4 644 000	3 082 352	2 450 000
1917	5 499 000	4 532 085	5 650 000
1918	6 533 000	5 283 676	5 880 000
1919	7 926 000	6 505 482	34 970 000
1920	8 348 000	6 417 910	26 570 000
1921	6 663 000	5 128 648	85 870 000
1922	5 625 000	4 369 268	19 850 000
1923	5 429 000	4 328 235	10 670 000
1924	5 544 000	4 350 982	8 420 000
1925	5 506 000	4 365 619	7 950 000
1926	5 219 000	4 163 994	162 230 000
1927	4 919 000	3 874 842	1 170 000
1928	4 806 000	3 673 144	1 390 000
1929	4 858 000	3 744 320	8 290 000
1930	4 842 000	3 719 401	4 400 000
1931	4 624 000	3 613 273	6 980 000
1932	4 444 000	3 367 911	6 490 000
1933	4 392 000	3 294 581	1 070 000

Source: Henry Pelling, *A History of British Trade Unionism*, 3rd edn (Harmondsworth, 1976), pp. 294–5.

From 1914 onwards the trade union leaders gave strong support to the war effort, and most entered into Treasury Agreements with the government in 1915, while many of their members chafed under the steady

rise of prices. Both the Clydeside engineering workers and the South
Wales miners came out in pursuit of higher wages in 1915. A further
point of contention was the government's attempt to dilute skilled with
unskilled and cheaper labour, and this was aggravated in turn by the
Munitions of War Act, which legislated a considerable degree of state
control. Suppression of the unofficial Clydeside leadership did not
prevent the spread of unrest and the formation of a national committee
of shop stewards.

Yet it would be misleading to suggest that the government relied on
the stick only, with trade union leaders serving as its prefects: Lloyd
George also dangled carrots before the unions and persuaded more
Labour representatives to serve in the coalition he formed at the end
of 1916 – and much of the post-war disputation began when the unions
claimed these promised carrots. One they did secure was the shorter
working day, for in virtually every industry the working day was
reduced to eight hours at the end of the war.

The more contentious claims concerned wages and wider issues of a
quasi-political nature. For in the immediate post-war period the old
distinction between industrial activity for industrial ends and political
activity for other objectives was far from clear. The unions were already
prepared to push industrial claims up to and beyond the point at which
the government disputed their legitimacy and claimed that the interests
of the state were endangered: now they were prepared to embrace
industrial action with explicit political objectives. In January 1919 the
miners demanded a reduction in hours, increases in wages and the
nationalisation of the mines (which had fallen under government
control during the war); Lloyd George set up a commission which did
in fact accept the principle of state ownership. In September 1919 the
railwaymen struck to protect their wages and secure a one-year agreement, and early in 1920 the dockers won improvements without
striking. The most important instance of this novel phenomenon of
'Direct Action' occurred in May 1920 when the London dockers
refused to permit the *Jolly George* to sail with munitions for use against
Russia, and in August a national conference of Labour set up Councils
of Action to enforce a general ban. A further aspect of the period was
the degree of solidarity: in October 1920 the threat of combined action
by the Triple Alliance between miners, railwaymen and transport
workers secured wages increases for the miners. Thus between 1918 and
1920 prices rose by approximately 30 per cent and average wages by
approximately 50 per cent. This abrupt account of the chief industrial

confrontations should suggest the militant atmosphere of the immediate post-war years, the formative period of a new wave of British Marxism.

But in the summer of 1920 the boom broke and within a year the unions were pushed back onto the defensive. In 1921 there was a series of crucial defeats. On 31 March 1921 the mines were handed back to the owners, who immediately lowered wages; then on 'Black Friday', 15 April 1921, the railwaymen and transport workers cancelled a planned sympathetic strike and the miners were beaten. The engineers were forced to accept cuts in 1921, and although they struck in defence of workshop rights the following year, they too were forced back to work with further reductions. Nineteen twenty-one was undoubtedly the turning-point, even though the left continued to exercise an influence in particular unions and even gained ground in the T.U.C. in the early 1920s. The militant industrial objectives – nationalisation, rank-and-file control, recognition of shop stewards, 'Direct Action' – disappeared from the agenda as the unions fought with mounting desperation to protect wages. Taking 1924 as the base rate, the weekly wage index dropped from 154.8 at the end of 1920 to 97.9 in December 1923; meanwhile the cost of living fell from 151.4 to 101.1.[17]

Nineteen twenty-six, the year when the last group of workers, the miners, were bludgeoned into submission, was the terminal date of this effort to defend living standards by industrial confrontation. The miners had held firm against another round of cuts in 1925, and secured T.U.C. suport for nine days in the General Strike of 1926, but their protracted defiance of the owners after the collapse of the General Strike crippled their union for at least a decade. The effect on the rest of the trade union movement was also severe.[18] The number of trade unionists had tumbled from a high point of over eight million in 1920 to six and a half million a year later; in 1927 it slumped to less than five million, of whom fewer than four million were affiliated to the T.U.C. (see Table 2). In the aftermath of the General Strike the Government passed the Trade Disputes and Trade Unions Act which, among other provisions, prohibited various forms of industrial action and introduced a 'contracting-in' system for trade union affiliation to the Labour Party. But such measures were hardly necessary in view of the widespread victimisation of militants, the profoundly pessimistic mood which swept the unions, and the new determination of their leaders to eschew conflict. The unions were capable of only sporadic resistance to the new inroads on living standards in the Depression, and

by 1933 there was a further paralysing division between the unions
and the unemployed.

Finally, we may point to some structural changes in the industrial
labour movement which were of major significance for working-class
Marxism. First, the unions of the old staple industries suffered particularly from unemployment and defeats at the hands of the employers.
Their decline was partially offset by the rise of unions based on the new
industries (such as the Electrical Trades Unions), unions which expanded their basis of membership (such as the Amalgamated Engineering Union) and, most importantly, the two giant general unions (the
Transport and General Workers and the General and Municipal
Workers). Nevertheless, organisation of the new industrial localities took
time and was hindered by various characteristics of the new workforce.
It was more geographically dispersed and harder to bring together; it
lacked clear-cut skills and was thus susceptible to a more complex
wage system and frequent demarcation disputes; it included more
women and juveniles who were often neglected by traditional trade
unionism and in any case frequently resisted it. Above all, 'as these
industries were relatively new, these sections of workers did not in most
cases possess the same experience or tradition of organisation and solidarity as groups like the miners and sections of engineers'.[19] The locus
of power within the unions also shifted: during the war and until 1921
the local work group and its elected representatives had assumed a new
importance; but thereafter the growth of national collective bargaining,
the increased complexity of industrial negotiations and the amalgama-
tions of many smaller unions all strengthened the hand of the national
executive and full-time officials. Within the T.U.C. also there was a
distinct trend towards centralisation, beginning in 1921 with the creation of the General Council. After 1926 this process continued and
dominant figures of the General Council, notably Walter Citrine and
Ernest Bevin, led the way in seeking a new and less belligerent industrial
strategy.

I turn now to the Labour Party. In 1914 this was an uneasy coalition
of trade unionists and members of the affiliated socialist societies, most
notably the Independent Labour Party (I.L.P.) and the Fabians, who
sought to give political leadership. Two separate threads of development can be discerned during the war: the majority supported the
government and was represented in it after 1915, while a minority
based on the I.L.P. was critical of the war and its conduct. That the
vast majority of the latter should have rejected Marxism and revolu-

tionary politics and returned to the fold in 1918, thus avoiding a major split, was a distinctive characteristic of the British labour movement and one which distinguished it from the continental norm. The reconciliation in constitutional gradualism was consummated in *Labour and the New Social Order* (1918), the new party programme which was prepared by representatives of the majority – even though Labour was now undeniably more independent and more advanced than before the war. More directly, the rejection of Marxism during the period of postwar militancy was due to the combined efforts of the I.L.P. leaders, Ramsay MacDonald and Philip Snowden, and that consummate organiser, Arthur Henderson, and we shall examine various aspects of their fight against Marxism in the body of this study. MacDonald assumed the leadership of the Party after the 1922 election and was able to form a minority Government after the 1923 election. His premiership and subsequent leadership of the party antagonised the left wing of Labour, whose stronghold was the I.L.P., but there was no serious challenge to his leadership either after the Government's defeat in 1924 or subsequently. Labour was returned to office in 1929 on the eve of the Depression but once again depended on Liberal support, and the administration was overshadowed by mounting economic difficulties. The Cabinet split over expenditure cuts in August 1931 and MacDonald formed a National Government. Labour was massacred in the subsequent election and still convalescent in 1933.

The story is a familiar one, yet there is surprisingly little research into the character of the Labour Party and the changes that took place in it during the period. We know for instance of the influx of middle-class ex-Liberals into the Party at the national level, but we lack any extensive social analysis of the lower levels. The 1918 constitution established local constituency parties, which ultimately superseded most of the functions of the socialist societies, yet their formation, early membership and activities are remarkably obscure (see Column 2 of Table 3). It had been common in many working-class communities for the relevant unions or the trades council to conduct the activities of the Party, especially at election time; certainly many were to be found in the two spheres of activity. This practice declined, particularly in the new industrial areas where the members of a single union were more dispersed, and the Labour activists of a given locality more heterogeneous. The closer supervision of the Labour Party by the trade union *leaders* in the aftermath of 1931 should not conceal the growing separation of the two bodies. McKibbin's valuable study *The Evolution*

Table 3 *Membership of the Labour Party, 1917–33*

Year	Trade union membership	Individual (constituency) membership	Co-operative Societies	Socialist societies	Total
1917	2 415 383	Nil	2608	47 140	2 465 131
1918	2 960 409	Not compiled	Nil	52 720	3 013 129
1919	3 464 020	,,	Nil	47 270	3 511 290
1920	4 317 537	,,	Nil	42 270	4 359 807
1921	3 973 558	,,	Nil	36 803	4 010 361
1922	3 279 276	,,	Nil	31 760	3 311 036
1923	3 120 149	,,	Nil	35 762	3 155 911
1924	3 158 002	,,	Nil	36 397	3 194 399
1925	3 337 635	,,	Nil	36 235	3 373 870
1926	3 352 347	,,	Nil	35 939	3 388 286
1927	3 238 939	,,	20 000	34 676	3 293 615
1928	2 025 139	214 970	20 000	32 050	2 292 169
1929	2 044 279	227 897	32 000	26 669	2 330 845
1930	2 011 484	277 897	32 000	26 213	2 346 908
1931	2 024 216	297 003	32 000	4847	2 358 066
1932	1 960 269	371 607	32 040	7871	2 371 787
1933	1 899 007	366 013	32 040	7970	2 305 030

Source: Henry Pelling, *Short History of the Labour Party*, 5th edn (London, 1976), p. 171

of the Labour Party 1910–1924 (1974) traces the growth of the Party administration, and its increasing control over various party organs, but beyond 1924 where his book concludes the picture remains unclear. Throughout this study we shall investigate the interaction of Marxism with Labour, and if the investigation appears too abstract and hypothetical that is due in part to the deficiency of our understanding of the Labour Party.

This abbreviated summary cannot do justice to the complexity of the phenomena under discussion, and many other important aspects of the labour movement such as the Co-operatives, the organisation of the unemployed and local government have been omitted altogether. It will suffice for our purpose if it has directed attention to the ferment among the organised working class at the beginning of our period, and given some impression of the shape of developments over the ensuing decade. The next task is to locate Marxism in this context.

1. The social and political basis of Marxism

Prior to 1917 there were only two Marxist organisations of any consequence.[1] These were the British Socialist Party (B.S.P.) and the Socialist Labour Party (S.L.P.) The B.S.P. was the direct descendant of the Social Democratic Federation (S.D.F.) founded in 1883 under the leadership of Hyndman, having been formed in 1911 as a coalition of the S.D.F., sections of the non-Marxist I.L.P., the *Clarion* movement and various local socialist societies. The membership of the S.D.F. during the nineteenth century never exceeded 4000;[2] the B.S.P.'s initial nominal membership of 40 000 declined to no more than a third that number by the outbreak of war, and active membership was considerably less. The S.L.P. had split away from the S.D.F. at the turn of the century. It was purer in doctrine and correspondingly much smaller; the membership never exceeded a thousand, the majority concentrated in Scotland.

Both grounded their Marxism in an extremely mechanical version of the materialist conception of history, which they interpreted as demonstrating the dominance of the 'economic factor'. The whole of human activity was controlled by economic forces independently of human volition. The state, politics, education and consciousness – all were mere epiphenomena of the techniques (and sometimes relations) of production. Just as feudalism had given way to capitalism, so the capitalist order would give way eventually to socialism. Their economic doctrines were equally rigid. They confidently expected a continually falling rate of profit, culminating in a final apocalyptic breakdown of capitalism. Some, though not all, subscribed to the 'Iron Law of Wages'; in any case they held that because capitalist profit derived from the surplus value of the workers, capitalist accumulation would reduce the working class to a state of misery and mass unemployment. Their different political strategies were each based on this prognosis: both believed that revolution would break out where capitalism had reached its highest pitch of development, and that the conditions of fully developed capitalism were automatically creating a socialist consciousness, so both were preparing for the time when the masses would rise up spontaneously against their unbearable conditions.

The chief task of the B.S.P. was evangelical: 'Their main function was the education of people in the principles of Socialism. . .'³ It considered most industrial activity diversionary, for since wages were determined by compelling economic laws, it was a waste of time for trade unions to try to improve them, and their resources would be better spent on socialist propaganda. Hyndman himself asserted that even 'the most successful strikes under existing conditions do but serve to rivet the chains of economic slavery, possibly a trifle gilded, more firmly on their limbs.'⁴ The B.S.P. did believe in parliamentary activity, as Henry Collins has shown, and it advanced a set of legislative demands to palliate the effects of capitalism; it also paid considerable attention to unemployment, education and housing. Yet these elements of local working-class politics never compensated sufficiently for its failure in the industrial field. T. A. Jackson looked back on his days in the S.D.F. in the early years of the century and recalled that its members 'thought their duty done when they had told the workers with reiterated emphasis that they had been and were being robbed systematically, and given them an exposition of how the trick had been worked. From this the workers were to draw a moral conclusion that the robbers ought to be stopped, and to reach a practical decision to wage a class war upon the robbers. When their audience didn't reach this decision, B.S.P. members were wont to conclude that "the bastards aren't worth saving" and gravitate to other fields of the labour movement.'⁵

The younger generation of Marxists, who were dubbed the 'impossibilists' and mostly found their way into the S.L.P., rejected this understanding of Marxism. For them the class struggle did not rest on such a fragile basis; it was immanent in history. Their political strategy was drawn from the American Marxist Daniel De Leon ('Old Dandelion' as he was irreverently dubbed by those who rubbed shoulders with his disciples and grew weary of his authority being constantly invoked). The S.L.P. scorned the existing trade union movement, but, unlike the B.S.P., wanted to establish an alternative movement of workers at the point of production organised on industrial rather than craft lines. De Leon and the S.L.P. held a more thoroughgoing class doctrine of the state than did the B.S.P. As capitalism collapsed, the existing state machinery was to be replaced by alternative working-class institutions, and the sole function of a working-class parliamentary majority was to prevent state power from being used during the crisis to defend the old order (though this would seem from a modern perspective to be one of the least likely achievements of such a majority). In the meantime the S.L.P.'s main activity was propaganda – from an aloof distance, for it refused to soil its hands by contact with gradualists of any kind, including those of the B.S.P. 'The true foundation of the Socialist movement', said De Leon during his Scottish tour, 'was the education of the working class. . .A genuine socialist movement must be narrow and intolerant as science, for there could be no compromise in the class war.'[6]

The characteristic feature of both these perspectives was their isolation from the British working class. It is dangerous to generalise on the membership and activities of the B.S.P. at the local level, and some branches were undoubtedly more involved in the daily round of the labour movement than this summary of its national strategy would suggest. Thus William Morris, a notable critic of the S.D.F., had drawn an earlier contrast between the 'good fellows' in the branches and the 'tone of arrogance' in the party as a whole.[7] In London, a distinctive set of economic and social conditions, and a particular tradition of radical politics reinforced by immigrants from the continent, sustained a diverse and fairly active membership. Elsewhere, with the exception of Lancashire, the B.S.P. was a loose federation and had less contact with the mainstream of the labour movement. The S.L.P. was similarly restricted to Edinburgh, Glasgow and neighbouring areas. Furthermore, with certain limited exceptions, both organisations were peripheral to the upsurge of rank-and-file working-class combativeness in the years immediately preceding the First World War.[8]

Yet between 1910 and 1920 British Marxism was transformed. The process began with the pre-war unrest, intensified during the war-time shop stewards' movement and associated developments, and came to fruition after the Russian Revolution. Two aspects can be considered briefly, first the changes within the Marxist organisations as a result of the altered industrial and political climate, and second the emergence of new organisations and forms of activity which extended and deepened Marxist influence.

The actual formation of the B.S.P. may be considered as a product of the pre-war militancy, but the influence of its S.D.F. nucleus was quickly reasserted and expressed as hostility both to rank-and-file industrial activity and to all other developments which fell outside the ambit of traditional Marxism. The turning point probably occurred in 1916 when the anti-war faction of the B.S.P. won a majority over Hyndman's own pro-war faction: the latter left to re-establish the S.D.F. Thereafter, under the influence of leaders such as Theodore Rothstein and Joe Fineberg, two Russian émigrés in London, and John Maclean in Glasgow, the B.S.P. began to criticise the war more strongly. In addition a number of B.S.P. members, of whom the Scot Willie Gallacher was most important, became active shop stewards, and at the 1918 Conference one delegate declared that the shop stewards' movement was 'the only active revolutionary movement in the country'.[9] The B.S.P. was also playing a far more active agitational role in the trade unions and Labour Party, for as one leading member testified, 'experience had taught him and others that instead of standing aloof from existing organisations, they should go into them' and win them to Marxism.[10] There is evidence of a similar tendency in the S.L.P. Whereas before the war its members were forbidden to hold office in existing trade unions, leading members such as Arthur Mac-Manus, John Muir and Tom Clark now discarded purism and explored the new methods of the shop stewards. In Glasgow especially, where most members worked in the engineering shops and shipyards and were thus more used to mixing with other members of left organisa-tions, the S.L.P. began to co-operate in joint action with the B.S.P. and I.L.P. By 1918, therefore, both Marxist groups were grappling with everyday problems and had forged a connection between their Marxist commitment and activity in the mass movement.

These new forms of working-class activity which operated on Marxism all exhibit a striking degree of spontaneity. The unrest which swept through the mining and transport industries between 1910 and 1912 was largely independent of union leadership; opposition to the war also emerged in spite of the patriotic activity of the great majority of most Labour spokesmen, and the very purpose of the shop stewards' movement was to fill the vacuum created by the inactivity of the workers' official representatives. In the course of struggle the rank and file threw up their own leaders and produced their own programmatic statements; and it is possible to trace a lineage from syndicalism via the shop stewards to post-war Marxism. But the historian must resist the temptation to read too much into such complex and uneven develop-ments. In a critical review of the main study of the shop stewards, Jean Monds has observed that the movement appealed as much to a desire to protect traditional craft privileges of skilled workers as it did to any revolutionary form of class consciousness, and the quasi-Marxist statements of leading shop stewards should not disguise the ambiguous response of the workers involved.[11] The unrest before the war had been less circumscribed and drew in wider sections of the unskilled working class, but it was also more ephemeral; and one needs to treat the pronouncements of its spokesmen with a similar caution.

The period between 1917 and 1921 was one of revolutionary unrest throughout Europe. If Britain escaped the crises that wracked the defeated powers as well as many of the victorious ones, there can be no doubting the heightened class tension. The admittedly alarmist reports to the Cabinet on 'Revolutionary Organisations in the United Kingdom' indicate a proliferation of various working-class movements and organisations on an entirely new scale. Several among them in which Marxism was influential can be distinguished, overlapping in membership and varying considerably in size and influence. Beside the B.S.P., the S.L.P. and the national organisation of shop stewards' committees, we may note the Plebs League, the National Guilds League, sections of the I.L.P., the Workers' Socialist Federation (W.S.F.) and the South Wales Socialist Society (S.W.S.S.).

The Plebs League had emerged from the strike of militant worker–students at Ruskin College, Oxford, in 1909, and at its foundation was strongly influenced by both Marxist and syndicalist currents. Its members established their own full-time Labour College, published the educational journal *Plebs*, and co-ordinated a network of local part-time labour colleges. As will be shown in chapter 3, these activities expanded rapidly in the immediate post-war years. The National Guilds League was a small and predominantly middle-class organisation interested in new forms of functional representation and organisation, which it propagated to any working-class audience which might be interested – and its left wing, which included such prominent Communists of the 1920s as Robin Page Arnot, W. N. Ewer, Walter Holmes and William Mellor, responded in the aftermath of the Russian Revolution to the Marxist critique of the state. The I.L.P. was estranged from the Labour Party because of its opposition to the conduct of the war – some branches and individual members such as J. T. Walton Newbold, Shapurji Saklatvala (the two Communists to be elected to parliament in the 1920s) and Helen Crawfurd also crossed the ill-defined boundary that demarcated the ethical socialism of the I.L.P. from Marxism. The W.S.F. was the successor to Sylvia Pankhurst's

Women's Suffrage Federation. It was small (maximum membership was about 300), largely dependent on Pankhurst herself, and limited to the East End and a constellation of tiny groups in industrial areas. Nevertheless, its newspaper, the *Workers' Dreadnought*, achieved the impressive circulation of 10 000 by 1917, for it had good contacts abroad and provided a very full coverage of domestic developments. The S.W.S.S. was even weaker, a loose confederation of local groups concentrated in the Rhondda, but it carried on and developed a recent tradition of syndicalist union activity.[12]

The list could be extended in two directions. There were other minor Marxist organisations as well as a vast miscellany of local socialist societies independent of the principal organisations; and there were individual Marxists within the ranks of the official Labour movement, such as the group of future Communists writing for the *Daily Herald*. The variety of these groupings testifies to a renaissance of Marxism within the larger context of the labour unrest, and this new popularity of Marxism is suggested by the recollection of one militant in the South Wales coalfield: 'it was said that one of the chief police officers in Glamorgan had heard so much about this Karl Marx, that he was responsible for this war-time propaganda and stirring up troubles throughout the coalfield, he had a warrant out to arrest him'.[13] This anecdote may tell us more about attitudes to police in the valleys than it does about the actual workings of the Glamorganshire constabulary, but it is one of many such references to this new influence. Rather than extending our catalogue, however, we need to consider a more important question – just what sort of Marxism was this?

The question defies an easy answer. At the beginning of the twentieth century there had been several well-defined groups of enthusiasts, each professing its own litany of Second International Marxism. Domestic events had then diffused Marxism over a much wider audience and provided a stimulus to broaden it to incorporate new forms of working-class activity. Finally, the Russian Revolution had introduced a radically new model to this country. These two stimuli, internal and external, now worked together and operated upon each other to produce the Marxism of our period, but they did not operate uniformly, nor do they lend themselves to simple generalisation. T. A. Jackson recalled of this period: 'I pulled my Marxism to pieces, examined every piece closely and critically in the light of objective practice. . ., helped by the works of Lenin as they appeared in English.'[14] While all Marxists may not have possessed Jackson's independence of intellect, an essentially similar process was occurring up and down the country. Here I shall review two important advances.

First, there was a new appraisal of the state. While there is evidence to suggest a degree of working-class mistrust of the state in its everyday forms,[15] the British labour movement had tended to insert both its industrial and political activities within the existing national political structure; in Gramscian terms it lacked a sufficiently hegemonic perspective to challenge the central institutions of state power. After 1910 there was a series of confrontations, among which the use of troops by Churchill in pre-war labour disputes and the military encirclement of Glasgow in 1919 were particular highlights, which alerted an increasing number of militants to this issue. Theoretical appreciation developed furthest among the shop stewards, who of course bore the brunt of government hostility; their new insights can be traced in their news-sheets and pamphlets.[16] The example of the Russian Revolution and the arguments presented by Lenin in *State and Revolution* thus fell on fertile soil, for as James Hinton has argued, it served a 'real theoretical need felt by British revolutionaries as a result of their own domestic experience'.[17] More than this, it demonstrated the practicality of the dictatorship of the proletariat to many who initially found the doctrine uncongenial. We may take the example of Eden and Cedar Paul, a married couple of earnest bohemians, who translated many Marxist texts during the 1920s and were active in workers' education. When they first heard of the dictatorship of the proletariat in 1917 they thought it 'repugnant to the truly civilised human being': yet by 1920 they found that 'the issues brought to the front by the bolshevik revolution have convinced the present writers that the dictatorship of the proletariat is an indispensable phase in the revolutionary transition'.[18]

The second lesson learned by British Marxists was the need to develop an immediate revolutionary strategy. They now realised that socialism was not guaranteed by some eventual breakdown of capitalism but must be won by immediate class struggle. 'The walls of the capitalist Jericho will not fall down in response to resolutions trumpeted by Labour Conferences, but must be stormed and ultimately levelled by the workers as a class for the purpose of taking all power into their own hands.'[19] As early as February 1918 one member of the B.S.P. discovered that 'our Russian comrades have shown us that the working class. . .can, under the most trying and difficult circumstances, assume power and maintain it'; he urged the British Marxists to develop a similar 'sense of power'.[20] The same point was put repeatedly by the section of the

S.L.P. who wished to join in establishing the Communist Party during their dispute with traditionalists. Along with the new activist outlook came a new conception of the role of the party. The pre-war Marxist groups, awaiting their historically ordained moment, had operated chiefly as propaganda societies. The public meeting and the educational class were their typical activities. Now they were called upon to abandon aloofness and throw themselves into every form of working-class activity. William Paul, another Scot who eventually left the S.L.P. for the Communist Party, wrote that 'Thanks to the Bolshevik Revolution we must no longer maintain our pre-war posture of scalping all those outside our ranks'; the 'melancholy procession of well-meaning but inactive revolutionary groups' confirmed Lenin's assertion that Marxists who refused 'to take their place in every fight and activity of the masses degenerate into sectarian "do nothings" '.[21] The call to participate in every activity had fallen on deaf ears before the war when Marxists had drawn an absolute distinction between their own revolutionary perspective and the reformist perspective of the mass movement. This distinction was no longer drawn after the war:

What was the position of the Communist Party? Their position was that every situation that cropped up, every cry that came from the working class, they took up, not as an issue in itself, but as an issue in the onward march of the revolution. They transformed it, they would precipitate that issue; they would deliberately take those issues presented to them, not in their separate character. . .but in the character of [their] part in the class struggle.[22]

This practical reorientation of Marxism was consummated in the formation of the Communist Party in 1920. The vanguard sections – the B.S.P., the W.S.F. (which had turned itself into the Communist Party, British Section of the Third International (C.P.B.S.T.I.)), the activists of the S.L.P., some leading shop stewards, a sprinkling of radical Guild Socialists – all reached the conclusion that it was necessary to form a united organisation of revolutionaries affiliated to the Third International.

The remainder of this study makes only passing reference after 1920 to other minor Marxist groups as the Pankhurstites (who soon followed her out of the Communist Party), the S.L.P. and the Socialist Party of Great Britain (S.P.G.B.); and none at all to the S.D.F. or to Trotskyists. The reason for their omission is that they were irrelevant. The S.L.P. and W.S.F. were important while they enjoyed a foothold among militant sections of the working class in London, Scotland and South Wales. After 1920, when their most active sections merged into the

Communist Party, the rump slipped away on the ebb tide of working-class militancy: the C.P.B.S.T.I. was soon wound up and the S.L.P. declined by the end of 1922 to a handful of enthusiasts. The course of the S.P.G.B. is more interesting, for it maintained a more or less constant membership of two or three hundred throughout the inter-war years, the same number as belonged before the First World War. Like the S.L.P., the S.P.G.B. had split from the S.D.F. at the turn of the century over the parent body's reformism. Its membership was concentrated in London with a handful of branches in Manchester, Glasgow and a few other large conurbations. In both theory and methods the S.P.G.B. was an extreme manifestation of the pre-1917 Marxist tradition. Its function was to educate the workers in the intractability of capitalism and the hopelessness of all trade union action or reform: its medium was the street-corner pitch where speakers would harangue passers-by and sell the *Socialist Standard*. Since prospective members were examined for their knowledge of Marxism and ability to speak in public, and since they prided themselves on their 'scientific socialism', propagandists of the S.P.G.B. enjoyed a reputation as formidable Marxists purists. Protected from change by their isolation from the larger movement, the continued existence of this group of highly committed Marxists is illustrative of a strand of London proletarian politics, but they exercised no significant political influence at any point during this century.[23] As for the S.D.F., when it was re-established by the followers of Hyndman after their war-time breach with the B.S.P., it was no longer a Marxist organisation. Like a grotesque parody of the right wing of the German S.P.D. in the same period, it carried patriotism and hatred of Communism to such lengths that its vestigial Marxism was buried under a mountain of vituperation against any kind of working-class militancy. A tradition of involvement in radical working-class politics was maintained for some years by particular branches, such as that in West Ham, but such branches either fell out with the national executive or else toed the line and lost their more radical members. The British S.D.F. continued as a declining organisation kept afloat by legacies until its primary function was an annual dinner of veteran right-wing Labour Members of Parliament.[24]

The omission of Trotskyism from this study of Marxism may seem in greater need of justification. The fullest available account of how British Trotskyism began shows how a group of dissident Communists emerged by the end of the 1920s, and there is prior evidence that some British Marxists were attracted to certain of Trotsky's criticisms of the

Communist movement. Yet no one comprehended a distinctively Trotskyist position and organised accordingly until the very end of our period.[25] It is a crucial feature of our period that there was no alternative understanding of Marxism to that of the Communists. Our study is not concerned solely with Communists, for a popular Marxism flourished in the labour colleges and sections of the trade unions and Labour Party, but it is very largely concerned with the Communist orientation to mass activity.

The Communist Party was formed in July 1920 some twelve months before the end of a period of working-class advance. In the previous few years the labour movement had extracted considerable economic concessions from the employers, successfully challenged the government on both industrial and political issues, and developed two new forms of local working-class organisation, the shop stewards and the Council of Action. The Party's formation enabled some of that experience to be consolidated and carried on through the 1920s, but conversely the circumstances of its creation stamped a pattern on the Party that was in some respects ill suited to the changed conditions that prevailed after 1921. For one of the features of the prior period was the diversity of organisation, strategy and social thought. If leading sections of the labour movement frequently found they had entered culs de sac and were forced to retrace their steps, such mistakes were a necessary cost of this diversity and even enriched the process of self-education. And even though the orientation of the new Communist Party was determined to a significant degree in Moscow, it is clear that the actual formation of the Party sprang from this process of self-education. The Party was designed to draw together the advances which had been achieved in different sections of the labour movement and carry them forward to a revolutionary conclusion. But almost immediately, within a year at most, the conditions for any immediate revolutionary perspective disappeared and the British Communists had to evolve a set of immediate tactics for a very different situation.

The most urgent problem was their relationship to the mainstream labour movement. From the beginning they numbered only a few thousand (see Figure 1) but in a period of flux this did not matter as much as it did a few years later. Convinced cerebrally if not emotionally by the arguments of Lenin, they applied for affiliation to the Labour Party with a similar status to that of the I.L.P.; but that application was unsuccessful for the Labour Party was already beginning to assume a new form with a correspondingly tighter political discipline. Hostility

Figure 1. *Estimates of membership of the C.P.G.B., 1920–33*

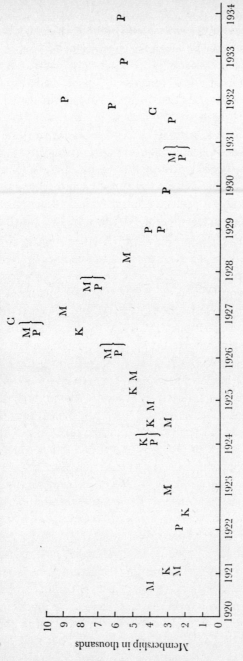

Code:
C *Communist International*, 1927, p. 154; 1932, p. 168.
K James Klugmann, *History of the Communist Party of Great Britain*, 2 vols. (London, 1968–9).
M L. J. Macfarlane, *The British Communist Party: Its Origin and Development until 1929* (London, 1966).
P Henry Pelling, *The British Communist Party: A Historical Profile* (London, 1958).
Note that Klugmann possessed information unavailable to the other writers.

intensified and the Communists were gradually driven out of every loophole – they were denied the right to affiliate, proscribed from individual membership and finally excluded from trade union representation on Labour bodies. By 1923 the Communist Party had shed a number of its better-known early members – Sylvia Pankhurst, Bob Williams (the secretary of the Transport Workers' Federation), Frank Horrabin (the editor of *Plebs*), William Mellor, Francis Meynell and Raymond Postgate (three middle-class intellectuals from the *Daily Herald*), as well as others, such as Arthur Cook (later secretary of the Miners' Federation) and Ellen Wilkinson (afterwards a member of the Attlee Cabinet) who would achieve full fame later. The Party was reduced already to the basis of its membership throughout the period, overwhelmingly working-class and concentrated in London, Scotland, South Wales, Lancashire, the West Riding and the North-East (see

Table 4.

Distribution of Communist Party branches by districts, 1920–30

District	September 1920	May 1924	May 1925	September 1926	October 1927	March 1930
London	34	23	29	36 (1560 members)	37 (1321 members)	30
South Wales	15	23	24	41 (1500)	38 (2300)	33
Scotland:						
Glasgow			13	17 (1105)		
Fife	27	17	6	8 (502)	45 (1500)	29
Dundee and Edinburgh			—	20 (1131)		
Tyneside		7	10	39 (1900)	22 (737)	24
Sheffield and E. Midlands		5	9	13 (1200)		17
Bradford		8	8	11 (250)	21 (420)	7
Manchester and W. Midlands	69	14	18	30 (680)	31 (534)	26
Liverpool		6	6	12 (576)	4 (104)	4
Birmingham		5	9	18 (326)	13 (55)	7
Others		27	30	2	16	—
Total: Branches	145	135	162	245	227	177
(members)	(approx.)	(3000)	(5000)	(10 730)	(7377)	(3000)

Sources: col. 1, Klugmann, *History of the C.P.G.B.*, vol. 1, p. 197; cols. 2–4, Organisation Reports held in Marx Memorial Library; col. 5, *Ninth Congress of the C.P.G.B.*, p. 15; col. 6, compiled from reports in *Daily Worker*, March-April 1930.

Table 4). In 1922 it adopted a new scheme of organisation on Bolshevik lines with greater co-ordination of activities and a formal hierarchy of national and district committees. This eventually transformed the Party from a federal basis inherited from previous socialist movements, and enabled it to benefit from some of the undoubted advantages of democratic centralism; but it also created two grave disadvantages. First, it erected an over-ambitious framework that could never be fully realised, as became manifest from the frequent retrospective admissions of failings (the membership statistics in Figure 1 seem more erratic than they actually were because of the temptation to revise previous claims downward in order to claim more recent advances). Second, it established a pattern whereby the Party attempted to resolve what were essentially political issues by administrative and disciplinary procedures.

The broad strategy of the Communists in this period was to provide a militant lead in the trade unions and win over radical sections of the Labour Party by agitation and exposure of the leadership. They met with little success in the political field, occasionally winning over individual constituency parties but failing to offer a more substantial challenge to Ramsay MacDonald and his colleagues. Indeed on the two occasions when Communism did clearly damage the Labour leader – with the editorial attributed to Johnny Campbell exhorting troops not to fire on workers which precipitated the 1924 election, and the more ambitious military advice allegedly offered by Zinoviev which helped to lose that election – the Communists were mere spectators. In the industrial field the Communist Party enjoyed greater success, for among its leaders were experienced and able trade unionists. In almost every case they worked within the existing unions, encouraging rank-and-file movements and working with the left trade union leaders. This dual emphasis was maintained in the 1926 General Strike, when the Party exerted a local influence out of all proportion to its numbers: thus it called both for an extension and intensification of the Strike, and for a strengthening of the General Council of the T.U.C. (which of course called the Strike off). The Communists then stuck doggedly to the miners during the long months they held out against the owners, and cemented close links with working-class communities on the Welsh, Scottish and North-East fields (see column 4 of Table 4). But after 1926 the Party's alliance with the 'left' members of the T.U.C. General Council collapsed. In an atmosphere of defeat and sectarian bitterness thousands of members were lost. With much prompting from the

Communist International, the British Party embraced the 'New Line' of 'Class Against Class' in 1928, whereby the principal enemies of the working class were the Labour and union leaders who deliberately betrayed them, and the special enemies were the Labour and union left whose function it was to disguise and facilitate the betrayal. This policy was relaxed in 1933 and finally abandoned in 1935, but hangs over the closing years of our study.[26]

The geographical limitations of the Communist Party – and, to a lesser extent, British Marxism generally – have been mentioned already, but the point cannot be emphasised too strongly. Table 4 indicates that the membership of the Party was, with the exception of London, concentrated overwhelmingly in the staple industrial areas and always strongest in South Wales and central Scotland. In London the principal strongholds were the East End and the south of Thames around Battersea and Clapham; in these areas the Communists carried on the work of the S.D.F. and at least in the early part of the 1920s they enjoyed comparatively harmonious relations with the local Labour parties. The basis of Communist activity in London, however, was non-industrial. A list of Communist factory groups in the capital in May 1925 reveals that the largest single group was that in the Russian Trade Delegation; and groups of 21 members in Tate's sugar works, 20 in the Nine Elms rail depot and 19 in the Woolwich Arsenal were the best that could be claimed elsewhere. There were in fact fewer than two hundred and fifty Communists active in London factory groups.[27] One expanding base of support was the Jewish community of London's East End, most of whom had arrived from eastern Europe during the second half of the nineteenth century. Prior to 1914 most Jews remained within their own community and created their own trade unions and socialist organisations; during the anti-fascist campaigns of the 1930s they became an important source of Party recruitment. For the transitional period of the 1920s we lack the necessary research, but it is at least evident that several leading Communists came from this background.[28]

Elsewhere in England the Communists were initially most successful among the industrial workers of Yorkshire and the area around Manchester; the General Strike fostered an expansion in the coalfields of the North-East and East Midlands. Communism in South Wales was concentrated overwhelmingly in the mining villages and towns, one of which will be examined below. The coastal centres of Cardiff, Swansea and Llanelly were noticeably more resistant. In Scotland the areas of greatest Communist recruitment and activity were far more varied.

The factories and shipyards of Glasgow and its surrounding area provided greater support in the first part of the 1920s than afterwards, when the I.L.P. and Trades and Labour Council repulsed the Communist challenge. The Party did better in areas further down the Clyde such as Clydebank and Greenock, though less well in Dumbarton. There was a considerable following in the Lanarkshire coalfield throughout the decade, and the Party made rapid strides among the Fife miners. The industrial towns on the East Coast were also significant. The outstanding feature of Scottish Communism was its ability to establish a significant and continuous presence, albeit in sime cases only, outside the traditional strongholds. The Vale of Leven, where the principal occupation was the bleaching, dyeing and printing of textiles, is an outstanding example, and I discuss it below at greater length.

There is little evidence for the occupational background of Communists before the 1930s.[29] During its first five years the Party seems to have been comparatively well represented among the more militant sections of the labour force: the engineers, railwaymen and miners especially. The sharp rise in membership in 1926 was undoubtedly caused in the main by an influx of miners – the jump in the number of branches in South Wales, Fife and the North-East provides statistical corroboration of claims made at the time. We then have two occupational breakdowns of Party membership which are of limited value – particularly so since one is based on 1930 when membership slumped disastrously to 2500, and the other on 1932 when the Party enjoyed an influx of several thousand recruits, many of whom were lost almost immediately. The occupations which are best represented are the miners, metal workers, transport workers and textile workers (the last group had recently been involved in bitter strikes.[30] There is considerable evidence that the Party tended to direct its full-time activists into industrial storm-centres and was thus able to recruit from embattled workers in this or that occupation, but such gains were often only temporary.[31] The largest single category of Communists, however, was the unemployed. They constituted just under half the total membership in 1930 and fully 60 per cent in 1932; and throughout the 1920s a large proportion of the Party was out of work either because of general unemployment in their particular trade or because of victimisation. It is difficult to generalise on the significance of this fact. In an unpropitious area like Birmingham it is clear that the unemployed Communists were cut off from those in work, yet in a mining community such as Mardy in South Wales unemployment was the common lot after 1925 and the local branch of the Unemployed Workers' Committee merged into the miners' lodge.[32]

The geographical and occupational distribution of membership are only part of the story. An equally important factor was the ability of Communists to command a local following – there is a fundamental difference between a branch of thirty which is isolated and estranged and one able to provide a lead which fellow workers follow. Election results can serve only as a strictly limited index of this capacity, and the results are difficult to interpret because most Communist candidates in the three General Elections between 1922 and 1924 either stood under the Labour banner or were uncontested by Labour. Nevertheless, we lack any more satisfactory evidence (with the exception of some important local studies[33]) and it is noteworthy that Communists commanded a far more impressive electoral support during the 1920s than ever since. In 1922 they put up seven candidates and won 52 819 votes (23.2 per cent of the poll); in 1923 nine candidates won 76 741 votes (25.3 per cent of the poll); and in 1924 eight candidates won 55 346 votes (10.0 per cent of the poll). In no General Elections since have they won higher percentages, even in 1945 when two Communists were elected, and of course no Communist candidate today expects to save his deposit.

Surveying the period as a whole, between 1920 and 1933 there were thirty-one occasions on which parliamentary candidates who stood as Communists received more than 10 per cent of the poll (I exclude from consideration the further eight candidatures under the official Labour banner). Only on two occasions did a Communist secure election – once in Motherwell (Lanarkshire) and once in the London constituency of Battersea North – and in both cases there was no Labour competition. These thirty-one relatively rewarding candidatures provide a good indication of areas of Communist influence. Thirteen were Scottish: Greenock (at the mouth of the Clyde) on five occasions; Motherwell (twice); Aberdeen North (twice); West Fife (twice); Dundee and Kelvingrove (Glasgow). Six were in Wales: Rhondda East (on three occasions), Rhondda West, Caerphilly, and Ogmore. Eight were in London: Bethnal Green North-east (on three occasions), Bethnal Green South-west, Battersea North (twice), Stepney Whitechapel and St George's, and Wandsworth Streatham. Only four were elsewhere in England; Birmingham West, Manchester Rusholme, Nottingham East, and Clay Cross in Derbyshire. Furthermore, if we restrict our attention to those occasions when the Communist was opposed by a Labour candidate, the pattern is more marked. There were eighteen such occasions: eight in Scotland, six in South Wales, three in London and only Clay Cross in the rest of England. And no English constituencies are comparable either with Greenock, where the Communist candidate received between one- and two-fifths of the poll from 1922 onwards, or with Rhondda East, where Arthur Horner, in a straight contest against the Labour candidate, built up from 15 per cent of the poll in 1929 to 31.9 per cent in 1931 and 33.8 per cent in a 1933 by-election – a level that was maintained right up to 1950.[34]

It should be reiterated that parliamentary election results are an extremely crude test of Communist influence, and I have used them only in the absence of regional and local studies which could support more fruitful comparisons. A line of demarcation was already fairly clear whereby the Labour Party served as the parliamentary expression of the labour movement, even in areas where it was not necessarily the organisation which conducted other forms of struggle. For this reason alone the election results for local government and poor law authorities, Co-op boards of management, trade union branches and so on are more accurate indicators of Communist strength. Nevertheless, the weakness of the Communist Party in national elections is undeniable and should remind us that in this country Marxist activity is normally conducted via non-Marxist organisational forms.

Turning now to the more general issue of the impact of Marxism, it is difficult to resist the temptation to continue the story in terms of Communist policy and influence. The periods of greatest impact, in 1920–1 and again from 1924 to 1927, coincide with strenuous Party efforts to build links with the Labour and trade union left; and the chief organisations – the National Workers' Committee, the British Bureau of the Red International of Trade Unions, the National Minority Movement, the National Left Wing Movement, the National Unemployed Workers' Committee, even for a time the National Council of Labour Colleges – were all under Communist control or influence. There would seem to be perhaps a hundred thousand militants enrolled in these various movements, giving Marxism a far greater presence than the membership figures of the Communist Party would suggest (see Figure 2). But the satellite interpretation is inappropriate. One defect is that the significance of Marxist doctrine and the level of theoretical understanding within these organisations varied greatly and was often extremely low. Conversely, a more serious problem is that Marxism had

Figure 2 *Some membership statistics for left-wing movements in the 1920s*

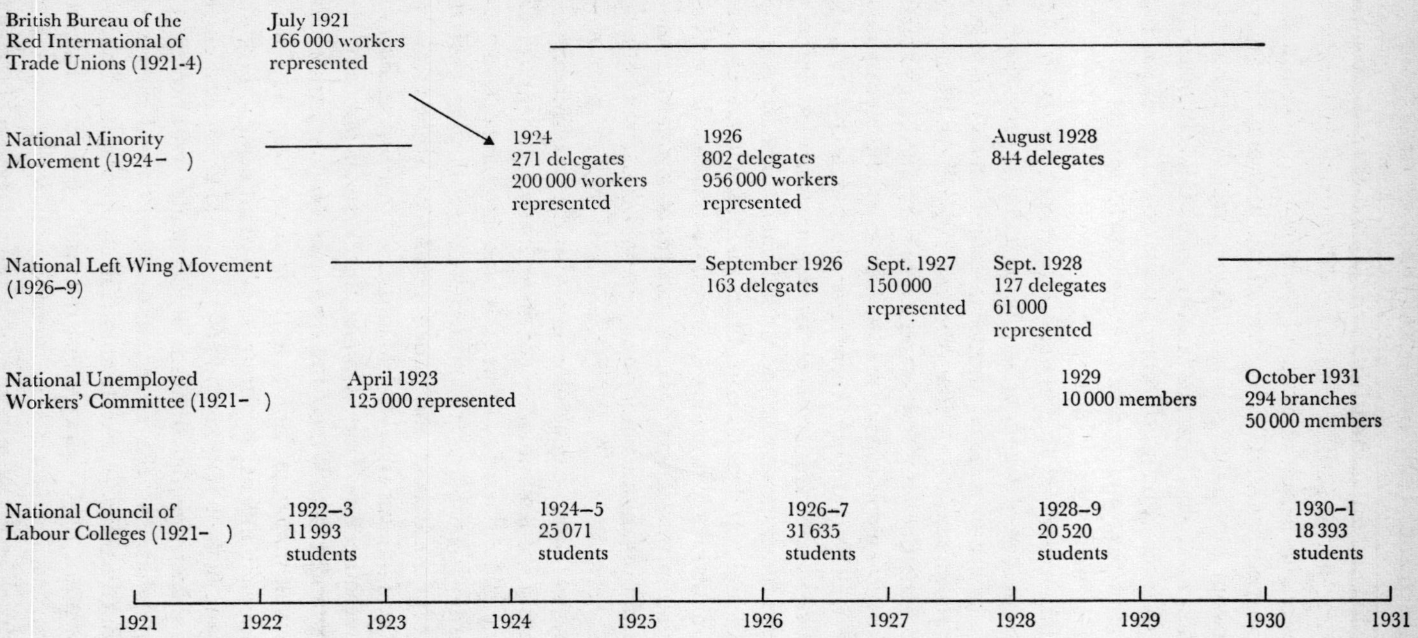

	1921	1922	1923	1924	1925	1926	1927	1928	1929	1930	1931
British Bureau of the Red International of Trade Unions (1921–4)	July 1921 166 000 workers represented										
National Minority Movement (1924–)				1924 271 delegates 200 000 workers represented		1926 802 delegates 956 000 workers represented		August 1928 844 delegates			
National Left Wing Movement (1926–9)						September 1926 163 delegates	Sept. 1927 150 000 represented	Sept. 1928 127 delegates 61 000 represented			
National Unemployed Workers' Committee (1921–)			April 1923 125 000 represented						1929 10 000 members		October 1931 294 branches 50 000 members
National Council of Labour Colleges (1921–)		1922–3 11 993 students		1924–5 25 071 students		1926–7 31 635 students		1928–9 20 520 students			1930–1 18 393 students

Sources: Reports of various organisations, supplemented by Klugmann, *History of the C.P.G.B.*; Martin, *Communism and the British Trade Unions 1924–1933* (Oxford, 1969); Macfarlane, *The British Communist Party*; and R. H. C. Hayburn, 'The Response to Unemployment in the 1930s with Particular Reference to South-East Lancashire', unpublished Ph.D. thesis (Hull, 1970), pp. 402–4.
Note that these figures include significant double counting and nominal representation.

deeper roots in the labour movement than is suggested by such a roll call. The efforts of two previous generations of Marxists may have been unsuccessful but they had not been completely barren. Certain aspects of Marxist thought, in an admittedly attenuated form, had passed into general currency and, as will be seen in the next chapter, this bowdlerised Marxism was one formative element of Labour doctrine.

The question of Marxist influence needs to be considered in two parts, the immediate post-war period up to 1921 and the period that followed. The periods are distinguished above all by the offensive character of the first and the defensive character of the second. In the first period when new types of mass activity cut across the established channels of the labour movement, the influence of Marxism was both more amorphous and more extensive. Few understood the precise meaning of Bolshevism but many responded to the broad notion of working-class power; similarly, many were attracted to new domestic phenomena such as the Councils of Action and the use of industrial 'Direct Action' for political ends, even though their precise affinities with the new Marxist perspective was far from clear. Such militancy declined after 1921 and the Labour Party and trade unions once again became the only major vehicles of working-class activity. As has been mentioned, during the 1920s a series of barriers was erected between the chief Marxist organisation, the Communist Party, and the mainstream of the labour movement. But the barriers were never completely effective. Many Communists continued to retain membership of the Labour Party until well into the decade, particularly in areas with a strong left tradition such as Sheffield where the leading Communist, George Fletcher, was still a member of the Labour Party Group on the Sheffield Board of Guardians until 1928, and Maesteg in South Wales where the leading Communist, Idris Cox, was vice-president of the Labour Party branch on the eve of the General Strike.[35] Communists were of course eligible for trade union membership, despite campaigns against them in particular unions, and they frequently won positions of local leadership. When all allowances have been made for inflated membership figures, the Minority Movement and National Left Wing Movement attracted significant numbers of trade unionists and a far from negligible number of local Labour Parties. But it is also necessary to emphasise the autonomous nature of this Marxism within the wider labour movement. Its clearest expression was the labour college movement, which was briefly led by individual Communists in the early 1920s but thereafter broke with the Communist Party and continued as an independent movement with a considerable Marxist content. A great many local socialists had been associated with the Communist Party in its period of formation and then severed their links in 1921 and 1922 (Figure 1 suggests that membership halved between 1920 and 1922). By then the choice of political allegiance was a simple one – Communist or Labour – and they chose to work with the mainstream organisation. Some would become extreme anti-Communists (the Braddocks of Manchester are an obvious example), but a great many others never entirely discarded their Marxist orientation. Fred Shaw of Huddersfield may be cited as one who left the Communist Party very early and become a stalwart Labour Party organiser and educationalist, but with a discernibly Marxist way of approaching political issues.[36] Similarly, many Labour and trade union militants drew on Marxism as one component of their creed, particularly in moments of revolt against dominant tendencies in the Labour movement. I shall attempt a more precise analysis of this wider Marxist influence in the body of the study.

There is a substantial body of literature dealing with 'traditional' working-class political culture. This literature deals with the working-class communities of the staple industries – mining villages, mill-towns, centres of the making and working of metal, as well as with dockside and railway communities – where the relationship of work life and home life was particularly close. These communities were dominated by a few companies, often only one, and were concentrated within a narrow range of jobs. Ties within the workplace were strengthened by family, leisure and residence, and are said to have supported a particularly strong form of internal solidarity. But this working-class solidarity focused inwards; it was concerned with the maintenance, and if necessary the militant defence, of existing standards and local values; it lacked any wider orientation which could provide a revolutionary impetus. Furthermore, so the argument goes, this working-class culture has been superseded by the new conditions of mass industrial society. The conveyor belt isolates workers in repetitive and unfulfilling labour; these workers live in nuclear family units in areas where their neighbours work in a variety of occupations and where recreation is centred in the home; their aspirations and perceptions of society are increasingly confined to income and consumption.[37]

Several criticisms have been levelled at this analysis of the traditional working-class community. It has been pointed out on the one hand that many of these traditional working-class occupational groupings did not manifest historically even the defensive form of class consciousness that is attributed to them, and deferred instead to bourgeois culture and political leadership.[38] On the other hand, these supposedly 'particularistic' communities *have* at various historical moments transcended boundaries of industry and locality.[39] Such criticism should remind us that the sociological model of the traditional working-class community is seriously incomplete and cannot serve as an adequate explanation of political behaviour. More particularly, it fails to provide any criteria for distinguishing between those traditional working-class communities in which Marxism flourished and those in which it languished. Yet the model does draw attention to certain structural features of the social constituency which shaped the Marxism of our period, and while its theorisation of these features may be faulted, the reality and significance of the phenomenon itself can hardly be ignored.

At the risk of freezing the historical process during a period of rapid change, and of constructing a stereotype out of widely divergent instances, we may hazard a composition sketch of the community in which the Marxists of the 1920s had emerged. The community was comparatively new, in most cases stretching back only three generations and sometimes only one or two. Its locale might be a village, a town or a distinct neighbourhood within an industrial city. Such separation was always a matter of degree but the absence of an influential local bourgeoisie was a general precondition. Life revolved around one or at most a handful of industries which (with the exception of the textile industry) employed only male labour. A variety of locally controlled institutions bound the community together – union, Co-op, institute, pub, club and chapel. Sexual roles were rigidly defined, but while the male exercised many privileges, the maternal influence within the home was marked and the mother exercised a crucial role in the childhood and adolescence of many Marxists. An elementary education ended at the age of fourteen, whereupon the adolescent entered the masculine world to learn his trade. Henceforth he was a man, with a man's privileges, for great emphasis was laid on his acquisition of the relevant occupational skills and his ability to bring a weekly wage into the household. The typical Marxist, like the typical Labour Party activist, took great pride in his prowess as a skilled worker and his responsibility as a wage-earner, and enjoyed a commensurate prestige within the community. (We can thus already appreciate that the massive increase in unemployment in the staple industries during the 1920s and the frequent victimisation of militants would have a particular bearing on the relationship of Marxists to their community.)

Like other political and industrial activists, the Marxist devoted his limited hours outside work to union activities and various other forms of self-improvement, and generally avoided the pub and leisure activities which occupied many other men. The crucial means of self-improvement was study. The young worker sometimes began to read into the night with an eye to acquiring clerical skills and securing entry into the salariat, or sometimes he simply wanted to learn how to write up the minutes of his union branch or to draw up a balance sheet. In either case the initial practical purpose was frequently replaced as the autodidact encountered a new world of literature, philosophy and social science. Alternatively, many were prompted to take up books by a sense of religious doubt or a more imprecise curiosity of an existential or social character. Until more substantial consideration is given to this complex subject, it is impossible to be more precise about its dynamics. The chances of embarking on such a course were higher in areas such as South Wales or Scotland where there was a stronger tradition of literacy, and among certain occupations conducive to mental enquiry: self-education was also more likely where the materials were readily to hand. Yet these facts merely point to certain relevant circumstances and in no sense constitute a historical explanation of what they describe. To take one significant source of working-class autodidacts, a miner of South Wales grew up with an inculcated respect for books, his work underground stimulated a curiosity about natural science, and he had access to a well-endowed library at his institute; but we still cannot explain why one miner should respond to these factors while another should spend his leisure time drinking and gambling. Whatever the reason, this 'earnest minority', as Richard Hoggart has called them, stood in ambiguous relation to the rest of their community. On the one hand, they were in the forefront of local life, hard-working, respectable, the natural leaders of opinion. Thus Robert Roberts locates such a stratum who 'talked more, read more and possessed a much larger vocabulary than their neighbours in general'; these were the men who 'gave pith and purpose to tavern talk, trade-union branch meeting and factory dinner-hour break'.[40] On the other hand, such individuals were frequently estranged from their fellows by contact with a wider world outside the community, the world of national congresses and conferences, of Ruskin College in Oxford and Central Labour College in London, and the still larger world opened by books. The man who

attended the Labour College was of course a marked man in the eyes of
the management, and was frequently unable to find employment upon
his return, but his isolation went further than this. As the young Jack
Lawson found when he began his studies – studies that eventually took
him to Westminster and Whitehall – he was 'simply voted "queer" by
the people' of his Durham mining village.[41] This earnest minority,
made up of a variety of trade union and labour activists and a sprinkling
of Marxists, were at once representatives of and strangers in their own
society.

In some cases this working-class elite assumed a distinct Marxist
form and was able to stamp its influence on the community at large.
Such communities frequently attracted the title of 'Little Moscow' or
'Little Russia' and became renowned for their deviant political culture.
Examples could be drawn from Fife or Durham but here I shall discuss
only two – Mardy in South Wales and the Vale of Leven in
Dumbartonshire, Scotland. An examination of them might uncover
the conditions of Marxist success and, if only negatively, suggest the
problems faced by Marxists in other areas.

The mining village of Mardy is situated at the top end of the
Rhondda fach, separated both from the main valley and neighbouring
Aberdare valley by steep mountain slopes.[42] The settlement was established after the first pits were sunk in the 1870s and it reached a
maximum population of between eight and nine thousand inhabitants
just before the First World War. The topography dictated the familiar
settlement pattern of parallel terraces above and below the main street
– a pattern which fostered the close-knit and highly self-enclosed community.[43] The hub of community life was the Workmen's Institute,
supplied originally by a philanthropic director of the coal company.
This was the biggest and most central building, with a large hall,
gymnasium, billiard room, reading rooms and library. Mardy had no
particular reputation for militancy before the First World War, but
there was a tradition of outstanding checkweighmen (the checkweigher,
a pivotal figure in the union structure, was elected by the colliers to
ensure that their trucks of coal were weighed correctly). The Mardy
miners had a tradition of electing men who had been victimised or who
were blacklisted elsewhere. In this tradition was Noah Ablett, a prominent advocate of union reform before the War and the leading Marxist
educationalist on the coalfield. He was succeeded by Arthur Horner,
the incorrigible rebel, who was soon to emerge as the leading Communist miner and who was elected on May Day 1919 while still in

prison for refusing to serve in the war. Horner's co-checkweigher was
Dai Lloyd Davies, another Communist. Between 1919 and 1925 Mardy
enjoyed full employment and high wage rates (higher than in Ferndale,
less than two miles down the valley), but the General Strike initiated an
economic crisis from which it never recovered. When the South Wales
miners began returning to the pits at the end of 1926, the colliery companies insisted on wage cuts; the Ocean Coal Company, which worked
Mardy, also took the opportunity to abolish various work customs won
over the past decade. The lodge refused to accept work on these terms
for the rest of the decade. Some of the inhabitants were forced to move
into England in search of work, settling in Slough, Coventry, Birmingham, Hayes and elsewhere, but a solid core stayed on. The misery they
experienced is recalled by one activist:

Mardy was so depressed, so poverty stricken, that people suffered from mal-
nutrition. Some people committed suicide, some people were taken into the mental home, and I can well remember visiting two at Bridgend Hospital, and when
I went in to see them, six months after they were put into the hospital, they were
standing by a wall, nothing in their hands but acting as if there was. And I asked,
'Well, what are you doing?' And he said, 'I'm trying to write out a list of where
I was looking for work last week.' And he'd been in the Mental Home six
months.[44]

The obduracy and unconventional procedure of the lodge (for example,
it allowed the Communist-controlled Unemployed Workers' Committee to be merged into it) led to trouble with the executive of the South
Wales Miners' Federation (S.W.M.F.) and Mardy was expelled from
the Federation in 1930. A new official lodge was established whose
members resumed work. In 1934 the militants finally came to terms
with the S.W.M.F. and merged their lodge with the official one, but
even this was no one-sided capitulation. Mardy maintained a reputation
throughout the 1930s that was celebrated in the novels of another local
Communist, Lewis Jones.

Mardy was part of the larger society of the Rhondda valley. Its comparative prosperity and recent growth attracted a heterogeneous population of miners from other areas, young men from further to the west,
and a sprinkling of Italians and Maltese. Yet its position at the head
of the valley fostered a strong local identity. The railway came in 1899
and the tramline from the main Rhondda valley in 1912; but these
were used more often by Mardy residents for trips down the valley than
by residents of Tonypandy, Porth or Pontypridd, who had little reason
to visit the smaller settlement. Like so many other working-class com-

munities dominated by a single staple industry, the texture of social relations was close-knit; familial, work and recreational ties interacted to bind members together. This did not mean that there was a uniformity of political views, and indeed there were active Conservatives throughout the inter-war period, but it did foster a more general sense of public and private morality, of right and wrong, which commanded broad acceptance across the political spectrum. This is best illustrated by the role of the lodge during the General Strike, when it turned itself into the strike committee and assumed an informal but total control. Commerce and transport were regulated and residents even forbidden to read newspapers sympathetic to the owners. The fusion of the lodge with other political activities was such that the same minute book was used to record the decisions of the 1927 Hunger March committee, the Distress Committee (consisting of representatives from the lodge, the institute, political parties, the chapels and the schoolteachers) which fed those thrown out of work in 1928 and 1929, the strike committee of 1931 and an election committee conducting Arthur Horner's parliamentary campaign in the same year. Furthermore, such working-class communities possessed a unity which was not present in more heterogeneous and fragmented social units. The Mardy Institute served as dance-hall, cinema, theatre, meeting place, reading room, library, sports arena and feeding place in times of distress – it was the focus of public life. The crucial achievement of the Communists in Mardy was to situate their Marxist ethos within this close-knit, communal tradition. Unlike the majority of British Marxists, they did not represent a minority sub-culture at odds with the majority; they were affirmative, rather than oppositional, appropriating the sense of community, rejecting or by-passing some of its forms but reproducing others, and always maintaining the underlying senses of continuity and solidarity. The Marxists supplied a pervasive political and social leadership through such institutions as the labour college class, the Communist Young Pioneers, the Miners Minority Movement and the International Class War Prisoners Aid, and such customs as the singing of socialist songs, secular funerals and reciprocal visits to the Soviet Union. It was the Party, for example, that organised public meetings of the miners and their wives to teach birth control. The Communist leadership of the lodge and the Institute was based on this more general hegemony.

The Vale of Leven extends some four miles, following the River Leven south from Loch Lomond to Dumbarton on the Clyde.[45] As with

Mardy, the slopes on each side of the valley mark the community off and reinforce a strong local identity – throughout the inter-war period the Natives and Residents Association had more than five hundred members. There are five settlements – Balloch, Jamestown, Alexandria (the biggest), Bonhill and Renton. The population grew during the nineteenth century along with the textile bleaching, dyeing and printing industry, whose works were strung out along the river. At the end of the First World War the population was a little over twenty thousand; thereafter the population declined quite sharply and this figure was not regained until the 1950s. The industry suffered from intensified competition and the development of new processes. It contracted sharply after the First World War, although some of the United Turkey Red Company's factories kept going on short-time throughout the inter-war years. The only other major industry was engineering. The Argyll Motor Company, Scotland's first manufacturer of motor cars, built a large factory in Alexandria in 1906 which employed 1300, but this failed on the eve of the war. Its premises were taken over by the Admiralty for the production of munitions, providing work for 2000, but this too ceased operations at the end of 1919; and the industry languished until 1936 when the government re-established a torpedo factory in the premises. Thus as early as 1922 58 per cent of the insured workers were unemployed, and after a partial recovery, two-thirds of the male wage-earners were without work for several years of the Depression. Many emigrated and others travelled in search of work to Dumbarton and further east along the Clyde, but the Vale was severely affected by unemployment for the whole of the inter-war period.

Like Mardy, the Vale had no reputation for undue radicalism before the First World War. There were local branches of the I.L.P. and S.L.P., but the local labour movement was dominated by a stratum of skilled craftsmen who enjoyed harmonious relations with the employers both in the workplace and in the thriving religious and recreational bodies which were a feature of local life. By 1918 eighteen societies representing some three and a half thousand workers were affiliated to the Trades Council: besides unions like the engineers and railwaymen, there were newly established branches of the Amalgamated Society of Dyers and Bleachers and the Workers' Union representing semi-skilled and unskilled workers. The Vale of Leven Co-operative Society was a thriving concern with some six thousand members and sales averaging £1 per week for every member. A new tone was first apparent during the 1918 General Election. Sir William Raeburn, a Glasgow ship-owner who was the successful Unionist candidate, was unable to hold election meetings at Renton, Bonhill or Jamestown. On each occasion his opponents, described by the local newspaper as 'socialists and discharged soldiers', heckled, moved motions of no confidence and finally marched through the streets singing 'The Red Flag'.[46] This post-war radicalism seems closely linked to the simultaneous collapse of the owners' authority and the impact of post-war unemployment. A branch of the National Unemployed Workers' Committee was formed and allowed to affiliate to the Trades Council. The Communist Party, most of whose members were unable to obtain work, was more successful in organising the unemployed than it was in factory politics, for its members were invariably blacklisted in all the major works. There were frequent marches on the parish council and county council involving several thousand disgruntled residents; and 'street captains' using hand megaphones to summon residents achieved considerable success in preventing evictions. The Communists were organised into district groups throughout the Vale but often came together for aggregate meetings, joint political activity, concerts, dances, socials, and so on. The Party also formed the Unemployed Band – tin whistles, supplemented by flutes, triangles and cymbals – and had a vigorous tradition of open-air activity. Its annual May Day celebrations frequently featured prominent national figures; its branch of the Friends of the Soviet Union was one of the largest in the country.

A notable feature of working-class politics in the Vale is the relative absence of sectarian rancour – a contrast with the pre-war S.L.P. branch which was 'never stuck for a virulent word' and whose general attitude had been 'bitter as hell'.[47] Except for a few years in the early 1930s, the Communists operated in electoral agreement with the local Labour Party and I.L.P. in elections for parish council, district council and county council, and joint meetings of the councillors of all three parties were a common occurrence. This local united front first achieved a majority on the parish council in 1922 and soon increased unemployment relief well above the permitted level. Each councillor was formally surcharged, but the first Labour Government took office shortly afterwards and, according to popular legend, John Wheatley ensured that the 'Bonhill file' was lost. A similar alliance operated within the Trades Council, where the Communists were well represented but did not attempt to create their own majority, preferring instead to work with Labour members and to develop their political attitudes. The same solidarity was evident during the General Strike: the local Council of

Action, nine of whose twenty members were Communists, used the Party rooms in Bonhill; the Council commanded general obedience and the authorities made no attempt to interfere or arrest the leaders, as they did in so many other Scottish areas. For much of the inter-war period, Hugh McIntyre, Dan O'Hare and David McKim represented the Vale on the county council. When the alliance broke up temporarily at the end of the 1920s, the Communist Party was sufficiently strong to maintain its electoral support: Hugh McIntyre won nearly three thousand votes in the Vale when he contested the Dumbartonshire by-election in 1932, and in the same year the Communists outpolled Labour in the local government elections. After the alliance was re-established, the united left again gained control and McIntyre became chairman of the district council.

In their different fashions the Vale of Leven and Mardy exemplify the strengths and weaknesses of the militant locality. Both were beleaguered communities whose struggle against mass unemployment and poverty brought them into conflict with the employers and the state – there, as in other Little Moscows between the wars, the police station was enlarged and the force strengthened. For them the doctrine of class struggle and the Marxist analysis of the state possessed a vivid reality, and the Communists derived their authority from an ability to win significant victories in defence of living standards. A comparatively wide spectrum of the inhabitants responded to their leadership – it was a prominent member of the Salvation Army in Mardy who led the band which headed demonstrations – and it was the calibre of this leadership which distinguishes them from equally stricken localities nearby which remained largely inert. The success of the militants in Mardy and the Vale lay in their permeation and mobilisation of existing social forms, for in so doing they capitalised on the qualities of close-knit local loyalty which elsewhere resisted the Marxist appeal. This does not mean that the Little Moscows were inward-looking or parochial – they hunger-marched to London, raised volunteers for Spain, and sent worker-delegations to Russia – but rather that they flourished through their achievement of a limited transformation of the locality. The Marx Terrace of Chopwell and the Engels Street of the Vale, the portraits of Marx and Lenin painted alongside Keir Hardie and other native patriarchs, the substitution of the *Daily Worker* for the *Daily Mail* in the public library, all formed part of a rich iconography which registered that the world had been turned upside down.

In every case a complete transformation remained an aspiration.

The red villages were subject to a constant attack from the local custodians of respectable opinion and, at moments of particular notoriety, from Fleet Street. This was accompanied by repeated police harassment. Mass arrests would occur at an eviction or street meeting, leading on to further arrests at the court hearing, and on one occasion in Mardy at a demonstration to welcome back released prisoners. By this means the leading militants of Mardy were removed for lengthy periods, and both the legal costs and fines were a further drain on limited resources. Then too there were lengthy battles with central authorities over the validity of local government policy when the latter was captured by the militants. But the most important limitation of the Little Moscows was internal. In each locality the militants were engaged in argument by moderate critics. This was not a class conflict in the strict sense of the term: in Mardy the authority of the coal-owners was always exercised indirectly; and the owners in the Vale, who before the war had been prominent residents engaged in various forms of patronage and leadership, subsequently withdrew. The petite bourgeoisie – the shopkeepers, small businessmen and professionals, the upper management of the dye and print works – were stronger in the Vale than in Mardy, but in neither locality were their collective interests sufficiently distinct from those of the working-class majority to constitute a clear alternative. Rather, the essential division was between those who advocated militancy and those who believed it brought ruin, and this division transcended class boundaries. The principal accusation brought against Arthur Horner, Dai Lloyd Davies and the other Mardy Communists was that their obduracy had prolonged the industrial strife and caused the closure of local pits; against Hugh McIntyre, Dan O'Hare and the Vale Communists that they cared only for confrontation and would not restore jobs. Here was a chink in the militants' armour which the employers exploited (for example, they responded to Horner's re-election as checkweigher in 1932 by immediately posting closure notices) but which had a genuine basis in the working-class consciousness. Furthermore, when this issue brought the militants into conflict with the national executives of the relevant unions, the position of the militants was especially vulnerable. Since Mardy, the Vale of Leven and other similar localities were no more immune from historical forces than any other section of the Labour movement, the notion of the Little Moscow as a militant citadel in defiance of the capitalist host must, in the last analysis, be rejected. The significance of the term lies in the postulation of an identity around which political struggles could be fought. Hence we may say that the precondition of a Little Moscow was the ability of the militants to win a sufficient following among the unemployed, the working trade unionists and the labour rank and file sufficient to displace working-class moderates from control of the local movement. If the particular circumstances of Mardy and the Vale allowed this to occur over long periods and with extensive results, it is also true that every Communist and Labour college militant was in this sense striving to build a Little Moscow.

2. Marxism and Labour Socialism

This study is largely concerned with the opposition of two doctrines, Marxism and Labour Socialism. Most readers will already be familiar with Marxism, at least in broad outline, but Labour Socialism demands immediate explanation. The term denotes the political perspective of the Labour activists of the period, along with the more general understand-of the social and economic processes which supported this perspective. This definition raises considerable problems, for doctrine was a secondary concern for the early Labour Party, and it needs to be shown as well that a distinct and reasonably coherent doctrine transcended the movement's internal differences. The primary basis of the Labour Party was, and still is, the trade unions, and Labour avoided imposing any precise ideological creed on its diverse membership. Of those Labour activists who were avowed socialists, few ever sought to systematise their views into a comprehensive general theory and they lacked the same legacy of accepted texts and broad methodological unity to which Marxists could appeal. It is sufficient to enumerate some of the many socialist organisations that existed before the First World War – the I.L.P., the B.S.P., the various *Clarion* groups, the Labour Churches and the Fabian Society – to appreciate the diversity of early British socialism. There was a plurality, an overlap of one organisation with another, and a general openness of debate that were largely lost after 1918.

Labour Socialism is usually identified with the leaders of the Labour Party, and above all with Ramsay MacDonald. It was MacDonald before the war who sought intellectual respectability for socialism with his ponderous essays *Socialism and Society* (1905), *Socialism and Government* (1909) and *The Socialist Movement* (1911); MacDonald again who shaped the post-war development of the Party with *Parliament and Revolution* (1919), *Parliament and Democracy* (1920), *A Policy for the Labour Party* (1920) and *Socialism: Critical and Constructive* (1921, with new editions in 1924 and 1929). These books were undoubtedly influential and there is sufficient repetition and

continuity in the development of his ideas to suggest that Labour
Socialism was a doctrine formulated by MacDonald and like-minded
publicists and handed down to the rank and file. MacDonald's own
study syllabus of *The History of the I.L.P.* (1922) certainly fostered this
sense of diligent missionary activity rewarded eventually by popular
acceptance, and it was reinforced by the heroic sketches of early pioneers
in such works as the lavish three-volume compendium *The Book of the
Labour Party*.

In fact the lineage of Labour Socialism is far more complex. It involved an interaction of the articulate minority and the social class on
which, in the last analysis, it depended – and their reciprocal relationship will be explored in the course of this study. A further flaw in the
evolutionary perspective of Labour Socialism is that it skips over certain
crucial shifts in the whole perspective of British socialism. Stephen Yeo
has argued that such a shift occurred in 1895. The movement that
arose in the 1880s was charged with an almost millennial ethical
fervour. Its insistence on an immediate moral response, reinforced by a
conviction that the current political order was fundamentally unstable,
shortened the time perspective to the point that the working-out of a
coherent political strategy was a relatively minor consideration. There
was an 'implicit view of the group as a strategy in itself – its increase
in membership, its collective missionary and other activities, just its
being there, however small, being a major part of what it was necessary
to do to bring socialism about'.[1] Yeo suggests that this phase of socialism
was replaced midway through the 1890s by a more fragmented socialist
movement which was more attentive to short-term pragmatic considerations. Because of the uneven character of socialist development in
different parts of the country, it is impossible to lay down hard-and-fast
chronological boundaries (by 1895 socialism had won a widespread
popular following in parts of the industrial north and London, but
twenty years later this remained unaccomplished in some industrial
areas, and ground had even been lost in London). The period from
around 1895 to 1914 is best characterised as displaying two main
tendencies. On the one hand is the tendency suggested by Yeo: the
leaders of the I.L.P. and the Labour Party were busy consolidating
their organisations by means of a parliamentary agreement with the
Liberals and a patient courtship of the unions. Here socialism was at a
discount. Then there was the tendency which maintained much of the
momentum and moral fervour of earlier days, carrying socialism into
new areas and harrying the leadership for its moderation. This was the

socialism of the *Clarion* vans, Victor Grayson, and George Lansbury's *Herald*. Without exaggerating the degree of social unrest in Edwardian Britain, it is clear that the working-class struggle to find new forms of expression assumed widely diverse forms.

Many of these differences were resolved in the First World War and the immediate post-war period. The 1918 constitution of the Labour Party seemed at last to have settled the controversy over the Party's political character, for Clause Four was sufficiently broad to secure union acceptance. The end of the Progressive alliance, and Labour's performance in the General Elections of 1918 and 1922 as well as in the post-war local government elections, suggested that it now enjoyed the support of a large proportion of the working class. And the collapse of rank-and-file militancy in the sharp slump of 1920–1 seemed to terminate the successive waves of syndicalist and shop-steward industrial politics. This historical moment thus marks a new shift in the development of British socialism. The vast majority of socialists seemed both to have accomplished their immediate aim of mobilising the working class and to have reached broadly similar conclusions about the necessity of working within the mainstream of the organised labour movement. In this context it became possible, indeed imperative, to clarify socialist ideology. The widely assorted attitudes of the pre-First-World-War period were resolved into two distinct ideologies, Labour Socialism and Marxism. They can be contrasted as follows:

Labour Socialism	*Marxism*
ethical	scientific
empirical	systematic
constructive	critical
idealist/educationalist	materialist
corporate	oppositional
reformist	revolutionary

Each of these co-ordinates will be explored further in the course of this study, and in the remainder of this chapter I shall suggest how they cohered during the 1920s into two relatively systematic ideologies.

We may begin with the contrast between ethical and scientific socialism. British socialism is sometimes characterised as a distinctively ethical tradition, in contrast to its more cerebral continental counterparts. Now it is undoubtedly true that the first British socialists in the early part of the nineteenth century based their doctrines on a moral critique of the emergent capitalist order. This is equally true of the first French and German socialists, and indeed it applies also to Marx himself before he became convinced of the need to understand the necessity of capitalism in order then to overthrow it. During the mid-Victorian era, when British capitalism had seemingly swept all domestic opposition aside to enjoy world supremacy, the chief criticism of utilitarianism and the dictates of the Manchester school came from Romantic and aesthetic spokesmen such as Carlyle and Ruskin – whose vast popularity among working-class autodidacts right into the twentieth century is of fundamental significance. Many British Socialists of the 1920s would echo Keir Hardie and 'mark the reading of *Sartor* [*Resartus*] as a real turning point' (even if they could not all claim to have read Carlyle's demanding essay 'until the spirit of it somewhat entered into me').[2] The revival of British socialism in the 1880s is closely linked to a general reaction against the high Victorian era, a reaction that assumed literary, intellectual, moral and religious forms. The example of Edward Carpenter, whose own spiritual crisis was resolved in the rejection of the moral norms of respectable society, is obvious. That the Fabians, who came to be seen as the coldly calculating New Machiavellians portrayed by H. G. Wells, also began as an ethical group called the Fellowship of the New Life, is less generally appreciated; and Willard Wolfe has recently reminded us of the visionary passions that stirred even the young Sidney Webb.[3]

The first generation of Marxists were an integral part of this movement.[4] The early S.D.F. compendium *How I Became a Socialist* reveals a common process of moral awakening and self-discovery that is characteristic of the period. It is apparent in Marxists as different in their origins and interests as Ernest Belfort Bax, a gentleman intellectual of independent means and Harry Quelch, a self-taught London worker who edited the S.D.F. paper *Justice*. And there was no more effective critic of Victorian materialism than William Morris, the most creative Marxist thinker of his generation. In the writings and activity of Morris the criticism of economic and social relations is indistinguishable from moral and aesthetic considerations.

The case of William Morris raises problems that bear on British Marxism generally. For the past eighty years two schools have fought over Morris – the one attempting to distinguish his literary and artistic achievement from later political aberrations; the other insisting on the substance of his conversion to Marxism, and indeed presenting it as a more realistic perception of his earlier concerns. The debate raged fiercely during our period, with the two principal adversaries, Bruce

Glasier and Page Arnot, reinforced by many equally partisan claim-ants.[5] More recent Marxist scholarship emphasises the complexity of Morris's struggle during the last dozen years of his life to integrate his pre-Marxist romantic impulses into historical materialism as it was then understood; and Edward Thompson has argued for the validity of Morris's moralism and utopianism, not just as appendages of this or that social theory but in their own right. Thompson claims that 'there is a sense in which Morris, as Utopian and a moralist, can never be assimilated to Marxism, not because of any contradiction of purposes but because one may not assimilate desire to knowledge'.[6] This con-ceptual distinction between desire and knowledge operates throughout the history of British socialism, but it became a practical distinction involving different political groupings only at the end of the nineteenth century.

During the 1893 coal strike a succession of prominent socialists came to address the Nottingham miners. Percy Redfern, then a young local activist and later a leading Co-operator, describes the Marxist spokes-man thus: 'Eloquent hands pictured the round cake of the national income. The workers made it; the capitalists and landlords took it. One slice only, a mere third, they gave back to the workers, just to keep their slaves alive.' Then came a spokesman for the I.L.P.: 'It was not this caricature, with its kernel of bitter half-truth, that Margaret Macmillan brought to the market place. She came with a vision of health, joy and beauty in working lives to be demanded and created by the people themselves. . .We listened with respect, touched by some-thing vaguely, unattainably fine, and then we went back to the strike.'[7] Not all Marxists were blind to the appeal of health, joy and beauty, but in popular perception there was an increasingly rigid division between this sort of ethical awareness and the Marxist creed. This can be attributed partly to the particular influence of Hyndman, but Hynd-man is too often used as a punching-bag by critics of the shortcomings of British Marxism. Frederick Engels was just as contemptuous of Morris's enthusiasms (which he once dismissed as the inadequacies of a 'settled sentimental socialist'[8]) and in hindsight it is possible to discern in the closing years of the nineteenth century a narrowing of Marxism along the lines of Engels's later texts, notably *Anti-Dühring* and *Socialism: Utopian and Scientific*. Options which had existed earlier were closed off in favour of a rigid, self-contained 'science' of society.[9]

Between 1917 and 1933 the temper of British Marxism was thus overwhelmingly scientific. The great achievement of Marx was to have rendered socialism scientific, and this was considered to be its crucial departure from Labour Socialism. 'It is for the scientific socialist to brush aside sentimental considerations', for unless socialism was 'based on a correct knowledge of the nature of conditions under which you work and live, [it] will not achieve much'.[10] No one challenged this interpretation during the 1920s, and it was left to John Middleton Murry, the literary critic of pronounced sensitivity (the novelist Katherine Mansfield, who was his wife, once told Murry that he made her feel 'you are going to uncover yourself and quiver'[11]), to do so when he discovered Marxism at the beginning of the 1930s. His claim that 'morality is at the very heart of Marxism' drew a storm of orthodox criticism. 'For Murry has made Marxism a matter of morals, whereas Marx showed morals to be a matter of material conditions. Marx explained morality, thus abolishing it; whereas Murry is now trying to reconvert Marxism into something mystical and ethical, instead of scientific.'[12]

If the schism between scientific and ethical socialism had a damaging effect on Marxism, its consequences for Labour Socialism were no less profound. Most non-Marxist socialists developed a far more pragmatic orientation after the 1890s. The exigencies of success in local government elections and of the closer relationship with the unions, and a working agreement with the Liberals, all served to moderate earlier attitudes. The principal leaders of the I.L.P. – Ramsay MacDonald, Philip Snowden, Keir Hardie and Bruce Glasier – were able to resist their more militant critics and strengthen their influence on the early Labour Party. In this emergent Labour Socialism the practical and the visionary co-existed in an uneasy relationship. Moderate socialists continued to exert a strong moral appeal. 'Coom to Jesus' Snowden became notorious for his appeal to the workers to 'come with us and call to the man with the muckrake, and tell him to lift his eyes from the earth and grasp the heavenly crown above his head' – Bunyan's man with the muckrake was freely cited in socialist literature of the period.[13] Glasier, who once described socialism as 'essentially a spiritual principle',[14] raised the art of pious, other-worldly sermonising to a new height; and neither Hardie nor MacDonald were slouches in this competitive field. There was, however, a new trend in ethical socialism. Because it was combined with an increasingly restricted political perspective, the ethical accompaniment became more rhetorical, less precise, with little or no practical import. Whereas with Owen, Ruskin or Morris, the ethical and the analytical had been fully integrated aspects of a unified ideology, the two aspects were now quite distinct. The call for a warmer, more loving transformation of human consciousness became an end in itself, no longer related to the material circumstances which shaped that consciousness. As Keir Hardie put it, 'Socialism is much more an affair of the heart than of the intellect', and it accordingly lost the cutting edge of rigorous theoretical enquiry.[15] A Lancastrian member of the I.L.P. has recalled that it 'attracted a type of Socialist who was not satisfied with the stark materialism of the Marxist school, desiring warmth and colour in human lives: not just bread, but bread and roses, too. Perhaps we were not quite sound on economics, as our Marxian friends took care to remind us, but we realised the injustice and ugliness of the present system.'[16] Thus for most socialists economics and ethics became shorthand terms for alternative creeds.

But the principal exponents of Labour Socialism were not prepared to surrender this corner of the field to their Marxist opponents so easily. They claimed that their economics and their view of social relations were sounder, more 'scientific', than those of the Marxists. When MacDonald wrote that 'the Socialist method is the scientific method' he meant that his 'constructive proposals' were 'founded not on any abstract Utopias which belong to the free imagination, but on the evolution of functions and institutions in his own time'.[17] This claim owed a good deal to Fabian influence, and the 1918 Party programme, *Labour and the New Social Order*, based itself explicitly on the 'Science of Society'. But Labour always stressed that its Socialism was more than scientific. 'The English people', one writer claimed, are 'a people practical, unphilosophic and at bottom religious. Economic theories divorced from ethics are repellent to them.'[18] Thus 'whereas continental Socialism was a product of dogmatic materialism, with the class war as its guiding idea, in this country humanism was the note of Socialist thought'.[19] The grip of this approach is revealed most clearly in a symposium, published in 1924, in which some 250 members of the Labour movement attempted to define socialism. One after another they described it as 'a fraternity of comradeship'; 'an attitude towards life'; 'a release from the overwhelming obsession of materialism to realisation of the higher spiritual values of life'; 'something greater than an economic doctrine. . .a way of life': 'an ethical–religious mass movement'; 'true brotherhood'. 'Our politics may be right and our economics sound, but unless we have caught the vision we shall fail, for "where there is no vision the people perish".'[20]

A further difference between Marxism and Labour Socialism was

the systematic character of the former and the pragmatic, piecemeal
character of the latter. The claims of Marxism to constitute an all-
encompassing science of society are well known; and the Marxism
which flourished in Britain at this time was particularly encyclopedic.
Following Engels's own lead in his later writings, British Marxists laid
claim to a universal science applicable to natural and social phenomena
alike: 'Marx's application of dialectic in the fields of history and
sociology was a special application. . .of a method that Marx and
Engels considered applicable to all nature and society.'[21] Marxists also
emphasised the methodological unity of their doctrine: historical
materialism, the dialectic, class analysis, economics and so on comprised a complete and indissoluble system so that it was impossible for
historical materialism, for example, to be understood separately from
Marxist economics. Furthermore, no aspect of human activity was not,
at least in principle, susceptible of Marxist analysis. Literature, art,
religion, sport and many other fields not normally regarded as political
were all grist to the Marxist mill. Such comprehensiveness might be
achieved at the cost of a tendency towards oversimplified dogmatism,
but it was one of the doctrine's most powerful appeals to the worker
who wished to make sense of his situation that it presented him or her
with a systematic explanation. As the young Nye Bevan discovered on
first reading Marx, 'The relevance of what we were reading to our own
industrial and political experience had all the impact of a divine
revelation. Everything fell into place.'[22]

British Marxists liked to think that their opponents held an equally
systematic set of beliefs. There was their own proletarian knowledge
and there was bourgeois knowledge, to which Labour Socialists wit-
tingly or unwittingly subscribed. A Communist like Rajani Palme Dutt,
the influential figure whose 'Notes of the Month' in the *Labour
Monthly* were a feature of the period, could always explain how
apparently random statements and unconnected events in the Labour
movement actually constituted a coherent Labourist or Social Democratic trend. But this trend was derived in the first instance from what
the leaders of the Labour Party did, and only afterwards was decked
out by reference to their speeches and writings. Dutt's personal library
of Labour conference reports, pamphlets, etc. is now deposited in the
Marx Memorial Library and his annotations reveal the procedure:
particular phrases and sentences are marked to appear, frequently out
of context, in future 'Notes of the Month'. Dutt could discern an underlying rationale in the most fragmentary bits of evidence, for in his

world there were no coincidences or random events, only tendencies and plots. But the truth of the matter was that Labour Socialism lacked both the consistency and comprehensiveness of Marxism, and that attempts to furnish it with such a general perspective failed to carry conviction.

Yet Labour Socialism *was* more systematic than Labourism, that earlier set of customs, habits and attitudes that continued to exercise such a powerful hold on the British working class.[23] At the very heart of Labourism lay a reluctance to express and thus examine the contradictions it embodied. Labourism resided essentially in maxims such as 'A fair day's wage for a fair day's work'; 'The labourer is worthy of his hire'; or 'You don't go cap in hand to the gaffer'. Trade union leaders and organisers from George Howell onwards might sometimes embroider these beliefs, but their glosses were designed primarily to tell a non-working-class audience what it wanted to hear and only secondly to influence the workers themselves. The purpose of Labour Socialism, on the other hand, was to lift the working class up from its lowly preoccupation with wages and conditions, and to endow it with a sense of social purpose. This involved the articulation of an elaborate theoretical edifice: a historical perspective of social progress in the nineteenth-century positivist tradition; an economic analysis to show that the worker was denied the full fruits of his labour; an organic view of society to indicate how this injustice ought to be corrected. These elements were assembled by MacDonald and others, but they were never completely assimilated into the everyday political practice of Labour Socialism. Nor did they ever cohere into a fully integrated theory of politics, since various historians of Labour Socialism have demonstrated both its eclecticism and the extent of its reliance on non-Socialist sources.[24] That its spokesmen should have erected such an elaborate scaffolding is significant, but it did not carry the weight of actual political practice.

One reason for the comparatively fragmentary character of Labour Socialism was its emphasis on constructive change. Unlike Marxism, it never comprehensively rejected capitalist society and indeed affirmed many of its aspects. Society was perceived in organic terms as continually eliminating its defects, moving ever closer to the Socialist Commonwealth. Right up to the First World War most of these reforms were pursued within the Progressive Alliance so that Peter Clarke has argued that 'There was. . ., before 1914, nothing in the Socialism of Tawney or MacDonald which made a gulf between their political philosophy and the Liberalism of Hobhouse, or Hobson, or Wallas.'[25] Even after the Progressive Alliance foundered on the shoal of heightened class antagonism in the war and immediate post-war years, Labour sought merely to carry on the programme of piecemeal social reform – 'to effect those changes in structure which the life of Society requires, and to launch the ship of state well manned and well equipped on its future voyages'.[26] There was never any question of scrapping the vessel and constructing a new one.

Two further aspects of Labour Socialism were its typically idealist perception of the process of winning converts to socialism and its general reliance on education as a political method. The tendency to operate in an evangelical fashion was common to all socialists in the late nineteenth and early twentieth centuries. At a time when socialists were largely isolated from the principal working-class organisations, the very act of conversion demanded a high degree of commitment and considerable self-sacrifice; and it was to these qualities that the socialist, in turn, addressed his appeal. Whether his socialism was derived from the English ethical tradition, from Comte and the positivist school, or from Marx, it involved an optimistic evaluation of human nature, a belief that there was a long-run tendency for rational insight and altruistic feelings to gain strength at the expense of ignorance and selfishness. To this extent all socialists were children of the Enlightenment.

These attitudes were common to Marxists and non-Marxists alike before the First World War. The S.D.F. and the S.L.P. both functioned primarily as propagators of socialism for whom doctrinal purity was more important than popular activity. But from the war onwards there was a new Marxist awareness of the material factors that operated on working-class consciousness and an increasing propensity to regard broad-based action as the precondition of advance. Labour Socialists, on the other hand, retained their faith in human nature, for they believed that 'The creative powers of Society are in men's minds, not in their pockets.'[27] Socialism was envisaged as a future stage in human progress which could only be attained when the people themselves were ready for it, and so present-day socialists concentrated their attention on this aspect of the problem. As MacDonald wrote, the socialist 'strives to transform through education, through raising the standards of mental and moral qualities, through the acceptance of programmes by reason of their justice, rationality and wisdom'.[28] Two consequences of this positivist vision may be distinguished. First, there was an enormous confidence in the power of moral appeal. Since mankind was essentially good it was only necessary to set the facts of poverty and oppression before the people to evoke a positive response. Katharine Bruce Glasier was perhaps unduly naive to expect that if a landlord 'had time given to him to think about' the evil consequences of private property, he 'would have clapped his hands and said the new way was ever so much the better';[29] but she was only pushing a general belief to its logical extreme. Second, there was an expectation that education, any education, would sweep all vestiges of ignorance and superstition away, and thus lay the intellectual basis for socialism. Unlike the Marxists, who paid attention to educational content, Labour Socialists pinned their faith to some unspecified notion of literate rationality. We may take the example of James Welsh, a Lanarkshire miner whose formal education ended at elementary school but who continued to study and published verse and novels of life in the Lanarkshire mining villages. Welsh rose to be checkweighman of his lodge and was elected to parliament in 1922 as the member for Coatbridge; and in the debate on the King's Speech he explained the inevitability of Socialism to the Conservatives thus: 'You gave us an Education Act 46 or 47 years ago, and such as it was, it gave us knowledge, and knowledge is power.'[30]

All this may seem to be taking us into a rather unproductive seam of the history of popular belief. But the foregoing had direct political consequences. 'Knowledge is power' was a favourite slogan of the Marxist labour college movement, but there were few Marxists who placed such total confidence in knowledge as Labour Socialists did. 'The workers have the numbers, the voices and the votes, and ought to be politically supreme. Their actual power is not a tenth of their potential power...What they lack is knowledge.'[31] Thus the Labour leaders preached and practised on the basis that there was no other impediment to socialism than the backward mentality of the masses – no Foreign Office officials with a penchant for circulating documents of doubtful provenance; no newspaper proprietors ready to publish them; no bankers with ultimatums concerning government spending. In this way the educationalism of the Labour Party stifled the prospects of the movement addressing itself to the actual balance of class forces.

This possibility was further retarded by the prevalence of a corporate view of society in Labour ranks. It is here that the distinction between Labourism and Labour Socialism is of crucial significance. Labourism was based on a deep-rooted, almost instinctive notion of a separate

working-class identity, of 'us' as against 'them'. While the precise
relationship of 'us' and 'them' remained undetermined, and only
fleetingly involved a clear sense of class conflict, there was a persistent
suspicion of those agencies of the state – such as police, education and
social services – which were perceived as intrusions into the working-
class domain.[32] This sense of separate working-class identity was to find
graphic expression in the 1920s, most notably in the General Strike,
and it was a factor that no Labour politician could ignore. Labour
Socialism certainly recognised that the working class bore genuine
grievances, but it perceived them as deviations from the norm, 'part of
the general disruption of social bonds and destruction of social fellowship which capitalism has produced'.[33] Each section of society had its
own proper function to contribute to the common good. Thus the whole
spirit of Labour Socialism was constructive, aiming to repair the social
fabric and integrate the working class into the larger collectivity.

Labour's effort, politically and industrially, must of necessity recognise the *fact* of
class warfare, and does recognise it...But our fundamental task is a creative one.
We are not seeking simply to wrest control from the class that exercises it to-day
in its own narrow and selfish interests. We are engaged in a positive effort to
bring the Co-operative Commonwealth into being.[34]

And this process of social regeneration was seen as proceeding gradually
and organically.

Marxism, on the other hand, emphasised the absolute incompatibility
of class interests and the need for the working class to seize power for
itself as a precondition of the abolition of class divisions. On trial for
sedition in 1921, John Maclean was asked what he meant by revolution. His reply was to hold out his hands, one above the other. The top
hand represented the capitalist class and the bottom hand the working
class. Then he reversed them. That was revolution.[35] Both in its literature and in its everyday working political practice British Marxism was
oppositional, dwelling on the defects of the existing order and seldom
pointing to a preferable alternative. Its reputation was that of the
troublemaker, the rebel, the hard case. As Daniel De Leon once put it,
'The Proletarian Revolution is Irreverent'. The chief exception to this
generalisation was the example of the Soviet Union, for the success of
the Russian Revolution furnished a storehouse of precept and example
whose significance is difficult to exaggerate. British Marxism now
ceased to be such a negative tradition of social criticism, and recaptured
something of the dream of John Ball – albeit in a form that Morris
would have found difficult to recognize. The austere columns of the

the pre-war *Justice*, *Socialist* and *Socialist Vanguard* gave way to a Communist press which argued the practical superiority of the Soviet system. There unemployment was abolished; education opened to all; production directed to real needs and not for private profit. (And those who looked for a daily dose of conventional pulchritude were rewarded with photographs of a smiling Komsomol member, or Moscow school-girls performing callisthenics – in this respect at least it is arguable that use made of the First Socialist State accommodated rather than challenged the dominant values of British society.) But the crucial limitation of this new affirmative aspect of British Marxism was that it was non-British. The isolated success of Marxists in Mardy, the Vale of Leven, Chopwell, Lumphinnans and a few other inter-war 'Little Moscows' was based on a capacity to demonstrate the positive aspects of the doctrine. Marxism achieved a palpable significance in the recreational, cultural and religious life of such communities. In the place of constant criticism of the local labour movement, the Marxists offered leadership; instead of costly campaigns against the Council, the Guardians and the School Board, they were sometimes able to turn them into citadels of the local working class. But British Marxists effected such a break-through in only a few cases, and in the vast majority of working-class communities, as well as nationally, they were fated to be the perennial critics.

The final difference between Labour Socialism and Marxism concerns their political methods. It is not particularly helpful simply to label Labour Socialism as reformist, for developments within the contemporary European left have surely demonstrated that an absolute distinction between reform and revolution is difficult to sustain. What matters is not so much the reformist or revolutionary character of a socialist party as the degree to which that party situates its policies within an overall strategy, a strategy which in turn rests on a theoretical analysis of its field of politics. In other words, there is nothing inherently unsound in compromises or the pursuit of limited objectives so long as they are recognised as such, and supported within an overall appreciation of their specific necessity. Judged by these standards, both Marxists and Labour Socialists were inadequate. The failure of the Marxists will be discussed subsequently, but briefly their weakness stemmed from an inability to reconcile the revolutionary commitment with regular political practice. The Communist Party pledged itself in its original constitution to 'relentlessly strive by industrial organisation, agitation, and revolutionary political and industrial action, to urge the working class on towards revolution';[36] and its writers constantly emphasised the follies of reformism.

Yet by 1921 at the very latest it was obvious that any immediate revolutionary initiative was out of the question, and that the working class was engaged in a desperate struggle to defend those gains it had made at the end of the First World War. The Communist Party's revolutionary rhetoric may have helped crystallise the deficiencies of Labour Socialism, but it also stood in the way of a frank recognition of the immediate tasks. On the other hand, those Marxists who abandoned the Communist Party for the Labour Party – most notably the group associated with the Plebs League and labour colleges, which included the Horrabins, Raymond Postgate, Morgan Philips Price, Ellen Wilkinson and J. T. Walton Newbold – were unable to loosen the grip of Labour Socialism on the Labour Party. They found themselves caught in the familiar quandary of a Labour ginger group: responding to the leadership on specific issues without ever advancing a coherent alternative strategy.

The fundamental weakness of Labour Socialism lay not in its reformism but in the aimlessness of its reformism. If the task of the Labour Party, as interpreted by MacDonald, was to repair the ship of state for future voyages, it manifestly lacked any blueprint which might instruct the efforts of the repairers. Historians of a social democratic sympathy such as Robert Skidelsky and David Marquand have drawn attention to the way in which the socialism of this period provided no guidance in the 'practical tasks of government'.[37] Sometimes the Labour leaders invoked socialism as carelessly as had Sir William Harcourt, confusing it with any and every form of collective activity. Sometimes they used the term to denote the policies a Labour government would pursue if only it possessed a parliamentary majority, an educated electorate, propitious economic circumstances. . .and so on. And sometimes they spoke of it in hushed terms as not even imaginable in the foreseeable future – thus Ramsay MacDonald looked back over the first eight months of his premiership and said that even after a further fifty years of Labour government the corn would still be green.[38] Whatever the usage, the subscription to socialism served as an excuse for lack of hard thinking about the methods and priorities of an effective programme of reform.

These elements, then, cohered into a doctrine that was ethical, empirical, constructive, educationalist, corporate and reformist. Between

1918 and 1931 this Labour Socialism commanded the general support of the labour movement and thus constitutes the prevailing ideology against which Marxism must be set. It remains, however, to discuss certain currents in the movement which were only uneasily assimilated into the Labour Socialist orthodoxy, and at some points actually opposed to it. I shall concentrate on three such currents: the trade unions, the Labour left and the middle class.

By 1918 the vast majority of British trade unionists were affiliated to the Labour Party, and in that year the Party committed itself 'To secure for the producers by hand and brain the full fruits of their industry. . . upon the basis of the common ownership of the means of production. . .'[39] It is clear that only a minority of trade union members were socialists and there is considerable evidence testifying to the general suspicion of Labour Socialists. Snowden and MacDonald had drawn particular criticism before the First World War for their lukewarm support of embattled workers; and the socialists' reservations about the war damaged their relations with these unionists further. While Arthur Henderson, Jimmy Thomas and others laboured to repair the breach, it was not until 1922 that MacDonald was able to resume the parliamentary leadership of the Labour Party he had resigned in 1914. At the root of these difficulties lay two radically different conceptions of the political Labour movement. The unions had been forced into politics by the need to safeguard their legal status, but parliament occupied only a small part of their total attention, for they went to Westminster as a pressure group without any more comprehensive political programme. Men like MacDonald, Snowden, Jowett and Lansbury, on the other hand, entered politics through the socialist societies with much larger aspirations. Their aim was nothing less than a political party based on the working class which could achieve national leadership. Initially this was obscured by their dependence upon an electoral agreement with the Liberal Party and before 1914 they had to hasten slowly, here coaxing reluctant trade unions to sever Liberal connections, there damping down more impetuous socialists. The war-time transformation of British politics ended this dependence on the Liberals and in so doing clarified the differences between the Labour Socialists and the unions. For if Labour was to be the second party of British politics, it must be something more than the mouthpiece of the unions; it must speak for a wider constituency and project a more comprehensive programme. And just as the Labour Socialists depended on the numbers and money of the unions, so the unions depended on the political leadership of the

Labour Socialists. They co-existed uneasily throughout the 1920s, quarrelling in 1924 over the Labour Government's attitude to industrial disputes and in 1926 over the Party leader's less than absolute solidarity with the General Strike, until they fell out finally in 1931.

This must suffice as a schematic summary of relations between the industrial and political sides of the Labour movement. But such a distinction could never be absolute in a movement where the unions are directly involved in the political organisation and, furthermore, at a time when a high proportion of Labour M.P.s and constituency activists were trade unionists. It is here that the conflict between a vestigal trade union and Labourist consciousness and the political exigencies of Labour Socialism was most acute. The final superiority of the latter can be suggested by consideration of the views of Ernest Bevin, for there was no more dogged champion of his union's interests than this thrusting young secretary of the newly amalgamated Transport and General Workers' Union, and Bevin was quite prepared to face down the 1924 Labour Government in support of his London transport workers' pay claim. At the same time he was closely involved in the affairs of the Labour Party; accordingly, he moved at the 1925 Party conference that Labour should never again take office as a minority government. In acting as Prime Minister without a parliamentary majority, MacDonald had failed to discharge the responsibility which any reputable trade union official owed his members: regardless of 'the politician's clever art' and 'whatever was done on the political side, on the industrial side they were going on with their organisation, uniting their forces and developing Trade Union consciousness, which would find expression on the political field as it did on the industrial field'.[40] But this appeal to the separate identity and block votes of the unions fell flat and Bevin's motion was easily defeated. It was enough merely to postulate the projection of a pure trade union consciousness into the political arena for its inadequacy to be generally appreciated, and Bevin himself was appreciative elsewhere of the need to build the movement on a more inspiring idea.[41]

There is another strand of opposition to Labour Socialism, one which found little direct expression within the Labour Party and was chiefly manifested in industrial action. Between 1910 and 1921 the belief was widespread that under certain circumstances it was legitimate to use industrial action to influence political decisions. Only a tiny minority of avowed syndicalists rejected the need for a working-class political party altogether, but many more can be described as quasi-syndicalist in their reservation of the right to achieve political objectives by industrial methods. This willingness to use 'Direct Action', as it was commonly known, was particularly noticeable between 1918 and 1920: thus the reluctant trustees of the Albert Hall were forced to make it available for a Labour meeting at the end of the war when the Electrical Trades Union threatened to cut power supplies; and the threat of more extended working-class action was generally believed to have forced the government to abandon military intervention against the new Soviet republic.[42] Sections of the trade union and Labour leadership were carried along on specific issues, but Labour Socialists fought a rearguard action against the underlying principle. 'To force upon the country by illegitimate means the policy of a section, perhaps a minority of the community, involves the abrogation of Parliamentary Government. . .'[43] The commitment to parliament and the constitution was re-established after 1921 when mass unemployment and a series of defeats undermined the quasi-syndicalist strategy. Yet even then, the trade unions retained the right to take industrial action regardless of its possible political implications, and this latter attitude was only abandoned as a result of the General Strike.[44] However, the crucial point concerning this strand of anti-Labour-Socialist practice is that its refusal to take part in politics left unchallenged the supremacy of Labour Socialists in the Labour Party.

The second major source of opposition to Labour Socialism was the Labour Left. While the Labour Left overlapped with militant sections of the trade union movement, its crucial characteristic was the commitment to parliamentary action. It never built a unified organisation but could be found in the I.L.P. (especially in Scotland), the Plebs League, the Ginger Group co-ordinated by *Lansbury's Labour Weekly*, and the National Left Wing Movement set up by the Communists through the *Sunday Worker*. In parliament its chief spokesmen were James Maxton and John Wheatley, the two leading Clydeside M.P.s, and George Lansbury. The Labour Left was impatient with the excessive caution of the Labour leaders and what it considered to be their obsession with respectability; it put greater emphasis on a proletarian identity and was more hostile to other classes, and in parliament and at conference it regularly attempted to push the Party in a leftward direction. MacDonald and the front bench found the Labour Left a nuisance (the Labour leader's skin was very thin) and for a brief period at the end of the First World War had to fight hard to keep the I.L.P. militants from affiliating to the Communist International. In particular localities, also,

the Labour Left were very strong. But in national terms it is clear that
the Left was unable to mount a serious challenge to Labour Socialism,
and as the decade wore on its attempts to do so by means of such
devices as the Cook–Maxton manifesto fell flat. The reason for the Left's
weakness was ideological. For all its criticism of particular aspects of
Labour Socialism, the Labour Left was itself constrained within the
same set of ideas; the same ethical tone which displaced systematic
analysis of the actual balance of class forces; the same faith in reason
and education; the same attachment to parliamentary methods as an
alternative to the other forms of working-class struggle. The Left's stick-
ing point was of course its insistence that the Labour Party should be a
class party, that 'the basis of the [Labour] political creed. . .is the recognition of the fact that present-day society is divided into hostile classes';[45]
yet even this rested on an historical myth. The frequent appeals to the
spirit of Keir Hardie and a lost proletarian purity conjured up a legend
that was at once spurious and irrelevant to the battles of the 1920s.

   The grouping which remains to be considered, if indeed it ever constituted an identifiable grouping, is the middle-class and upper-class
members of the Labour Party. I shall concentrate on figures of some
national significance even though local worthies also exerted their own
more limited influence. Some were long-standing members of the pre-
war Fabian Society, I.L.P. or university socialist societies such as the
Webbs, Leslie Haden-Guest, Hugh Dalton, Susan Lawrence, Fenner
Brockway, Rosslyn Mitchell, Clifford Allen, the Coles, Will Mellor or
Clement Attlee. Some had come from the Liberal Party, usually during
the war by means of the Union of Democratic Control: Noel Brailsford,
the Buxton brothers, J. A. Hobson, H. B. Lees-Smith, E. D. Morel,
Arthur Ponsonby, Helena Swanwick and Charles Trevelyan. Some
again were progressive intellectuals with a looser attachment to
Labour: Norman Angell, Harold Laski, A. D. Lindsay, Bertrand Russell
and R. H. Tawney were most prominent of these. Those who had
figured in the radical wing of the Liberal Party found a degree of
continuity with their earlier Progressivism, and usually picked up the
orthodoxy fairly readily. Others found the homespun intellectuality and
windy rhetoric of Labour Socialists both distasteful and more than a
little ridiculous. A handful, of whom Laski and Cole were outstanding,
actually subjected Labour Socialism to a rigorous criticism owing
something to the Marxist tradition, and since they also applied themselves to the correction of Marxism they occupy a crucial position in
the theoretical debates of the British Labour movement, and are given

some space in subsequent chapters. Leaving this last group to one side, however, it is noticeable that the middle-class Labour figures never attempted to replace Labour Socialism as a general body of thought. While their education and background gave them a privileged position in the life of the Party, and this enabled them to contribute their own expertise to this or that area of policy, they always operated within an already established ideological discourse. Not for another twenty-five years would a later generation of middle-class intellectuals confront the deep-rooted traditions of the Party with a thoroughgoing revisionism.

I would therefore claim that during the 1920s there was a distinct Labour Socialist ideology to which Marxism was the only complete alternative. Both conventional and quasi-syndicalist trade unionists, as well as the Labour Left and middle-class converts, all displayed their particular viewpoints, but Labour Socialism alone spelt out a comprehensive view of society and of the methods whereby it would be changed. Clynes and Thomas, Swales and Cook, Lansbury and Maxton, and Ponsonby and Trevelyan were all to be heard echoing MacDonald and Snowden. And the decisive influence of Labour Socialism emerges even more clearly in the local organisations of the Labour movement. It is a limitation of this study that it draws so heavily on the published views of a relatively small number of national figures – though in extenuation it should be said that few of our efforts in the collection of oral testimony and other forms of historical retrieval have so far been focused on the ordinary Labour activist. By their very nature the rank and file – the men and women who bought and sold literature rather than wrote it, and listened to speeches rather than gave them – produced very little material of their own. We need to know more of these anonymous men and women who swelled the ranks of the trades councils, constituency parties and I.L.P. branches up and down the country. But such testimony as we do have, supplemented by the local Labour press and other historical records, testifies to the pervasive influence of Labour Socialism. Particular phrases such as 'a higher social consciousness', 'the social organism', 'the Socialist Commonwealth', 'let us call to the man with the muck-rake', 'ballot boxes and not bullets', etc. are encountered repeatedly. Correspondence published in the Labour press is often suggestive. Decisions taken at conference often indicate the way opinion ran. More often, however, we have to work indirectly through the writings of the few, seeing how they constructed their arguments and noting symptomatically arguments they considered and those they omitted to consider.

3. Literature and education

'In Britain we are very deficient in the fundamental works. Many are not available, the body of works of commentary and application is not written, or written badly, many of the works are not as well translated or cheap as they should be.'[1] So wrote the organiser of the Communist Party bookshop in 1932. This was perhaps an unduly severe judgement, for British readers were not as badly served for the literature of Marxism as is often supposed and the majority of the more important works of Marx and Engels had been translated into the English language by 1917. Admittedly the standard of these translations varied a good deal and reliable translations of many texts were not made until the 1930s. It is also true that many of the original translations existed only in the expensive editions of Swann Sonnenschein and that a good many others were available only through the cheaper but still fairly costly American editions of Charles H. Kerr, the socialist publishers in Chicago. The American price of most Kerr volumes varied between fifty cents and two dollars, but they were sold in this country at a higher price than their strict sterling equivalent. Before 1917 *Capital* came at 6/6 a volume, Morgan's *Ancient Society* cost 5/- and Joseph Dietzgen's two books 3/6 each; in 1922 James Clunie paid 6/9 for his *Critique of Political Economy*, 7/6 for Morgan and 6/9 for a volume of Dietzgen.[2] Such prices made the purchase of a book a significant item in a working-class budget (though groups of Marxists took advantage of a scheme whereby they paid $5 to become shareholders in Kerr's and bought the books at half price). Before the establishment of the Communist Party the task of publishing cheap editions was beyond all Marxist groups except the S.L.P., who printed mainly pamphlets, mostly selling for a few pence, on their own press. Furthermore, most editions of Marxist texts were restricted to runs of no more than two or three thousand. The problem of buying or gaining access to the rarer items was to some extent overcome collectively: members of a local political branch or informal study circle would each subscribe a few

pence a week and gradually acquire works that would otherwise have
been beyond their means.

I have endeavoured elsewhere to list all the English-language translations of the writings of Marx and Engels that were available by 1933,
and the results are summarised in the Appendix to this chapter.[3] It may
be worth while running over what Marxists had at the start of our
period. In 1917 the *Communist Manifesto* and the first volumes of
Capital existed in several editions, while Kerr supplied a translation of
the later German edition of Volume One as well as the second and
third volumes. These Kerr editions were distributed by the S.L.P. and
afterwards by the Communist Party and the labour colleges. They were
generally readily available in left bookshops, though sometimes an
English publisher of the same work would prevent their import; for
example, Allen and Unwin prevented the sale of the Kerr edition of
the first volume of *Capital* in the early 1930s.[4] In addition there were
several cheap editions of the first nine chapters of *Capital* – a somewhat
daunting selection – and of both *Wage Labour and Capital* and *Value,
Price and Profit*. The *Contribution to the Critique of Political Economy*
had also been published. Of the historical essays there were available
the *Eighteenth Brumaire of Louis Bonaparte, Revolution and Counter-
Revolution in Germany*, the *Civil War in France* and the three volumes
edited by Eleanor Marx from her father's articles for the New York
Herald Tribune (*The Eastern Question, Secret Diplomatic History of
the Eighteenth Century* and *Story of the Life of Lord Palmerston*).
Engels's *Conditions of the English Working Class* went through many
editions. Of Marx's early philosophical works only the *Poverty of
Philosophy* and the *Theses on Feuerbach* were available. Engels's
*Origin of the Family, Private Property and the State, Anti-Dühring,
Socialism: Utopian and Scientific* and *Ludwig Feuerbach and the Close
of German Classical Philosophy* had all been translated.

Neglect of continental writings on Marxism was more noticeable.
Among the classic works of the Second International there were available only Kautsky's *Class Struggle, Social Revolution* and *Ethics and
the Materialist Conception of History*, and Bebel's *Women in the Past,
Present and Future*. They had Böhm-Bawerk's *Karl Marx and the Close
of His System*, Bernstein's *Evolutionary Socialism*, Croce's *Historical
Materialism and the Economics of Karl Marx*, and Labriola's *Essays on
the Materialist Conception of History*. Defenders of Marxism could read
the philosophical books of Joseph Dietzgen and works of the Americans
Louis Boudin and Daniel De Leon. But the works of Plekhanov – apart

from his *Anarchism and Socialism* – Luxemburg and Lenin were all as yet unavailable.

In retrospect it can be seen that the list encouraged rather distorted notions about Marxism. The concentration on the later writings of Engels, and the absence of most of Marx's early works as well as the *Grundrisse* (which did not appear in any language until 1939) reinforced a crude positivist approach to philosophy. The voluminous notes on economics taken by Marx which were eventually published as *Theories of Surplus Value*, and which clarify his approach to classical political economy, were also unknown (and would remain so until Maurice Dobb began to discuss them with Marxist students in Cambridge during the 1930s). But the most immediately significant absence was Marx's various writings on politics: most notably the *Critique of the Gotha Programme*, but also his correspondence and the many incidental writings and addresses in which he set forth his strategy for the workers' movement. Looking back on his days in the S.L.P., the Scottish Communist Tom Bell later suggested that he and his colleagues might 'have been saved from numerous errors of sectarianism' in the pre-war period if they had been able to read of the importance Marx himself came to attach to the trade unions and mass labour movement.[5]

Between 1917 and 1933 a vast quantity of secondary Marxist writings became available, yet no great change occurred with regard to Marx and Engels themselves. The *Critique of the Gotha Programme* and some other political writings and addresses were published, as well as *Class Struggles in France* and the *Peasant War in Germany*. In addition, H. J. Stenning's rather erratic selection of Marx's early writings was published in 1926. It was not until 1933 that the situation was greatly improved when the Communist publishing house Martin Lawrence, in conjunction with the Marx–Engels Institute in Moscow, began more systematic publication of the works of Marx and Engels. Even they did not attempt a complete series on the scale of the German or Russian Collected Works, and such a series has only begun to appear over the past few years. The *Correspondence* and Marx's *Letters to Kugelmann* were published in 1934 and several collections of addresses, manifestos and newspaper articles followed. Moreover, a number of works which had already been published were then provided more cheaply and to improved textual standards. Two other important translations in the 1920s were the biographies of Marx by Beer and Ryazanoff, the director of the Marx–Engels Institute, for until then

John Spargo's execrable *Karl Marx: His Life and Work* had been the only available biography.

A miscellany of Bolshevik writings began to appear after 1917. Between 1917 and 1920 emphasis was on contemporary political pamphlets, particularly those of Lenin. In this category fall, among others, *The Collapse of the Second International, April Theses, State and Revolution, Chief Tasks of Our Times*, the *Proletarian Revolution and the Renegade Kautsky*, and finally *Left Wing Communism: An Infantile Disorder*, which referred specifically to the British situation. It was not until 1926 that Lenin's pre-war writings began to appear. *Imperialism* was followed the next year by *Materialism and Empirio-Criticism*, then by the article on Marxism he wrote for the Granat Encyclopaedia, and finally *What Is To Be Done?* A Collected Works of Lenin was begun in 1927 but only five volumes appeared. Fifteen volumes of a cheap and handy Little Lenin Library had appeared by 1933. In addition, other Soviet texts appeared, including Plekhanov's *Fundamental Problems of Marxism*; all Bukharin's principal books; Trotsky's *History of the Revolution, Towards Socialism or Capitalism?* and *Where is Britain Going?*; and Bogdanov's *Short Course of Economic Science*. Stalin's *Theory and Practice of Leninism* was published in 1925 and followed by two volumes of writings entitled *Leninism*. Among non-Soviet writers published between 1917 and 1933 the most important were Kautsky's *Dictatorship of the Proletariat* and *Economic Doctrines of Marx*. Other seminal Marxist theories such as Luxemburg, Lukács, Korsch and Gramsci were unknown to British readers. It can thus be seen that in our period the Leninist version of Marxism was the only one to which British readers had real access. They had an incomplete but substantial selection of the writings of Marx and Engels, and of Marx's major mature works only the *Theories of Surplus Value* was lacking. In attempting to understand Marxism, however, they were dependent upon the guidance of Soviet interpreters.

But this conclusion runs ahead of the actual historical circumstances. The Soviet interpretation was assimilated into an already established native Marxism – indeed, throughout our period it was publicised by men and women who had cut their teeth on this pre-Bolshevik tradition. Much of this study is therefore concerned with the interaction of the new with the old and for this reason I shall dwell at some length on the variety of Marxist educational forms prior to the First World War.

The study and comprehension of Marxist ideas at the beginning of the twentieth century must be set first in a general and then in a particular cultural context. The general context is the movement for intellectual self-improvement and adult education that flourished during the nineteenth century among sections of the working class. A passion for education had been a distinctive feature of the radical movements in the first half of the nineteenth century, variously manifested in coffee-house reading rooms, Owenite Halls of Science and the flourishing popular press, and these had evoked a series of middle-class interventions into the field of popular education. These propagators of individualism and 'Self-Help' were active in different areas, taking control of the Mechanics Institutes, founding their Society for the Diffusion of Useful Knowledge, moulding the form of the public library, and, later in the century, playing a central role in the University Extension movement.[6] Such agencies helped to fix the distinctive character of late-nineteenth-century adult education with its earnest and generally uncritical tone and progressive assumptions; but it would be wrong to regard them on such ground as simple projects of the bourgeoisie or instruments of social control. Even at the high-point of the Victorian era, when the Chartists had given way to a new generation of orderly and respectable labour leaders, education remained a powerful catalyst of the proletarian consciousness and worker–students continued to discover that 'Knowledge is Power'. There remained what Barry Smith has described as 'that culture. . .of ardent hopes and fears, inexhaustible fact-hoarding, dogmatic speculation, excitement in disputation, and taut morality which shaped the thoughts of aspiring working people in the Victorian Age'.[7]

It is noticeable that the intellectual development of our working-class activists began as a process of individual self-discovery. Since formal schooling ended at the age of ten, eleven, twelve or thirteen, and provided only basic literacy and numeracy, the worker–student's initial efforts were often based on a cheap second-hand dictionary. His or her initial reading might be among the burgeoning popular literature of the period, leading on to Eugène Sue, Dickens or Jack London, or it might be among the cheap editions of Shakespeare, Milton, Scott and other respectables that appeared in the second half of the nineteenth century. It would be impossible to exhaust the variety of starting points: witness George Sims, afterwards a carpenter and the original secretary of the Central Labour College, who began work at the age of eight and whetted his intellectual curiosity by reading *The Times* to the master of the Park Lane mansion in which he was a page.[8] Irrespective of initial impulse, these individual intellectual odysseys were likely to share certain common features. Religion was usually important, if only because the Bible was one book which most had read, but more particularly because the question of religious belief preoccupied the late Victorians and a great many autodidacts came to base their education on the secular press and literature. Thus on the eve of the First World War Stella Davies married into a family of skilled engineers who were members of the Openshaw Socialist Society. The grandfather had been a follower of Bradlaugh and based his reading on Paine, Darwin, Huxley, Mill and Spencer; to which, probably in the 1890s, her father-in-law had added Marx and Engels.[9] Beyond religion, a worker–student's interests would move in different directions according to his interests and opportunities. Some, like Mr Polly, would read simply for private escape from the drudgery of everyday life, some with a more social orientation. A crucial influence might be a literate workmate who would recommend or lend particular books, such as the Christian Socialist who pressed copies of *Merrie England*, *News From Nowhere*, *Sesame and Lilies* and *Sartor Resartus* on the young Robert Roberts in Salford, and his secularist rival who offered Haeckel and the *Freethinker* as an antidote.[10] And in whichever direction their interests lay, these autodidacts exhibited a characteristic intellectual tone: they were great respectors of fact and intellectual authority; earnest, even reverential, in their treatment of the text; and they brooked no short cuts in the search for knowledge. Alongside this deference to literary authority, one must put the fact that it remained *their* education, for they defined both the purpose and the boundaries of their intellectual exploration and the books they read assumed significance in this light. Thus an original interest in the doctrine of the creation could lead from the *Freethinker* to Darwin or Huxley, and thence to Haeckel's *Riddle of the Universe*, Morgan's *Ancient Society* and sometimes Engels's *Origin of the Family, Private Property and the State*; or an interest in history might commence with Gibbon, Macaulay, Lecky or Buckle and subsequently assume an increasingly sharp focus on the basis of the current social order, thus leading to Marx's historical writings.

An outstanding feature is the sheer energy and determination with which these self-taught worker–intellectuals pursued their knowledge – men such as Harry Quelch, who had come to London in the 1870s as a shop-boy and was later a factory worker and warehouse packer. Quelch taught himself French in order to read *Capital* and subsequently progressed to German and Latin as well. He became secretary of the S.D.F., edited its newspaper, managed its press and translated *The Poverty of Philosophy*. He may also be taken as illustrative of some of the tensions in the relationship between the worker–intellectual and his untutored fellows. In chapter 1 I noted how Jack Lawson was generally regarded as 'queer' by his fellow miners in Durham when he surrendered himself to the world of books, and suggested that others like him occupied an ambiguous role in most working-class communities. The degree of acceptance of the working-class autodidact depended on a host of factors related to the community's level of social and cultural development, but one important determinant was the attitude of the worker–student himself. Quelch and others like him commonly manifested a contempt for the mentality of the ordinary worker: this emerges with particular clarity in the heavily moralistic short stories he wrote for the S.D.F. and the B.S.P. press in which the sober, self-reliant socialist was repeatedly sponged upon, ridiculed and abandoned by his brutal and fickle workmates.[11] Even in defending their reading, such autodidacts frequently manifested the same estrangement. Tom Barclay, a Leicester secularist, found that his colleagues 'attempted to make fun of him because of his fondness for books, and then Tom would take an impish delight in mystifying them by speaking bookish language about common things, and by using many syllabled words to indicate what they were to do'.[12]

Marxist education before the First World War, then, was rooted in this larger tradition of individual workers' search for knowledge, the tradition from which sprang Harry Quelch and Ben Tillett, and which George Sims, T. A. Jackson and other autodidacts carried over into the 1920s. It must also be set in the particular context of party training. The B.S.P., S.L.P. and S.P.G.B. all paid particular attention to the training of new members in Marxist doctrine. This education bore a markedly more pedagogical tone in which the roles of teacher and pupil were clearly defined and the pupil was expected to master a corpus of established truth. The S.L.P. classes were particularly rigorous and the successful completion of an initial course was a precondition of membership. Tom Bell, a leading member of the S.L.P. in Glasgow and later in charge of Communist education, has recalled how such classes operated:

Our method in the classes was to open with an inaugural survey of the whole field we proposed to traverse, and make the workers familiar with the subject as a whole...Each student was given a series of definitions of terms used by Marx.

These had to be studied, memorised and discussed thoroughly, for perhaps the first four weeks. The student would study *Wage Labour and Capital* at home. At the class we would read it over paragraph by paragraph, round the class. This practice aimed at helping students to speak fluently and grammatically. At the following class meeting questions would be put and answered, and the points raised thoroughly understood by everyone, the results of each lesson being summarised by the leader.[13]

Finlay Hart, who later became a Communist organiser, was an apprentice in Beardmore's yards on the Clyde when he attended such a class:

We went through *Wage Labour and Capital* in twelve lessons; then we took *Value Price and Profit* in twelve lessons; then we did the first ten [sic] chapters of *Capital* which was the beginning of your studies in economics. But besides that, you weren't really an appreciated member of the S.L.P. if you hadn't read Morgan's *Ancient Society*, Gibbin's *Industrial History*, . . .[etc.][14]

S.P.G.B. classes were similar, as were those of the B.S.P., though the latter were less rigorous. Such methods tended to make Marxism into a catechism, for they fostered a thorough literal knowledge of the text at the expense of any attempt to develop Marxism further. Yet there was no hard-and-fast division between the idiosyncratic milieu of the working-class autodidact and the formal class in Marxism; and leading S.L.P. theorists such as George Yates, Willie Paul and Tom Bell bore the hall-mark of the worker–intellectual polymath, just as did Alex Anderson and Moses Baritz of the S.P.G.B. or Will McLaine of the B.S.P. Such proletarian Marxists had an extremely wide range of interests but, above all, they shared an extraordinary hunger for reading. Books were a drug for which they would sacrifice almost anything. Imprisoned in 1926, Jackson reread his beloved Dickens and Gibbon, and renewed his familiarity with Smollet and Macaulay. Finally, for want of anything better, he picked up a volume of Jane Austen. He read with 'mounting ecstasy', pressing the book up against the fading light coming from the barred window until it was impossible to read any longer, then woke at dawn and went without breakfast in order to finish the book. Similarly, J. T. Murphy used his spell in prison to read Macaulay and Conrad, and continued his study of German and Russian.[15]

These two aspects of Marxist education, its exegetical format and its links with a wider working-class intellectual culture, came together in the labour college movement. The labour colleges originated before the First World War and continue beyond our period, yet they are of primary significance as a vehicle for Marxism in the

1920s, and repeated reference will be made to them throughout this
study.[16] They had their origins at Ruskin Hall (later Ruskin College),
which was established in 1899 as a centre of working-class education
with a Christian Socialist emphasis. Its students, who were all men in
residence, were financed either by their unions or by wealthy patrons:
in addition there were provincial Ruskin Halls in industrial cities and a
considerable network of correspondence students. Within a few years
the majority of students were trade unionists from the industrial areas,
with miners from South Wales and the North-East to the forefront.
Some of these brought S.D.F. and S.L.P. doctrines to the College and
were involved in the considerable industrial turmoil of the period.
Among them were Durham miners like George Harvey of Follonsby
and Will Lawther of Chopwell; Welsh miners like Noah Ablett and
Noah Rees; George Sims who was now a carpenter in Bermondsey and
who had been expelled from the S.D.F. in 1908 because of his support
of industrial unionism; and W. W. Craik, a militant railwayman.
Such students pressed for a greater Marxist content in the syllabus and
organised their own extra-curricular classes in Marxism. As the result
of curricular and disciplinary disputes which are too complex to
summarise here, the students formed the Plebs League – the title was
taken from Daniel De Leon's pamphlet *Two Pages of Roman History*
– and launched the journal *Plebs*. In 1909 Dennis Hird, the principal,
was asked to resign because of his failure to maintain discipline and
general sympathy with the students, and the majority of students went
on sympathetic strike. A group of them established their own Central
Labour College with Hird as principal and persuaded the S.W.M.F.
and the Amalgamated Society of Railway Servants to support it.
The College began in Oxford and moved to London in 1911. It was
hampered by poverty but struggled on until 1917, when the conscrip-
tion of W. W. Craik, the Acting Warden, and George Sims, its secretary
and tutor, forced suspension of activity until 1919.

If the full-time educational project was dogged by financial difficulties, the regional movements for independent working-class education
prospered in the pre-war years. In different parts of the country
members of the new Plebs League who had been at Ruskin took the
lead in forming branches of the League and promoting local labour
colleges and evening classes. The most common subjects were industrial
history, evolution and economics, though the content of labour college
education varied considerably. Until the end of the First World War
the movement flourished on informal, local and spontaneous lines of

development, and the most that can be said is that the general emphasis was Marxist, with a strong dash of syndicalism and industrial unionism. The classes often merged with the existing efforts of Marxist groups and where possible they won the support of local trade union branches. The Central Labour College produced an annual supply of new tutors and organisers, and the Plebs League and its journal served as a National link. No firm statistics are available, though Craik claimed later that there were 'at least a hundred' classes operating in England and Wales by 1914, and by 1917 there were forty in South Wales alone.[17]

It is important to emphasise the variety of educational activity in the decade before the First World War. In Lancashire, for instance, a host of individual classes sprang up more or less independently of each other in Bury, Oldham, Openshaw, Rochdale, Liverpool, Warrington and Wigan. Plebs Leaguers were often instrumental in running such classes but 'each class was run as an adjunct of and housed by the local Socialist Society', as Harry Pollitt's description of the Openshaw class makes clear.[18] In South Wales, also, besides the classes associated with the League, which often enjoyed lodge support (these were restricted in the main to the Rhondda), there was a miscellany of local groups. Two examples will suggest their range. A fraternity of miners congregated at the 'White House' at Ammanford, near Swansea, which had been bought by George Davidson, a wealthy American anarchist, and turned into a Marxist educational centre.[19] Wil Jon Edwards, a self-educated miner in the Rhondda, conducted his own unofficial evening classes whose students bought their own copies of *Capital* on the instalment system, 'swallowed Marx whole and mentally disgested him with enthusiasm'.[20] Such projects could proliferate in the mining valleys, where lodge libraries afforded an easy access to Marxist and other literature – surviving library copies of *Capital* in the South Wales Miners' Library reveal that they were read by hundreds of borrowers. Sometimes also Marxists took advantage of the facilities offered by the local authorities or those of the newly formed Workers' Educational Association (W.E.A.). Thus in Scotland John Maclean, the best-known and most successful Marxist educationalist of all, taught classes in Marxist economics during this period under the auspices of the school boards. Lastly, there were free-lance socialist propagandists, such as Bill Gee, T. A. Jackson and the Welshman Nun Nicholas, who made a precarious living from lecturing wherever local groups could raise money to hire a hall and pay the lecturer's expenses. Little wonder, then, that the Commissioners who enquired into war-time industrial unrest in Scotland and Wales reported that 'the development of civic spirit and sense of solidarity' had been 'seriously retarded' by the spread of Marxist education, and urged the provision of remedial civic education in these areas; or that in the same year the secretary of the rival W.E.A. should have written to the Cabinet to support his request for state support with a warning that this proliferation of the study of Marxism was having a dangerous effect on the workers.[21]

In the last years of the war and during the immediate post-war period the labour college movement grew significantly, consolidated its membership and developed its educational methods. These years of political and industrial turmoil were the heyday of the labour colleges as a vehicle for Marxist education: they drew larger numbers into their ambit, popularised their teaching by means of new textbooks, and forged new links with the organised labour movement – without yet yielding, as they would by the end of the decade, to the exigencies of union paymasters. The success of the Marxist educational movement during these years was assisted by the fact that it was not yet rent by the rivalry between the labour colleges and Communist Party.

The three areas of greatest growth were Scotland, South Wales and Lancashire. In Scotland Marxist classes had flourished in the central industrial belt, and the proposal to unify efforts in a national Scottish Labour College attracted very considerable support. In 1916, 471 delegates representing 271 trade union branches and other local organisations attended a conference in 1916 and elected a national committee. In 1918 the committee claimed that fifteen hundred students were attending its classes; in 1920 the number had increased to a little under three thousand, with full-time tutors in Glasgow, Aberdeen, Edinburgh, Fife, Kilmarnock and Stirling; and by 1922 a high-point of over three thousand was achieved. John Maclean's particular ambition was to establish a residential college and this did operate briefly in Glasgow with two tutors and a dozen full-time students studying economics, industrial history, political history, evolution, English, public speaking, economic geography, mathematics and Esperanto – as this was only part of Maclean's activity during the period, it is not surprising that his health soon gave way. The several thousand part-time students were organised in rather larger evening classes in self-supporting local labour colleges.[22] In South Wales the characteristic form was the evening class held in the Miner's Institute and often sponsored by the local lodge. From these classes eight miners in 1919, and thereafter twelve each year, were awarded two-year scholarships to the Central Labour College in London. In Lancashire the various pre-war classes were linked up and a daily Labour College opened in Manchester at the end of the war, which enrolled nearly five hundred students for the 1919–20 session.[23] A common feature of these local classes was the new volume of support they attracted from local union branches, trades councils and party branches. In London, for example, there were forty-six classes and eleven hundred students in 1920–1, and the list of affiliated organisations included twenty-nine branches of the National Union of Railwaymen (N.U.R.), ten branches of the Amalgamated Engineers Union, even a branch of the National Union of Police and Prison Officers, seventeen metropolitan Labour Parties and Trades Councils, and eleven branches of the Communist Party.[24] An undated pamphlet, probably published in 1917, on *How to Start a Social Science Class* provided detailed advice on how to win trade union and trades council support.[25]

The usual form of such classes was a lecture followed by a discussion, but this depended on the availability of lecturers. The great majority were worker–intellectuals, who had sometimes learnt their Marxist economics and historical materialism in the B.S.P. or S.L.P., and in many cases had attended the Central Labour College. By the end of the war their numbers were outstripped by the increased numbers of classes, and this problem was not eased until later in the 1920s when the re-opened Central Labour College had trained a fresh supply. If no lecturer – or tutor, as they were generally known – was available, then the class usually worked by the collective reading of a text, possibly with the help of a more able student-leader. The text might be *Capital*, the *Communist Manifesto*, or perhaps Gibbin's *Industrial History* or Dietzgen's *Positive Outcome of Philosophy*. Despite the success of such reading groups there was a pressing need for more popular texts, and indeed in lecture-classes as well there was now a general relaxation of the somewhat austere standard that had prevailed before the war. One important achievement of the Plebs League was to produce cheap and relatively simplified literature such as Noah Ablett's *Easy Outlines of Economics* (1919) and *A Worker Looks at History* (1918 and subsequent editions) which was written by another South Wales miner, Mark Starr. Over thirty thousand of these textbooks were sold in the first three years after the war. The League also distributed Fred Casey's *Thinking* (1922) and Craik's *Short History of the British Working Class*

Movement (1918). During this period the labour colleges gave attention
to making their courses more easily intelligible in other ways. Shorter
courses were devised in a wider range of subjects; diagrams and lantern
slides supplemented lectures; freer discussion superseded rote-learning;
the journal *Plebs* was enlivened with shorter articles and imaginative
illustrations. For the colleges were no longer catering for a working-
class elite: they were seeking a more popular audience, with the *Plebs*
alone selling between six and seven thousand copies each month.

During this immediate post-war period, the basic unit of Marxist
education was the local labour college, which managed itself and was
financed by individual class fees and affiliation payments. The national
Plebs League consisted of some six hundred individual labour college
activists whose main activities were the general promotion of independent working-class education and the production and distribution of
literature. Since the League's energies were thus directed, and the
Central Labour College did not wish to extend its functions, a National
Council of Labour Colleges (N.C.L.C.) was established in 1921 as an
umbrella organisation to which were henceforth affiliated the Central
Labour College, the Plebs League and the local labour colleges. Its
purpose was the co-ordination and extension of the rapidly expanding
movement, and in particular it endeavoured to persuade trade unions
to affiliate on a national basis. Within a few years it attracted the
Building Trades Workers, the Distributive and Allied Workers, the
Engineers and several other more restricted unions. Furthermore, the
number of students enrolled in classes rose steadily from 11 933 in
1922–3 to a high-point of 31 635 in 1926–7. By then, however, powerful centralising forces were at work, undermining the autonomy of the
local labour colleges and altering the character of educational work.
These changes were to a considerable degree attributable to J. P. M.
Millar, a young and indefatigable Scot who succeeded George Sims as
General Secretary of the N.C.L.C. in 1923. It was Millar who super-
vised the reorganisation of the labour colleges into eleven divisions, each
with its council, executive committee and full-time organiser reporting
to the national head office. The freedom of action of these regional
divisions rapidly diminished: in 1925 the London Divisional Council
protested against the National Council vetoing their nominee for the
vacant post of divisional organiser; and in 1928 a majority of the
labour colleges which made up the Scottish division (still called the
Scottish Labour College) actually withdrew in protest against the
disaffiliation of the Glasgow Labour College. Nevertheless, the process

of centralisation continued, for the factor which tipped the balance in favour of head office in such disputes was the fact that union fees were channelled through it.[26]

Various accusations have been brought against Millar by John Maclean, James Younie and other aggrieved labour college figures: that he was an interloper from outside the working class, that he was hostile to Marxism and the left, and that he was determined to gather power in his own hands.[27] Such charges seem to me to be partially inaccurate and largely beside the point. Millar certainly came from a lower-middle-class background (his father was an accountant) and was exceptional as a privately financed student at the Central Labour College; he soon evinced his hostility to the Communist Party and fought left-wing opposition with undying determination. Yet it is impossible to deny his commitment to the cause of class-conscious education with a Marxist emphasis. In fact, beneath the frequent inter-war disputes in the labour college movement there lay two fundamentally different conceptions of that movement's purpose. Millar envisaged the N.C.L.C. as the educational arm of the trade unions and was determined to eliminate those political adventurers and organisational irregularities which deterred greater union support. Because the N.C.L.C. found itself competing for this support with the W.E.A. and, more directly, with the Workers' Educational Trade Union Committee, it increasingly tailored its syllabuses to trade union requirements. And in providing a training for the prospective shop steward, branch secretary or trade union official, more emphasis was placed on techniques of industrial negotiation and union management, and less on such apparently esoteric subjects as Marxist economics, historical materialism and dialectical materialism. Most of Millar's opponents, on the other hand, came from a Marxist tradition which was more critical of the unions and Labour Party, and wished to safeguard their autonomy as an independent educational movement with a rank-and-file emphasis. As Millar wrote of his critics among the regional organisers in 1932, 'Many of them have been rebels all along. Because they were rebels they went to the residential Labour College. There they kept up the rebel tradition by striking and threatening to strike.'[28] It is hardly surprising that such individuals were impatient with Millar's highly detailed organisational circulars; and it is indicative of Millar's attitude that he could imagine no greater criticism against such organisers than that they wrote their letters to head office by pencil.[29]

Beside this conflict in the labour colleges, further problems arose

between the N.C.L.C. and the Plebs League. By the 1920s the League
gathered together several hundred working-class educators, led by a
knot of mainly middle-class and ex-Communist left-wingers who were
bound together by ties of kinship and friendship. There were Frank
Horrabin, the cartoonist and cartographer, and his wife, Winifred, who
had come down to London from Sheffield before the war; between
them they edited the *Plebs* from 1914 to the end of the 1920s. Frank
Horrabin's sister, Kath Starr, was in charge of the Plebs League office.
Her husband was a South Wales miner who began his studies at the
Central Labour College before the War, and completed them when the
College re-opened; he was now a full-time tutor and organiser and the
author of two important textbooks. Raymond Postgate, another regular
contributor to the *Plebs*, was the son of a Cambridge classics professor,
the brother of Margaret Cole and son-in-law of George Lansbury;
Postgate had been a young conscientious objector and was now a
journalist on Lansbury's *Herald*. Both the Horrabins, Starr and Postgate had been members of the Communist Party for its first eighteen
months, as had also Ellen Wilkinson (the trade unionist and future
Labour politician, with whom Frank Horrabin was romantically involved by 1926) and two university-educated socialists, J. T. Walton
Newbold and Morgan Philips Price. Finally, there was a smaller group
who kept their Communist associations while working within the
League: Eden and Cedar Paul, Willie Paul, T. A. Jackson and Maurice
Dobb, a young Cambridge economics don. The majority of the
League's executive broke with the Communist Party between 1922 and
1924, for reasons that will shortly be recounted, and took up a position
on the left of the Labour Party: five of them were either Labour
Members of Parliament or parliamentary candidates during the middle
part of the decade. They acted as a ginger group in the N.C.L.C. – using
the *Plebs* and *Lansbury's Labour Weekly* as a platform – and there
were periodic ructions between them and the more moderate members
of the labour colleges who expected uncritical loyalty to the Labour
Party. For example, at the League executive meeting in January 1926,
Jack Hamilton, a Lancastrian stonemason who was briefly a Communist and then a Labour councillor and the first president of the
N.C.L.C., 'said that the League was being used by certain disgruntled
people to ginger up the Labour Party, instead of carrying on Independent Working Class Education propaganda'.[30] The gradual consolidation of the N.C.L.C. during this period relegated the Plebs League to
an increasingly marginal role, and in 1927 its publishing activities were

taken over by the N.C.L.C.; but the journal *Plebs* remained an important focus of Marxist educational activity throughout the 1920s.

No account of the internecine conflicts in the labour college movement would be complete without reference to the stubborn independence of the Central Labour College in London. This was controlled by a Board of Governors, largely appointed by the S.W.M.F. and N.U.R., on which extinct volcanoes like Noah Ablett (whose political activism declined as his dependence on alcohol increased) were prominent. The Central Labour College directed hostility impartially at the middle-class intellectuals of the Plebs League and the empire-builders of the N.C.L.C. alike. When it fell on hard times after the General Strike, it refused to accept an N.C.L.C. offer to take it over and closed in 1929. Finally, coming full circle, the Plebs League in its turn was a consistent critic of the Central Labour College both for its parochialism and for the heavy-handed discipline it exercised over students.

Before turning to the activities of the Central Labour College in more detail, it is necessary to deal with yet another discordant factor, the educational strategy of the Communist Party. The initial effect of the formation of the Party was to consolidate existing educational efforts. The B.S.P. and a section of the S.L.P. merged into the Communist Party, along with their Marxist classes. Many of the leading figures of the Labour colleges and Plebs League also joined, and the Party in turn delegated most of the responsibility for Marxist education to them. The chairman of the Party announced in 1921:

We have already decided at a recent meeting of the Executive to urge and advise the linking up with the Plebs League of all branches engaged in the running of these classes, thus assisting to place the whole matter of working-class education into one definite department, under the guidance and direction of those specialising in that particular field.[31]

This arrangement lasted until 1922, when a breach opened between the League and the Communist Party. An examination of the rupture reveals two different views of Marxist education.

The Plebs conception of education was political. Its stated aim was 'To develop and increase the class-consciousness of the workers, by propaganda and education, in order to aid them to destroy wage-slavery and to win power.'[32] However, by 1922 the Communist Party wanted to make education more directly and completely political, and to subordinate it to the Party. Beside teaching Marxist theory, the pages of the *Plebs* had always provided an open forum for debate over political and industrial strategy among labour militants. Now, however, the Communist Party was assimilating both a particular interpretation of Marxist theory and a particular doctrine of politics. It looked on further debate as a waste of limited resources. As a German Communist put it in 1922 at the Fourth Congress of the Communist International, 'It is quite impossible for a financially weak party, engaged in a hard political struggle, to indulge in teaching any branch of science that might be quite useful in itself, but serves no direct purpose in promoting the task of the Party.'[33] Thus guided, the C.P.G.B. set about correcting defective (non-Leninist) understandings of Marxism and turning the Plebs League and labour colleges into adjuncts of Party activity.[34] The ensuing conflict was confused by the fact that the leading defenders of the Plebs conception of education were themselves members of the Communist Party who during the same period were discovering that they disagreed with the Party on a number of issues besides education. The Horrabins, Starr, Postgate, Wilkinson, Price and Newbold all left between 1922 and 1924. In March 1923 a temporary compromise was reached between the Executive of the Plebs League and the newly established Party Training Department of the Communist Party. It was agreed that the League's role was 'the training of workers into class-conscious revolutionaries' and that of the Party Training Department 'the training of Party...members in the principles and policy of the Party and the methods of its work and organisation'.[35] This was only a temporary lull, for while the Communist Party believed that 'working class education can only achieve its object under the leadership of the Party', the League insisted that 'such education can best be provided by a specifically educational organisation, supported by all workers' industrial and political organisations and uncommitted to any sectional policy'.[36]

The breach was complete by the end of 1923 when most leading Plebs figures had either left or were about to leave the Communist Party, while the majority of Communists left the League. The League, and the N.C.L.C. into which it was dissolved soon after the General Strike, continued to play the major Marxist educational role, and some Communists – notably Maurice Dobb, T. A. Jackson and Willie Paul – continued to write and teach for the journal and the colleges, and even to win election on the League's Executive.[37] At a local level some Communist branches continued their affiliations to labour colleges and many other individual Party members worked in them.[38] Yet the split with the Labour colleges undoubtedly weakened the educational influence of the Communist Party in the 1920s. Numerically the labour colleges were far more important than Communist classes: in 1923 the N.C.L.C. claimed 11 993 students and by 1925 the figure had risen to 30 398; meanwhile the total membership of the Party was no more than 5000, of whom fewer than eight hundred attended educational classes.[39] The principal effect of the breach was therefore to isolate the Communists from many young militants who instead received an education whose Marxist content subsequently diminished.

Having traced this split, we can better appreciate the stormy history of the Central Labour College between its re-opening in 1919 and its closure in 1929. The fullest account is that of W. W. Craik, who replaced Dennis Hird as principal until 1925, when a financial scandal led to his replacement; and while Craik's account possesses many virtues, not least its vivid evocation of the intellectual tone of the Labour College, he perhaps understandably glosses over the degree of discord. In retrospect it appears that the original Ruskin revolt of 1909 initiated a tradition of student rebellion that punctuated the history of the Labour College on an almost annual basis. Student dissatisfaction sprang partly from political disagreements, partly from dissatisfaction with the teaching, and partly from a refusal to accept the fairly strict discipline imposed by the principal and Governors (whose own financial improprieties can only have fuelled discontent).

The College admitted twenty-nine students when it re-opened in the autumn of 1919 (the course lasted two years) and these were joined by thirty-nine more a year later. Of approximately three hundred students who attended the College during the next decade more than half were from the S.W.M.F. and the N.U.R. The students lived in a large house in Earls Court and for a few years the College also used a property in Kew. Craik acted as principal in the absence of Hird (who died in the following year) and lectured on history and logic; Will Mainwaring, another South Wales miner, lectured on economics; and Alec Robertson, a Glasgow schoolteacher, taught sociology and history. In their first year students studied economics, industrial history, the history of socialism, sociology, English and logic or the Science of Understanding. In the second year economics and philosophy were studied at a more advanced level, along with extra classes chosen from such subjects (offered by guest lecturers) as imperialism, economic geography, trade union law, literature, psychology, languages, etc. This syllabus remained substantially unchanged throughout the 1920s, though it was cut back in the last years. Study was by lecture, group discussion and essay, though this imposed an intolerable burden of work on the full-time staff and only the lectures could be counted upon.

By the end of the first term students were raising a variety of complaints against the restrictions on the use of lights, the quality of the food, the need for a pass-key, the lack of essay work and the fact that they were not represented on the Board of Governors; they further resolved at their house meeting 'that we request the staff to desist from making general accusations against the students'.[40] In 1921 two miners from South Wales and one from Nottingham were expelled, ostensibly for their 'gross insubordination' in refusing to attend one of Craik's lectures, but more substantially because they insisted that the teaching of Mainwaring and Robertson was incompetent. In a phrase that was to recur throughout the decade, Craik also alleged that there was 'evidence that the aid of the Communist Party has been invoked'. For their part, the Governors approved the expulsions, drew the time-honoured distinction between liberty and licence, and observed that 'students are at the college for study'.[41] In 1923 there was a new student manifesto: dissatisfaction was again expressed with the lectures of Mainwaring and Robertson, and also with the behaviour of Craik. The terms of this student criticism are particularly interesting. Mainwaring's lectures were condemned because of their exegetical character. As the students put it, 'The Labour College should be anything but a monastery for retiring Marxists beaten or frightened by a world of orthodoxy', and they accordingly demanded more neo-classical economic theory, and some practical instruction in bookkeeping, statistics and so on. Craik was alleged to be shirking his duties and his course on the history of socialism was found unsatisfactory because it was restricted to English socialism only.[42] This time the students backed their complaints by lobbying the annual general meetings of the S.W.M.F. and N.U.R., who were after all the financial supporters of the College; and the Governors clearly decided that renewed homilies would not suffice. They set up a sub-committee to investigate student complaints. The lectures were found satisfactory (in any case Mainwaring resigned his post shortly afterwards to become miners' agent in the Rhondda); Craik was instructed to spend more time in the college; a joint consultative committee of the students and the Governors was established; and, finally, outside influences were again accused of fomenting discontent.[43]

Trouble recurred in 1924. The students went on strike at the beginning of the year because they had not received their book grants and found the library inadequate. This issue may have been related to a series of scandals uncovered between 1924 and 1926 involving the misappropriation of College funds by George Sims, Craik and W. T. A. Foot, the secretary of the Board of Governors. (Craik was replaced as lecturer by Jack Jones, a South Wales miner, and as principal by Robertson and then by Thomas Ashcroft, a railwayman.) Yet it is also clear that by the mid-1920s the Labour College was in a state of almost constant political turmoil. A large proportion of the students were Communists (no less than seventeen out of thirty-one in Idris Cox's year in 1925 were Party members[44]) and they used the classes, house meetings and the students' journal, the *Anvil*, to publicise their views: by 1924 a counter-group of non-Communist students had emerged and it complained to the Governors about a 'campaign of intrigue'.[45] There is some evidence also that the College authorities attempted to keep known Communists out of the College wherever possible. With the exception of Mainwaring no member of the teaching staff was a Communist, and when T. A. Jackson was elected to a post at the end of 1921, the Governors insisted that he should first give up all Party work.[46] Nevertheless, members of the Communist Party remained sufficiently influential to recruit other students and carry militant resolutions at house meetings, so that further disputes and expulsions occurred in 1926, 1927 and 1928. In 1928 no fewer than seven students were expelled because they had refused to take part in College celebrations of the centenary of Joseph Dietzgen – instead they had sung in a Communist choir elsewhere in London.[47] The resulting furore played no little part in the decision of the N.U.R. and S.W.M.F. executives to rid themselves of responsibility for the College. In the aftermath of the General Strike they found the expenses a heavy burden and were in any case less disposed to support a centre of Marxist education which was a citadel for their critics. They severed their links and the College closed in 1929.

We can now turn to the education of the Communist Party. As has been explained, this was entrusted initially to the Plebs League. As part of the re-organisation of the Party at its Congress in October 1922, Training Groups were established, but these did not operate systematically for several years and in 1924 the results were admitted to be 'unsatisfactory'.[48] Most groups were left to their own resources and we may take as typical one Lancashire group whose members took turns in reading from William Paul's distinctly pre-Communist book *The*

State.[49] The inadequacy of such arrangements can be illustrated from the experience of another group at Crosskeys, near Newport, which was conducted by a prominent Communist, Len Jeffries. Every Sunday they would ascend a nearby hill with a copy of the first volume of *Capital*. None were familiar with it and Jeffries 'thought well, if we've got to start this education, the only way to do it is to do it like they did in Sunday School'. So each member of the group took turns in reading a paragraph to the others, which the group would then discuss. 'And I tell you,' Jeffries recalls, 'there wasn't one of us out of the nine that could damn understand Marx.'[50] The problem was compounded by the fact that the best Party teachers were caught up in the labour colleges, and were often not prepared to drop this work in order to concentrate on Party education. When Jim Backhouse, a foundation member of the Communist Party, was instructed to resign from the secretary's post in the Bradford branch of the Plebs League in order to become Yorkshire educational organiser for the Party, he refused and subsequently left the Party altogether.[51]

Only after the inadequacy of Communist education had been under-lined at the Fifth Congress of the Communist International in 1924[52] did the C.P.G.B. make an effort to develop a systematic alternative to the Labour colleges. Training notes and syllabuses were published in Party periodicals, and a manual on Party training was prepared by Tom Bell. A Central Training School was established in London which conducted intensive six-month courses to classes varying in size from ten to twenty.[53] The members trained at this school were then sent out to set up and conduct training groups at district and branch level, and by 1930, when an educational census was made, it was claimed that there were eighty-six of these trainers teaching 192 members in District Schools and a further seven hundred in the branches.[54] A further source of education was the Lenin School in Moscow. This was established in 1924, and from 1926 the British Party periodically sent a handful of select younger members to train in it. The syllabus was demanding, and probably not inferior to that of the Central Labour College: each student 'had to learn Russian thoroughly, and go through advanced courses of economics, history, political theory, philosophy, dialectical materialism, history of the Russian Communist Party, etc.'.[55] The first graduates of the Lenin School returned to this country in 1928 and undoubtedly raised the level of Marxist understanding in the Communist Party at a time when the non-Communist alternative, the Central Labour College, was about to close.

In general, Communist education retained much of the pedagogic character of the pre-war S.L.P. and B.S.P. education. The 'trainer' or 'instructor' would set his or her pupils to learn sections of standard texts and then test their knowledge through 'the question and answer method'. 'The instructor must all the time be clear where he is leading the discussion, and see that it reaches the right conclusions', a manual on Party training insisted.[56] Later in the 1920s these methods were relaxed and the Party announced that it had 'broken with the past': 'In place of the barren lecturing of the Labour College type, our students are encouraged to take an active part in the school as a whole. Personal research, enquiry, mutual interrogation of each other and with tutors, common discussion of theoretical problems, essays writing and debate are the means. . .' Yet the increasingly rigid content of Communist education prevented any real change from established habits, for by now the Party claimed a monopoly of Marxist understanding and its Marxism was treated as unproblematic truth to be assimilated by the uninitiated. Hence this same announcement of new methods contrasted the practical character of Communist education with the 'pedant', 'bookworm' and 'superior person' found in the labour colleges.[57] Classes in dialectical materialism never questioned the validity of this Soviet doctrine: rather, they learnt off by heart standard passages from Engels, Plekhanov, Lenin and Stalin, with appropriate exegetical commentary. Those trained in such a manner acquired a good textual knowledge of Marxist literature and a formidably coherent interpretation, but their ability to compare it with other interpretations or to subject it to critical scrutiny was correspondingly limited.

Besides the labour colleges and the Communist Party, there were other sources of Marxist education between the wars. The Proletarian Schools, a variant of earlier Socialist Sunday Schools, catered to working-class children in several localities mostly in the central industrial belt of Scotland and South Wales. Their tenor is suggested by the Ten Proletarian Maxims which replaced the Ten Commandments. The first was 'Thou shalt inscribe on your banner, "Workers of all lands unite. You have nothing to lose but your chains. You have a world to win." '; the fifth was 'Thou shalt teach Revolution. . .'; the sixth 'Thou shalt demand on behalf of your class the complete surrender of the capitalist class'; the seventh 'Thou shalt wage class war'; and the last 'Thou shalt remember that the economic structure of society determines the legal and political super-structure. . .'. The organiser of these schools was a Glaswegian, Tom Anderson, and he published a series of pamphlets on working-class heroes, episodes of popular revolt, *The Fat Bourgeois*, etc.[58]

More typically, most co-operative societies supported an education sub-committee as an integral part of their activities, and these usually provided lectures and entertainments. Before the First World War these lecture programmes were unlikely to cater for the serious proletarian student; certainly in the Vale of Leven he would not derive much help from offerings such as 'Sidelights on the Siege of Mafeking', 'A Winter at Monte Carlo' or 'Literary Life Behind the Scenes'. However, at the end of the war the younger militants won control of the Vale of Leven Co-op and it subsequently served as a platform for James Maxton, John Maclean and others.[59] The necessary research on the educational work of co-operative societies in the 1920s largely remains to be done, but we may point to one impressive example, the Royal Arsenal Co-operative Society. Here the Liberal education secretary was replaced in 1918 by Joseph Reeves, an I.L.P. socialist of the old school with a strong sense of class education and culture. Reeves soon encouraged an impressive set of activities. Besides orchestras and dramatic societies, there were in 1928–9 three thousand students enrolled in classes on a variety of subjects including social science.[60] This was a context in which an interest in Marxism could flourish among working-class students.

Individual Marxist teachers also continued to make use of facilities offered by local educational authorities. Thus in Wales Nun Nicholas, who had worked as a free-lance propagandist, was now paid by the Glamorgan County Council for Marxist classes he took at Ystalyfera in the Swansea valley, and a schoolmaster named Lewis gave similar classes in Monmouthshire.[61] Elsewhere too use was made of Fisher's Education Act to establish evening classes with a Marxist emphasis which qualified for official grants. The most important provider of adult education was of course the W.E.A., which expanded rapidly during the 1920s. The W.E.A. received state financial assistance, its teachers were predominantly university-trained from outside the ranks of the working class, and it explicitly repudiated any partisan approach to education. Its educational philosophy can be characterised as liberal pluralist, and it resisted any clear-cut doctrine such as Marxism. Yet since its enrolment was at this stage predominantly working class, and since the tutorial groups enjoyed the freedom to choose their own courses of study, Marxism was often taken up and discussed.[62] Two important introductions to Marxism were written by academics active in the W.E.A.: A. D. Lindsay's *Karl Marx's Capital* (1925) and G. V. Portus's *Marx and Modern Thought* (1922), which was published by the Australian W.E.A. and distributed in Britain. Some W.E.A. tutors were in fact committed Marxists and this was the basis of their teaching.[63] Furthermore, pressure was often exerted by the students themselves for a less detached and more partisan treatment of subjects. In Scotland the chief demand was for classes in economics, and the orthodox economist Henry Clay remarked at a meeting of tutors that 'When our students ask to study economics, they mean social ethics.' R. H. Tawney immediately corrected him, 'They mean to denounce the evils of capitalism.'[64] Another student remarked that his reason for attending W.E.A. classes was to equip himself 'with the knowledge and desire to defeat the capitalist class'.[65] We may generalise by saying that the W.E.A. classes bore the character of their locality, and that in areas where Marxism was strong, the gulf between the labour colleges and the W.E.A. was not great. If there was no labour college class in such a locality, the Marxist activists would often use W.E.A. facilities to spread their own ideas. Finally, another important medium of working-class education was the classes of the W.E.T.U.C. This was established in 1919 with the financial support of a number of unions and it relied for teaching staff on the W.E.A.[66] As with the W.E.A., there was ostensibly no effort to impart an explicit doctrine, Marxist or otherwise, and the W.E.T.U.C. was in direct conflict with the union schemes of the Marxist N.C.L.C. Yet in some cases these classes could provide another forum for Marxist literature and the discussion of Marxist ideas.

The problem with compiling such a list of institutional openings for Marxist education is that adult education is not an ideological neutral activity whose political character simply reflects the dispositions of teacher and student. Rather, the development of adult education in the inter-war years was an integral aspect of official social policy, as was indicated in the quotation from the 1917 Commissions into Industrial Unrest which urged the provision of civic education in order to rectify the effects of Marxist classes. The W.E.A. was the chief instrument of this state policy of adult education. In making this assertion, I do not mean to impugn the honesty of Lindsay, Tawney and others sympathetic to the labour movement who laboured in this field. It is their educational objective that lends itself to this characterisation. In essence the mission of the W.E.A. was to break down the isolation of working-class students and integrate them in a national culture; in political terms the proletarian intellectual was encouraged to widen his narrow class horizons for a broader progressive polity; in cultural terms the old, dogmatic, autodidact knowledge was discredited in the light of university studies. A W.E.A. course on economics, for example, was usually based on Henry Clay's *Economics. An Introduction for the General Reader* (1916), which was more descriptive than analytical; and insofar as such classes touched on economic theory, they would not teach Marxism but rather compare it with other doctrines. Much the same can be said of the educational settlements that were set up between the wars in distressed areas. Here religious organisations and other concerned bodies engaged in social missionary work among the un-employed, once again combating the appeal of Marxism with what the Merthyr settlement defined as 'adult education in a broad, tolerant disinterested spirit'.[67] Again in South Wales, the Glamorgan Education Committee appointed an able and progressive young teacher, Harold Watkins, to conduct tutorial classes in the county. In attempting to step gingerly across the political minefield, Watkins repeatedly came up against a quite different and avowedly partisan approach to education. Thus a Neath student came to the first class in that area and insisted on asking the crucial question: 'before I join I want to ask you a question: "Do you teach according to the materialist conception?" '.

The same conflict between a pre-existing proletarian intellectual culture and the new apolitical relativism is apparent in another con-versation related to Watkins by an older student who was a miner. This man had a daughter who had become a teacher and he was dis-cussing her syllabus.

I told her she ought to teach history according to the materialist conception.
  'Oh, no, dad, you're too narrow,' she said.
  'Oh, so you don't think I can teach you anything.'
  'About coal mining, yes dad, but not about history. I learned all about that at college. I don't think there's anything I can learn from you about that.'[68]

This exchange is not just about the impatience of a younger generation with the wisdom of an older one. It points to the supersession of a con-ception of history that is self-constructed, deeply political and intim-ately related to a complete world view; and its replacement by a new conception of history as a formal academic discipline, stripped of meta-physics, and based on the ultimate authority of the 'college'. That transition seems a suitable point at which to conclude this survey of Marxist education and turn to a consideration of its character.

APPENDIX TO CHAPTER 3
English-language editions of Marx and Engels

This appendix is based on pp. 336–46 of my thesis 'Marxism in Britain, 1917–1933', where a much fuller bibliography is provided, with title variants and publication details. Subsequent editions by the same publisher are here denoted by 'etc.'; and new editions or new translations are separated by a semicolon.

Text	Foreign English-language edition	British edition
Correspondence	–	Selections, 1934
Marx, *Critique of Hegel's Doctrine of the State* (1843)	–	–
Marx, *On the Jewish Question* (1843)	–	1926
Marx, *A Contribution to the Critique of Hegel's Philosophy of Right*	–	Excerpts, 1926; 1933
Marx, *Economic and Philosophical Manuscripts* (1844)	–	–
Marx, *Critical Notes on the Article 'The King of Prussia and Social Reform. By a Prussian'* (1844)	–	1926
Marx and Engels, *The Holy Family* (1844)	–	Excerpts, 1923; 1926
Engels, *Condition of the English Working Class* (1844–5)	1887	1892; 1920; 1926
Marx, *Theses on Feuerbach* (1845)	1903	1929; 1932
Marx and Engels, *The German Ideology* (1845–6)	–	Excerpt, 1933
Marx, *The Poverty of Philosophy* (1846–7)	Excerpt, 1888; 1900 etc.	1900
Marx, *Wage Labour and Capital* (1847)	1891, etc.	1885, etc.; 1893, etc.; 1918; 1925; 1932
Marx and Engels, *Communist Manifesto* (1848)	1883; 1888; 1901; 1902, etc.	1850; 1886; 1888, etc.; 1921; 1930, etc.
Marx, *Speech on Free Trade* (1848)	1888; 1907; 1917, etc.	–
Marx and Engels, *Articles in the Neue Rheinische Zeitung* (1848–9)	–	Excerpts 1923; 1926
Marx and Engels, *Address to the Central Committee of the Communist League* (March 1850)	Canada, 1923	–
Ditto (June 1850)	–	–
Marx, *Class Struggles in France* (1850)	1924	1934
Engels, *Peasant War in Germany* (1850)	1926	1927
Engels, *Revolution and Counter-Revolution in Germany* (1851–2)	1896, 1907, etc.	1896, 1933
Marx, *Eighteenth Brumaire of Louis Bonaparte* (1852)	1898, etc.	1926; 1934

Marx, *Revelations on the Cologne Communist Trial* (1852)	–	–
Marx, *Grundrisse* (1857–8)	–	–
Marx, *Contribution to the Critique of Political Economy* (1859)	1904 etc.	1904
Marx and Engels, articles in *New York Daily Tribune* (1852–61)	–	Excerpts, 1897; 1899; 1925; 1926; 1929
Marx, articles in *Die Presse* (1861)	–	–
Marx, *Theories of Surplus Value* (1861–3)	–	Fragments, 1923
Marx, *Proclamations on Poland* (1863)	–	–
Marx, *Inaugural Address of the International Working Men's Association* (1864)	Canada, 1923	192?
Engels, *Prussian Military Question and the German Workers 'Party* (1865)	–	–
Marx, *Value, Price, and Profit* (1865)	1897 etc.; 1901	1898 etc.; 1908, 1925 etc.
Marx, *Capital*, Volume One (1867)	1890 etc.; 1899 etc.; 1906 etc.	1887 etc.; 1909 etc.; 1928 etc.
Marx, *Writings for the International* (1867–9)	–	–
Marx, *Two Addresses to the General Council on Franco-Prussian War* (1870)	–	1870; 1921; 1933
Marx, *On the Paris Commune* (1871)	–	–
Marx, *The Civil War in France* (1871)	1900 etc.; 1912 etc.	1871 etc.; 1921; 1933
Marx, *Further Writings for the International* (1871–2)	–	–
Marx, *The Housing Question* (1872–3)	–	–
Marx, *On Authority* (1874)	–	–
Marx, *For Poland* (1875)	–	–
Marx, *Critique of the Gotha Programme* (1875)	1922 etc.	1919; 1933
Engels, *Anti Dühring (Herr Eugen Dühring's Revolution in Science)*	Incomplete, 1907	Excerpt, 1908; 1934
Marx, Notes on Wagner's *Lehrbuch der politischen ökonomie* (1879–80)	–	–
Engels, *Socialism: Utopian and Scientific* (1880)	1892; 1900 etc.	1892; 1908; 1920
Marx, Introduction to programme of the French Workers' Party (1880)	–	–
Marx, article in *Revue Socialiste* (1880)	–	1933
Engels, articles in *Labour Standard*	–	1934
Engels, *Dialectics of Nature* (1873–83)	–	–
Engels, speech at Marx's graveside (1883)	–	1933
Engels, *Origin of the Family, Private Property and the State* (1884)	1902	1940
Marx, *Capital*, Volume Two (pub. 1885)	1907 etc.	–
Engels, *Ludwig Feuerbach and the End of German Classical Philosophy* (1886)	1903	Excerpt, 1932; 1934
Engels, *Socialism in Germany* (1891)	–	Excerpt, 1931
Marx, *Capital*, Volume Three	1909 etc.	

4. Marxism as a class culture

A crucial feature of British Marxism before the 1930s was its working-class character. Members of the middle class played an indispensable part in its formation, and the intermediate strata of shopkeepers, clerks, schoolteachers and tradesmen were prominent at an early stage in local S.D.F. branches, just as they were in the other socialist organisations.[1] But by the turn of the century, the class basis of the doctrine was fully apparent: the breakaway S.P.G.B. and S.L.P. were aggressively pro-letarian and a new generation of working men were assuming control of the S.D.F.

The First World War, the Russian Revolution and the upsurge of domestic radical activity then brought an influx of middle-class radicals and intellectuals into Marxist ranks. Young converts like Page Arnot, Maurice Dobb, the Dutt brothers, Ralph Fox, Allen Hutt, Eden and Cedar Paul and Tom Wintringham contributed to the newly-established Communist Party their university education, knowledge of foreign languages and general contact with a wider world which was more or less unknown to most proletarian Marxists. Yet the outstanding common feature of these recruits was their youth, for they had literally grown up in the aftermath of the Russian Revolution. The Marxist movement in this country failed to attract established intellectuals of national significance (with the single possible exception of George Bernard Shaw, whose enthusiasm for the Russian Revolution was surely intended above all to *épater le bourgeois*). Unlike other countries where this did occur, there was thus no interpolation of Marxism into the centre of cultural and political life. Rather, the potboilers on Communism and the articles that appeared in *The Times* and elsewhere at the end of the war bearing such titles as 'What Is Bolshevism?' offered either a garbled account of foreign events or else a domestic picture of developments on the Clyde or in South Wales – developments that lay completely outside the ambit of 'national' life. Furthermore, just as a great many progressives were assimilated into Labour ranks at this time, so the progressive thinkers like Cole, Hobson, Lindsay, Russell, Tawney, the Webbs and H. G. Wells all rejected Marxism in favour of a social philosophy conducive to more gradual social reform.[2] Finally, the majority of those younger writers, journalists and public figures who were attracted initially to Marxism abandoned it again within a few years. These birds of passage were a mixed bunch, comprising journalists and writers such as Gerald Gould, William Mellor, Francis Meynell, Raymond Postgate and Morgan Philips Price; the erratic Colonel L'Estrange Malone M.P. and J. T. Walton Newbold; and a prominent suffragette like Sylvia Pankhurst. Their early departure from the Communist Party at once indicates the uncongenial nature of the Party to such middle-class interlopers and served to seal Marxism off from this milieu. The Party recruited a few university graduates like Freda Utley and Leslie Morton during the remainder of the decade, but Marxism was effectively isolated from the academic and cultural mainstream. If one had to nominate the field in which Marxist intellectuals were most prominent in the 1920s, it would probably be typography and bibliography, where Allen Hutt, Walter Holmes, Francis Meynell, Stanley Morison and Graham Pollard were all engaged, and the crucial point here is that their Marxism was largely incidental to their engagement.[3]

All this changed in the 1930s. The Communist Party began to recruit in considerable numbers from the middle-class intelligentsia and to become an established part of the Oxbridge scene. Erstwhile critics such as Cole, Laski and even the Webbs revised their anti-Marxist attitudes, and Cole wrote in 1933 that 'To look around on the world of to-day with seeing eyes is to be a Marxist, for Marxism alone explains what is going on.'[4] Prominent scientists like J. D. Bernal, J. B. S. Haldane, Hyman Levy and Joseph Needham became interested in dialectical materialism. A new generation of poets, playwrights, literary critics, musicians, historians and teachers discovered Marxism and began to explore its ramifications in their fields.[5] In short, Marxism ceased to be a separate proletarian phenomenon, and its proletarian manifestations in the domain of theory were swamped.

The earlier working-class character of Marxism shaped its form and content. It inherited the tradition of working-class education described in the previous chapter whereby the individual read in search of understanding. This was an essentially individual pilgrimage. The autodidact might share his interests with fellow workers, and in some workplaces the atmosphere could be extremely conducive to intellectual discussion.

Walter Haydn Davies remembers his section of the Bedlinog pit thus:

The conveyor face down the Number 2 pit was a university...Night after night in this Alma Mater, well-read, intelligent, clean-minded men discussed the burning topics of the day, the changing religious trend, the theory of evolution, the nature of spiritualism, Christian Socialism, Communism, and all the other isms that then did abound. The ideas expressed by Charles Darwin, R. J. Campbell, Sir Oliver Lodge, Keir Hardie, Ramsay Macdonald, Karl Marx, Noah Ablett were treasured in their minds as well as in the books they carried in their pockets.[6]

Both this sort of informal education and the formal education discussed in the last chapter offered a collective forum which shaped the process of learning. Nevertheless, among the vanguard of advanced worker–intellectuals the search for knowledge rested perforce on books, which are a primarily individual medium of education. There was an enormous confidence in the authority of the text, a belief that the ultimate solutions to questions which perplexed these questing minds were locked up in the printed page. In a passage that captures the tone of the phenomenon particularly well, Jack London describes his Martin Eden reading Herbert Spencer: 'And here was this man Spencer, organising all knowledge for him, reducing everything to unity, elaborating ultimate reality...All the hidden things were laying their secrets bare. He was drunken with comprehension.'[7] It is this sense of revelation that British worker–autodidacts experienced with Marxism, and various examples will be provided elsewhere in this study. Here we may take the example of George Sims, writing from the front in 1918 to Winifred Horrabin with reminiscences of his discovery of Marx:

I had tried for years to get a feeling of reality in religion, to feel that God and the Christ were of me and with me, the reality never came...But with the first reading of the *Communist Manifesto*, how the pamphlet appealed to something in me, some revolt against things as they are...We are neither fatalists, nor believers in miracles – simply people who know...the inevitability of social evolution, of development and progress based upon material needs as a stepping-stone to our higher selves.[8]

It is undeniable that this working-class Marxism was over-simplified and dogmatic. The very project of founding a distinct and complete 'proletarian science', as it was sometimes called, lent itself to such tendencies. A highly revealing medium of Marxist education was the wall-chart which was used in all subjects and possessed a much greater significance than as a mere pedagogic device. In history, economics, philosophy and politics knowledge was represented by means of such charts whose geometrical complexity does not disguise their essentially simple methodology – in each case reality was reduced to direct causality and simple equivalence. Thus historical wall-charts recorded advances in technology in chronological order down one column, and the corresponding changes in social relations, politics and so on in parallel columns; or alternatively the prevailing mode of production in a particular epoch was represented as the 'base' and the other phenomena arranged as the 'superstructure'.[9]

Yet even in its most dogmatic moments this Marxist intellectual culture possessed a sense of wonder and intellectual curiosity. The best working-class Marxists always retained their interest in a wide range of subjects and displayed a genuine humility. This sense of continuing wonderment can be illustrated in the following declaration from a student at the Central Labour College: 'Having set out upon an educational mission we are given an insight into the abstract conception "Knowledge". What appeared before to be something small and limited, and which could be easily overcome, now appears as something which has no limits. Indeed it is the contrary. It is man's power to understand the understandable that is limited.'[10]

During the 1920s this cultural tradition fused with a particular set of political conditions. As we have seen, between 1917 and 1920 British Marxists largely overcame their earlier purist isolation from the existing forms of working-class organisation and activity. The formation of the Communist Party consolidated this fresh emphasis on involvement in day-to-day issues at a time when the labour movement was engaged in an intensive programme of industrial and political struggle. In these circumstances it is hardly surprising that there was a pronounced tendency to understand Bolshevism primarily as a doctrine of action. A concern for theory came to be regarded by many as an obstacle which had been blocking the path of revolutionaries and which the Russians had demonstrated could now be removed. As one working-class student of Marx put it at the time, 'The Communists of Russia, and elsewhere, are not doctrinaire maniacs who are so engrossed in Marxistic theory that they are unable to take their place in the common struggle of the masses.'[11] Raymond Postgate put the same idea more simply in his book *The Bolshevik Theory* when he said that on the last analysis Bolshevism was simply 'Socialism now'.[12] Even when this misapprehension was corrected and the Party insisted that the Third International was founded upon and alone understood Marxism, the same attitude lived on. Nor was this surprising. The typical member of a Party branch in an industrial area was thrown into a round of ceaseless activity: trade union work, organisation of the unemployed, literature sales, outdoor meetings, local government elections, and so on. All too often such a comrade's educational class, which was the least pressing commitment, was squeezed out. Some even attempted to turn exigency into principle: Helen Crawfurd, a prominent Glasgow Communist (and significantly one not from an S.L.P. but an I.L.P. background), said in 1928 that the Party's newspaper 'wants fewer theoretical articles and more facts regarding the wholesale robbery of the workers that is going on'.[13] Such heresies did not go unnoticed in Moscow. In 1925 the Agitation and Propaganda Department of the Communist International condemned the 'aversion to theory' which 'revealed itself everywhere' in the British Party's work; and three years later the Party's training manual was publicly censured for its 'serious omission' of 'the Marxist world conception'. 'How many active Party workers are there', asked Allan Hutt on behalf of the leadership yet again in 1932, 'who have not heard time and again, Party members. . .speaking of "theory" as of some strange thing far removed from them, something in which perhaps a handful of leading comrades might be expected to be interested, but which was of neither interest nor importance for the mass of the membership?'[14]

But it would be misleading to leave the matter there, or to judge British Marxism by the self-flagellatory confession of Party members. For every antitheoretical statement like that of Helen Crawfurd one can find a dozen instances of the importance attached by Communist activists to a proper understanding of Marxism. Len Jeffries, for example, has said that he did not 'regard anybody as being a Marxist unless they have thoroughly digested, and not only thoroughly digested but be able to relate Marxism to every question that arises'.[15] What has to be emphasised above all is that the Marxism of the 1920s was first and foremost a tool of politics. These circumstances often resulted in an indifference to the niceties of theoretical discussion, but this should not be confused with indifference to theory as such. Indeed it was because they grasped their Marxism with such eagerness as the key to understanding, and hence to social action, that many British Marxists showed little interest in its critical elaboration.

If the exigencies of the period therefore tempered the quality and range of Marxist thought, they also enabled the doctrine to achieve a greater practical significance than ever before. Until the sectarian barriers went up in the aftermath of 1926, Marxism was an active component in the ideology of the post-war labour movement, enabling the self-educated working-class enthusiasts to reach a much wider audience through trade unions, trades councils, ad hoc organisations, and even many local Labour parties as well as the labour colleges. The fact that Marxism rested in working-class hands at a time of mass struggle meant that it was acutely aware of the larger historical circumstances of that class, giving it a relevance and immediacy that it has seldom possessed in this country. Such opportunities were closed off later in the decade; but in any case this distinctive culture was then itself in decline.

There are several reasons for this. The first generation of Communist leaders – men like Tom Bell, Johnny Campbell, Arthur MacManus, J. T. Murphy and William Paul, who all combined practical experience with a thorough grounding in this culture – were relegated to positions of secondary importance by the end of the decade. Politics and theory no longer possessed the same unity in the new leadership, for intellectuals like Palme Dutt now exercised unchallenged theoretical authority to which the working-class militants in leading political posts like Harry Pollitt and Willie Gallacher tended to defer. This is not to say that these working-class Communists lacked a thorough Marxist grounding; Pollitt and Gallacher had both undergone the painstaking process of self-education described in the last chapter, and younger cadres like Finlay Hart in Scotland or Idris Cox in Wales received a thorough training in the labour colleges and the Lenin School. (It could be argued that Pollitt's instinctive feel for the class struggle was in fact superior to that of Dutt.) Yet in matters of theory they deferred to the theorists. Furthermore, the earlier wide-ranging and diffuse discussions among Marxist autodidacts are no longer evident by 1933, partly because they had yielded authority to the new Marxists in the universities and partly because the new Party orthodoxy restricted such discussion in Party life – and specific instances of this marginalisation of the proletarian intellectuals will emerge in subsequent chapters.

A more fundamental reason for the contraction of this working-class intellectual culture surely lies in the changes in British education and social structure. From the beginning of the twentieth century there was a major expansion of secondary education and of the educational opportunities available to the gifted working-class child. The odds against a child in an English elementary school gaining a scholarship to a secondary school in 1894 were 271 to 1; by 1934 the odds were 11 to 1.[16] Inequality of educational opportunity persisted, as it does today, but there was an increasing likelihood that the bright and ambitious student from a working-class home would make his way on to secondary school and thence to a non-manual occupation. It is precisely these highly intelligent individuals whose route had been blocked prior to the First World War, and whose aspirations and interests often assumed an autodidact form outside the established intellectual culture. In the Rhondda, for example, two intermediate schools of five hundred pupils served for more than one hundred thousand inhabitants of the valley.[17] It is hardly surprising that some of the young men who went down the Rhondda pits should have been attracted by the opportunity to study at the Central Labour College, nor that the standard reached by those who sat the competitive examination to win a union scholarship should have been so high. Not all of those who went off to London intended to return to the coalfield, and it was a recognised problem that some students found jobs with the management, insurance companies, and so on: as Nun Nicholas put it, 'in taking a youth from his occupation for say two years, he either becomes "intellectual", i.e. anxious to ascend the movement; or ambitious [to] make the movement subservient to his purpose'.[18] Against these instances of the educated miner choosing to abandon his occupation or use its union hierarchy for his own ends must be put other cases where the returned student was blacklisted. When D. J. Davies returned from the College in 1921 and asked for a job at the local colliery, he was told by the manager to 'Go and ask Lenin for a job.'[19] Such victimised students might find work at another pit; some became checkweighers or miners' agents; alternatively they became full-time organisers for the labour colleges, and in such cases they usually retained a relationship with the labour movement. But just as this leavening process among the miners and railwaymen came to an end in 1929, so the gifted children in many working-class communities (like the miner's daughter in the previous chapter who went to teachers' college) were now brought into the ambit of state-controlled, secondary education.

Some light is thrown on the erosion of the autodidact culture by an examination of particular episodes where it came into contact with university learning. In the labour colleges, for example, there was considerable resentment against the middle-class intellectuals who came into the Plebs League during and immediately after the war. Two books written by Eden and Cedar Paul, *Creative Revolution* (1920) and *Proletcult* (1921), attracted criticism for their obscure vocabulary – they coined words like 'ergatocracy' to replace the ugly 'dictatorship of the proletariat' – and generally schoolmarmish tone.[20] The young Raymond Postgate was especially resented for his flippant style and disrespect for revered authorities like Joseph Dietzgen. Postgate's standards of judgement were in fact those of an Oxford tutor, and when asked to read the manuscript of the autodidact John S. Clarke's *Marxism and History* (1927) he commented that it was 'past amendment' – 'a clever opponent could make this a matter for laughter in twenty minutes', for it was 'hopelessly inaccurate and question-begging, and just the stuff I'm afraid the N.C.L.C. will like'.[21] And yet it is noticeable that a great many labour college teachers were intimidated by Postgate and deferred to his superior historical knowledge. When Jack Hamilton was asked to write a new short history of the British labour movement for the Plebs League, he wrote back an aggrieved letter suggesting that as Postgate seemed to be better appreciated by *Plebs* readers, he should do it himself.[22]

In the Communist Party Postgate's prestige was more short-lived. He was one of several 'Lansbury's lambs' – middle-class journalists on the *Herald* – attracted to the C.P.G.B. on its formation, and along with Francis Meynell he took charge of the first Party newspaper, the *Communist*, early in 1921. They managed the paper as a highbrow socialist magazine, with great attention to typography, graphics and layout, highlighted by elaborate Pelican Press settings and featuring long, discursive essays. Meynell subsequently admitted that the *Communist* was 'addressed almost wholly to middle-class intellectuals' and that his main interest was in the opportunity it afforded for typographical innovations.[23] Meynell yielded the editor's chair to Postgate in July 1921, but the *Communist*'s coverage of the pressing issues facing the British working class at the time remained unsatisfactory. He put the pugnacious Willie Gallacher's back up when he attempted to pay 'Mr Gallacher' for an article, and the Party's press came in for particular criticism from the Commission on Party Organisation established in March 1922.[24] Postgate resigned the editorship in May 1922 and soon drifted out of the Party.[25] Notwithstanding his case, however, there is evidence to suggest that middle-class intellectuals enjoyed considerable prestige within Communist circles.

The outstanding example is J. T. Walton Newbold. Newbold was born in 1888 into a prominent Quaker family which had a large house near Buxton in Derbyshire. At Manchester University he joined the Fabian Society and two years later the I.L.P. A man of independent means, he achieved prominence during the First World War as a researcher, labour college lecturer and I.L.P. propagandist who specialised in detailed investigations of company structure, interlocking directorates and their relationship with the state. He used these gleanings of Somerset House to argue that the war was a capitalist conspiracy, his other main theme being the impending collapse of capitalism. His articles appeared in both the I.L.P. and the Marxist press, and many were reprinted as pamphlets. Active in the Plebs League and the L.R.D., he joined the Communist Party shortly after its formation. In the General Election of 1922 he stood as a Communist candidate for the Scottish constituency of Motherwell, where he previously had been the endorsed Labour candidate, and with the support of the Trades Council he won a four-sided contest.[26] As one of two Communist Members of that parliament he was particularly prominent, contrived to be suspended from the House, and had several of his speeches reprinted as pamphlets. However, he lost his seat by a narrow margin at the next General Election in 1923, subsequently drifted away from the Party and resigned in September 1924. By now his frequent articles on economic affairs were suffused by a new optimism about the new industries. He rejoined the I.L.P. in 1925, stood as Labour candidate for Epping against Churchill in 1929 (he lost but was rewarded with membership of the Macmillan Committee on Finance and Industry), and followed MacDonald out of the Labour Party in 1931. By 1935 he had moved so far across the political spectrum as to recommend Churchill to the electors of Epping, and shortly afterwards he converted to Roman Catholicism and emigrated to Eire, where he died in 1943.

Newbold was never popular among working-class Marxists. At the foundation conference of the Communist Party he antagonised delegates by accusing them of bleating 'capitalism, capitalism', without realising all that the term implied. 'Then he went on to talk of the ramifications of capitalism until we were all dazed. Through the maze of the international banking system he led us: Western and Eastern Europe, the Near and Far East, the Americas and the British Empire.'[27] He achieved some notoriety for his conduct on propaganda tours; his slovenly appearance did not impress his hosts (his wife Marjory, who was a far more popular Communist, would send him off with a suitcase full of clean clothes, which would remain untouched until his return), nor did his ungracious manner and his reputation for asking exorbitant expenses. One working-class hostess was instructed to keep her 'brat' quiet, another ordered to serve his tea without delay. In short, there is a strong resemblance to the scandals of Edward Aveling some thirty years earlier.[28] Newbold was a prominent exponent of the school who held that the working class was too irredeemably stupid to be saved, and he was once heard to complain of his audiences that he had 'had better response in a workhouse'.[29] Furthermore, during his year at Westminster he became notorious for theatrical displays and managed to antagonise even the small group of Labour M.P.s with whom the Party enjoyed good relations. Willie Gallacher has recalled being telephoned one evening in London from King Street and asked to hurry down to the House of Commons to save Newbold. Upon his arrival he found a group of Clydeside M.P.s hammering on a locked door behind which was the Communist Member, and Neil Maclean was swearing that he would knock Newbold's block off.[30]

All the more remarkable, then, is Newbold's major reputation as a Marxist theoretician. The quality of his writing is poor, and his understanding of Marxist economics extremely weak, showing none of the subtlety or insight into the tendencies of capitalist development that was demonstrated over the same period by, say, Morgan Philips Price or the working-class Marxist J. T. Murphy. Newbold's work consisted of the endless compilation of data, all demonstrating the simple propositions of bourgeois villainy and capitalist crisis. In fact it was his sheer factual knowledge that was the basis of his reputation. Bessie Braddock, then a young Liverpool Communist and later a right-wing Labour M.P., remembered the veneration with which she held Newbold in the early 1920s, and the feeling of awe when she was allowed into his study to see his large library and the massive wall-charts of finance he had compiled.[31] Newbold never enjoyed the warmth of working-class regard extended to Maurice Dobb, whose modesty contrasts with Newbold's inflated ego, yet he clearly basked in general admiration. His reputation should warn against the danger of regarding the autodidact culture as autonomous or thoroughly critical.

The same point can be made by turning to a working-class intellectual. T. A. Jackson – known both as T.A.J. and Tommy – was born in Clerkenwell in 1879.[32] His father was a compositor with radical views and Jackson began reading in the home before commencing school. His education at the local board school would seem to have been unusually good, for helpful teachers encouraged his extracurricular interest in a range of subjects, notably science and Greek mythology; and at home he read widely among Dickens, Scott, Fielding, Smollett and others. An astigmatism discouraged him from playing games (though he retained a lifelong passion for all sport) and his spectacles gave him a bookish appearance. He also became notorious for his utter carelessness about his dress and personal appearance, but whereas the wealthy Newbold's dirtiness was taken as an affectation,[33] Jackson made do with shabby clothes because he preferred to spend his limited money on books and entertainment. He left school before his fourteenth birthday to become a reading-boy in the print shop where his father was foreman, and subsequently completed an apprenticeship as a compositor. This was the period during which he bought and read books with an avidity he retained to the end of his life. By the last year of his apprenticeship he was a socialist and joined the S.D.F., but as a younger 'impossibilist' he afterwards associated with both the S.P.G.B. and the S.L.P. By now regular work was hard to find because of his political views, and from 1909 he became a professional lecturer, eking out a living for his wife and young family by speaking in various parts of the country. He was prosecuted for sedition during the First World War but escaped imprisonment and was later granted exemption from war service. At the end of the war he became a labour college organiser and lecturer in the North-East. From 1921 to 1929 he was a full-time worker for the Communist Party, engaged mainly in London in editorial and educational capacities. Life remained extremely hard, and in 1925 he and his family were evicted and their possessions seized (including Jackson's precious library) because of arrears of rent. His wife died in 1927. Jackson went to live in Sussex with his second wife in 1929, and after she died he continued to live in Sussex with a friend; during this period he wrote several books. The Party called him back to full-time work as a touring speaker during the Second World War; he retired in 1949 and died six years later.

No summary account can do justice to Jackson's courage, vitality and mental curiosity: and his autobiographical *Solo Trumpet* is a record of fundamental significance for this subject. He was renowned for his idiosyncrasies and every veteran of the period has his own anecdotes of Tommy Jackson – how he was so enraged not to have been included among the twelve leading members of the Party who were arrested in 1925 that he wanted to print an article in the Party weekly asking who was the shadowy mastermind the Home Secretary had overlooked. His quirky individuality, Rabelaisian wit and impish sense of fun gave him a reputation for political unreliability – his well-known paraphrase of Lenin in 1921 to the effect that the Communists wanted to take the Labour leaders by the hand as a preliminary to taking them by the throat was taken up and exploited by Labour opponents.[34] This reputation led to his political eclipse by the end of the 1920s. Finally, as an opponent of the new policy of 'Class Against Class', he was dropped from the Central Committee in 1929.

Jackson's educational and theoretical activities, which are our immediate concern, exemplify the strengths of the autodidact tradition to a particularly high degree. His writings display a freshness and vigour that clearly reflect his prowess as a lecturer and teacher of working-class audiences. A strong sense of the identity of his readership is evident, enabling an appreciation of the need to win and keep their attention by use of metaphor and example, combined at the same time with a belief in their fundamental intelligence.[35] On the other hand, he was an impetuous polemicist and was sometimes guilty of verbal overkill – Jackson's adversaries were seldom mistaken and frequently dunderheaded knaves. His interests were amazingly wide-ranging, for literature, philosophy, history and anthropology were all grist to his mill, and his tastes were neither narrow nor sectarian, as his delight in the mannered world of Jane Austen demonstrates. Yet a corollary of this catholicity was a tendency towards a sometimes uncritical veneration for the acknowledged authority, coupled with a view of Culture as something standing in its own right beyond the range of Marxist criticism. Jackson himself observed retrospectively that the canon of classics through which he and so many other autodidacts gained their knowledge encouraged such a tendency, for it 'caused a student to slip into regarding Culture as a fixed Mind-world into which one either ascended with the geniuses to supreme heights or sank with the dullards and dunces to the uncivilised slime', and this in turn fostered a contempt for the 'vulgarity and sordidness of everyday life'.[36] Jackson did subject certain of his beloved masters to critical analysis.[37] But he did not extend this reappraisal to other areas of his learning so that his historical materialism, for example, was built on a foundation of nineteenth-century evolutionary materialist and anthropological knowledge. Jackson retained a lifelong enthusiasm for James Frazer, author of the massive *Golden Bough* and other writings on primitive religion, to whom he wrote in admiration in 1929 and whom he later met.[38] It was precisely this body of learning which the autodidact Marxist took as the foundation of their culture and which gave that culture an increasingly threadbare appearance between the wars.

A useful comparison can be drawn with Germany. Prior to the First World War the German S.P.D. was the largest Marxist party of all,

with a panoply of political, social and cultural institutions, a thriving
party press and an express commitment to Marxist theory. Such a
movement would seem to be in complete contrast to the small Marxist
groups of Britain, struggling under the most adverse conditions to
spread Marxism among the largely indifferent labour movement. Yet
on further consideration, the differences are perhaps not so great. First,
in both countries, as in Europe generally, Marxism was still essentially
a working-class phenomenon. Despite the prominence of national
leaders and of theorists drawn from the intelligentsia, the Second International remained largely autonomous from the state, the university,
the bourgeois world generally. Second, research into the reading habits
of German workers suggests that only a distinct minority were interested
in philosophy, history, and the social and natural sciences, and that
even this minority was considerably removed from orthodox Marxism.
The most popular Marxist writing by far was Bebel's *Women under
Socialism*, and there was a widespread interest in natural history and
social Darwinism of a similar evolutionary tenor: besides Darwin's
Origin of Species and Aveling's popularisation of the master, they read
Haeckel, Büchner, Hesse and other German books of biology and
natural history.[39] With the exception of Hywel Francis's work on the
South Wales miners' libraries and other scattered local studies, the
same sort of investigation of British workers' libraries remains to be
done; yet these German findings are surely in accord with our general
conclusions. In both countries in the early twentieth century there was
a reasonably well-defined minority of serious readers, and in both cases
they read for an understanding of social development based on
nineteenth-century evolutionary and positivist doctrine. In Germany
this elite was part of a nominally Marxist mass movement; in Britain
they were as likely as not to be unorganised or else enrolled in secularist
societies, and this difference in location is crucial. But the similarity of
doctrinal content is clear.

5. Historical materialism

What we now recognise as the disciplines of anthropology, history and sociology were largely mapped out and established on a 'scientific' basis during the nineteenth century. Their lines of demarcation, later so heavily scored, were then faint. None of the founding fathers would have recognised the disciplinary boundaries which operate today because their own intellectual habits were comparative and systematic; they made use of geology, geography, biology, philology, phrenology, or whatever else was necessary to construct a general science of their subject. This mid-Victorian social science was heavily influenced by rationalist and positivist assumptions in its search for universal patterns of development, and a dissatisfaction with these assumptions underlay the criticisms of Weber, Durkheim, Freud, Bergson and others towards the end of the century.[1] But just as working-class readers clung to Carlyle and Ruskin long after their influence had waned among the literary avant-garde, so there was a keen working-class interest in mid-Victorian science. Right up to and beyond the First World War proletarian autodidacts continued to buy and read the works of T. H. Buckle, Charles Darwin, Ernst Haeckel, T. H. Huxley, G. H. Lewes, Sir Charles Lyell, Lewis Morgan and Herbert Spencer.

There is a variety of evidence testifying to the extent of this interest. Jim Connell, the S.D.F. activist and author of the Labour anthem, 'The Red Flag', had a favourite lecture entitled 'From Protoplasm to Man'. It was a most erudite performance, recalled Philip Snowden, but Connell never got beyond the introduction and, after lecturing for two hours, had to stop from sheer exhaustion.[2] Dennis Hird, principal of Ruskin College and later of the Central Labour College, also gave popular lectures on 'the history of the earth', illustrated with lantern slides. Tom Stephenson, a Lancastrian working man, remembers the tremendous interest in natural history among working people in north-east Lancashire in the early part of the century. While on a field-trip with a weaver who was a keen naturalist, they met a coalminer on his way home from the pit, sitting by the wayside examining a dandelion: the miner and the weaver were soon 'arguing most learnedly as to the exact species of this particular dandelion'.[3] Similarly, an earnest American social investigator who lived among the miners in Kelty, Fife, listened to a conversation initiated by a miner who said 'I dinna ken how the coal got into the pits.' Another workmate replied, 'I dinna ken muckle aboot it, but I hae read a book by a mon, Professor Geikie', and then explained the geological principles of James Geikie of Edinburgh University (or perhaps those of his elder brother, Archibald) for nearly an hour.[4] And as late as 1929 there was a heated controversy over the pros and cons of Haeckel in the correspondence columns of the *Daily Herald*.

One aspect of this popular materialism is the nineteenth-century secularist movement, for the freethinkers seized on advances in natural history and evolutionary doctrine to discredit Church teaching. Thus Edward Clodd, the self-educated son of a mariner, produced *The Childhood of the World. A Simple Account of Man in Early Times* (1873) with the object of 'explaining to children how the Bible must be understood in the light of new knowledge'.[5] The secular societies reached a membership of approximately five thousand by the 1880s (of whom a very high proportion were working men and women); but the movement was then undermined by a division between the Liberal-inclined majority, led by Bradlaugh, and those who became attracted to socialism. The latter element, comprising *inter alia* such prominent early socialists as Edward Aveling, John Burns, Tom Mann, Ben Tillett and Will Thorne, drifted away from the secular movement; and this, along with the passing away of an older generation of working-class leaders, encouraged less horny-handed and more respectable agnostics to join the society and increasingly to assume its direction. What might be described as the secular tradition in British socialism was always outweighed by the religious element; and this distinction is in any case a murky one since, on the one hand, so many believers fell outside the ambit of orthodox Christianity, and, on the other, most freethinkers found the loss of faith was 'not an intellectual but a moral matter'.[6] Secularism and religion could thus come together in the late nineteenth century to produce the ethical societies, the Labour Churches and the Socialist Sunday Schools. Nevertheless, there was a significant body of socialist opinion which was hostile to the Church and which subscribed to a militant materialism. Robert Blatchford used the *Clarion* to explain how 'science traced man's steps in evolution from the jellyfish to Shakespeare';[7] he frequently publicised the writings of Haeckel and wrote his own controversial critique of orthodox religion, *God and My Neighbour* (1903). Throughout the early part of the twentieth century the Watts publishing house and the Rationalist Press Association continued to publish cheap editions of the nineteenth-century authorities – 75 000 copies of Haeckel's *Riddle of the Universe* (first British edition 1900) were sold by 1903 alone, and by 1928 the Rationalist Press Association claimed to have published four million books.[8] The experience of religious doubt, an interest in materialism and the process of radicalisation are closely related in the personal development of many working-class Marxists: and the crucial influence of this materialist corpus emerges clearly in the autobiographies of such prominent Marxists as Tom Bell, Willie Gallacher, T. A. Jackson, Harry McShane and J. T. Murphy.

It should be made clear that we are dealing with an atypical section of the working class. Anyone who has tackled the ponderous systematising of Ernst Haeckel's *Evolution of Man* will appreciate the effort such a text would demand of a self-taught worker, working with a dictionary at his elbow after a ten-hour shift; and Haeckel's propensity to coin new words – ontogeny, phylogeny, hemihedric, etc. – would limit the usefulness of most dictionaries. Why, then, did the 'earnest minority' persist with such grim fare? The answer seems to be that they were motivated by an intense desire to understand the situation of their society and their class. How had the present division of labour come about? Was there a pattern they could discern in the past which would make their present lot intelligible? This corpus of nineteenth-century social science offered a consistent framework within which such questions could be answered. It suggested how the life and thought of other societies reflected the influence of their environment, and how a chain of progress could be discerned. The worker–student drew from this literature a conclusion along the lines suggested by Daniel De Leon: 'The Socialist is not like the chicken in the fable that, having on its back a bit of the shell of the egg from which it just crawled, looked out into the world and said, "Why, as things are, they have always been and will be".' Instead, the socialist perceived a 'succession of well marked social changes'.[9]

British Marxism was rooted in this popular materialist tradition. By means of the *Manifesto, Socialism: Utopian and Scientific,* and the *Origin of the Family, Private Property and the State* it derived a conspectus of history with the same formulation of general principles and the same emphasis on human agency operating with specific material restraints. One Communist activist on the South Wales coal-field has recalled how in his youth he 'read terrifically in the history of social periods' in search of an explanation for 'why things happened'. He encountered 'the materialist conception of history...with the result that history began to take on a different form to me' and he became a convinced Marxist.[10] This realisation of the historical contingency of the present order was a potent aspect of Marxism, endowing the convert with a wider social awareness and sense of mission – 'a new enthusiasm, a purpose in life', as one individual testified.[11] Or as T. A. Jackson puts it in his autobiography:

I was groping for a working-concept of the 'becoming-process' of human society. Here before me [he was reading the *Communist Manifesto*] was the vital clue I had searched for. All the myriad fragments of my miscellaneous learning slipped easily into place, and I had – something better than a hope – a Faith, a rational certainty by which to live and guide my steps.[12]

Nor was such a general notion of social development peculiar to the Marxists. Labour Socialists also subscribed to a positivist scheme of specific historical stages in what Philip Snowden called the 'social evolution of mankind'. As he put it, 'Just as tribal communism, slavery and serfdom have disappeared, giving way to a higher form of organisation, so the present system of wage labour and capitalism will give way to the higher form of organisation we call Socialism.'[13] It is noticeable, however, that the Labour Socialist scheme was much less rigorous, resting not so much on a substantial materialist analysis as on a general belief in inevitable progress: 'Socialism is that state of Society evolving out of Capitalism. Sociologists tell us that in the upward march of mankind towards freedom and security, society evolves through five "doms". Beginning with Savage-dom, it went Slave-dom, then Serf-dom, then into Wage-dom (that is Capitalism). We are now anxious to bring in the final "dom" – Freedom.'[14] As with many other aspects of doctrine, Labour Socialism and Marxism were drawing on a common stock of ideas; the former diffusing them into a loose synthesis, the latter preserving them in a fundamentalist code.

Linked to this vague notion of social progress was a fairly common tradition of populist historiography, which projected the characteristics of the present-day class struggle back into earlier periods. For Marx 'the existence of classes is only bound up with particular historic phases in the development of production'; and the existence of a working class depends on the separation of the labourers from their means of production.[15] Therefore the form and object of the political activity of earlier social groups – a peasantry for example – will, from a Marxist standpoint, necessarily differ from those of a working class. Yet British socialists displayed a pronounced tendency to posit a pre-industrial Merrie England and then trace a more or less uninterrupted line of resistance against the oppressive ruling class. Hyndman's *Historic Basis of Socialism in England* (1883), which may be regarded as the first native Marxist text, draws a contrast between 'The Golden Age of the People' and their subsequent fall. There is some continuity here with the earlier Radical tradition of 'free-born Englishmen' whose rights had been usurped by Crown and nobility (and it is precisely this persistent tendency to romanticise the past and mistake the new class enemy which Paine, Owen and Marx, as sons of the Enlightenment, all aimed to eradicate). The populist tendency was by no means confined to Britain, since its most prominent exponent was a German socialist, Max Beer. Beer lived in Britain between 1894 and 1915 as the correspondent of the German S.P.D.'s journal *Vorwärts*, and returned here after the Nazi seizure of power. Besides his *History of British Socialism*, Beer published an ambitious series of five books entitled *Social Struggles in Antiquity*, *Social Struggles in the Middle Ages*, etc., of which G. D. H. Cole caustically remarked that the author's 'interpretation of Communism seems wide enough to include almost anyone who said it would be nicer if we all took our meals together'.[16] Yet Cole's own popular history, *The Common People*, written in collaboration with his brother-in-law Raymond Postgate, is by no means free of the same tendency, and it can be found also in Tom Johnston's *History of the Working Classes in Scotland* (1920) and much Marxist historical writing besides. Even Willie Paul, who was reared in the stern orthodoxies of the S.L.P. and was a leading theorist of the early Communist Party, overlooked Beer's elision of the specific characteristics of these different historical stages.[17] The De Leonist Marxists of the S.L.P. were indeed particularly prone to treat history as a reservoir of universal precepts, as is evident in De Leon's own *Two Pages from Roman History*, from which the Plebs League took its name.

Populism has received rough treatment of late at the hands of certain Marxist theorists, and I think it is worth observing that the essential object of populism – which is to unite oppressed classes and social groups into a progressive alliance – is by no means incompatible with Marxism, and indeed such a project remains relevant to contemporary politics. Much of the weakness of the left in the 1920s stemmed from its inability to construct this wider alliance. My criticism is directed towards the blurring-over and flattening-out of differences whose recognition is a precondition of a viable popular alliance. In other words, the combination has always to be negotiated, and the assumption that it has a natural historical existence stands in the way of its construction.

In view of the foregoing it is a paradox that British Marxists were scrupulous in their distinction of the specific character of each historical stage, feudalism, capitalism and socialism. The Marxist materialist conception of history (or 'm. c. h.' as it was commonly abbreviated) was an extremely precise and formal doctrine. As summarised by T. A. Jackson, it proposed that 'human history is born out of the needs of man. . .to make a living by action upon external nature. Man's dependence upon Nature, his need to subdue it to the satisfaction of his needs, constitutes the basic fact from which all historical development proceeds.'[18] Marxists placed particular emphasis on the economic aspect and the importance of class conflict, but the texts they produced were characteristic of the popular materialist genre. We may cite *Socialism. Its Growth and Outcome* (1893), in which Belfort Bax and William Morris traced 'social evolution' from the tribes, gentes and clans to the contemporary nation–state; in each stage of social organisation they laid bare the economic basis of family relations, morality, religion and politics. Later examples are William Paul's *The State: Its Origin and Functions* (1917), a book quarried out of the resources of the British Museum in much the same spirit as Engels's own treatment of the same subject; or Mark Starr's *A Worker Looks at History* (1918), a Plebs textbook that sold 10 000 copies in its first year and went through three subsequent editions, which similarly conducted the reader through an analytical summary of world development.

Just as F. J. Gould distributed a leaflet 'Table of World History, or Evolution' which distinguished the main stages of world history ('Time Before Man', 'Early Age', 'Catholic–Feudal Age', 'Age of Expansion') and listed the main advances of each (in the Age of Expansion one finds factories, trade unions, and popular education side by side with public sanitation);[19] so the Marxists also used to devise similar tables with distinct stages (Ancient Society, Feudalism, Capitalism, etc.) and their corresponding main features. Tom Bell prepared five such wall-charts for the Communist Party education classes on which he tabulated 'Inventions, Events abroad and at home, Trade conditions, and Prices and Wages'. We may also recall the evolutionary trees of Darwin, Haeckel and other nineteenth-century evolutionists. In this and several other respects the materialist conception of history carried on the intellectual assumptions of nineteenth-century popular materialism. T. A. Jackson later observed with insight that he and other Marxist autodidacts treated the materialist conception 'much too much as an improved version of Buckle's geographical and climatic determinism'.[20]

During the 1920s an unmistakable change occurred in this aspect of British Marxism, even though it is difficult to interpret. The change reflected a general decline of interest in the old nineteenth-century learning, for working-class students were simply no longer prepared to wrestle with these ponderous texts – this emerges with particular clarity in the argument (cited above) among the readers of the *Daily Herald* over the value of Haeckel. There was a manifest preference for a simpler, more practical and politically oriented materialist doctrine, shorn of its abstruse knowledge and turned more directly to class ends. This was accompanied by what might be termed a Bolshevisation of British Marxism, the introduction of the new orthodoxies of Lenin (or, more accurately, of Stalin, since the change occurred in Lenin's name but after his death). But the change also involved a recognition among British Marxists of real theoretical limitations in the old m. c. h, and a desire on their part to rescue Marxism from these difficulties. Thus between 1917 and the end of the 1920s the old m. c. h. was replaced by a Leninist doctrine of historical materialism. In the following pages I shall describe the change by reference to some of these difficulties: the ones I shall discuss are the problems of evolution, of fatalism, of historical causation and human motivation, of ideology, and finally of the relation between theory and practice.

Those who believed in the principle of social evolution – and this included Marxists and Labour Socialists alike – understood it as a process equivalent to biological evolution. This was encouraged by nineteenth-century writers such as Haeckel and more directly by Dennis Hird who, in his influential *Easy Outline of Evolution*, laid it down that 'In planets, in organisms, in societies, this law holds good.'[21] We may take as typical the statement that 'the only satisfactory explanation of social phenomena yet supplied to the inquiring mind is the materialist conception of historical social development and the formulae used for its conclusions are based on the same fundamental principles as that of the evolutionary explanation of life'.[22] Frequent reference was made to Darwin – though in fact there was greater familiarity with popularisers such as Huxley than with Darwin himself.

The Labour Socialist understood society as an organism subject to
the same evolutionary 'laws' as a plant or a living creature and like
them changing gradually in response to its environmental conditions.
Thus Ramsay MacDonald claimed that 'biology alone was competent
to give the clue to the proper understanding of the process of evolution',
and dismissed Marxism for its unscientific belief in abrupt, revolutionary change.[23] In short, the Labour Socialists employed Social
Darwinism to discredit Marxism. The Marxists of the late nineteenth
century were mindful of Marx's own admiration for Darwin and
attempted to claim him for themselves. Hyndman had written that
'Those who try to draw a distinction between evolution and revolution. . .misunderstand the entire theory of sociological development as
formulated by the whole scientific socialist school. Revolution simply
means that the evolution of society has reached the point where a
complete transformation, both external and internal, has become
immediately inevitable.'[24] In the 1920s, too, Marx's conception of
social development was frequently likened to Darwin's conception of
evolution, for example by J. P. M. Millar of the labour college movement, who wrote that 'The man whose name is most clearly associated
with evolution as applied to society is Karl Marx.'[25] There was also an
attempt to provide biological metaphors for the revolutionary perspective. Marx himself had described force as the midwife of progress,
delivering the old society pregnant with the new, an analogy followed
by Kautsky in *The Class Struggle* (1892) and Trotsky in *Where is
Britain Going?* (1926) and used frequently by British Marxists.[26] But
the organicist implications of this evolutionary tradition were more
difficult to refute, and by the end of the 1920s Marxists were much
more wary about drawing such close comparisons. A syllabus on
historical materialism published in 1927 stipulated that Marxism did
not transfer biological concepts to the study of society, and recognised
the 'distinctive laws of the social process'.[27] They increasingly insisted
also that the concept of evolution must be interpreted dialectically, a
statement whose meaning will be examined in the next chapter.

A further problem raised by the materialist conception of history was
that it seemed to impose severe limits on the capacity of men and
women to control their own destiny, that it reduced them to mere
puppets who must play out their allotted role in the historical process.
Most Marxists certainly believed that Marx had guaranteed the ultimate triumph of socialism, a belief that had comforted them during
long years of fruitless propaganda before the war and simultaneously

justified their abstention from many areas of working-class activity on the grounds that it was irrelevant to the larger forces of work. 'Comrade History' would vindicate them in the end, and there was little purpose to be served in rushing him. This attitude was contradicted in the most graphic manner possible by the Bolsheviks, who managed to seize power from the capitalist class in a country so backward that this was thought impossible by 'orthodox Marxists', a country where it had been held that nothing could be done prior to a lengthy maturation of social forces. While the success of the Bolsheviks had a galvanising effect on the practice of British Marxism, its implications for Marxist theory were more difficult to assimilate, for they undermined the entire bedrock of positivist assumptions. Witness William Paul, who in 1920 voiced the traditional belief that 'Marxism asserts that Capitalism must collapse as a result of its inherent and insoluble contradictions'; a year later he embraced the Leninist attitude that 'Communists and Marxists do not believe in the automatic theory that capitalism *must* collapse and Communism *must* emerge from the ruins'; a further year later he had reverted to the old habit of comforting the comrades that they were 'fighting *with historical evolution on their side*', for 'history is moving in the same channels as their work, and is helping them to realise their mission'.[28] Nor did the well-meaning intellectuals Eden and Cedar Paul clarify this vexed issue with the suggestion that 'in *theory* Lenin was a determinist of the hard-shelled, the oriental, the fatalist kind', but in practice he exemplified 'freedom to change the course of the world'.[29]

How then was the contradiction resolved? The orthodox solution was that men were subject to blind necessity only so long as they remained unconscious of the historical pattern Marx had uncovered: when they understood and accepted this pattern, the laws that had dominated them became subject to their will. Freedom, in short, 'is the appreciation of necessity'.[30] This definition of freedom was taken by Engels, Plekhanov and Lenin from Hegel, and is thus related to problems about the relationship of the Hegelian to the Marxist dialectic, which will be examined in the next chapter. In the present context, British Marxists simply assumed its validity, and this asssumption exhausted their interest in the problems of necessity and contingency raised by their conception of historical determination. 'Lenin shows the futility of opposing historical necessity to personal effort. Historical materialism shows us under what conditions are personal activities assured of success...' 'The materialist is, therefore, anything but a fatalist. He is simply logical and practical', for he 'works in a direction which he knows must bear fruitful results.'[31] Those who shared this understanding of historical materialism, and few challenged it, did not have to concern themselves any further with the problem; after briefly relaxing their inherited rigid determinism under the influence of Leninism, British Marxists had now reimposed a new teleological doctrine based on his authority.

The only challenge came from the American Max Eastman. After he had left the American Communist Party Eastman produced an important critique, *Marx, Lenin and the Science of Revolution* (1926), which owed more than a little to the German revisionist Bernstein's *Evolutionary Socialism*. Eastman contended that Marxism subordinated all human activity to a predetermined goal, and thus rested on an unjustified 'animistic personification of "history" '. His argument was taken up in Britain by the group of ex-Communist intellectuals who were active in the labour college movement and whom he met on a visit to this country in 1924, but it had little impact.[32]

The question of historical causation aroused much greater controversy. Most were familiar with Marx's dictum that 'The mode of production of material life conditions the general process of social, political and intellectual life',[33] but they understood it only by reference to particular historical essays such as *Class Struggles in France*, for he had never systematically elucidated a general theory of historical development. Three interpretations of historical materialism can be distinguished. The first understood it as a theory of economic motivation; the second took it to be a technological explanation of history; and the third used the concept of an economic base to explain historical development in structural terms.

It was widely believed that Marxism rested on a particularly pessimistic evaluation of human nature because it attributed all action to material self-interest. The Labour Socialists certainly interpreted it thus. 'The materialist conception of history', wrote MacDonald, 'is the view that the motive for historical change has been primarily economic', that the progress of man is 'solely inspired by his pocket'; and he contrasted this 'one-sided and inadequate' doctrine with the Labour Socialist belief that 'the creative powers of Society are in men's minds, not in their pockets'.[34] This was an established Fabian criticism and it was common to most commentators on Marx during the 1920s. Harold Laski, for instance, wrote that the Marxist interpretation of history 'may be summarised by saying that all the phenomena of history are the result of economic motives'; Bertrand Russell agreed that Marxism 'means that all the mass-phenomena of history are determined by economic motives'; similarly Graham Wallas stated that the materialist conception consisted in 'reducing all motive to the simple desire for pecuniary gain'; and Cyril Joad frequently claimed that Marxism was based on the premise that 'man's ideal was to obtain money'.[35] Common to all these expositions of Marxism as a theory of economic motivation was a rejection of the doctrine on the grounds that it was too narrow. To quote Laski again, 'The impulses of men, in fact, are never referable to any single source.'[36] Hence, it was argued, all actions could not be attributed to any single impulse, for nationalism, religion, and, most important, selfless idealism also played their part. Like other forms of materialism, this particular doctrine diminished the human personality and undermined creativity, emotions and even morality.

Labour Socialism broadened the assault on materialism by linking together a number of senses in which the term could be used. In particular they destroyed any distinction between materialism as a philosophical doctrine asserting the primacy of matter and materialism as an ethical doctrine meaning an obsession with narrowly material interests. Materialism was thus both an 'outworn metaphysical theory' and a morally repugnant 'outgrowth of capitalism'.[37] The Labour Socialist campaign against materialism was also directed indiscriminately at two targets which were actually quite separate. It was firstly aimed at the preoccupation of traditional Labourism with narrowly economic issues. In their past struggles for better wages and conditions, the trade unions were in danger of succumbing to the acquisitive morality of capitalism, and Labour Socialists called upon the movement to shed these 'swaddling clothes which capitalism provided'.[38] The campaign against materialism was aimed secondly at Marxists who were sliding back to this pre-socialist mentality. Bruce Glasier complained that the over-emphasis of Marx's materialist doctrine had 'hardened the spirit of socialist propaganda, and weakened its aesthetic and idealist appeal to imaginative minds'.[39] This was the reason that many British socialists gave for their inability to accept Marxism:

Those of us who learned Socialism not from Marx but from experience of life and its heartless egoisms want a better world for ourselves and our children. But we want to feel our heads touch the stars. Man cannot live by bread alone...

The false philosophy of to-day is 'money' theism. Neither Marx nor any of the economists of Socialism has impunged [sic] the worship of the false god.[40]

This campaign against materialism reached its height during the immediate post-war years of industrial and political turmoil, for it seemed to many that the ethical socialism of the I.L.P. which had flourished before the First World War was in jeopardy. 'The revolutionary and materialistic frames of mind created by the war have been a serious menace to the Socialist spirit of common service', wrote MacDonald; and many leading Labour figures joined in warning of 'The Perils to the Workers from Materialism'.[41]

How accurate was this characterisation of British Marxism? Its publicists certainly repudiated the equation of Marxism with the notion that man was influenced by selfish motives only, and they doggedly chased this hare whenever it was set before them by Laski, Russell, Wallas, Joad and others.[42] Nevertheless, there was a pronounced tendency to conduct political propaganda in this spirit. The system of capitalism was commonly presented as the consequence of human cupidity, and the class enemy was believed incapable of following any consideration other than personal profit. While the working class was the repository of higher virtues, these would never find proper expression while that class remained wage-slaves; in other words, 'until a man's urgent material needs are satisfied, his intellectual side does not begin to function'.[43] Such views were not without a certain measure of justification in a context of constant hardship and deprivation, particularly when juxtaposed against the ethical, other-worldly excesses of Bruce Glasier and company; yet they signal a particular narrowness and doctrinal rigidity which was commonly associated with British Marxism. This may be illustrated by an anecdote concerning an S.L.P. propagandist who had explained to his audience how history demonstrates the primacy of economic considerations. He was asked, 'If that is so, why is it that because of an event which is alleged to have taken place two thousand years ago, the price of herrings has just risen on Farnworth market?' It was the beginning of Lent and the price of fish had been increased to meet higher demand from Roman Catholics.[44] Religion was indeed the Achilles' heel of more than one Marxist: witness Raymond Postgate's assertion that the Reformation was 'engendered in beastly lust'.[45]

Most Marxists approached the problem of historical causation in more impersonal terms, regarding it not as a mechanism of individual motivation but as the outcome of more fundamental forces. Following Marx, the conventional interpretation distinguished an economic 'base' and a 'superstructure' comprising the legal, political and other forms of social practice. The superstructure was erected on the base and hence dependent upon it; the crucial problem was the nature and limits of this dependent relationship.

Until the 1920s many British Marxists understood this schema as asserting the absolute priority of technology. To use the terms employed by Marx in his Preface to *A Contribution to the Critique of Political Economy*, they concentrated entirely upon the 'forces of production' and paid no attention to 'relations of production'. History was determined by the introduction of successive techniques of production:

Thus in the final analysis, all changes in society of whatever kind – political, social, religious, philosophical – are shown to result from a development in the productivity of human labour power, which production is conditioned upon man's ability to improve his tools...Hence from the standpoint of historical materialism, technical progress forms the foundation of the development of human society.[46]

This technological interpretation was common among pre-war Marxists and continued to enjoy some popularity in the post-war years. Almost at random we may quote the following two examples drawn from the period 1917–19:

It was the recognition of the important part played by tools upon social development that enabled Karl Marx and F. Engels to formulate their celebrated theory – the Materialist Conception of History.

The Marxist believes that the clue to the current social order, moral codes, ethics, laws and politics of any particular period is to be found in the means by which the people obtain their livelihood, the tools they use, and the way in which these tools are owned and controlled.[47]

Such an interpretation of social change is admittedly widespread; how many accounts of the Industrial Revolution, even today, are based on technical advances in the methods of production? But the prevalence of such statements in Marxist texts suggest that not many can have read the passage in the first volume of *Capital* where Marx rejects such an interpretation,[48] and during the 1920s there was an increasing awareness that this narrow understanding of the economic base led to a hopelessly rigid theory of historical causation. The usual way of demonstrating its inadequacy was to point to its circularity, for mechanical inventions did not operate in the abstract, since their successful application depended upon appropriate economic and social conditions. Though it never disappeared entirely, the technological interpretation was eclipsed in the writings of most Marxists well before the end of the 1920s.

Its abandonment was only an aspect of a much wider discussion of the meaning of Marx's proposition that the economic base determined the superstructure. As might be expected, there was general agreement at the beginning of the period that the relationship was one of simple determination. Followers and critics of Marx alike shared this understanding. This initial agreement about the meaning of Marx led to two fundamentally different responses: most Marxists came to appreciate the unsatisfactory nature of the narrowly economic interpretation of Marxism, and therefore they modified it to meet some of the difficulties; whereas non-Marxists insisted that this interpretation was indeed an accurate representation of what Marx had meant, and therefore they rejected Marxism. The critics never repudiated the economic interpretation of history altogether and they always acknowledged the importance of the 'economic factor', but they criticised Marx for neglecting other, non-economic factors. Their pluralist conception of history was juxtaposed against their monistic understanding of Marxism.[49]

Now it was certainly an ingrained habit of British Marxism to regard every aspect of social activity simply as a reflection of an underlying economic force. Yet from time to time some Marxists were moved to protest against excessively crude economic determinism and sometimes to draw a distinction between the popular 'Economic Interpretation of History' and Marx's own 'Materialist Conception of History'. The economic interpretation, which Palme Dutt once described as the 'British–American substitute for Marxism', saw history in purely economic terms and did not link it to an overall class analysis: this made men mere puppets of abstract economic forces. He was echoed by Ralph Fox, the Communist intellectual, who said that 'the misuse of the materialist conception has brought much well-deserved ridicule on our movement'; similarly, John Clarke, a Scottish Marxist active in the labour colleges, thought that 'the narrowing down of the Marxian concept by some of his past disciples has been chiefly responsible for much of the antagonism shown towards it. There has been an inclination to "harp upon one string", *the economic*, to the exclusion of all others'.[50]

The problem for these more sophisticated Marxists was to find a formulation which avoided these oversimplifications. The Russian exile Joe Fineberg's criticisms of economic reductionism illustrates this problem. He took exception to a passage in Mark Starr's popular textbook *A Worker Looks at History*, where it was claimed that 'the change which precedes all changes in the superstructure of society, in politics, morals, laws, religion, etc., is a change in the economic foundations of society'.[51] Fineberg was clearly concerned with the implications for Marxist theory of the Russian Revolution which, he thought, had demonstrated the inadequacy of the platitude that 'political power is the reflection of economic power'.[52] Indeed it is tempting to interpret Fineberg's dissatisfaction with the conventional materialist interpretation as another instance of traditional British Marxism being broken down in the doctrinal ferment which followed the Russian Revolution, for we have already seen how the success of the Bolsheviks forced Marxists to reappraise much of their theoretical heritage. But in the case of the materialist conception this interpretation can be taken too far. Even though Marxists in this country sensed difficulties in the old formulation, they were unable to improve it. Thus in the controversy which followed Fineberg's criticisms, no one could clarify the relationship of the economic and political levels: Mark Starr and Frank Jackson argued that political power sprang from economic power; Fineberg, the reverse.[53] Thus defined, the argument defied resolution.

Even when Soviet Marxism began to exercise a more direct influence in this country, the situation did not change significantly. In his authoritative codification of the *Foundations of Leninism* Stalin had denounced Kautsky for his adherence to the outdated theory that productive forces determined all aspects of social life; and, after this text was introduced into this country, British Marxists also began increasingly to lay stress on the causal interaction between base and superstructure.[54] They often cited Engels's statement to Bloch that if the materialist conception were 'twist[ed] into the statement that the economic element is the *only* determining one', it would be reduced to 'a meaningless, abstract and absurd phrase'; and such oversimplifications were labelled 'vulgar Marxism' by Communist theorists. In this vein T. A. Jackson criticised a draft version of A. L. Williams's little pamphlet *What Is Marxism?* (1933) for its assertion that 'changes in ideas were to be explained by changes in economic life'. 'Marx did *not* turn everything into economics', protested Jackson, and although the class struggle arose from 'economic facts', once arisen it included 'a lot of things beside economics'. Here was a fairly substantial objection to vulgar Marxism, and yet in its published version Williams's pamphlet merely substituted the word 'social' for 'economic' and left the matter there.[55] In short, British Marxists' belated recognition of the activist nature of the superstructure – their realisation that political, ideological and other elements could help shape history – made their materialist conception hard to distinguish from the pluralism of the non-Marxists. They still lacked the concepts with which to construct a more sophisticated understanding, for the concepts of 'base', 'superstructure' and 'interaction' represented a semantic obstacle to more precise development of Marxist theory.[56] The notion of 'interaction' undermined the concepts of 'base' and 'superstructure' to the point that historical explanation based on these terms was more verbal than real.

Those who attempted to pursue such difficulties in the materialist conception of history were thus liable to encounter problems that within orthodox discourse remained intractable. Maurice Dobb found this through hard experience. In his seminal essay *On Marxism To-Day*, he criticised the 'abstract separation of events into "material" and "ideal" ', and maintained that the precise influence of the politics and morals of an epoch could only be determined by a careful examination of the social relations of that epoch.[57] Hugo Rathbone, who was one of Palme Dutt's assistants as guardian of Party orthodoxy, seized on this deviation with relish. Dobb had distorted Marxism and must be made to recognise 'the fact that the material basis (to which belong mechanical inventions) is primary, and the superstructure (to which belong ideas and property relations) is secondary'.[58] Under limitations such as these, the new orthodoxy on the question of historical causation generally remained lifeless dogma.

These various approaches to the central problem of the materialist conception, the nature of historical causation, also impinged on other aspects of Marxist doctrine. One such aspect, ideology, requires further comment. The Marxist tradition interprets human thought and knowledge as aspects of a social consciousness which is closely related to its material circumstances. But while British Marxists regarded ideas as manifestations of a class in a particular historical situation, they were uncertain whether this was the result of a deliberate intention to propagate a class viewpoint or whether such ideas should be treated as a necessary consequence of the general process of historical causation. Should ideology be interpreted according to the psychological version of Marxism, whereby all phenomena were the result of economic motives, or should it be treated as an aspect of the superstructure and thus as the result of more impersonal forces? Were ideas natural products of the historical situation or were they falsehoods to trick the workers?

The one interpretation of ideology applied the model of base and superstructure to explain the production of ideas and their dependence upon the base. According to this interpretation, men's ideas were reflections of productive and social relations, and always corresponded to the particular stage of social development. Put in a more popular form, this materialist conception enabled the worker to 'prove a connection between thoughts and economic conditions'.[59] Such a bald assertion may have lacked theoretical sophistication but it did promote a comparatively advanced interpretation of ideology, for ideology denoted not just a class's self-awareness but its whole philosophical, intellectual and artistic outlook. This understanding of the Marxist theory of ideology was fairly widespread, but it was overshadowed by the other more popular understanding. Here ideology was 'dope', false ideas that were deliberately produced and inculcated by the dominant class in order to deceive and manipulate the working class. I shall deal with this conspiratorial view of ideology at greater length in chapter 9, where it will be suggested that most sections of the labour movement used the conspiratorial view to explain the British worker's absence of class consciousness. My point here is that the historical materialist view that ideology was socially produced was clearly inconsistent with the conspiratorial view that it was class produced. British Marxists, however, were unaware of the inconsistency (only the American Max Eastman seems to have recognised it),[60] and slid quite haphazardly between one interpretation and the other. Within a single paragraph one writer could first explain how 'justice, morality, religion. . .and all the other superstructure of capitalist society are predetermined in character and scope by the foundations of the systems of economic exploitation': and add as a supposedly 'logical consequence' of this explanation the proposition that 'the whole of culture, intellectual and aesthetic, is coloured and fashioned in order to provide a world of slaves with just what is needed to keep it quiet'.[61]

The confusion induced by such inconsistency is evident in Marxist views on education. Marxist educationalists believed that all education bore a class character, and that all education other than their own served the interests of the bourgeoisie. Other teachers were simply 'hirelings of the master class' employed to hypnotise the workers with 'soothing lullabies of social solidarity'. This conspiratorial view of non-working-class education was an article of faith with Communists and members of the labour colleges, but they also urge the historical materialist view that the culture of each class reflected the social relations of that class and necessarily 'differs from the culture of the rest'. In this light the class character of existing education was a matter of necessity, not design, since 'untendentious economics, untendentious sociology, are, we would urge, as impossible as. . .untendentious football'.[62]

What, then, was the status of Marxist education? Was it simply political indoctrination or could it claim to be objective? Marxists thought it was both. The constitution of the Plebs League stated that its aim was 'to develop and increase the class consciousness of the workers by propaganda and education'. 'It is impossible to draw any hard and fast line between "propaganda" and "education" ', wrote the Horrabins, because 'education, in the view of the Plebs League, is necessarily propaganda; the only question for the working class being: what kind of propaganda?' Therefore fields of knowledge had to be 'wrested from the bourgeois, refashioned and used for proletarian ends'.[63] Yet in practice the Marxists never accepted the implications of this position. They grafted on to their propagandist purpose a distinctly positivist notion of working-class education, for which they claimed the 'objective method so successfully employed in natural science'. Thus they stoutly denied that their studies were merely propagandist and always argued their superiority to bourgeois knowledge on 'objective educational grounds'.[64]

But in what sense could it be claimed that Marxism was more than a particular class viewpoint? Up to the 1920s this was a question to which British enthusiasts devoted scant attention, contenting themselves instead with claims such as that of John Maclean: 'Our teaching is true because it is the philosophy of the Working Class War against capitalism.'[65] In this general sense it was taken for granted that Marxism was valid because it theorised actual reality: but such claims were not advanced as serious epistemological propositions and should be read as rhetorical assertions. Then, during the 1920s, Stalin began to lay down a new theoretical catechism which stated the scientific basis of Marxism in more formal terms: in essence, he asserted that Marxism was grounded on indissoluble unity of theory and practice which simultaneously guaranteed its truth and explained its necessity – 'theory out of touch with revolutionary practice is like a mill that runs without any grist, just as practice gropes in the dark unless revolutionary theory throws a light on the path'.[66] These homely metaphors would have seemed fairly platitudinous when first translated into English in 1925, and their full significance only became apparent at the end of the decade. In 1920 Stalin intervened in a debate among philosophers in the Soviet Union about the role and status of Marxist theory, and his

declaration that 'theoretical thought is not keeping pace with our practical success' not only stretched credulity to breaking-point but also
opened the door to a far more political attitude to theory than ever
before.[67] Henceforth the unity of theory and practice meant that every
aspect of Communist policy received *a priori* theoretical consecration,
and every aspect of Marxist theory became binding orthodoxy.

This is in some respects a misleading note on which to conclude a
survey of developments in the doctrine of historical materialism, for the
influence of Soviet Marxism was not wholly unfortunate. A group of
Russian historians of science came to an international congress in 1931,
and delivered papers of seminal influence in the attempt to construct a
materialist approach to the subject.[68] J. D. Bernal, J. B. S. Haldane,
Joseph Needham and others would carry forth this project in the
1930s; and there were similar developments in literature, history and
other fields. What this renaissance of Marxism in the 1930s represented,
however, was a shift from self-educated workers to university-based
intellectuals. I have suggested the various deficiencies of the working-
class Marxists' understanding of historical materialism, and in formal
terms it is undeniable that the Soviet innovations avoided such deficiencies. Nor was this new orthodoxy simply foisted on British Marxists:
I have tried to show how it addressed itself to difficulties and oversimplifications of which native Marxists were increasingly aware. The
problem was that the Soviet rectifications were introduced in such a
dogmatic manner. By the end of the 1920s the new formulations had
become binding orthodoxy; they were expressed in an increasingly alien
language, and they failed to create any substantial understanding of
the issues with which they were meant to deal. Insofar as this new
orthodoxy no longer reflected the same familiarity with the broader
tradition of popular materialism, it was so much the more likely to
operate as lifeless dogma.

It remains to provide an estimate of the influence of historical
materialism on the Labour movement. Such an estimate must remain
highly speculative since we lack research into most aspects of the
phenomenon, and perhaps the most useful approach will be to consider
the question of working-class materialism in conjunction with working-
class religion. To pose the question in such terms runs the risk of suggesting that the early-twentieth-century working class fell into one of
two camps, Christian and materialist, whereas all the evidence suggests
that the great majority were simply apathetic. Still, religious belief was

strong and pervasive in those industrial working-class communities in which Marxism flourished between the wars. In South Wales, Scotland and the north there was substantial working-class membership of the chapels. It seems clear that while the chapels typically emphasised an 'other-worldly' mentality and sought to heal class divisions, significant sections did take up the demand for social reform, and large sections of the working class in these areas had strong links with them. In most cases these links weakened in the course of our period, though it is difficult to generalise over a field in which there were profound regional and denominational variations. A useful study of South-West Wales suggests that 'in the 1920s and 1930s working class people began to withdraw from the chapels', among them the majority of trade union activists and militants of the Labour and Communist parties.[69] Furthermore, in this anthracite area of the coalfields the break with the chapels occurred later than it did in the more politically advanced region to the east – whereas the labour movement made rapid progress in the Rhondda after the turn of the century, the turning-point in the anthracite region may be set as late as 1925.[70] Studies for South Wales as a whole suggest that the 'gap between the Chapels and industrial communities was widening' before the First World War, and it is noticeable that the socialism that spread through the valleys during this period was secular and often anti-religious.[71] These findings for South Wales, an area in which popular Marxism made as much progress as in any other, may be contrasted with a mining valley in Durham where the influence of Methodism persisted during the 1920s and retarded the development of a militant working-class consciousness.[72] Furthermore, there is the hypothesis put forward earlier that Marxism found little support among Roman Catholic workers: thus the Communists of the Vale of Leven were rebuffed by the Irish community down in Dumbarton. All this is not to deny that throughout the country many socialists continued to be practising Christians – our point is that religion and Marxist socialism, with its materialist basis, were common rivals. We should also note the effect of the First World War on the popular mentality. A widespread disillusionment with 'God, King and Country' was apparent in the aftermath of the war; in most cases the mood was apolitical and passive, resulting only in an indifference to the previously potent amalgam of nationalism and religion, but in other cases the war stimulated a radical reappraisal of earlier beliefs.

What sort of materialism was it that contested traditional religion? A great many workers who became interested in social questions reached a point where their received attitudes of social harmony and their religious upbringing came into conflict with a class analysis of politics. At this point – and the process can be traced in many working-class memoirs[73] – they found that the study of natural science and history undermined religious belief, and after a period of deep uncertainty they abandoned the old faith for a broadly materialist interpretation of history. They came to the conclusion that man made his own history and that in doing so he passed through definite stages of development which corresponded to the prevailing method of economic production. This convinced them that socialism must be won according to the principles of this historical pattern by organising the working class to overthrow capitalism. When popular materialism confronted religion it struck at the ethical, other-worldly orientation of the old faith, as can be seen in the following discussion among some South Wales miners:

C. Why all this Marx, why no Christ? We have it all in the Bible, we've lost the vision.
D. We should return to the 'sermon on the mount', it's all there.
E. But it's conditions that make people what they are, that's what Marx shows.[74]

The adoption of a materialist view undermined traditional Labourism because it promoted a fuller class awareness. In the materialist light all sorts of previously sacrosanct institutions and aspects of British culture – church and chapel, monarchy, law and order – were revealed as accoutrements of the present class order. 'Once we realise that the economic conditions necessitated the formation and evolution of these institutions, then we shall be better able to appreciate that as they are the creation of the economic needs of their ages, so they will inevitably give place to other institutions. . .'[75] The materialist conception showed that organisation at the point of production or the election to parliament of workers' representatives was not the limit of working-class emancipation but only a first step on the road to power.

6. The dialectic

Part of the conventional wisdom about British Marxism is that it has always been deficient in the philosophical sphere. Marxists are thought to have shared the lack of interest of other British socialists in philosophical and epistemological questions, and also to have displayed the same empirical and non-metaphysical bent of the national culture.[1] Now it is true that most schools of thought in this country have lacked familiarity with the German tradition of metaphysics and dialectics which culminated with Hegel, and to which Marxism owes a considerable debt. Admittedly, there was a British school of neo-Hegelian philosophy in the nineteenth century whose notable figures were T. H. Green and Bernard Bosanquet, but it left little lasting mark and its contemporary influence did not extend to the socialist movement.[2] With the notable exception of Ernest Belfort Bax, the nineteenth-century Marxists in this country remained blissfully uninterested in Hegel's influence on Marx. It is also true that most socialists who had received a university education, and who were therefore trained in the dominant modes of thought, were extremely wary of mixing politics and philosophy. Bertrand Russell thought it a mistake to 'base a political theory upon a philosophical doctrine', for he maintained that while the materialist position in philosophy might be true or false, it did not affect the validity of historical materialism, nor did it bear directly on the merits of the case for socialism. This argument was freely used by other socialist critics of Marxism and was usually attributed to Russell.[3]

We must also notice that a deep suspicion and ignorance of 'this rather unhappy term, dialectics'[4] persisted in intellectual socialist circles throughout the 1920s. As late as 1933 Raymond Postgate was able to raise laughter with his parody of the dialectic: 'It is a confusion of terms such as humourless relatives torment schoolchildren with: "Are you getting on well with your arithmetic, Georgie? Then tell me: if you multiply six kangaroos by six herrings how many fresh eggs do you get?

Ha, ha, ha! That's a good one isn't it?" '.[5] And an inability to grasp
the Hegelian tradition is apparent in the writings of Cole and Laski,
who, in their summaries of Marxist theory gave only the most perfunctory attention to this aspect and employed the most hackneyed
generalisations. The dialectic was merely the principle that 'all living
things are subject to constant change'; it was 'a kind of rhythm which
moves from the concrete hardness of some definite idea to its opposite';
'thesis meets antithesis; and out of these comes a higher synthesis'.[6]
Whereas A. D. Lindsay had absorbed at least the neo-Hegelian tradition of his Balliol predecessors and could show in his W.E.A. primer,
Karl Marx's Capital (1925), how the dialectic was a dynamic principle
which animated the Marxist system, for Cole, Laski and most others it
was a purely formal and lifeless component. It is significant that the
American universities were much less isolated from the continental
philosophical tradition and were able to subject Marxism to a far more
penetrating examination. In 1925 Rebecca Cooper wrote a carefully
researched monograph on The Logical Influence of Hegel on Marx,
which concluded that 'the connection between the Marxian and
Hegelian systems is for the most part a purely external and verbal
rather than an integral one'.[7] Her publication went unnoticed in
Britain; and Sidney Hook, who as professor of philosophy at New York
University wrote a series of works on Marxist theory in the 1930s, was
perhaps the first American academic writer on Marx to attract attention in this country.

We may therefore accept the propositions that British socialist intellectuals were averse to systematic philosophy in the continental tradition and that their interest in Marxist philosophy was not awakened
until the 1930s. But it is not true that no earlier Marxist interest in
philosophy existed; nor is it true, as Max Beer claimed, that in his Life
and Teaching of Karl Marx (1921) he 'showed to English readers for
the first time the philosophical connection between Hegel and Marx'.[8]
In fact there was a keen interest in these questions in workers' educational circles prior to the First World War, and this dialectical tradition continued unbroken during the 1920s. Working-class Marxists
assimilated dialectics through two principal sources: first, through the
writings of the German writer Joseph Dietzgen; and second, through the
Soviet Marxist doctrine of dialectical materialism. This working-class
philosophical tradition is a hitherto neglected aspect of British Marxism
and is of considerable interest. In contrast to the dominant modes of
thought in contemporary British intellectual life, it was non-empiricist,

metaphysical, systematic and highly dogmatic. Representing the minority subculture of one section of society in a highly hostile environment, it afforded a potent philosophical justification of the Marxist faith. We shall therefore begin by describing the doctrine derived from Dietzgen and the Communist doctrine of dialectical materialism. Then we shall examine the opponents of the dialectic and some later developments, and finally discuss the significance of this body of ideas for the wider labour movement.

A young academic philosopher who taught at the Maes yr Haf Educational Settlement after the General Strike was astonished, 'when taking classes among the Welsh Miners during the past winter, to find that almost invariably when Philosophy was suggested as the subject for the class, the immediate reply was, "That's Ditchkin, isn't it?" '[9] For many thousands of worker–students during the first three decades of this century, the name Joseph Dietzgen was indeed synonymous with the study of philosophy.

Joseph Dietzgen was born near Cologne in 1828.[10] An active socialist, he practised his tanner's trade in Germany, Russia and America, where he died in 1888; and he also wrote a series of books and articles on philosophical aspects of socialism. Marx considered that these 'contain[ed] much that is excellent', and Engels subsequently credited Dietzgen with the independent discovery of the materialist dialectic.[11] Dietzgen's aim was to bridge the dualism of thought and reality, a task inherited from the German classical tradition and specifically from Feuerbach, so that Dietzgen shared the same philosophical point of departure as the young Marx. As did Feuerbach and Marx before him, Dietzgen began by rejecting all speculative, *a priori* thought as metaphysical and hence serving to reinforce the duality of the phenomenal and the noumenal that he wished to overcome. Dietzgen held that this duality could only be bridged by a philosophy that was inductive and identified itself with the natural sciences: 'From the standpoint of the inductive system the world and all it contains forms but one homogeneous object.' Dietzgen therefore claimed to reconcile idealism and materialism in a monist philosophy which bore a close similarity to the monism of Haeckel and other nineteenth-century materialists. Furthermore, as Dietzgen's initial antagonism to Hegel weakened, this monist philosophy came increasingly to rely on the Hegelian dialectic for its method; it 'absorbed the Idea...and overcame the antagonism between the mechanical and the spiritual view of life.' The dialectic came

to serve as the principle of unity in his monist philosophy for it mediated contradictions which arose from this antagonism: 'Everything is
large, everything is small, . . .everything a whole and a part, because
everything is the essence of everything, everything is contained in the
all, everything related, everything connected, everything interdepen-
dent.'[12] From this brief summary it should be evident that Dietzgen had
provided a turgid and far from clear attempt to spell out a materialist
world view, but one relying on the dialectical tradition for its inner
dynamic.

As was the case with many Marxist texts, the chief works of Dietzgen
were made available to British socialists in two volumes of translations
published by Charles H. Kerr in 1906, and these account for almost
two-thirds of his German collected writings. They were immediately
taken up by the working-class education movement and became the
principal texts for courses in philosophy given by the labour colleges.
Dietzgen appears to have been especially popular in Scotland, South
Wales and Lancashire: in Glasgow there were special Dietzgen Study
Circles, and when John Maclean first read of Einstein's theory of
relativity he claimed that it was implicit in the writings of Dietzgen;
while Maurice Dobb has recalled of his days as a Labour College
lecturer that 'if one stayed overnight. . .in a South Wales miner's household, there were his works. . .in a prominent place and treated with
reverence as a sacred text'; and Rex Batten, a leader of the Educational
Settlement scheme in South Wales, prepared himself for debate with a
Rhondda Communist by studying *The Positive Outcome*.[13] Dietzgen
was described as the 'basic work for materialists in those days' and
served as an introduction to the philosophical foundations of Marxism
for many young working-class autodidacts, one of whom stated that 'not
until I got a thorough grip of the monism of J. Dietzgen was I ever able
to give a logical backing to my economics'.[14] Such examples could be
multiplied tenfold, and Dietzgen crops up in autobiographies, oral
testimony and even working-class fiction – we are clearly dealing with
a surprisingly extensive readership which has until recently been almost
entirely forgotten. His followers claimed that he had expanded and
deepened Marxist thought and even that Marxist philosophy should be
termed 'the Marxian–Dietzgen dialectic'.[15]

The Dietzgen cult can be seen as the complement of the popular
materialist conception of history described in the last chapter. The
worker who believed that the whole of human activity was determined
by material forces needed some further doctrine to account for change

and development. If social classes, the form of government, even men's thoughts, were all determined by the prevailing method of production, how did mankind progress from one stage to the next? Dietzgen was used as the clockwork motor of this static mechanism, he provided what one devotee described as 'the scientific explanation of how and why human society develops'.[16] Again there is an affinity with the vitalist tendencies of other nineteenth-century materialists such as Haeckel, whose later writings exhibit a similar teleological element amounting to an almost mystical belief in the inevitable laws of development of the life-force – Hegel's Cunning of Reason under a new guise.[17] While British Marxists derived such general principles of evolutionary development from the materialist canon, it was to Dietzgen that they turned for a fully worked-out scheme. 'The Materialist Conception of History shows how changes in ideas result from changes in social conditions, and these from changes in economic conditions. Dietzgen explains *how* our conditions determine our thoughts.'[18] Only this can explain why so many worker–students would laboriously underline their way through the two Kerr editions and annotate their margins with phrases such as 'part-whole', 'Motion stillness', etc.[19]

A precondition of Dietzgen's popularity was the absence of any more authoritative alternative based on the writings of Marx and Engels themselves. In the early part of the twentieth century British Marxists lacked the early philosophical writings (with the exception of the *Poverty of Philosophy*) and a considerable proportion of Engels's later codifications. During the 1920s this ceased to be the case as British Marxists gradually became acquainted with the Soviet doctrine of dialectical materialism; but as dialectical materialism did not attain its mature form until the beginning of the 1930s, and as there was a further delay in its British assimilation, the differences between the new Communist doctrine and the old Dietzgen one took some time to emerge. It will be easier to compare the two theories after we have summarised dialectical materialism.

Dialectical materialism was a universal science which Communists claimed to derive from Marx (though in fact the term was coined by the Russian Marxist Plekhanov, and Marx never used it). Marx was supposed to have taken the dialectic as the 'rational kernel' of German idealist philosophy. This interpretation rested on Marx's oft-quoted Afterword to the second German edition of *Capital*:

The mystification which dialectic suffers in Hegel's hands by no means prevents him from being the first to present its general form of working in a comprehensive and conscious manner. With him it is standing on its head. It must be turned right side up again if you would discover the rational kernel within the mystical shell.[20]

Marx never elaborated this somewhat cryptic formula but Engels did, first in Marx's lifetime in the polemical *Anti-Dühring* (published in Germany in 1878 and by Kerr in 1907) and the notes which comprise *Dialectics of Nature* (written between 1873 and 1886, but not published in Engels's lifetime and not translated into English until 1940); and subsequently in the more systematic *Ludwig Feuerbach and the End of German Classical Philosophy* (published in Germany in 1886 and by Kerr in 1903). These texts constructed a complete philosophical system which was thereafter generally taken as the theoretical basis of Marxism. *Anti-Dühring* was to be particularly hallowed among British Marxists – Tommy Jackson regarded it as 'the most fundamental document in all Marxism' with the possible exception of the *Manifesto*; another thought it 'the most fundamental work of Scientific Socialism after *Capital*' – but its full popularity was not apparent until the 1920s.[21] Engels, however, obliterated the distinction Marx had drawn between a rational kernel and a mystical shell *within* Hegel's dialectic, for he believed that the Hegelian dialectic itself constituted the rational kernel and its idealist context the mystical shell. According to Engels, 'Hegel was not simply put aside. On the contrary, one started out from his revolutionary side described above, from the dialectical method. . . [T]he dialectic of Hegel was placed upon its head; or rather, turned off its head, on which it was standing before, and placed upon its feet again.'[22] Here we have a new, less subtle, distinction between Hegel's method and his philosophical system: Engels rejected the system but kept the method.

Soviet Marxism systematised Engels's interpretation and developed it into the doctrine of dialectical materialism. In a pamphlet on the subject written by a member of the Marx–Engels Institute in Moscow and specially commissioned for a British readership, Hegel was credited with the discovery of 'the real laws of movement of the world' which he mistakenly took to be 'laws of the movement of the absolute idea'.[23] A leading theorist of the British Party made the same claim: 'Marx took the dialectic content while rejecting the idealist form.' Or, as it was put in the *Daily Worker*, Marx 'acquired his dialectics from Hegel'.[24] Furthermore, Soviet Marxism codified and greatly extended the dialectic's field of operation. Dialectical materialism was now the science of the general laws of all motion, incorporating both social and natural phenomena, for 'Marx's application of dialectic in the fields of history and sociology was a special application. . .of a method that Marx and Engels considered applicable to all nature and society.'[25] Communists also emphasised Engels's claim that dialectical materialism was a science both of the external world and of human thought, meaning that it supplied a logic for comprehending reality and at the same time was fully exemplified in reality. Engels had even laid down three fundamental laws – the law of transformation of quantity into quality, and vice versa; the law of interpenetration of opposites; and the law of the negation of the negation – and these laws were accepted by Communists by the 1930s. It was these laws which particularly interested the famous group of Marxist scientists of the 1930s, and they frequently claimed that their colleagues were unwitting practitioners of them. 'They do not see how it [dialectical materialism] applies to the experiments they are actually performing', lamented J. D. Bernal in 1934.[26]

In the last paragraph I have quoted from British publicists of this Soviet doctrine of dialectical materialism, but have yet to show how it was introduced into this country and the nature of its confrontation with the earlier understanding based on Dietzgen. From a contemporary perspective the two doctrines share a common belief that the dialectic was a universally applicable tool, and that all forms of social life could be reduced to one essential contradiction. The dialectic justified and reinforced the dogmatic tendencies in British Marxists' historical materialism because, rather than encouraging them to analyse the specific nature of a social formation at a given moment, it established *a priori* truths about history and politics. Yet between the two doctrines there is an unmistakable difference in tone. Whereas the Soviet doctrine was invested with the textual authority of Marx and Engels, and was precise, rigorous and all-encompassing, Dietzgen's 'proletarian logic' had a distinctly makeshift quality, consisting as it did of a series of speculative and discursive essays. Much of its attraction lay in the fact that its author was himself a self-taught worker, untainted by the influence of 'cringing, unphilosophical bourgeois philosophers'.[27] The Soviet Marxists had recognised Dietzgen's achievement in the 'independent attainment by a worker to dialectical materialism', and they continued to give him guarded approval, even though, as Lenin remarked, 'he is not always giving the right interpretation of the teaching of Marx and Engels'.[28] He was criticised for subsuming thought within the category of matter and thus blurring the distinction between materialism and idealism. Lenin developed this criticism of Dietzgen in *Materialism and Empirio-Criticism* (1909), which was first translated in 1927 and caused British Marxists to make a more critical reappraisal of Dietzgen. Though 1927 was clearly the turning point in Communist attitudes to 'proletarian logic', Dietzgen was never dismissed absolutely, so that as the new orthodoxy was being introduced in the course of the 1920s, Dietzgen was still taught in British Communists' educational classes (as well as the labour colleges) and the Communist bookshops continued to stock his works.

The difficulty was that Dietzgen's British disciples were not prepared to accept their master's relegation to a minor role in the Marxist pantheon. Just as Dietzgen's own son, Eugene, and his translator, Ernest Untermann, had engaged in prolonged controversy with orthodox continental Marxists before the war, so his British followers also claimed for him a leading and independent status. His leading champion until 1925 was W. W. Craik. Craik lectured the students on 'Logic and The Science of Understanding', and in 1926 helped Eugene Dietzgen to prepare a new translation of *The Positive Outcome* to replace the original. ('Permit me to write', began the German, 'that your English diction is without stilted grandezza and still very choice, graceful and translucent like a pure water-colour technique which avoids squash colouring.')[29] Roneoed sets of his 'Outlines of Lectures on Logic' and a similar pamphlet published by the Halifax Labour College were circulating during the 1920s. However, in 1925 Craik was involved in a scandal concerning Labour College funds which resulted in a warrant being sworn for his arrest, and he removed himself to Germany for several years before returning in the 1930s to take up union work. His lectures were taken over by the Welsh miner Jack Jones, who had attended Craik's lectures, but in Craik's absence the mantle of 'proletarian logic' passed to Fred Casey.

Fred Casey was one of those eccentrics thrown up by a movement who have such an unshakeable conviction in the absolute validity of their own views and the muddleheaded incompetence, or worse, of others, that they estrange themselves even from their own supporters. He was born in Bury in 1876 and trained as a plumber until at the age of seventeen he lost his right leg in an accident. Thereafter he worked in Bury as a watchmaker for more than fifty years. I have no direct evidence concerning his educational and political activities prior to the First World War but he seems to have become particularly interested in Dietzgen's books soon after their introduction to this country after

1906. He produced a major textbook on *Thinking. An Introduction to its History and Science* which the Labour Publishing Company published in 1922 and which was widely used in the labour colleges (it passed through a second British and an American edition). This book was supplemented by wall-charts illustrating the development of philosophy which were of such complexity that the most intricate railway shunting yard seems comparatively simple: one shudders to imagine their effect on the newly enrolled student. In subsequent articles and pamphlets he became increasingly preoccupied with Dietzgen, to the exclusion of all others. He believed that while Marx and Engels had 'worked out dialectics' in a practical sense in their writings on science and society, they had 'never worked out the dialectic of the thinking process' and had therefore failed to construct a 'complete science of thinking'. According to Casey, 'Dietzgen's work ...[was] the reduction to law of that which Marx and Engels themselves used but never completed in finished form'.[30] Casey's understanding of dialectics differed significantly from the Communist doctrine of dialectical materialism: where Engels and Communists after him understood the dialectic as a process of movement and development, Casey interpreted it statically. He thought 'the keynote of dialectic...thinking lies in knowing how a thing can be so and yet not so at one and the same time'.[31] This claim probably had its origins in Dietzgen's observation that the thinking subject attributes relationships to objects depending on the particular context, and his related proposition that these different mental conceptions must be accommodated in a monist outlook. But while Dietzgen's attempt to deal with subjectivism was applied to society, Casey's was applied to the individual and reduced to such banal paradoxes as 'Sitting in one's chair while the world swings along in its orbit is a case of being still in relation to the chair and yet moving.' Another example of how 'one minute we can say a thing is so, yet the next minute it isn't so' was the human body, for 'we say a man is living, but since a great number of his bodily cells are at all times dying, so is he dying'.[32] Casey also used his principle of 'the ONE-ness of the contradictory parts' to assault the Communists' new understanding of the dialectic, and in particular their 'widespread misunderstanding...to the effect that things are constantly moving and therefore never still'. This was 'mistaken, of course, for the stillness has an existence just as much as the motion'. Further, Casey claimed that his Applied Logic could provide answers to questions such as 'Are strikes unreasonable?' 'Are majorities always right?', 'Should workers serve on trade union executives?' and even 'Should I be a Communist?' By the second half of the 1920s the last question was answered in the negative, for the Communists were mechanical determinists whose very opposition to the Labour Party illustrated their failure to appreciate the dialectic of history.[33]

It is difficult to see how any coherent meaning could be extracted from such an arbitrary and absurd logic as that of Casey. Of his dictum that 'if the whole is absolute then every part is absolute because the whole is the parts and the parts are the whole', Jackson once remarked that '*qua* Casey, the spare wheel of a car will carry you to London as well as the "whole" car would'.[34] Nevertheless, there was a considerable British following for Dietzgen's philosophy and Casey's version of it. The Communist response to Casey, as well as their increasingly intransigent criticism of Dietzgen himself, seem to have been motivated as much by a desire to reply to the political criticisms of the Party made by Casey in his later books as by specific doctrinal differences. Communists had given Casey's first book, *Thinking*, a warm welcome in 1922, and as late as 1927 Jackson had written that 'whatever its incidental shortcomings, Casey's book is unquestionably right in its main drift'.[35] However, in 1928 the *Sunday Worker* refused to publish his critical review of Lenin's *Materialism and Empirio-Criticism*. As was suggested earlier, the appearance of an English translation of Lenin's critical comments on Dietzgen caused Communists to re-evaluate 'proletarian logic' and this process was accelerated by the increasingly anti-Communist tone of the Dietzgen cult. In 1928 both the Central Labour College and the South-East Lancashire Labour College, in which Casey was a tutor, held celebrations of the centenary of Dietzgen's birth, and while the Communist Party gave lukewarm support to the anniversary, some Party students at the Central Labour College were disciplined for, *inter alia*, their refusal to attend the London ceremony.[36] In 1930 there occurred a major scandal in the South-East Lancashire Labour College when Casey accused a Communist tutor, Sam Knight, of having given lectures on Dietzgen to a class in Wigan, using Casey's notes but distorting them so that criticism of the Communist Party and of Leninist epistemology was omitted. These allegations were brought before a series of meetings of the Tutors' Committee at which Casey spent hour after hour explaining the errors of dialectical materialism and the treachery of the Communists, followed by public debates between Casey and Knight in the Warrington Labour Club and elsewhere.

Throughout this period Casey was firing off thirty-page typed, single-spaced letters to anyone who seemed sympathetic, and while he retained the support of the N.C.L.C. regional organiser it would appear that an increasing number of Marxists began to treat him with that particularly polite caution one accords the unstable. Casey's problems were exacerbated by a singularly dour manner. When T. A. Jackson met him early in the 1920s he 'found him to be more completely devoid of humour than any human being I have ever met. The traditional Scot who "jokes with difficulty" would be a flippant jester by comparison.'[37] The N.C.L.C. had already declined to publish the little book entitled *Dietzgen's Logic* which he produced himself in 1928, and his talks on 'proletarian logic' were delivered to increasingly unlikely audiences such as the Oldham Health Society (for he was now an osteopath and a vegetarian), to whom he explained the close relationship between correct dialectical thinking and mental health.[38] By now the Communists were adamant that 'whatever may be the merits of Dietzgen's works. . ., the work of his pupil, Mr Casey, is one mass of muddle-headed confusion and crude *idealism*'. And when T. A. Jackson took up Casey's *Method in Thinking* (1933) while in bed with neuralgia, he was plunged into such a 'frenzy of disgust and indignation' that he threw off his bedclothes and began writing a reply. Three years and many drafts later, the reply was published under the title *Dialectics* with a sixty-page appendix devoted to a refutation of the 'idealistic bemuddlement' of this 'High Priest of neo-Dietzgenianism'.[39]

Casey continued to lecture in the North-West throughout the 1930s and the Second World War and even into the 1950s, and he continued to display the same unfortunate ability to fall out with friends over the most absurd reaches of 'proletarian logic'. In 1935 Dr Edward Conzé, a Marxist exile from the Continent, wrote a new edition of his earlier *Introduction to Dialectical Materialism* (1926) entitled *The Scientific Method of Thinking*, in which he adopted Casey's example of the stationary chair and the moving planet; Casey's response was to write him a violently critical letter.[40] The Bury watchmaker continued to write and publish material on 'proletarian logic', and his *How People Think* (1949) triggered off yet another debate about the significance of the study of Dietzgen to the Labour movement. But classes in this 'proletarian logic' became an increasingly unusual eccentricity, encountered in the backwaters of the S.P.G.B. or the dwindling classes of older labour college lecturers. On the other hand, Jackson's own book on *Dialectics* belongs unmistakably to the same tradition as the writings

of Craik and Casey: eclectic and idiosyncratic, representing the elaborate world-view of a highly intelligent but philosophically unsophisti-
cated autodidact. As Jackson himself put it, 'My *Dialectics* is as full of
faults as a dog is of fleas...., but with all its faults it did embody the
results of the reading of a lifetime.'[41] And neither Jackson nor any
other veteran working-class Communist ever fully assimilated the new
orthodoxy of dialectical materialism. Exposition and discussion of the
new doctrine was left to university-trained Communists such as
Clemens Dutt and to a group of professional scientists and philosophers
with no previous interest in Marxism. Jackson's generation of working-
class intellectuals whose understanding of dialectics sprang from their
struggle for a general knowledge, and who had cut their teeth on such
general philosophical surveys as Lewes's *Biographical History of Philosophy*, was replaced by a new generation of workers who learnt dialectical materialism as a formal component of Soviet Marxism without
any other knowledge of philosophy. The endlessly detailed notes on
ancient Greek philosophy taken by Craik while a student at Ruskin
have no modern equivalent.[42] And as Jackson enquired, 'What do they
know of Marxism who only Marxism know?'[43] Thus the disappearance
of Dietzgen from the shelves of British Marxists and the eclipse of
working-class study of 'proletarian logic' should not be attributed
simply to Communist hostility. It is more usefully seen as a further consequence of the exhaustion of the working-class educational tradition
discussed in chapter 4.

Within the labour college movement it is also possible to observe a
confrontation over dialectics between working-class Marxists and
university-trained Marxists. As we have seen, a prominent group of
writers and teachers in the Plebs League, among them Postgate,
Philips Price and the Horrabins, came from a middle-class background
and shared the undialectical temper of British academic culture. These
teachers never shared the general enthusiasm for Dietzgen and periodically called down the wrath of the labour colleges by questioning his
value. Thus in 1923 Maurice Dobb urged students to 'get away from
mid-19th century philosophy and academic dissertations on the absolute, and get just a few clear and essential notions about the scientific
method and modern science'. Amid a storm of complaints in the next
issue of *Plebs*, Postgate supported Dobb and suggested 'we abandon
Dietzgen teaching altogether and respectfully, but firmly, put old
Joseph on the shelf'. Again in 1926 Eden Paul antagonised a number

of worker–students at the Central Labour College with his assertion in a lecture on psychology that Dietzgen was out of date.[44]

With the exception of Dobb, these critics of Dietzgen were not merely hostile to his turgid and unorthodox presentation of the dialectic, they were opposed to the entire dialectical tradition; and in 1926 they broadened their assault to include the new Communist doctrine of dialectical materialism. Their criticisms were taken from the American intellectual Max Eastman, whose *Marx, Lenin and the Science of Revolution* was published in that year. Eastman had already antagonised Communists in the previous year with his book *Since Lenin Died*, which criticised recent political developments in the Soviet Union. He now set out to rescue Marxism from the 'vast mystic–intellectual legend' which had been imposed on it and which he rejected as 'an unintelligible mixture of emotional mysticism and psychological half-truth'. While admitting that Marx received a Hegelian education, Eastman claimed that he threw it over with the *Theses on Feuerbach* and thereafter that 'his whole scientific life shows the struggle of those practical and realistic instincts against that education'. Unfortunately, because Marx concentrated upon economics, he 'left to Engels the task of formulating their common philosophy', and Engels had reverted to the Hegelian tradition; Soviet Marxism had compounded Engels's error and was 'merely Marxism in its purest Hegelian–metaphysical form'. Now was the time, Eastman concluded, to shake off this irrational legacy of 'Hegel and the Soviet priesthood' once and for all: 'The philosophy of dialectic materialism is not to be confused with the practical science of Marxism, and wherever and whenever it gets in the way, it is to be kicked out.'[45]

As was noted in the last chapter, Eastman enjoyed the friendship and support of the group of ex-Communist intellectuals who clustered around the Plebs League. They quickly took up *Marx, Lenin and the Science of Revolution*, and Jackson remarked subsequently that the group imbibed the book 'surreptitiously as a sort of intellectual "bootleg" '.[46] This remark attests to the influence of Eastman but is not strictly correct, for the group made no secret of their agreement with Eastman and publicised his book widely. J. F. Horrabin said that Eastman had thrown some 'well-aimed brickbats', while Raymond Postgate thought that he had conclusively discredited the dialectic and Marxists should now 'say goodnight to it'.[47] Eastman's importance stemmed from his ability to make explicit the ingrained hostility to dialectics which was shared by so many British Marxists with a university education. While these intellectuals always interpreted Marxism in an emphatically positivist sense, apart from their earlier attacks on Dietzgen they had previously avoided discussion of the general issue of Marx's Hegelian heritage: such was their unfamiliarity with the German idealist tradition that they were probably incapable of tackling the problem. 'And now', as John Strachey wrote at the time, 'Max Eastman comes along to tell us that we have been perfectly right all along: that the British Socialist has instinctively grasped the valuable, scientific and important part of Marx's teaching, and rejected the lumbering, out-of-date, and quaint systems of thought and philosophy which Marx had to take over from Hegel...'[48] Eastman was thus interpreted as justified the natural aversion to dialectics, and during the remainder of the decade no one outside the Communist Party bothered themselves any further.

It was not until 1933 that British intellectuals began to produce more original arguments in this field. John Macmurray, professor of philosophy at the University of London, did so in his generally sympathetic essay *The Philosophy of Communism*. He thought the chief weakness of dialectical materialism was its assumption that 'reality is an organic process and, therefore, can only be understood dialectically'. Macmurray stressed what he called the 'superorganic element' of human relations. E. F. Carritt, an Oxford lecturer in philosophy, also believed that dialectical principles might apply to natural science but obscured the unique aspects of social science.[49] These two writings marked an upsurge and widening of interest in this aspect of Marxism, further augmented as the Marxist circle of scientists were drawn into discussion. A series of articles followed in the *Labour Monthly* in 1933, and the collection of essays entitled *Aspects of Dialectical Materialism* appeared in 1934. They helped to define the new intellectual range of post-1933 Marxism, and detailed discussion of them falls outside the scope of this study.[50]

In any case, this strand of the intellectual Marxism of the later 1930s was prefigured in certain crucial respects by the earlier imposition of a more formal Soviet orthodoxy. As we have already seen, the doctrine of dialectical materialism was introduced into this country in the course of the 1920s; but it did not take on its final form until the end of that decade, and only emerged then from a protracted debate between two major groups of Soviet theorists. One group, usually known as the mechanists, were hostile to the dialectic, and the other group, which was led by the philosopher A. M. Deborin, insisted that the dialectic was an essential element of Marxism. They argued throughout the 1920s and the debate was finally settled at the beginning of the 1930s by Stalin's imposition of the official interpretation of dialectical materialism. Although there was no contemporary awareness of this argument in Britain, it had important repercussions for Marxism here. The interpretations of Marxist theory advanced by Nikolai Bukharin, who was a leading mechanist, had clear affinities with the anti-metaphysical tendencies of British Marxists, and Bukharin's writings were extremely influential in this country during the 1920s. Furthermore, while British Marxists were introduced to the controversy only after it had been resolved and the doctrine imposed by Stalin had become obligatory, this retrospective and clearly tendentious explanation of the errors of the mechanists and Deborinites alike did nevertheless shape the final British understanding of the dialectic. We shall therefore briefly summarise the Soviet debate in order to trace its subsequent impact here.[51]

The mechanists believed that all phenomena, including human activity and thought, could be deduced from organic matter and explained by mechanical laws. They believed they were helping to construct a unified science which would make all philosophical speculation antiquated and redundant. Marxism was particularly concerned with social phenomena, but it could be considered fully consistent with this science so long as it was purged of all metaphysical Hegelian trappings: the mechanists drew an absolute distinction between the Hegelian dialectic, which took the erroneous metaphysical view that there was dialectical movement in nature itself, and the Marxist dialectic. The Marxist dialectic was taken to be simply a method of research. The Deborinites, who began replying to these attacks on philosophy in 1924, rejected the mechanists' positivist notion of a unified science based on mechanical laws. Their view was that there were distinct areas of knowledge, and the function of Marxist philosophy was to provide the methodology and theoretical basis for them. Deborin also maintained that the dialectic was an essential element of Marxism, and that it was not simply a method of research but was fully exemplified in nature itself. By 1929 the Deborinites had won control of the chief Soviet publications and institutions of learning. Their victory coincided with the political defeat of Bukharin and the Right Opposition, and mechanism was condemned by the Party as a theoretical deviation of political significance. The same fate overtook the

Deborinites shortly thereafter, however, for Stalin's speech to the Conference of Marxist Agrarians at the end of 1929 encouraged the final subordination of philosophy to politics – a culmination of the doctrine of the unity of theory and practice which was outlined in chapter 5. The immediate effect of Stalin's speech was to strengthen criticism of Deborin and his associates for the scholastic and insufficiently practical nature of their work, and they were removed from positions of influence by the end of 1930. The defeat of the two groups ended free discussion of the general questions of science and philosophy, and of the particular issue of dialectics, for the mechanist and Deborinite debate gave way to the official version of dialectical materialism.

I have already observed that British Marxists did not learn of this dispute until 1931. Yet it is clear that many possessed already and quite independently a positivist attitude to science which was remarkably similar to that of the Russian mechanists. Their object of exorcising the ghost out of the machine was common to much of the literature in the nineteenth-century popular materialist tradition which was examined in the previous chapter, and British Marxists carried a similar belief in science across to their study of society. The very name given by the S.L.P. to Marxist educational classes – Social Science Studies – suggests their positivist temper. As one member of the S.L.P. who subsequently joined the Communist Party put it:

Science is exact knowledge about the universe of which we form a part. Its methods are those of reason, observation and experiment. After a long struggle ...through the ages against the forces of reaction, superstition and ignorance, science has triumphantly overthrown its enemies in one field after another, and today offers to the world's workers the truth.

This outlook left no room for philosophy: indeed, philosophy was specifically condemned by a leading Communist intellectual as 'metaphysical speculation', mere 'juggling with words' and 'a waste of time'. He insisted that 'any progress we make must be the work of science in correlating experience'.[52]

This native hostility to philosophy was reinforced by Bukharin, whose work was more readily available in translation in England than that of any other Bolshevik after Lenin. There was the popular textbook he wrote with Preobrazhensky, *The ABC of Communism* (first translated in 1921, a superior edition in 1922), the essay *Lenin as a Marxist* (1925), *The Economic Theory of the Leisure Class* (1927) and *Imperialism and the World Economy* (1929). His *Historical Materialism*, an important if not entirely typical exposition of the mechanist standpoint, was translated in 1926 and was extremely influential among British Marxists. In it he sharply distinguished the Marxist dialectic from that of Hegel, and presented it as a mechanical theory of equilibrium. T. A. Jackson wrote that 'it is impossible to speak too highly of this volume', and Bukharin's interpretation was regarded as definitive in this country for the next few years.[53] For an example of the uninformed mechanism of British Marxists we may turn to a Communist review of the Russian physiologist Pavlov's *Conditioned Reflexes*: 'The importance of the work to Marxists will be evident. We have here the possibility of a complete materialist conception of the mind to the exclusion of foundationless theories of "soul", "life force", "universal idea" and such sentimental imaginings.'[54] In short, science had driven out philosophy.

There was little opposition to these views. Max Eastman wrote that Bukharin's attempt to interpret the dialectic as mechanically as Newton's laws of motion simply reduced the entire 'dialectic metaphysics' to absurdity, but Eastman was of course a more vehement opponent of dialectics than Bukharin, and what he wanted was a clean sweep. The only defence of dialectics to appear in Britain during the 1920s came from Deborin. In 1927 he provided a foreword to the English translation of Lenin's *Materialism and Empirio-Criticism*, in which he polemicised against certain unspecified 'positivist' misinterpretations of Marxism and claimed rather artfully that 'it is to the credit of Russian Marxism that, in both theoretical and philosophical fields, it continued to develop the dialectic method'.[55] Such a veiled protest could only pass over the heads of his British audience and there is no evidence that anyone in this country recognised his distinctive position. The dispute was first explained to British Marxists after Stalin had concluded it – in October 1931 by Dmitri Mirsky. Mirsky's article was a faithful summary of the new Stalinist orthodoxy; Bukharin and his colleagues had rejected the dialectic under the erroneous belief that 'science is its own philosophy'; the Deborinites were also at fault for 'academic scholasticism' and their 'unduly emphasising Dialectic as distinct from Materialism'. In place of these two erroneous positions, Communists must insist on 'a philosophy which is consistent with the revolutionary interests of the proletariat'. That philosophy was dialectical materialism.[56] This interpretation was faithfully reproduced by all Communists subsequently writing on the subject. It undoubtedly oversimplified and distorted the views of both discredited groups, and the American Julius Hecker's *Moscow Dialogue: Discussions on Red*

Philosophy (1933) was the only available account that came close to an appreciation of the complex philosophical issues which had actually been raised in the dispute. There was indeed a general ignorance in this country of the continental alternatives to orthodox dialectical materialism. The Hungarian Communist Georg Lukács and the German Karl Korsch, whose theoretical writings earlier in the 1920s were widely discussed in the European movement, were known in this country at this time only for their political activities.[57]

The only British challenge to the official account came from Lancelot Hogben, then a young left-wing biologist with Plebs experience, who agreed with and continued to defend the position of Bukharin. This brought him into dispute with Clemens Dutt, elder brother of the better-known Rajani Palme Dutt, who argued for the official doctrine of dialectical materialism. Examination of the debate allows a fuller appreciation of the conflict between the mechanist attitude, which had been general among British Marxists, and the new orthodoxy. Hogben first advanced a mechanist view of science in 1930. In his book *The Nature of Living Matter* he claimed that 'it would be difficult to specify in a living system any single activity which could not be reproduced by a mechanical system'. Hence 'we can now envisage the possibility that the methods of physical science will one day claim the whole field of what can be properly called knowledge'.[58] This forthright mechanist credo was complemented in the following year by an attack on what he called the 'anti-mechanist' character of Soviet philosophy. Hogben criticised those Russian scientists and philosophers who 'proudly proclaimed themselves in the Apostolic succession of Hegel' and suffered from 'the habit of borrowing from Hegel verbal conventions which have only the most superficial relevance to the logic of science'. Hogben said that he preferred to follow Bukharin. Indeed he went further along the mechanist road than Bukharin in his assertion that the dialectic was a mere 'epistemological principle', for Bukharin had at least conceded that dialectics were also inherent in nature.[59]

Clemens Dutt joined issue with Hogben in a belated review of *The Nature of Living Matter*. The chief defect of the book, wrote Dutt, was its undialectical character. Hogben's 'materialism with all its qualifications is still nothing more than the naive "vulgar" materialism of the scientist engaged in scientific research. In fact, his whole tendency is to hark back to the eighteenth century materialists and to lay stress on the reduction of all phenomena of life to terms of physics and chemistry'.[60] This criticism is typical of that directed at the Soviet mechanists, Bukharin included, who had long since retracted. Yet Hogben did not. In a cautious and far from consistent reply to Dutt he paid lip-service to dialectical materialism but said his views were still 'in essential agreement' with those of Bukharin. He also claimed that the dialectical system, while it may have assisted science in the last century, was increasingly irrelevant to modern science. Engels 'would have been the first to admit that Hegel's negation of negation has less relevance to the technique of scientific reasoning than the chapter on the dialectic would signify'.[61] Dutt then returned with a restatement of the orthodox doctrine. He acknowledged that the dialectical mode of thinking was not immediately congenial to many scientists who had an instinctive mistrust of philosophy, but they should realise that 'dialectical materialism represents the scientific outcome of philosophy'. Scientists such as Hogben were deluding themselves if they believed they could ignore it, for it was 'the only adequate scientific foundation for investigation and knowledge of nature, human history and processes of thinking'.[62] There the controversy ended.

It is difficult to assess how far British Marxists understood the Soviet debate. Leading Communists learnt the official attitude on these questions and inveighed at length against the dangers of mechanism on the one hand and Deborinite idealism on the other. Yet there remained something stilted and imitative about such performances, suggesting a lack of genuine interest in the philosophical problems themselves. And on a more popular level, the Party never completely threw off its inclination to profess a simple (or 'vulgar') materialism. In 1932, for instance, the *Daily Worker* began printing a series of letters from the rank and file on materialism which read like testimonies for a patent medicine: 'I too have only recently experienced within myself that marvellous infusion of new life and purpose which can only result from the absolute conviction that the fundamental laws of existence are materialistic.'[63] One non-Communist reader was driven to protest that 'your correspondents give no indication in their letters that they are not mechanistic materialists, who merely reduce all the varied phenomena of life and humanity to nothing but aggregations of some element vaguely conceived as matter'.[64] This criticism of popular materialism has considerable general validity for the period and it is significant that the later debates on dialectical materialism were restricted in the main to university-trained Marxists only. The old enthusiasts for proletarian logic were generally silent.

A labour college student once protested that 'the two words "dialectical materialism" were enough to completely put the wind up workers having just completed a shift in the mine, a day on the footplate or nine hours in the factory'.[65] For the vast majority of workers this judgement is undoubtedly true, and it is therefore tempting to conclude that the dialectic was a negligible aspect of British Marxism. But it would be wrong to do so. Such a judgement ignores the grim determination with which the small minority tackled the works of Dietzgen, Engels and other popularisers of the dialectic. One student wrote that she could often have wept from self-pity as she wrestled with Dietzgen, and others like her painfully accumulated their understanding.[66] Individual teachers such as the Welshman Nun Nicholas devoted the greater part of their energies to popularising Marxist philosophy. It is true that the great majority were uninterested and that there was a general antagonism to the language and concepts of the dialectical mode of thinking; but a far more useful way of looking at this minority enthusiasm is to see it as a case of intellectual apartheid. Because English empiricism was so uncongenial to metaphysics, those workers who discovered the dialectic were likely to regard it as the key to all knowledge. They came to constitute a circle of uncritical enthusiasts, convinced that they alone understood the foundations of reality. The Soviet doctrine which displaced this native working-class dialectical tradition was forced on to the members of the Party, most of whom spoke the new orthodoxy with halting unfamiliarity. Yet even under these conditions it continued to supply its adherents with a world outlook which they would otherwise have lacked and a philosophical guarantee for their politics. For these reasons Engels's *Anti-Dühring* was perhaps the most potent of all Marxist texts. Even after she had left the Communist Party, Charlotte Haldane remembered it as 'perhaps the most brilliantly written of all its holy texts', and said it had caused in her 'that heightening of consciousness and resolution that are symptomatic of a true religious conversion'.[67] She was not alone.

7. Economics

In the late nineteenth and early twentieth centuries the economic aspect of Marxism was better known in this country than most other aspects. While the historical and philosophical works of Marx were mostly unknown to British readers, a good selection of his economic writings were freely available in English translation. The S.D.F., the S.L.P., and the S.P.G.B. had all given primary emphasis to the economic doctrine drawn, though not necessarily accurately, from these writings. Great importance was attached to a thorough understanding of them: J. T. Murphy recalled later that if a prospective member of the S.L.P. 'could not give a satisfactory definition of a commodity and explain something about the concentration of capital, the applicant would be advised first to attend some educational class and to acquire the necessary knowledge'.[1] Moreover, the Marxist critique of capitalism had considerable impact on the rest of the labour movement. Simplified in technical argument and emptied of revolutionary content, its influence can be detected in the popular outlook of many members of the Labour Party. In this chapter I shall first describe British Marxists' understanding of the general doctrine, then discuss some particular issues in dispute, and finally investigate aspects of the wider impact of Marxist economics.

Before 1917 Marxist economics was usually taught from the first nine chapters of Volume One of *Capital*, or perhaps from Edward Aveling's summary of it – both daunting starting-points. Those who wished could then work their way through the remainder of the first volume and the two subsequent volumes in the Kerr edition.[2] These were the textbooks for the course in economics at the Central Labour College, supplemented by the American Louis Boudin's *Theoretical System of Karl Marx* (1907) as well as Smith, Ricardo, Mill, Marshall, Hobson and Jevons. But by the 1920s there were three popular textbooks. Noah Ablett, the South Wales miners' leader and early Plebs activist,

published his *Easy Outlines of Economics* in 1919. In 1922 the Plebs
League produced an *Outline of Economics*, drafted in the first instance
by the engineering shop steward Will McLaine on the basis of his
earlier roneoed 'Economics Without Headaches'; the *Outline* sold
14 000 copies over the next decade. Then in 1925 another Plebs
activist, Mark Starr, published *A Worker Looks at Economics*. To
these may be added the briefer printed notes which accompanied
John Maclean's lectures on economics and which were published by
the Scottish Labour College at the end of the war.

As Marx had done in *Capital*, British popularisers usually began
with the commodity. A commodity was a product of human labour
made primarily for exchange. The production of commodities was not
an immutable feature of human history, for in earlier times people
produced articles for their own use. In the popular texts we can already
detect a tendency to oversimplify, and Ablett and Starr, like many
Marxists before them, sometimes mistook commodity production for
capitalism. William Paul also defined capitalism simply as 'a social
system wherein the fundamental aim of all production is the creation
of goods for the market in order to realise profit – and not for use' (this
was the obverse of his reading capitalist class relations back into earlier
periods of history which was discussed in chapter 5).[3] In their influential
ABC of Communism (translated 1921) the Russian Marxists Bukharin
and Preobrazhensky warned against the widespread misconception
that commodity production was synonymous with capitalist production
and observed that goods had been produced for exchange long before
a capitalist class came to control the means of production. British
writers came increasingly to respect this distinction, and it was generally observed by the end of the 1920s. According to the orthodoxy,
then, capitalist production differed from simple commodity production
by its division of labour into two new classes, capitalist and proletarian.
The capitalist class owned the means of production: the propertyless
working class or proletariat 'owns no means of production and can
only get a living by selling its labour-power to the capitalist class' in
return for a wage payment.[4] For Marxists the *differentia specifica* of
capitalism was the buying and selling of labour-power.

The labour theory of value formed the keystone of Marxist economics and British Marxists accepted it without question. They
usually began explaining the theory by distinguishing between use-
value and exchange-value. Every commodity was produced to satisfy
some need and therefore possessed utility or use-value: however,

although use-value was an attribute of all commodities, it was not a satisfactory measure for economic analysis because of its subjective and variable character. This left exchange-value. 'Marx explained that if you set aside the useful qualities of the commodity (for which we can't find a standard) then you are left with a "common property" ', namely that commodities exchange on the market and therefore bear an exchange-value. The concept of exchange-value led British writers on to the labour theory of value. For what determined the exchange-value of a commodity? 'The exchange-value of any commodity is measured, as it must be, according to how it stands in relation to the value of other commodities; and the only standard by which values can be really compared is the standard set by the amount of social labour power needed to produce them.'[5] The quantity of labour needed to produce a commodity determined the value of that commodity.

It will be apparent that the only justification given by British Marxists for the labour theory of value was that all commodities had labour embodied in them. Because this was their 'one thing in common', their 'common property' and 'common denominator', it must somehow determine their value.[6] No further arguments were thought necessary. A common procedure was simply to assume the validity of the labour theory of value and defend it against hypothetical objections. Hence Mark Starr answered a series of stock criticisms: 'In order to prove the Labour Theory to be incorrect, gold nuggets fall from heaven without the agency of human labour...[But] if gold continually fell like rain no S[ocially] N[ecessary] L[abour] T[ime] would be needed to produce it, and therefore it would have no value.'[7] Such criticisms were in fact frequently encountered by Marxist propagandists, and one Clydeside I.L.P. activist sympathetic to Marxism remembers how his lectures on economics frequently drew objections from sceptics in the audience who cited exceptions to the labour theory of value – a valuable painting, for example, was worth far more than the cost of the labour embodied in it.[8] William Paul used to ridicule such objections by asking in return questions such as 'What is the value of a frying pan at the North Pole?'[9] British Marxists were always better versed in such exercises in the imaginary than they were in the more fundamental debate over the labour theory with which their continental counterparts were familiar, and it was not until Maurice Dobb published his essay 'The Requirements of a Theory of Value' in 1937 that the doctrine was put on firmer foundations.[10]

Greater emphasis was placed on the theory of surplus value, which in the presentations of British Marxists depended on the labour theory. Some undoubtedly preferred to concentrate on the theory of surplus value and lambast capitalist appropriation of wealth, while avoiding the question whether labour was the sole source of this wealth, but on the whole Marxists denied that other factors of production did create value. Their view was that the raw materials and machinery used in the productive process merely transferred value to the finished commodity and could never add extra value. Accordingly, the extra value embodied in the finished commodity, which gave the capitalist his profit, was imparted in the labour process. To explain how this occurred they used the distinction between labour and labour-power. The difference between the two was likened to 'the difference between the machine and the operations that machine performs' – 'labour power is the energy in its static form' and labour 'the energy flowing outward', the 'dynamic form'. Or as John Maclean put it, labour-power could be compared with the water stored in Loch Katrine and labour with that water flowing through pipes. The capitalist bought labour-power from the worker in return for a wage payment; the worker then performed labour. 'Labour-power is a commodity and is bought on the market by the capitalist in the same way as any other commodity; its value is equal to the value of the commodities necessary to produce and maintain it, i.e. food, clothing, shelter, etc.'[11] To this extent labour-power was like any other commodity, being exchanged for its value equivalent; but in one respect it was unique – 'unlike any other commodity, it is capable of producing more than its own cost'. For 'during the hours they are forced to work, the workers create things, or perform services, whose value exceeds what they receive in wages, and this excess value, or surplus value, is pocketed by the capitalist class'.[12] This was the essence of capitalism: 'The capitalist who employs labour therefore buys labour-power (pays wages to the workers) and gets back in products an equal value plus a surplus.' Or, to put it more simply, 'profit is unpaid labour. It is a glorified, legalised burgling expedition against the working class.'[13]

It will be apparent already that the popular British expositions of Marxist economics lacked both originality and theoretical sophistication. But while it is easy to criticise both the simplicity and the narrowly exegetical scope of this literature, such criticism runs the danger of overlooking its real purpose. It aimed to simplify and explain the basic principles of the Marxist critique of capitalism to a working-class audience. The most imaginative and vigorous popularisation, Noah

Ablett's *Easy Outlines,* is a far more skilful piece of educational writing than might appear at first sight, and the *Plebs Outline* and Mark Starr's *A Worker Looks at Economics* display the same qualities to a lesser degree. With two exceptions, their authors were self-educated (Maclean was a schoolteacher, and McLaine had attended university extension classes in Manchester) with considerable experience in the working-class educational movement and an intimate familiarity with the problems a worker–student was likely to encounter in his attempt to grasp Marxist economic principles; each had learnt, through lengthy trial and error, the best methods of solving these problems. In these respects the British efforts stand comparison with the equivalent Russian textbook, Bogdanov's *Short Course of Economic Science* (published in Britain in 1923; new edition 1927). Where the British expositions are deficient is in their application of Marxism to the contemporary situation, for they treated Marxist economics as a final and complete system whose applicability to current events could be taken for granted; and it is significant that one grievance among the students at the Central Labour College in 1923 was that there was inadequate attention to non-Marxist economics, both formal theory and the more practical subjects like statistics and accountancy.[14] Marx's critique of capitalism was presented more as an illumination of the extraction of surplus value from the worker – the 'glorified, legalised burgling expedition', as Willie Paul put it – than as a dynamic analysis pointing to the future development of capitalism. Palme Dutt drew attention to this characteristic when he launched the Communist campaign against the Plebs League in 1923. In 'the British–American substitute for Marxism, as taught in such works as Ablett's *Outlines of Economics,*' he alleged, 'the essence of Marx is left out. The economics . . .is taken in unreal abstraction, and the history and politics is slurred over or omitted.'[15] Marxist economics in Britain, rather like the traditional m.c.h. and 'proletarian logic', tended to be a self-contained set of ideas possessing little contact either with the intellectual mainstream or with the march of events. There are exceptions to this generalisation. John Maclean used to lecture on economics to packed lecture halls, and would commonly begin with a newspaper clipping of some local company's annual report. He would explain the meaning of the financial terms, draw the contrast between the declared dividend and the workers' wages, and relate this analysis to the immediate political considerations of the workers' movement on the Clyde. While very few possessed Maclean's gift for popular exposition, the weaknesses were overcome to a certain extent by the development of Marxism in the 1920s. We can illustrate this by following three particular areas where Marxism was vulnerable to criticism – the 'Great Contradiction', wages, and capitalist crises – and by seeing Marxists' growing expertise in meeting such criticism.

Of all criticisms of Marx's theory of value, by far the most important was that which came to be known as the 'Great Contradiction'. It was put most tellingly by the Austrian economist Eugen von Böhm-Bawerk in his book *Zum Abschluss des Marxischen System* (1896) and repeated by many of Marx's opponents. Here we examine how British critics took up the Great Contradiction and how Marxists attempted to refute it.

Marx, it will be recalled, contended that labour, or variable capital, was the source of surplus value, whereas raw materials and machinery, or constant capital, merely transferred value to the finished product. It would therefore seem that an enterprise with a greater proportion of variable to constant capital would yield a higher rate of surplus value than an enterprise with less variable and more constant capital. In the first volume of *Capital* Marx assumed equal organic composition of capitals – that is, the same proportions of constant to variable capitals throughout industry – but in Volume Three he conceded that this was only an approximation to actuality. He also admitted that two enterprises with different organic compositions could produce the same apparent rate of surplus value. The reason he gave for this apparent aberration was that each entrepreneur received as profit a share of the general pool of surplus value according to the total capital (variable plus constant) employed in his particular industry. Under capitalism, exchange took place and entrepreneurs were rewarded at prices of production and not at real values. Hence prices deviated from their strict value equivalents.

Böhm-Bawerk seized on this admission as the Great Contradiction on which the Marxist system foundered. 'Marx's third volume contradicts the first. The theory of the average rate of profit and of the prices of production cannot be reconciled with the theory of value.'[16] His book was published in Britain as *Karl Marx and the Close of His System* in 1898 and became a source book for Marx's British detractors. It became standard practice to show how Marx had been forced to abandon his labour theory of value and resort to a new and contradictory theory in order to take account of constant capital, which was after all contributed by the capitalist. The 'elaborate and laboured arguments in the First Volume are all thrown away'; the labour theory is 'dropped', and Marx is forced to abandon his claims for labour.[17]

British Marxists were well served with material with which to contrive a reply to these critics. In addition to the Charles H. Kerr edition of Volume Three of *Capital*, and the lengthy introduction in which Engels attemped to deal with the problem, they had the American Louis Boudin's *Theoretical System of Karl Marx in the Light of Recent Criticism* (1907) and translations of Hilferding's *Boehm-Bawerk's Criticism of Marx* (1919) and Bukharin's *Economic Theory of the Leisure Class* (1927). All contained lengthy replies to Böhm-Bawerk. Yet British Marxists exhibited obvious discomfort in their attempts to answer the Great Contradiction. Thus Max Beer accepted that there was a discrepancy between values and market prices, but fell back on a metaphysical notion of value: 'behind the empirical movements and appearances' of the market 'there is a law, a principle, underlying and controlling them, and to which, despite all deviations and refractions, they conform'.[18] If the critic would merely don Beer's Hegelian spectacles he would see that his Great Contradiction was an empirical chimera! Equally unsatisfactory was Ralph Fox's effort: according to him the third volume was meant to show 'that while the capitalist obtains profits from the circulation process he merely *realises* in the course of the process the profits created in the form of surplus values during the process of production'.[19] This might be the case but it was hardly adequate.

The working-class educationalists, particularly Ablett, did better. In his chapter entitled 'The Great Contradiction', which clearly benefits from study of Louis Boudin, Ablett acknowledged that there were differences in profit rates on the market, and claimed in reply that value in the market sense was only realised in the market. But at this point in his cogent summary of the problem he faltered: 'It is not a contradiction that equal capitals, whatever their composition, receive equal profits. But the difference between producer and receiver is not known to our critic...'[20] This was merely a restatement and not an explanation of the Great Contradiction, for it still did not show why equal profits on different compositions of capital occurred.

The only writer to demonstrate a convincing understanding of the issue was Maurice Dobb, for he alone sought to provide an intelligible explanation for the divergence of market prices from value equivalents. He pointed out for the first time that this reflected 'the need imposed

by the competition of capitals for profit to be spread out so as to yield
an equal rate per £, as water finds a common level given a sufficiency
of connecting pipes'. This requirement of the market altered the distribution of the Marxist surplus between different sections of industry,
'but it did not affect the size of surplus-value in the mass'. Thus the
conditions of modern capitalist exchange modified but did not invali-
date the labour theory of value.[21]

Another common criticism of Marx's economics was that he had
prophesied a steady and irreversible decline in wage levels. Before
1917 most Marxists had accepted this allegation and interpreted Marx
to mean that workers were paid the minimum necessary to survive and
that their condition was bound to deteriorate. Against this view, which
was often called the 'Iron Law of Wages', an increasing number of
Marxists after 1917 argued that the determination of wage levels
involved consideration of other factors.

We can begin by summarising the basic principles that were common to both interpretations. It was agreed that wages represented the
price paid for the commodity labour-power, and that like all commodities the value of labour-power was determined by the value of
the commodities needed to produce it. In this case 'the amount paid to
the workers for the use of their labour-power is the equivalent of what
they need in the way of food, clothes, shelter and other necessities for
themselves and their families, to maintain them in a fit state to work
and to bring up and train their children to work after them'.[22] British
Marxists also detected a downward tendency in wage levels. Because
capitalist industry sought continuous technical improvement, which
tended to substitute machinery for labour, an increasing number of
wage labourers were thrown out of employment. This 'reserve army of
labour' exercised a continuous downward pressure on wage levels.
Furthermore, as only variable capital could create surplus value, a
reduction in the proportion of variable to constant capital (i.e., an
increase in the organic composition of capital) caused a profit squeeze
which capitalists tried to overcome by further wage cuts. More and
more unsuccessful capitalist and previously independent producers
went to the wall and swelled the ranks of the proletariat. 'Unemployment becomes chronic and exploitation intensifies.'[23]

Some Marxists interpreted this analysis as a literal and complete
description of the workings of the capitalist system. Hyndman and
De Leon had done so; so had the pre-war S.D.F., S.L.P. and S.P.G.B.;
and Raymond Postgate wrote as late as 1920 that Marx had stated 'in

most unequivocal terms that the wage slaves could not improve their condition, which must grow worse and worse until it was absolutely intolerable'.[24] A few writers even attributed to Marx himself the proposition known as the Iron Law of Wages which held that wages could never rise above bare subsistence level (even though Marx had specifically repudiated the proposition in his address *Value, Price, and Profit* and his *Critique of the Gotha Programme*).[25]

This economic fatalism was an aspect of pre-war Marxism that was eclipsed after 1917. The Communist Party always insisted that it did not believe in any Iron Law of Wages. Yet the Party did not throw off the old attitudes altogether. It frequently depicted the process of wage determination as the operation of inexorable and purely economic forces: 'The worker slaves for a miserable wage, just sufficient to keep him sufficiently fit to carry on working...[He] only receives sufficient to enable him to keep going as a producer of profits, and to raise a new family of profit producers.' More importantly, towards the end of the 1920s Communists were expected to subscribe to a new 'Marxian law of absolute impoverishment of the working class'.[26] The law of absolute impoverishment was pressed as part of a new strategy of the Communist International and was the subject of considerable argument in Communist ranks. The argument turned on whether the working class was suffering an absolute decline in its condition or was merely receiving a smaller proportion of total capitalist production – in the latter case an increase in total production might compensate for the decrease in the share passing to the working class. Hugo Rathbone, whom we have seen earlier as an enforcer of orthodoxy, was one who insisted on absolute and irreversible impoverishment.[27] He was supported by the authoritative *Marxist Study Course* (a series of pamphlets prepared by the International and published as a fortnightly series from 1932 onwards). The course on Political Economy rebuked those comrades who believed that an absolute impoverishment was not inevitable. Wages might rise, it conceded, but inflation, increased hours and more onerous conditions of work, and reduced employment all constituted an overall decline which must intensify.[28] Such a doctrine seems to imply that the increased rate of exploitation – the diminished share of the product accruing to the workers – could not be compensated for by an increase in total production brought about by improved methods, but the advocates of the doctrine did not pursue such an argument. The doctrine was supported not by analytical reasoning from Marxist economic principles, but by descriptive reference to the manifest poverty of British workers, as in Allen Hutt's major survey of *The Condition of the Working Class in Britain* (1933).

There was, therefore, a definite tendency among British Marxists to espouse an extremely rigid law of wages, if not an iron one, and the metallic content increased at the end of the 1920s. But an opposing view was also current. Palme Dutt, for example, condemned in 1927 'the old misconception of the "theory of increasing misery", the idea that Marx taught that the absolute poverty of the workers must grow steadily greater. This is a mere confusion. Marx made very clear that real wages may rise...' Dutt also drew a distinction between the quantity of value paid to the workers, which might increase, and their share of the total, which would decline. He thought this second measure, the rate of exploitation, was the more important, for 'the decisive question is the movement of *relative wages*, the relative position of the workers in relation to the general development of society and accumulation of capital'.[29] His view was shared by other opponents of the theory of increasing misery, who also stressed other aspects of wage determination than the purely economic. The wage level was not absolutely fixed. Its lower limit was set by the amount necessary to maintain and reproduce the workforce, its upper limit by the organic composition of capital and the rate of surplus value; within these limits was worked out the 'traditional standard of life' which took account of 'the social conditions of the time and district'.[30] It was worked out through the class struggle. As John Maclean put it, the capitalist class constantly tried to increase their profits by reducing wages 'to the bare animal existence', while 'workers get above this by organisation and fighting the "Huns at Home". The better the organisation and the stronger the fight, the greater the chance of the workers to keep their standard of living above the animal level.'[31] (And this incidentally illustrates how Maclean had a less fatalistic conception of Marxism than most of his B.S.P. and S.L.P. contemporaries.) In such fashion the simple economic beliefs of pre-war Marxists gave way to something more like a political economy.

The Marxist theory of wages was closely linked to a more general theory of a falling rate of surplus value expressed in deepening economic crises, and there was considerable controversy over the nature and outcome of capitalist crises. Briefly, the orthodox theory went thus. The centralisation and increasing organic composition of capital produced an inherent tendency for the rate of surplus value to decline. Since production under capitalism was for profit, the declining rate of

profit periodically precipitated a sharp curtailment of activity as well
as a thinning of capitalist ranks. This led to an increase in the number
of the unemployed and hence a cheapening of the price of labour-
power; and this in turn restored conditions for an increased rate of
surplus value so the economic process could thus resume. But resump-
tion allowed the replacement of human labour by machinery to continue, augmenting the reserve army of labour, reducing again the rate
of surplus value, and preparing the way for the next crisis. The theory
thus postulated an increasing polarisation of society into the two classes
of capitalism, and ever-deepening crises as the organic composition of
capital steadily increased.

Was capitalism, then, bound to break down under the weight of
these internal contradictions? The question had divided continental
Marxists prior to 1917, especially after 1899 when Bernstein pronounced Marxism inadequate because of its unacceptable 'theory of
breakdown'.[32] Kautsky and most orthodox Marxists denied that Marx
had ever subscribed to such a theory and disclaimed it themselves
(though elsewhere they displayed a belief that capitalism was indeed
bound to collapse). More radical Marxists, such as Rosa Luxemburg,
reaffirmed that capitalism would break down.[33]

Before 1917 most British Marxists, and especially those of the S.L.P.,
expected a capitalist collapse – though this was more an article of faith
than a reasoned position informed by the continental debate; the
American Marxist Boudin provided the only link with the foreign
literature, which otherwise remained untranslated.[34] For pre-war
Marxists displayed little interest in the breakdown controversy. In their
writings capitalism was typically treated as a static system of unequal
exchange, and they were more interested in exposing the process of the
extraction of surplus value than in analysing capitalism as a mode of
production with its own dynamic tendencies of development. This did
not mean that they held no views on the future of capitalism, but
rather that their cataclysmic forecasts were derived from general
expectations and not from actual economic analysis. In the stormy
period from 1917 to 1920 they felt these expectations of a breakdown
were being confirmed and they shared an apocalyptic faith in 'The
Coming Crash', as Walton Newbold liked to call it:

Society goes hurtling to the universal catastrophe which the writer of *Capital*
foretold. Capitalist civilisation is reaching its culmination, impelled by the most
fearful momentum of its ever more frenzied career.

The tide of capitalism is fast going out, leaving in its wake the wreckage of human lives and ideals; its waters are scarlet with the blood of slaves, and its moaning echoes the despairing cries of the millions who have sunk in its reeking depths.[35]

Such judgements still took no account of the debate outside Britain and lacked any process of reasoning. As was suggested in chapter 5, the belief that capitalism would inevitably collapse, giving way to a new socialist order, performed an essentially psychological function, comforting its authors that 'history is moving in the same channels as their work, and is helping them to realise their mission'.[36]

And as a remnant of traditional Marxism it came into increasing conflict with the new Bolshevik perspective which looked beyond purely economic factors to political considerations. The new perspective did not discard the view that there were economic obstacles to the unlimited expansion of capitalism, nor that capitalism would undergo ever more severe crises, but it insisted that capitalism would be ultimately destroyed only by the concerted action of the working class. The first British challenge to the prevailing economic fatalism came from John Maclean, who took issue with a new Kerr publication entitled *The Collapse of Capitalism* (1919) in which it was announced that 'the coming of that great event' was 'a matter of figures and entirely independent of even the collective will of men'.[37] Maclean took issue both with the actual prediction of an imminent capitalist collapse and with the more general determinist approach to the question:

Many comrades seem to have been carried away by Cahn's *The Collapse of Capitalism*. My impression is that capitalism is more vital today in Britain, Japan and America than it ever was, and is preparing for expansions such as never made before, that if capitalism is to be 'sent west' it will only be as the result of the delivery of the greatest knock-out blow ever given, and that this blow must be given by a united, revolutionary working class.

View it as I may, I cannot see the possibility of a financial collapse automatically arising out of the contradictions of the capitalist process of production. The great contradiction is the opposition of classes leading to the collapse of the system through the mighty, resounding blows of a world-united Labour.[38]

The Communist Party continued Maclean's approach and bolstered it with theoretical support. Its theory of crises contained two elements: the tendency to a falling rate of surplus value, which I have discussed already; and a new aspect, the problem of realising surplus value on the market. This new aspect, sometimes known as the disproportionality thesis, had been extensively analysed by Rosa Luxemburg and possessed a long pedigree. But Luxemburg's treatment of the disproportionality thesis in her *Accumulation of Capital* did not become available to English readers until 1951, and the introduction of the argument into Britain in the 1920s came about indirectly through its popularisation by Soviet writers. The Soviet *Outline of Political Economy* provides a typical example of the thesis as it was understood by the Communists. It began by distinguishing between two 'branches of production', one producing means of production and the other means of subsistence. In periods of full employment, it was argued, the demand for production goods outstripped supply and there was overproduction of consumption goods, leading to mass unemployment; only after the glut of consumption goods had been cleared at reduced prices did renewed demand stimulate a recovery. As presented in the Soviet *Outline* (though not by Luxemburg), the disproportionality argument constituted a theory of cyclical crises in a 'very deep and acute' form, but not a theory of final breakdown. Indeed, the same reasoning which accounted for these crises explained their regenerative function: 'a prolonged disproportion between production and the purchasing power of the market, if not discovered in the form of crises, would lead to the decline of the capitalist system. Crises bring the concealed infection to the surface and thus make possible its rapid cure.'[39] Along with the more familiar doctrine of the falling rate of surplus value, disproportionality suggested that capitalism would be racked by ever-deepening crises – but the resolution of these crises could not be foretold in advance. The orthodox Communist position was that capitalism produced its own gravedigger, the proletariat; and the final destruction of capitalism was ultimately a political question.

Most socialists remained unconvinced by the Marxist doctrine of crises and assumed that a Labour Government could modify and patch up capitalism. A small group of ex-Communists in the Labour movement also directed a stream of criticism at the Communist pre-diction of a 'speedy and catastrophic collapse of the whole capitalist system', as they rather inaccurately described it.[40] The most important of these critics were Morgan Philips Price and J. T. Walton Newbold. Their essential argument was that new techniques of production, particularly in the chemical and electrical industries, seemed to herald a new era of capitalist prosperity.[41] Communists waxed indignant at this 'curious would-be "Marxist" section of the I.L.P. . . .who preach the Revival of Capitalism', and the debate had some significance in the mid-1920s.[42] The ex-Communists were able to capitalise on the confusion felt by many Marxists. For on the one hand Communists

now rejected the fatalist view that capitalism must collapse of its own
internal contradictions: on the other, they embraced a doctrine of
deepening capitalist crises from which there was no logical escape. The
dilemma persisted until the end of our period, when it was laid down
in Moscow that capitalists could always find a way out of the deepest
crisis at the expense of the workers; but this new twist is of limited
significance to our study.[43]

How far was the British labour movement influenced by Marxist
economics? The question has not been answered – nor indeed asked –
by Labour historians and here we can only make some provisional
suggestions. The influence of Marx will be assessed in two stages: first,
by considering what Labour spokesmen had to say about it; and
second, by examining their own economic doctrines for evidence of
what can at this stage be imprecisely called a Marxist perspective.

Explicit attitudes to Marxist economics came largely from spokesmen for rival doctrines. Their assessments were inaccurate, derivative
and yet significantly equivocal. From the gradualist viewpoint of
Ramsay MacDonald, 'the validity of [Marx's] economic theories is
more than doubtful', even though they bore the intellectual stamp of
'a master mind' and had provided the socialist movement with form
and direction. According to the young Harold Laski, 'Marxian economics is in no small degree self-contradictory', even though the broad
outline of his conclusions was 'unanswerable'. J. A. Hobson thought
that Marxism deserved its considerable reputation for the demonstration of 'capitalist robbery', even though 'the fallacies of the Marxian
theory of value and surplus value' were indisputable. These apparently
confused judgements indicate a simultaneous acceptance of Marx's
indictment of capitalism and rejection of the theory on which it was
based (and the revolutionary conclusions which Marxists drew from
it). Sidney and Beatrice Webb put this point more plainly:

The theoretic mistakes of Marx are as patent nowadays as the mistakes of Moses;
but nobody who has ever read the historical chapters of *Das Kapital* can ever
again fall under the illusion that capitalists, as such, are morally respectable.
Marx, in spite of his pretentious blunders in abstract economic theory. . ., succeeded magnificently in suddenly turning the banners of capitalism with their
seamy sides to the audience. . .[44]

Marx was therefore given credit for his painstaking work on the Blue
Books and his unparalleled description of the hardships suffered by the
working class. But as a theorist he was found unsatisfactory. It was

frequently suggested as well that his theory had been plagiarised from English predecessors, in particular Thomas Hodgskin, William Thompson and John Francis Bray. The British originator of this canard was apparently H. S. Foxwell, a professor at London University at the turn of the century, and it was repeated by many others.[45]

The writings discussed so far were characterised by an extremely poor understanding of the doctrines of Marx. Few socialist critics distinguished between labour and labour-power. Many attributed to him the Iron Law of Wages, a doctrine he had expressly disowned.[46] The writer of an educational series in *Forward* misunderstood surplus value as the difference between what a capitalist charged and the 'actual value' of a commodity.[47] In a celebrated passage in *Religion and the Rise of Capitalism*, R. H. Tawney expressed the belief that Marx accepted the economic role of the producer and reserved his hostility for the speculator or middleman.[48] In short, the statement made by the editor of a Labour newspaper seems to hold for most sections of the Labour movement: 'We have a vague idea of Karl Marx, and have tried, without success, to fight our way through *Das Kapital*.'[49] T. A. Jackson put the same point more pungently when he observed of Herbert Morrison, when he used to carry *Capital* under his arm, that only a limited amount of Marxism can be soaked up by the armpit.

Nevertheless, further investigation of the economic outlook of the Labour movement reveals some aspects in common with Marxism. To begin with, the terms 'capitalism', 'capitalist class', 'working class' and 'exploitation' were commonly used in the Labour movement, however imprecisely; and the declared aim of the Labour Party was 'the gradual supersession of the capitalist system by an industrial and social order based on the public ownership and democratic control of the instruments of production and distribution'.[50] These terms and the attitudes they expressed were not unique to Marxism, and several other socialist sources – Owenism, for example – helped to implant them in Labour Socialism. But we can point to more specifically Marxist themes. In setting out their socialist programme Labour spokesmen typically characterised capitalism as a historically specific economic system based on the private ownership of the means of production.[51] Society was divided, they thought, into 'two distinct and antagonistic classes', and the class which owned the means of production treated labour simply as a commodity in its ruthless pursuit of wealth. Furthermore, they perceived that the basic mechanism of capitalism was wealth accumulation and that the capitalist produced goods without concern for the needs of the community.[52] So far the standard analysis is proceeding on Marxist lines, even if they are not exclusive to Marxism. Eric Hobsbawm has even asserted:

Insofar as the British labour movement developed a theory about how capitalism worked – about the nature of capitalist exploitation, the internal contradictions of capitalism, the fluctuations of the capitalist economy such as slumps, the causes of unemployment, the long-term tendencies of capitalist development, such as mechanization, economic concentration and imperialism, these were based on the teachings of Marxism, or were accepted insofar as they coincided with them or converged with them.[53]

Hobsbawm qualifies this by adding that it is the rank-and-file understanding of economics which was influenced by Marxism, and that the leaders of the movement drew on other traditions. Even then his claim seems pitched too high. Let us begin our investigation with these economic alternatives to Marxism.

Labour Socialists were aware that capitalism functioned by extracting surplus value in the sphere of production. But occasionally in their writings on economics, and more often in general political practice, they presented inequality and poverty, and not the making of profit, as the fundamental characteristic of a system which they wished to end. The misallocation of national resources, whereby 'luxury production for the few takes precedence [over] the provision of necessaries for all',[54] was attributed to the fact that the few possessed a preponderance of wealth. As Philip Snowden put it in a major Commons debate on socialism, the fault lay with the 'method of wealth distribution'.[55] Policies were accordingly devised by the Labour Party to redistribute wealth and provide social services in the expectation that industry would then satisfy social needs. The basis of Labour's economic programme in the 1920s represented not a critique of the production process, Marxist or otherwise, but a critique of the social effects of wealth distribution.

The most coherent non-Marxist critique of the *economic* effects of wealth distribution was the theory of underconsumption. A recent study has demonstrated that this theory has a long history in economic thought,[56] and while an articulate Labour minority were conversant with the theory, a much larger number simply subscribed to the notion that there was insufficient purchasing power to maintain full production and that this was capitalism's essential defect. The essential argument was only an extreme version of the disproportionality thesis, using the same distinction between the two branches of production to diagnose a permanent and chronic disproportion of production and consumption. Capitalism suffered from what one underconsumptionist called the 'inherent and congenital defect of creating an unmarketable surplus'.[57] While wage-earners were unable to buy consumption goods sufficient for their needs, the owners of capital consumed only a fraction of their profits. These accumulated as savings or were used to buy more means of production: in either case the problem of inadequate demand was exacerbated. The productive capacity of capitalist industry was unrealised because of inadequate demand, and only 'an organic change in the distribution of wealth', as Hobson put it, could overcome the imbalance and provide sufficient demand to revive the economy.[58] The attraction of the theory was that it provided economic justification for an urgent and drastic redistribution of wealth. And although the Labour Party could not be persuaded to adopt the underconsumptionist Living Wage proposals of the I.L.P. (the most influential proposals to be based on the theory),[59] the notion that capitalism was decaying for lack of demand was shared by many socialists. Besides J. A. Hobson, the father of modern underconsumptionism, it was popularised by H. N. Brailsford, G. D. H. Cole, Fred Henderson, the young John Strachey, and John Wheatley, to name but a few important writers.

British Marxists lacked consistency in their attitude to underconsumption theory, for while they condemned it explicitly, they frequently employed similar arguments in their own writings. In this respect their hostility seems to have been directed primarily towards the reformist political perspective of the popularisers of underconsumption theory rather than against the economic doctrine itself, with which they showed little familiarity. Palme Dutt's book on *Socialism and the Living Wage*, by far the most important Communist attack on the I.L.P.'s underconsumptionist Living Wage proposals, spent less than twenty pages discussing the actual economic doctrine. Direct criticism was generally perfunctory and it was more important to show the 'un-Marxist' character of underconsumption theory than to subject it to systematic analysis.

Nevertheless, we can summarise the Communist critique of the theory as follows. Communists denied that demand was reduced by capitalists taking their profits out of circulation: such profits were not locked up but were either directly spent or else released by the banks. But while Communists denied that the realisation of profits in itself reduced total demand, they did say that it altered the proportion of demand between production goods and consumption goods, and this disproportion periodically manifested itself in crises – to this extent they were rejecting one market theory, underconsumption, for another, disproportionality. However, they also maintained that while market problems were a 'facet' of capitalist crises, they were not the explanation.[60] Advocates of underconsumption theory were not regarded simply as defective Marxists, for their fallacy was more than a failure to distinguish between total and proportional demand. According to Communist critics, they were unable to comprehend the basic mechanism of the capitalist mode of production – the extraction of surplus value. The underconsumptionist proposal to augment demand by increasing wages was ridiculous, for while the capitalist must maximise his surplus value or perish, the underconsumptionist was suggesting he pay part of his profit to the worker in the form of a wage increment. Such a suggestion was blind to economic and political reality.[61]

The underlying difference between Marxism and Labour Socialism lay in their opposing views of the production process. Like the Marxist, the Labour Socialist believed that capitalism robbed the worker of the fruits of his labour; but unlike him, he did not derive this belief from a labour theory of value. The Labour Socialist certainly believed that labour played a uniquely important part in the creation of wealth, and sometimes went so far as to claim that 'all wealth is obtained by the application of labour in some form or another'.[62] But that proviso 'in some form or another' was what distinguished the Labour view of economics from the Marxist one. Labour writers thought the strict doctrine of the labour theory of value was untenable because it suppressed the role of other factors of production. Beside the contribution of manual labour, they usually singled out two particular factors: 'brains' and 'capital'.[63] All three were necessary to the productive process and helped to determine the value of the finished commodity. Labour Socialism was a corporate and not a class doctrine.

Even though Labour Socialists did not accept the labour theory of value, they did accept the theory of surplus value to a limited extent on the grounds that labour received less than its proper *share* of the total: 'labour is exploited in the sense of receiving as the reward of its energy less value than it produces'. This proposition was accepted by moderate figures in the movement; Philip Snowden, for example, wrote that 'labour does not receive all that labour creates', and he thought the Party's aim was 'to secure for the community the surplus value which now goes to landlords and capitalists'.[64] The slogan 'The Surplus for the Common Good' was inscribed on the Party programme *Labour and the New Social Order* (though once again Labour was speaking here 'in the interests not of the wage-earners alone, but of every grade and section of producers by hand or brain' who joined in creating the surplus).[65] Because Labour Socialists made no distinction between labour and labour-power and had no strict concept of surplus value, their plan for a greater return to the worker was acceptable to a wide spectrum of opinion within the movement. The plea was after all inherent in the traditional Labourist maxim of 'a fair day's wage for a fair day's work', and could be invoked by the most conciliatory trade union leaders to support campaigns for increased wages. Thus J. R. Clynes explained that 'While I want to give the brain worker, the inventor, the captain of industry and the director the best of rewards in point both of pay and thankfulness for his services, I ask him to be a little more considerate to the bottom dog.' This was, he wrote elsewhere, the worker's right.[66]

Unlike Marxism, there was a pronounced ethical strain in Labour's economic doctrine. It recognised the justice of a return to all who made a positive contribution to the productive process. 'The true separation in society', wrote MacDonald, 'is the moral and economic line of division between the producer and non-producer. . .'[67] Taken to its logical extreme, this doctrine spawned absurd distinctions such as that drawn by a parliamentary candidate: 'Our quarrel is not with those who have worked very hard all their lives and are looking forward to spending their declining lives in ease and luxury. Labour's quarrel is only with those who are in the habit of leaving their money to inheritors who spend without having to earn.'[68] As a corporate doctrine Labour Socialism allotted a place to every active member of the community. Even those such as H. N. Brailsford who challenged the magnitude of the reward to the entrepreneur did so only on the grounds that modern industry had reached a point where capital accumulation no longer required skill, judgement or risk. Since in Brailsford's view the capitalist was no longer making a positive contribution, he had ceased to be a producer.[69] Parasitic rentiers were always a special target of Labour criticism, and the proposal for a Capital Levy was infinitely more attractive than schemes for wholesale nationalisation of industry.

How then was the worker deprived of his proper share? The Marxist answer was that he was forced to perform surplus labour beyond the price he had received for the sale of his labour-power, but this proposition, and the whole distinction between labour and labour-power, was ignored by Labour writers. Their answer seemed to be that the capitalist robbed the worker by buying cheap and selling dear. He forced the wage level down to the bare minimum and sold the product at an inflated price, thus robbing the worker of a just reward for his contribution. Sidney and Beatrice Webb claimed that 'the capitalist's profit is found essentially in the margin between the price he gives for other men's services and the price which he gets in selling the product of these services'.[70]

While most members of the Labour movement made use of this notion of a capitalist surplus of which labour was entitled to its just share, few attempted a coherent statement of the principle or bothered to compare it with Marxist doctrine. For this reason alone it is worth examining the views of the small number of socialist intellectuals who did so, and who made their own theory of value the basis of their case for socialism. Perhaps the most original was the Master of Balliol, A. D. Lindsay, who attempted to drive a wedge between the labour theory of value and the theory of surplus value. He claimed that 'Marx's theory of surplus value can certainly be stated in a form which is independent of the general theory of value', and argued that the essential flaw in the latter was that it was individualistic: 'It seeks to unravel from a complicated system of production and exchange the separate contribution of each separate individual, to discern what each severally creates and reward him accordingly.' On the grounds that the complexity of economic relations in modern industrial society made this impossible, Lindsay sought to set the labour theory of value aside as a theory of prices and consider it instead as an ethical theory of natural right.[71] Harold Laski very soon appropriated Lindsay's argument to 'demolish the foundations of individualistic society'. According to Laski, it was not simply Marx's theory of value that was obsolete but the whole system of individual property relations on which the labour theory was based.[72] Here there would seem to be a confusion of what was with what ought to be – Marx had not condoned capitalist property relations, he had used them in order to lay bare the dynamics of the capitalist mode of production and show how such a system could be overthrown. A similar confusion is evident in the thinking of G. D. H. Cole during his period as a Guild Socialist. Cole rejected the labour theory on the grounds that it was 'fundamentally inconsistent with the recognition of the fact that "Labour" consists of human beings' and that 'the whole question of the control of industry is not economic but ethical'. 'The attempt to found "justice" on the theory of value merely revives the old conception of individual natural rights in its least defensible form. The right of Labour to a life of comfort and self-expression is quite independent of whether it creates all wealth or not.'[73] Here again the Labour Socialists unwittingly trod the ground traversed by the young Marx and construed his subsequent labour theory of value as a surrender to the spirit of capitalism rather than as an attempt to understand capitalism's laws of motion.

Lindsay, Laski and Cole all concluded by ethical means that there were no clear-cut individual rights to the fruits of industry. Other Labour Socialists reached the same conclusion by a different route, which we can describe through an I.L.P. tract written by Alban Gordon. He claimed that land and machinery located in industrial areas attracted a 'surplus value' over and above their intrinsic value; thus a factory in London would be more valuable than the same factory in the Outer Hebrides. While this 'surplus value' accruing from location was really created by society at large, in fact it enriched the owner only. 'It is therefore right and just that the "economic rent" of the land should go. . .to the community who by their aggregation created the "surplus value" of the land.'[74] This doctrine of surplus value, which should not be confused with the Marxist one, had its roots in the Ricardian theory of land rent and was widely diffused by the second half of the nineteenth century. The general principle had been popularised by Henry George in the 1880s and by Robert Blatchford in *Merrie England* (1893), perhaps the most widely read socialist work of all. The Fabians had also extended the theory from land to other factors of production.[75] There can be no doubt that in the early part of the twentieth century this so-called Law of Rent was widely accepted in the British Labour movement, and we can observe the Webbs in 1917 employing it as the rationale for the new Party programme's claim that the surplus rightly belonged to the community and should be claimed for the common good.[76] Such an argument is commonly encountered during the 1920s and performs much the same function for Labour Socialists as does the labour theory of value for Marxists. A typical example of what might be called the communal theory of value is contained in Brailsford's popular *Socialism for To-Day*:

The product of all our efforts is therefore for Socialists a common possession, a pool to which no class, or group, or individual has any separate or privileged claim. The prior claims which are based on ownership of land or machinery, the various unequal 'pulls' which groups exert because some accident of scarcity has given them a commanding strategic position – these we dismiss as anti-social. They are, for us, only so many ways of robbing the pool.

The pool should be protected by nationalising the means of production and thereby taking the power to exert 'pulls' out of private hands.[77]

To conclude, there was a more or less coherent Labour Socialist alternative to Marxist economics, and the two schools of analysis display basic differences. Yet we can detect in the writings of Labour figures some concepts and doctrines common to Marxism, even though they were reconstituted in Labour hands. It is this very process of transformation which can shed valuable light on the ideological debates of the British labour movement. For example, the apparently dogmatic insistence of the Marxists on the labour theory of value only makes sense in the aftermath of an examination of Labour Socialism; the labour theory was the weapon with which Marxists sought to undercut Labour Socialists' plea for other agents of production.

It is more difficult to estimate the extent to which Marxist economics prevailed over Labour Socialist economics in the wider movement, and the problem demands far greater attention than it can be given here. It would appear, however, that economics was the Achilles' heel of Labour Socialists, for during the 1920s their preference for the interests of the community frequently estranged them from workers actually engaged in wage struggles. As a senior recruit to Labour, Viscount Haldane perhaps unwisely observed that the natural corollary of the Labour leaders' corporate doctrine was that the proceeds of industry should be distributed in accordance with actual services rendered, and that 'people contributing capital should be paid just the market value of such services'.[78] This recognition of the property rights of the owners often clashed with the instinctive and implicit claims of workers, for while union claims were generally restricted to wage demands (though not always, as the miners' demand for nationalisation illustrates), it was frequently impossible in a period of declining profits to reconcile the claims of owners and workers. And in such instances it was difficult to persuade trade union members to recognise the priority of owners' claims. George Lansbury wrote in 1920 that 'It is true most British workers have not read Marx, [and] do not know or want to know anything about the theory of "surplus value"...They do know, though, that they are the wealth producers...'[79] Marx had of course repudiated the Ricardian socialists' notion of a right to the 'whole produce of labour', but it would seem that such ethical precepts came to be identified with the Marxist tradition. Hobsbawm has suggested that most militants absorbed basic Marxist theory in a similar fashion to the process whereby Americans who diagnose their personal problems use Freudian concepts, even though they have never read Freud.[80] There were a great many workers who lacked any familiarity with *Capital* or even *Value, Price, and Profit*, but who subscribed to Lansbury's view; and they interacted with the several thousand who had worked their way through the texts of Ablett, Starr or McLaine and could offer more systematic support. Because Marxist theory was consistent with the daily economic struggle, the Labour Socialists were far from successful in their attempt to persuade such workers that it was not they but the whole community who were the real producers of wealth. In this sense Marxism was a potent influence.

APPENDIX TO CHAPTER 7
Marxism and orthodox economics: Maurice Dobb

In the inter-war years the impact of Marxism on the academic study of economics in this country can be traced in the writings of one man, Maurice Dobb. During the 1920s he was indeed the only Communist to hold an academic post, and can now be recognised as one of the few British thinkers to have made a significant contribution to Marxist theory. He was born in 1900, studied economics at Cambridge from 1919 to 1922, returned from the London School of Economics in 1924 and remained in Cambridge until his death in 1976. He belonged to the Communist Party continuously from 1922.[81]

His first major publication was *Capitalist Enterprise and Social Progress*, the result of postgraduate research at the L.S.E. between 1922 and 1924. It is a critique of the dominant marginalist and neo-classical theory, in particular its doctrine of the entrepreneur. Dobb argued that the economic functions of the entrepreneur, whose role was enshrined in marginalist theory, could be provided without private ownership of capital. In particular, he contended that orthodox economics depended on a series of assumptions about the way society worked, a sociology and philosophy of 'classless individualism'. According to Dobb, these assumptions were no longer valid as a description of modern capitalist society, for they neglected the effect of monopolies. As he put it elsewhere, the theories of academic economists 'would be admirable wisdom in a classless society' but did not apply to reality.

Until economists revised their science in accordance with actual conditions, it could be legitimately criticised as an 'unscientific system of apologetics'.[82]

This critique of orthodox economics made a considerable advance on the efforts of contemporary British Marxists, for where they had simply condemned all non-Marxist economics as *ipso facto* 'defences of capitalist procedure',[83] Dobb wrote from a thorough and up-to-date knowledge of modern economic theory. Yet there remains something equivocal about his contribution. Though written from a Marxist standpoint, *Capitalist Enterprise and Social Progress* employs throughout the language and concepts of the system of thought he wished to discredit. Dobb himself regretted 'the bourgeois form and style which the circumstances of its production [as a research student at the L.S.E.] imposed on it'.[84] And even though his later writings were more outspoken, the essential problem continued and was perhaps aggravated by his extreme modesty which led him to present original insights in old clothes. Dobb's strength lay in his mastery of two schools, the Marxist and the neo-classical, and in his ability to bridge them with a clarity of thought and expression that made one school intelligible to someone trained in the other. His role posed two difficulties which were inherent in the attempt to bridge such fundamentally different systems of thought. The first was that academic economists were loath to accept the Marxist foundations of his work. Lionel Robbins's ill-tempered review of *Capitalist Enterprise and Social Progress* may be taken as an example, for he accused Dobb of 'having smuggled Marx in by the back door of "monopoly"' and therefore of having vitiated his argument by reliance on this 'great anti-rationalist of nineteenth-century economics'.[85] As Hobsbawm has observed, Maurice Dobb was only marginally accepted as an academic. The second difficulty was that in attempting to surmount the first, Dobb continually skirted the fringes of Marxist heresy. He was frequently reprimanded by certain Party theorists (for whom Hugo Rathbone was usually spokesman) who made up for their intellectual mediocrity with imitative vituperation, and the letter of apology Dobb wrote for one particular transgression testifies to the difficulty of being both an economist and a Communist during this period.[86] Partly as a reaction to such criticism and partly because he was convinced that the Party had been wrong to break with them, Dobb's main energies during the 1920s went into the labour colleges and only in later years were his talents more fully utilised in the Party.

One important contribution was his emphasis upon classical political economy. He showed how Marx drew upon the classical tradition, and Ricardo in particular, and how the common approach of Marx and Ricardo was superior to the neo-classical tradition that replaced it.[87] Dobb undoubtedly helped to rescue Ricardo from neglect. Yet this achievement also was not free from difficulties as he tended to minimise the differences between the Marxist and Ricardian systems, particularly when he later came under the influence of the neo-Ricardian school of Piero Sraffa, whose work Dobb believed could provide the solution to a number of problems whose treatment by Mark was unsatisfactory.[88] A new generation of Marxist economists have criticised him for this but none deny his crucial pioneering achievement.[89] There are, of course, many other aspects of Dobb's work: his *Studies in the Development of Capitalism* (1946), which remains the best Marxist account of the genesis of British capitalism; his major contribution to the debate on the transition from feudalism to capitalism; successive editions of *Russian Economic Development since the Revolution* (first published in 1928), and subsequent work on socialist economies. It is impossible to discuss them here. Suffice it to say that with unfailing courtesy and great personal courage in the face of harassment and innuendo he established Marxism as a subject for serious consideration and passed on his own knowledge to later generations.

8. Class, state and politics

At the heart of the great divide between Marxists and other British socialists lay fundamentally different conceptions of politics. Much of the political disagreement could of course be traced to differing understandings of nature, society and economics – but only the Marxists possessed explicit and fully worked-out views on these subjects. It was over politics that the rival doctrines came into direct and immediate conflict. In this chapter I endeavour to illuminate these differences by a preliminary examination of the two key concepts of class and state, followed by a more general discussion of the political perspectives of the British labour movement.

The Marxist view of class may be summarised briefly. British Marxists believed that men and women were divided into classes according to their relationship to the means of production. Ever since human society had produced an economic surplus, there had been 'a succession of different forms of class-society and class-domination, corresponding to different stages of production, and developing through a series of class struggles'.[1] In the era of the capitalist mode of production the two basic classes were those controlling the means of production, the bourgeoisie or capitalist class, and those who possessed only their labour power, the proletariat or working class. The gulf between the two classes was such that few workers could expect to move out of their class, and the laws of capitalist development were resolving other social groups into these two primary categories. Conflict between them would increase until the abolition of private property ended all class divisions. All this was accepted as elementary by British Marxists and the class standpoint pervaded every popular activity of organisations such as the Communist Party and the Plebs League.

Several observations seem appropriate. First, it is indeed true that the vast majority of British families earned their livelihoods by wage labour. The data of the 1921 census are difficult to interpret but suggest that of the total occupied population, some 90 per cent were employees of one sort or another and approximately 75 per cent were engaged in some form of manual labour.[2] While neither of these statistics should be confused with class in the Marxist sense, they undoubtedly reflect the existence of a large industrial proletariat. It is also true that property ownership in Britain was (and is) concentrated among a very small proportion of the population. It has been estimated that on the eve of the First World War 87 per cent of aggregate personal wealth (we are unable to distinguish ownership of means of production from other forms of wealth) was owned by the richest 5 per cent of the population. In the period 1924–30 this proportion fell slightly to 84 per cent, but even then 90 per cent of the total population owned less than 10 per cent of aggregate personal wealth.[3] Second, these economic divisions in British society were reinforced by a complex set of non-economic factors – such as education, dress, residence, accent, recreation, and so on – which made both the owner and the worker fairly readily identifiable. Such distinctions were more marked then than they are today, and more systematic in British society than they are in most others. If the symbolic value of the cloth cap and top hat is unconvincing in current Marxist polemic, such emblems possessed a vivid reality in the 1920s; and indeed the graphic representation of working-class politics both in cartoon and banner form was then more prominent and of a higher artistic standard. This highly specific sense of class is of major significance. Third, the class structure of British society was nevertheless far more complex than Marxists allowed. Referring again to the 1921 census, there were significant social elements who cannot be assimilated with the capitalist and proletariat as these were understood: leaving aside the senior managerial, administrative and professional groups, we have more than one million self-employed (mainly shopkeepers and tradesmen) and many more in minor professional and salaried non-manual occupations. Furthermore, the industrial working class was itself highly stratified. British Marxists recognised the existence of craft and other divisions but they expected that these various craft skills and privileges would be progressively eroded and displaced by machinery and changes in methods of production; and it is true that the rigid hierarchies that characterised so many occupations before the war were largely broken down after it. Yet subsequent experience suggests that this erosion of skills was counterbalanced by the acquisition and establishment (often involving protracted struggles) of new ones, and that the segmentation of labour did not disappear but was merely transformed in the new industrial units. Since British Marxism was rooted in the old staple industries where change was less marked, where the 'intermediate strata' were less significant and where the general attack on wage standards tended to bind the working-class community together, they tended to neglect these complex issues. Fourth, the industrial working class was itself undergoing a transformation. As I suggested in the Introduction, there was a shift from the old staple industries to the new ones, especially the electrical, chemical, consumer durable and service industries, and the censuses for 1921 and 1931 also disclose a marked growth in the non-manual occupations. The boundaries of the working class in modern Britain are the subject of keen debate, and my point is merely that the understanding of class held by British Marxists in the 1920s could not encompass the significant changes in class structure that occurred in the inter-war period.

There is a fifth and final point of crucial significance. The British conception of class was narrowly economic – the class was derived from an economic category in the capitalist mode of production and it was this common interest that defined its existence and determined its behaviour. There was thus a pronounced tendency to reduce politics to its economic essence and see the political merely as an expression of a prior reality. It was because British Marxists lacked a political definition of class and class alliances that it found great difficulty in accommodating the highly complex social relations of inter-war Britain, and I shall return to this problem later in the chapter.

The rest of the labour movement felt the same lack. I am not concerned here with the responses of the trade unions to the changes in economic and social structure, though the statistics for trade union membership in Table 2 indicate that they were unable to respond effectively to the new employment sectors before the 1930s. My attention is concentrated on the Labour movement's understandings of class and their significance. I referred earlier to the powerful tradition of Labourism, of 'us' against 'them', which was based on a narrower and less reflective conception of class than that of the Marxists. There undoubtedly existed a widespread feeling of antagonism to the employer and of interests in common with other workers, and such sentiments were readily expressed during the 1920s by trade unionists and members of the Labour Party. But this deep-rooted Labourist consciousness was generally a long way removed from full class consciousness in the Marxist sense. It fell short because it lacked a hegemonic perspective – that is, it was restricted in scope to the protection of immediate working-class interests and did not involve any notion of the incompatibility of those interests with the capitalist class.

Within the Labour Party there was a fundamental difference between those who subscribed to the notion of class, either in the Marxist sense or in one akin to the Marxist, and those who sought to replace it. In the second, Labour Socialist, camp were the great majority of the Labour leadership who, while recognising and sometimes appealing to this feeling of 'us' versus 'them', always sought to play down the class struggle. During the 1922 election a Labour leaflet written by Philip Snowden replied indignantly to the Liberal canard that 'the Labour Party exists for the benefit of one class'. 'The Labour Party is the very opposite of a Class Party', insisted Snowden, for its object was 'justice for all men and women of every class who live by honest and useful work'.[4] While Labour Socialists acknowledged that their Party was based on existing social divisions, they attributed this to the pernicious influence of capitalism. 'It believes in the class conflict as a descriptive fact, but it does not regard it as supplying a political method.'[5] The Labour Socialists held an organic view of society, rooted in the economic distinction they drew (which was noted in the last chapter) between those making a positive contribution to the productive process and those 'who made no productive effort of any kind but lived idly and luxuriously upon the fruits of the labours of others'. The rich idlers were excluded from the community.[6] Society was therefore composed of all 'those whose toil enriched the Community', in whatever manner. In this sense 'the workers are not a class, they are the nation. Talk of the class war is obsolete.'[7]

Existing class divisions were 'only part of the general disruption of social bonds and destruction of social fellowship which capitalism has produced'. Although this was an 'inevitable result of the present condition of society', MacDonald regretted it as the 'worst thing that can overtake society'.[8] There was class antagonism, to be sure, for the obduracy of the possessing class had sometimes driven the working class to extreme measures. Such conflict was likened by MacDonald to 'the pattern on a web of cloth': it was always secondary to 'social unity', which was 'the web – the stuff itself'.[9] For these spokesmen, therefore, socialism was not a class doctrine, it was a creed for regenerating the whole social fabric:

Labour's effort, politically and industrially, must of necessity recognise the *fact* of class warfare, and does recognise it: the very existence of an independent political party of the workers can mean nothing else than that the producing class has recognised the need of organising for its own protection and for the destruction of the system which keeps the producers in subjection to an exploiting and profiteering class. But our fundamental task is a creative one. We are not seeking simply to wrest control from the class that exercises it to-day in its own narrow and selfish interests. We are engaged in a positive effort to bring the Co-operative Commonwealth into being and we appeal to the support of all classes. . .

It is the anti-Socialist who makes class appeals; the Socialist makes social appeals.[10]

It might be argued that the Labour Socialist usage of 'class' was more attuned to the complexity of and changes in British society to which I have referred. Such an argument would suggest that the Labour leaders were attempting to reconstruct a party that had originated with the industrial trade unions so that it could incorporate other sections of the workforce – the salariat, the professions, the self-employed, and so on. There is, however, little evidence to suggest that the Labour Socialists attempted any analysis on these lines. Like other sections of the movement, they understood the working class in the strict sense to mean the organised sections of industrial, transport and distributive wage-earners, and this was the sense in which they habitually used it. The wider constituency to which they appealed and which embraced the productive community – entrepreneurs, labourers and consumers alike – remained an aspiration based on the vision of an organic society and not on reasoned political analysis. Insofar as it possessed any theoretical foundation, it rested on an extremely loose redefinition of the producer, and there was no attempt to work out the specific class identities within this productive community or to identify the extent to which their class interests overlapped. It remained an economic understanding of class, and an extremely woolly one at that.

Only an ideologically articulate minority of the Labour movement followed the Party leaders in explicitly repudiating the class viewpoint. Traditional Labourism was still widespread in the 1920s, and the Labour Party still consisted in the main of men and women drawn from the working class who retained a strong sense of their own origins. There is also considerable contemporary writing which suggests that in the period immediately after the First World War there was a heightened sense of class consciousness and of an impending confrontation, with capital and labour sometimes likened to opposing armies.[11] In moments of confrontation, leaders such as Lansbury, Turner, Smillie and Smith would appeal for class solidarity against the class enemy. But always they would shrink back from the full political implications of such a stance.

By the end of the decade, when Labour was elected into office on the programme *Labour and the Nation*, the national standpoint had undoubtedly triumphed, and the Party spoke therein 'not as the agent of this class or that, but as the political organ created to express the needs and voice the aspirations of all who share in the Labour which is the lot of mankind'.[12] Prevarication in the face of class conflict became an established characteristic of the Party, allowing it to sympathise broadly with the working class in struggle and yet draw back from the full political consequences of challenging the existing class order. While this Janus-like attitude to the class question was propagated by the Party leadership, their emphasis on social harmony and ultimate rejection of disharmony left the door open to Marxism. Over the past century the British labour movement has puzzled observers by its ability to display simultaneously peaceful legality on political questions and obdurate militancy in pursuit of industrial objectives. Throughout the 1920s the emphasis which the Labour leaders placed on social harmony resulted in a deep rift between the political and industrial wings of the movement, and Marxism became more attractive just to the extent that Labour Socialism either ignored or regretted the industrial turmoil. However, what separated most industrial militants from the fully-fledged Marxism of the Communist Party, and what kept them in the Labour fold, was their acceptance of MacDonald's political strategy of winning a parliamentary majority for socialism. Grumble as they might about the watering-down of Labour's programme, they would not accept *in toto* the Marxist doctrine of the state. It is to this doctrine that we must turn to understand the fundamental political division of the labour movement.

It is best to begin discussion of rival doctrines of the state with a summary of the Labour viewpoint as it had emerged during the period before the First World War. The Labour leaders regarded the state as the political expression of the community. It was 'the organisation of a community for making its common will effectual by political methods'. They allowed that because the state represented society at an incomplete stage of development, it was sometimes misused. Individual classes had been able to 'impose their will upon the State'. Indeed Philip Snowden went some way to accepting the Marxist claim when he admitted that 'in the past the State has always been the representative of the oppressing and exploiting class'.[13] But the leaders of the Labour Party never accepted the argument that because the state had historically misrepresented the community, socialists should therefore discard it. This argument seemed to them a nonsense. The state was the embodiment of the communal will; it was 'as essential to individual life as is the atmosphere'.[14] Furthermore, they believed that it was evolving towards its democratic essence so that socialists would be able to 'use the organic state to transform itself'. Through the state the community would take control of economic life; it would confiscate private wealth and take industry into public ownership. MacDonald thought that such a programme of state social reform could be the means through which the 'ugly caterpillar becomes the magnificent butterfly'.[15] And on such a basis the parliamentary leaders of the infant Labour Party clung to the coat-tails of the Liberal Party while they implemented the first stages of unemployment insurance and state pensions.

During this pre-war period MacDonald and Snowden had already been forced to consider the Marxist critique (though they commonly confused it with syndicalism). After 1917 this became all the more necessary, for the Bolsheviks revived an uncompromising class interpretation of the state. Not that this was unknown to British Marxists before 1917. They were already acquainted with Engels's classic *Origin of the Family, Private Property and the State* (Kerr edition, 1902), and on the eve of the Russian Revolution William Paul of the S.L.P. produced his major book *The State* to demonstrate anew that it was 'the weapon of class rule'.[16] Nevertheless, with the Bolshevik Revolution the question moved to the forefront of Marxist agitation and acquired an immediacy hitherto lacking in the somewhat abstract criticisms of the B.S.P. and the S.L.P. As Palme Dutt quickly recognised, 'The theory of the Communists begins with an analysis of the modern state as a machinery of class rule.'[17] Lenin's *State and Revolution*, a methodical exposition of this analysis, was first published jointly by the B.S.P. and the S.L.P. in 1919 and was republished many times during the 1920s.

Where the Labour leaders viewed the state as the natural expression of the community, Marxists held that it was 'not a thing of eternity' but was created at a particular stage of historical development. 'The State did not always exist. It arose out of the institution of private property and the creation of classes.' When a section of society came to own property they had created the state 'as an instrument in the hands of the economically dominant class for holding down and suppressing the subject class'.[18] For this reason Marxists rejected the Labour

Socialist view that British capitalists had corrupted the state or prevented it from playing its properly representative role. The very function of the state was class coercion. They also rejected Labour's belief that the state could be wrested from capitalists by the democratic process. Whereas previous revolutionary classes had won control of the state and adapted it to their own purposes, the task facing the working class was much greater. Previous revolutions such as that of the bourgeoisie had 'no need to completely break up the existing State apparatus' because they were limited in scope to replacing one exploiting group by another. The purpose of the proletarian revolution, on the other hand, was to abolish all class divisions. 'That is why it must break up the old State machine...'[19] British Marxists also appreciated that the capitalist state was far more complex than earlier forms of state organisation. It comprised 'not Parliament alone, but the apparatus of coercion: the armed forces, the police, the law-courts and prisons, besides the administrative apparatus of the civil service...and the ideological apparatus of the educational system, the church, the capitalist Press – and only then, Parliament'.[20] In this respect they were more acute than the Labour leaders, who had an essentially parliamentary conception. Even though MacDonald and Snowden recognised the political influence of the civil service and armed forces, they assumed that these were completely loyal to parliament and hence susceptible to democratic socialist control.

But while Marxists were in this sense more appreciative of the complexity of the capitalist state, in another sense they were more simplistic. They regarded every 'organ' of the state as a simple tool of the capitalist ruling class. Instead of analysing the specific nature of parliament, the civil service, the Church, the press, etc., they interpreted them simply as devices for 'ensur[ing] that the process of exploitation be carried on with the requisite smoothness and efficiency'. Indeed they frequently went further and described these institutions as mere camouflage for capitalism: thus they were 'only the screen behind which the operations of finance capital go on, which is the real Government of the country'.[21] Education, as we saw in chapter 5, was considered not as an aspect of social activity which was mediated by its capitalist environment, but purely and simply as a device of capitalism. This propensity to regard political phenomena as 'simply the concentrated and most highly organised expression of the economic struggle'[22] was pervasive in British Marxism, and is closely related to its oversimple view of the materialist conception of history.

One method of reducing politics to economics was particularly popular in the war and immediate post-war period. Above all it was the method of J. T. Walton Newbold, and consisted of compiling long lists of politicians and company directors, tracing their financial and familial associations and relating these to aspects of government policy. In Newbold's study were huge wall-charts, like genealogical tables, laying bare the hidden skeleton of the capitalist state: to write a study of foreign policy he would simply abstract information dealing with overseas traders and the armaments industry; for Middle East policy he would take the oil industry, and so on. Using this method from 1913 onwards Newbold produced a torrent of pamphlets and articles bearing such titles as *The Gang behind the Government...(Exposure of a 'Capitalist Conspiracy')*, *The War Trust Exposed*, *Bankers, Bondholders and Bolsheviks* etc., all exposing the state as the executive arm of big business. It was 'the screen of Parliamentary and propagandist camouflage, which they have rigged across the stage to conceal their real manoeuvres and identity'.[23] This was a popular method. Another contemporary practitioner was C. H. Norman, who like Newbold was a middle-class member of the I.L.P. campaigning in the immediate post-war years for its affiliation to the Third International. Norman had been part of the *New Age* circle before the war and even then was renowned as 'the malcontent of malcontents',[24] a man who used to sniff out remissness in high places with outstanding ingenuity, driving home his arguments with details of interlocking directorates and their political affiliations. His articles and pamphlets also bore such titles as *The Conspiracy against the People*, 'The Dictatorship of the Plutocracy', 'The Hidden Causes of the Financial Crisis', etc. The same sort of analysis of financial, political and governmental personnel was performed subsequently in Simon Haxey's *Tory M.P.* (1939), and it is by no means a negligible element in Ralph Miliband's *The State in Capitalist Society* (1969). There is nothing distinctively Marxist about this tradition, which had been practised earlier by Radical critics of British foreign policy such as Hobson and Morel and was continued in Brailsford's *War of Steel and Gold* (1914) and Brockway's study of the armaments industry, *The Bloody Traffic* (1933). But in the 1920s such analysis was commonly associated with Marxism.

The Marxist doctrine provided one challenge to the prevailing Labour Socialist view of the state. Another challenge came from Guild Socialism, which flourished during the decade spanning the First World War. The Guild Socialists drew on the pluralist school of political theory to construct a fundamentally new objective and strategy of socialism. Essentially, they wanted to invest in associations of producers the powers and functions currently exercised by the state and the owners of industry. There are several reasons for making space for them in this chapter. The influence of Guild Socialism should be calculated not by its accomplishments, for it failed absolutely to achieve its objects; nor by the membership of its organisation, the National Guilds League, which was never more than a thousand;[25] but by its indirect influence in the wider labour movement. Its warning of the dangers of state socialism caused many to reconsider their assumption that state ownership was synonymous with socialism. And its restatement of a utopian strain in English socialism provided Guildsmen such as G. D. H. Cole with a wider vision of the socialist society of which he never subsequently lost sight. Furthermore, because the Guild Socialists were so sensitive to the question of the state, they were quick to pick up and discuss the Leninist contribution to the topic. Here I shall discuss the writings of three prominent socialist intellectuals: Cole, who was the most radical leader of the National Guilds League; Bertrand Russell, who also served for a time on its executive; and Harold Laski, who from a greater distance also shared the pluralist viewpoint at this time. Analysis is focused on these three because all of them, and Cole and Laski more than anyone else with the possible exception of R. H. Tawney, subsequently exercised a profound intellectual influence on the British labour movement, and it is therefore particularly significant that they were all initially drawn into working-class politics with a political outlook sharply different to that prevailing in the Labour Party. While they subsequently came to terms with Labour orthodoxy, their earlier experiences left them acutely aware of the force of the Marxist critique.[26]

Like the Labour Socialists before them, Cole, Laski and Russell all believed that the state was meant to serve the community and had ceased to do so. Unlike the Labour Socialists, however, they refused to merge the identities of the state and community, believing that the 'general will' or 'Commonwealth' resided in the community alone and could never be institutionalised. They remained equivocal over the class analysis of the state and baulked at attributing all the shortcomings of the existing political order solely to the domination of the capitalist class. Cole paid most attention to this question in a prolonged dialogue with the 'Marxian thesis' that the state was a class instrument. He was prepared to admit that the 'political superstructure' of modern communities always 'reflects the economic basis of that society' and that 'while Capitalism exists as the dominant social form, the State will be forced to do the bidding of Capitalism'. But he insisted that 'what occurs under Capitalism is a perversion of the true function of the State'. The state was not simply an instrument of class oppression, as Marxists claimed, and 'the need for the State does not arise out of the institution of property, or out of Capitalism'. Hence Guildsmen 'do not say with the Syndicalists and Marxian Industrial Unionists that all States are to be swept away with the downfall of capitalism: they say that on the ashes of the capitalist State there must rise a very different thing, a democratic State'.[27] Russell also rejected the class analysis of the state – even though he recognised that capitalists misused it – on the characteristic grounds that the underlying malady was lust for power and this was a universal trait of human nature. 'Marxians never sufficiently recognise the love of power is quite as strong a motive, and quite as great a source of injustice, as love of money'.[28] And while Laski admitted that the state was a 'reflexion of what a dominant group or class in a community believes to be political good', he too looked for changes which could return the state to its proper purpose.[29]

It would therefore seem that the Guild Socialists did not believe that the state was merely a reflex of class interests, nor that it would be possible to abolish it in the manner Marxists urged. As Cole put it, the state was necessary 'because certain jobs want doing, and it is the organisation best suited to do them'.[30] What were these jobs, and what was the role Guild Socialists allotted to the state in the transition to socialism? Paradoxically, while Marxists insisted on seizing the capitalist state in order to destroy it, Guild Socialists left it out of their immediate strategy for change but intended afterwards to reconstruct it. Their tactic was encroaching control through industry, their ultimate objective a system of functional representation. The precise blueprint of this new system of government changed several times during the lifetime of the National Guilds League, and different sections disagreed over its composition. But all agreed there must be a sovereign body to enforce the collective will: even Bertrand Russell, who was by far the most libertarian of the three, insisted that 'the State, in some form, must continue'.[31] The essential purpose of Guild Socialism was to create functional representative institutions to control the 'Servile State', but it never questioned the need for a state.

The eclipse of Guild Socialism and the aspirations it represented were of lasting significance for the British labour movement. The actual disappearance of the National Guilds League, which was wound up in 1923, conforms to the general pattern whereby the different schools of pre-war British socialism gave way after the war to an increasingly monolithic Labour Party. The richness and diversity which had been expressed through the I.L.P., the *Clarion* and the *Herald*, Plebs League and syndicalists, as well as in myriad local socialist societies, were lost and all socialists were required to answer one fundamental question: will you accept the programme and discipline of the Labour Party and remain within the host; or will you cling to your beliefs in the wilderness? Cole abandoned Guild Socialism because whereas before the war it 'could afford to seek after perfection because it was not in a hurry; post-war Socialism needs practical results'.[32] The path marked out by Cole was the one Russell, Laski and most Guild Socialists followed, into the Labour Party; and a smaller group led by Page Arnot, Palme Dutt, Walter Holmes and Will Mellor took the other path, into the Communist Party (though Mellor and others soon crossed over to the Labour fold).

It is instructive to follow the writings of Cole, Russell and Laski during the 1920s after they had settled for the Labour strategy of social reform by means of the state. Cole did not offer any substantial reappraisal which might justify this strategy and it seems he retained some misgivings of a broadly Marxist character. His underlying attitude was that in the struggle immediately confronting them from 1921 onwards, the workers must make use of any weapon, however limited, that was available to them.[33] The political development of Russell is clearer. He continued to mistrust the state and to urge the creation of new associations to balance it, but this objective was not incorporated into a political strategy based on the Labour Party. Socialism would be won by turning all land and capital into 'the property of the State'. Indeed, the initial effect of the socialist transition would simply be to turn the managers of capitalism into 'civil servants'. Russell now clearly believed that the state was susceptible to popular control.[34] Laski also abandoned Guild Socialism for the Labour Party at the beginning of the 1920s. Like Cole and Russell, he went some way towards accepting the Marxist view that 'political power is the handmaid of economic power', but he believed a proletarian revolution to be impossible. Further, the 'emergence of the Labour Party has altered the general perspective' of British socialists, for it held out the prospect of democratic changes which could go 'deep into the fabric of the State'.[35]

This revision of earlier beliefs and expectations is one way of plotting the decline of Guild Socialism, a decline which in turn reflected the demise of shop committees after the war. Another and more illuminating way of reflecting on the problem is to examine the reverberations of its ideals within the Labour Party. When G. D. H. Cole wrote his post-mortem on the Guild movement he judged that it had at least 'killed dead. . .the old Collectivism which thought of the mechanism of nationalisation as a mere extension of the political government of the State'. He claimed that 'every Socialist who is not merely an ante-diluvian now recognises that the growth of socialisation involves the development of a totally new technique of public industrial administration and control'.[36] There is some superficial evidence that Guild Socialism did have this effect. At least in the short term it induced MacDonald, Henderson and Snowden to deny that they were state socialists and to emphasise that ' "socialisation" meant more than "nationalisation" '.[37] The pluralist approach may also be detected in the proposals for the joint control of industry urged at this time by the miners, and in the Webbs' proposals in *A Constitution for the Socialist Commonwealth of Great Britain* (1920) for a new functional administration of industry. Such ideas and the general topic of industrial democracy were extremely pervasive in the early 1920s, but they left little lasting influence. Thus while in 1918 the Labour Party committed itself in principle to the nationalisation of the mines and the railways, the meaning of this principle was left unclear and became increasingly hazy as the decade wore on. It was during and immediately after the second Labour Government of 1929–31 that the Labour Party and the T.U.C. hammered out the new model of the public corporation whose board of management would be appointed by the appropriate government minister and whose workers and consumers would be excluded from any significant influence. Herbert Morrison, the leading architect of this new form, pronounced: 'This buses for the busmen and dust for the dustmen stuff is not socialism at all. . .It isn't a busman's idea; it's middle-class syndicalist romanticism.'[38] An effective voice for industrial democracy did not revive for another quarter-century.

Before concluding this survey of attitudes towards the state, something ought to be said about the impact of the events of 1931. We have seen how during the 1920s Cole, Russell and Laski recognised the force of the Marxist critique of the state but held out from accepting it until a workers' government had tested the possibilities of parliamentary action. This attitude was widespread among other socialists and Labour militants during the 1920s. We may cite Bernard Shaw's comment that the Labour Party 'can no more make our political system produce Socialism than they can make a sewing machine produce fried eggs', though he nevertheless continued to support it; or H. N. Brailsford's perceptive writings on the limits of state action, even though he urged one final attempt to wrest its control from the capitalists.[39] Such socialists felt that the Marxist doctrine was difficult to refute, and expressed considerable doubts about MacDonald's confident constitutionalism, but believed they must at least put the matter to the test. The Welsh trade union organiser Ben Griffiths expressed this attitude with particular clarity as early as 1918: 'We know that the historic role of the State is that of "The Executive Committee of the Capitalist Class", as Marx and Engels warned us long ago, and as men like Newbold, Paul and Ablett din in our ears today. But we are not yet convinced that the workers have *tried* to use the State in their own interests.'[40] For such Labour militants the circumstances of the collapse of the second Labour Government in 1931 provided compelling evidence that the Marxists were right and that, as one disillusioned member of the I.L.P. wrote after the formation of the National Government, when in crisis 'capitalist dictatorship throws off the mask of Parliamentary democracy'.[41] There were three responses to this realisation. The first was to become a Communist, the second to create an independent working-class party with a new strategy for winning state power, and the third to stay in the Labour Party and disseminate these lessons more widely.

It seems clear that comparatively few followed the first option, more the second, and the great majority the third. Figure 1 suggests that as many as five thousand recruits may have joined the Communist Party in the last three months of 1931, though more than half were lost almost immediately. To these members of the C.P.G.B. we may append fellow-travellers like John Strachey who, although he never actually joined the Party, was perhaps the most notable and articulate convert to its cause. His conclusion that parliamentary methods were unworkable and that it was necessary to 'smash the capitalist system and to build up a new system from the very bottom' was expressed forcibly in the influential series of Marxist tracts he produced during the 1930s.[42]

The second course was to work independently of the Labour and Communist parties with a new strategy for winning state power. This was the course taken by the seventeen thousand members of the I.L.P., whose leaders broke with the Labour Party in 1932, ostensibly over their refusal to accept the standing orders of the Parliamentary Labour Party but fundamentally because they had reached the point of departure from Labour's political method.[43] The attitude towards the state adopted by the I.L.P. after 1931 was greatly influenced by Marxism, and their object was now nothing less than 'the complete overthrow of the economic, political and social organisation of the Capitalist State and its replacement by a Socialist Commonwealth'. Yet closer examination reveals continuing prevarication and uncertainty in this new 'quasi-revolutionary' perspective, as Brailsford described it at the time. I.L.P. members still seemed to regard the state as responsive to the will of the electorate and continued to look forward to the election of a real socialist government, 'enabling us to proceed boldly with our Socialist purpose'.[44] For the I.L.P. the essential lesson of 1931 was the need to tackle capitalist institutions such as the banks which had frustrated the Labour Government. Capitalist influence was external to the state itself; it came from the City. Thus the I.L.P. insisted that 'it would obviously be an initial advantage to have control over administration and the armed forces and civil services which governmental power would secure';[45] and despite Communist strictures it never accepted the Marxist argument that 'governmental power' alone would not secure such control. But its acrimonious dispute with the Communists over this and other aspects of Marxist doctrine was overshadowed by the I.L.P.'s rapid decline, until by 1935 it had shrunk to a mere four and a half thousand members.

The final way of responding to the new insights into the state gained in 1931 was to communicate them to the rest of the Labour Party, and this was the course followed by Cole, Laski and the members of the Society for Socialist Information and Propaganda and the Socialist League. In the words of a prominent convert, Stafford Cripps, these activists now realised that 'Democracy under capitalism. . .is more than half a sham. We know, if we read the lessons of the last few years aright, that Money Power will either use or limit or altogether abolish democracy and democratic machinery according to its view of its own interests.'[46] In calling his pamphlet *Can Socialism Come by Constitutional Methods?* Cripps was the first Labour politician since the war to address himself to this fundamental question, and whatever else they have lacked, Cripps's writings of the period certainly display a new awareness of the obstacles in Labour's path. As to the extent to which his views and those of other men and women in the reconstituted

Labour left of the 1930s were now influenced by Marxism, we may turn again to the revised opinions of Cole and Laski.

After 1931 Cole came close to accepting the Marxist analysis he had previously resisted. He now found it 'impossible to believe that any country will ever achieve socialism by parliamentary means'. Not only would the capitalist class resist a socialist government, but it was clear to Cole that such a government could not rely on the civil service, judiciary or army. The only effective course of action was 'transitionally some form of dictatorship'. Yet he continued to cling to the hope of changing the capitalist state from within. An elected Labour government must make a simultaneous 'frontal attack on the key institutions of Capitalism' and a 'radical reconstruction of the machinery of legislation' and administration. If backed by a class-conscious and politically educated working class, it might thus transform the institutions of government. The essence of Cole's new position was a reluctance to take responsibility for class war, for while he thought such a conflagration was extremely likely, he insisted that it must be instigated by the capitalists.[47] Laski was equally adamant in rejecting the proposition that the state stood above classes and just as equivocal about the political implications of such an insight. 'The centre of effective authority', he wrote, 'lies in the hands of a small knot of financiers', and 'The legal order is a mask behind which a dominant economic interest secures the benefit of political authority.' Laski recognised that the logical consequence of his view was that 'Socialist measures. . . are not obtainable by constitutional means', but, like Cole, he shrank from advocating an open challenge to the constitution.[48]

It is apparent that these converts to an avowedly Marxist view of the state tended to see capitalist control in conspiratorial terms; in the Newbold tradition they focused on the surreptitious activities of the City or a 'small knot of financiers'. This fact might help to explain why these new Marxists in both the I.L.P. and the Labour Party remained so hopeful of gaining control of the state by constitutional means – for if the state was capitalist simply because particular groups had surreptitiously imposed their will upon it, it was conceivable that their machinations might be exposed and democratically frustrated. To adopt the formulation of Fenner Brockway in an I.L.P. pamphlet published immediately after the crisis, the alternative was *The City or the Nation*. Perhaps this suggests why Cole, Laski, Cripps, Brockway and many others remained hopeful of changing a state they had now apparently rejected. Their attitude may be likened to that of those well-meaning Marxist littérateurs of the 1920s, Eden and Cedar Paul, who in the light of the bankers' ramp now distinguished between two aspects of the state, the Marxist and the Platonic. In the Marxist sense the state was an instrument of capitalist authority, but in the Platonic sense it served some universal and essential social functions. Thus the Pauls argued that it was 'only in the Marxian sense that the State can "die out"...There is a wider sense of the state in which...that institution will not merely persist, but develop towards the Platonic ideal.'[49] Like the Pauls, many clung to a residual Platonic conception of the state as the expression of the communal will which must be defended against capitalist usurpers. Yet it would be naive to think that British socialists' political views were determined solely by doctrines of the state. It is to politics, therefore, that we turn next.

British Marxists had remarkably little to say about their political method. They spilt much ink on the iniquities of capitalism and the advantages of socialism, but were surprisingly reticent about how they proposed to lead Britain from the former to the latter, and so while they could inveigh at length against Labour's political naivety they experienced great difficulty in advancing a credible alternative. To a considerable extent this failure stemmed from sheer uncertainty. As was explained in chapter 1, the future Communists who were caught up in the war-time industrial ferment had realised the inadequacy of the politics of the B.S.P. and the S.L.P., and they threw aside much of their doctrinal purity to advance the industrial movement with all its imperfections. Convinced by the Bolshevik example, they abandoned the educational role attendant upon a distant capitalist breakdown in favour of an immediate revolutionary push for power.

However, shortcomings were soon revealed in this initial transformation of British politics. It depended on two factors, a militant offensive by the Labour movement and an international atmosphere of revolutionary instability. Both factors disappeared by 1921 at the latest, and the return to more stable conditions left a legacy of weakness for British Communists. Furthermore, earlier attitudes which had never been completely eliminated tended to revive in the more barren environment. Yet there was a more fundamental difficulty. Under the influence of the Communist International and persuaded in particular by Lenin's advice in 'Left Wing' Communism – An Infantile Disorder (first British edition, 1920), they adopted, in principle at least, a strategy of agitation and participation in the mass organisations of the labour movement. But this strategy was based on a wildly optimistic estimate of the strength of British Marxists. The result was that from 1920 to 1933 the C.P.G.B. pursued two basic policies – first that of the United Front, and after 1928 that of 'Class Against Class' – which were both premised on a mass Marxist party and which, given the Communist Party's lack of strength, were both unsuccessful. Communist politics, a mixture of old and new, were characterised by unreality and improvisation in varying proportions.

It is easiest to explain the British Marxists' understanding of politics, as they did themselves, by comparison with the prevailing political method of the Labour Party. We saw in chapter 2 how Labour Socialism conceived of society in organic terms, with the state as its proper instrument, and postulated certain modifications whereby the Labour Party could remedy its existing defects. The ambit of Labour politics was extremely narrow and most forms of extra-parliamentary political action were emphatically repudiated. Thus the Labour leadership always insisted that 'a new and permanent Social Order can never be established on any other basis than the consent and co-operation of an enlightened democracy'.[50] On the other hand, they set strict limits to the efficacy of parliamentary politics, for the real regulator of political progress was public opinion. Socialism was still widely conceived in the late-nineteenth-century sense of a transformation of the collective social conscience, and while the Labour Party was now assuming an increasingly narrow electoral concern, there remained a vestigial scepticism about the very possibility of legislating a social transformation – and this contradiction is of fundamental significance to the failure of Labour Socialism. No Labour government could move faster than the popular mentality would allow: indeed, Snowden could imagine 'no greater disaster to the Labour Party than that it should be called to power on some passing wave of indignation', for a premature socialist administration would antagonise public opinion and set back the movement.[51] Labour's political method thus depended on a delicate interaction of state activity and the civic culture, illustrated by Sidney Webb's presidential address to the 1923 Labour Party Conference. In this address Webb specifically repudiated Marxism's influence on the politics of the Labour Party: 'For the Labour Party, it must be plain, Socialism is rooted in political Democracy; which necessarily compels us to recognise that every step towards our goal is dependent on gaining the assent and support of at least a numerical majority of the whole people.' Thus socialism 'would be accomplished, and could only be accomplished, by the nation as a whole, acting by a majority of citizens, as a common economic and political transformation, called for by a preponderating public opinion'. In short, Labour worked by 'the inevitability of gradualness'.[52] I shall further explore this understanding of public opinion as the regulator of socialism in the next chapter.

Most Labour writers believed that their reliance on majority support distinguished them from the Marxists. They frequently alleged that Communists wanted an armed insurrection to impose their will on a reluctant majority.[53] This allegation was inaccurate insofar as it portrayed Communists as putschists of the Blanquist variety who conceived their politics in insurrectionary terms, for the Communists always insisted that 'individual terrorism and acts of sabotage are useless', and that 'unless it is able to win over to its standard a decisive majority of the working class it cannot realise the social transformation'.[54] Yet the Communist attachment to majority support was always qualified in a class sense: it was a majority of the workers they sought, not of the nation as a whole. And the Labour spokesmen's allegations seem to have been generally accepted at the local level. Thus we find an I.L.P. member active on the South Wales coalfields during the 1920s echoing MacDonald's phraseology: 'There was a sharp line between those who wanted the ballot and those who wanted the bullet, and we used to regard those who wanted the bullet as half-baked in British conditions.'[55] Perhaps unjustly, Marxism and Communism were popularly regarded as doctrines of force and violence; they represented an impermissible short cut. This was a popular image which was generally accepted; in a piece of oral history which is all the more valuable because its source is an inactive and apolitical Labour supporter, we find a Glasgow carter describing his local Communists as the rough element, those who were out to cause violence.[56] And the revolutionary road was not merely undemocratic and anti-social, but also impractical: as John Wheatley put it, 'I should be very doubtful as to my ability to convince a man to take up a rifle for his class if I had failed to persuade him to take up a pencil and vote Labour.' Labour therefore believed its principal task was one of persuasion. 'The sole way leading to Socialism is the way of education'; 'If the people cannot will the Socialist State there will be no Socialist State: if they do will it there need be no violent dictatorship.'[57]

Marxists denounced this confidence in constitutional democracy as a dangerous illusion. They believed parliament could be used as a 'revolutionary forum' only, for 'Parliament merely registers and gives legal sanction to the decisions arrived at by the ruling class elsewhere.' They also believed that socialism could only be achieved by a forcible overthrow of capitalism: 'As history does not reveal any ruling class willing to abdicate voluntarily, the Communists unhesitatingly declare that civil war, the most acute form of class struggle, is the final means whereby all ruling classes will be overthrown.'[58] However, British Communists did not at any time take active steps to prepare for civil war, and their distinctive non-revolutionary character was noted by an early student of international Communism.[59] Their explanation for the lack of revolutionary preparation was that such steps would be premature, for an immediate revolutionary situation was not apparent in Britain. But this admission merely heightened the unreality of their calls for 'the violent overthrow of the bourgeoisie',[60] calls which diverted the political debate between the Labour and Communist parties into a debate about the feasibility of an armed seizure of power in Britain.

It was frequently alleged by critics of Marxism that a revolution in Britain was impossible for military reasons: the mobility and firepower of the modern army were thought too great for workers armed only with rifles, and the new factor of the air force was sometimes added. Moreover, the critics claimed, Britain was dependent on overseas supplies and a revolutionary regime could be quickly brought down by international boycott.[61] The response of Marxists to these arguments betrayed considerable weakness. There were some highly optimistic military and logistical calculations: Ralph Fox, for instance, claimed that aircraft could be driven from the skies by rifle fire and others insisted that tanks and poison gas could be overcome by a workers' militia. As for the international capitalist blockade, the 'Red Army' and the Russian people were thought sufficient.[62] Certainly, the success of liberation struggles in China, Vietnam and elsewhere should remind us that the possession of superior armaments does not in itself guarantee victory, yet success in the face of such odds is dependent on both a high degree of popular support and a fairly weak ruling-class adversary. The British discussion of the subject assumed that the conflict would be fought out between the armed forces and rest of the population – and seemed to imagine that the vast squadrons of suburban middle classes, the groups that eagerly volunteered to defeat the General Strike, would look on passively during a civil war.

We should not be too quick to condemn this strand of thinking.

There was a long tradition of Marxist rumination on the general theme, for the experiences of the Paris Commune and Trafalgar Square possessed an immediate relevance for Engels, Morris and many others. As I have already pointed out, British Marxists in the 1920s always stipulated that they were not interested in fomenting an insurrection and that they were considering the military issue only in the context of a *capitalist* recourse to armed force. That is, they were anticipating problems involved in a process of transition without prejudicing the question of the initial form of the transition. Nor was the question purely hypothetical – Ralph Fox would die in Spain alongside many other British volunteers. But the underlying weakness of the Communist defence of armed force was that it bore no relation to their everyday political practice. They were committed to a strategy of mobilising the working class on the basis of their everyday activities and aspirations. From such a perspective the armed forces were more appropriately seen not as 'machines and engines of destruction' but 'rank and file. . .influenced by their past experience as workers' who should be mobilised along with the rest of the working class.[63] It was in this light that Marxists approached some of them at the end of the war, in 1931 and more intermittently during the intervening decade. But the Invergordon mutiny apart, there was very little likelihood of fomenting serious unrest and in any case it would have been premature to do so in advance of a substantial working-class challenge to the authority of the state. Thus while Marxists certainly bore a responsibility to warn the Labour movement of the hazards of a transition to socialism, their dwelling on these particular military hazards seemed all too often to confirm the Labour Socialist allegation that they were irresponsible adventurers engaging in quixotic daydreams.

What then of immediate Marxist politics? Before 1917 they were not so far removed from those of other socialists. Both placed great emphasis on education and propaganda, believing their gospel to be transparently evident. The special feature of the B.S.P. and S.L.P. derived from their rigidly determinist view that the gospel would not find a mass audience until capitalism collapsed. This pre-war attitude to political conversion was upset by the post-war emphasis on action. Partly as a result of direct experience and partly as a response to the success of the Bolsheviks, British Marxists came to see a need for participation and agitation in all spheres of working-class activity. They rejected 'the belief that reason is the main force of human action' and that the working class was, 'if properly educated, always prepared to accept programmes by reason of their justice, rationality and wisdom'; and they turned instead to a more activist method of political agitation.[64] The new method was explained most systematically in Lenin's *'Left Wing' Communism – An Infantile Disorder*, which was written in 1920 and immediately translated into English, and which contained a chapter specifically aimed at the British movement. Here Lenin condemned the purist isolation of British Marxists from the mass of the working class and called on them to 'work by every possible means wherever the masses are to be found'. He added that it was the duty of Communists to 'penetrate into the humblest taverns' – the translation was makeshift – and to 'find [their] way into the unions, societies and chance gatherings of the common people, and talk with them, not learnedly'.[65] This new orientation was immediately accepted in principle by the British Communist Party and it instilled 'a new political conception regarding the progress of the working-class movement in this country'. The Constitution adopted by the Party on its formation pledged it to participate in every aspect of working-class activity, to 'relentlessly strive by industrial organisation, agitation, and revolutionary political and industrial action, to urge the working class on towards revolution'. And the same principle was to be found in all subsequent literature: 'Everywhere and anywhere the Communists work. Wherever there is a working-class grievance, no matter how trivial, there the Communists are to be found. . .'[66]

In practice, of course, the Communist Party never became the mass party Lenin had prescribed. For its first two years it continued with the inherited structure as a federation of what James Klugmann has described as 'vague propagandist territorial groupings'.[67] Even after the *Report on Organisation* was adopted and the Party 'Bolshevised' in 1922, the elaborate structure of 'fractions' and 'nuclei' which were established as organs of mass activity had little more than a nominal existence. On the industrial field the Party certainly achieved an importance in particular unions and exerted an occasional influence on the T.U.C., but it was never able to integrate its industrial strength into a revolutionary political movement in the Leninist mould. In their important essay, James Hinton and Richard Hyman have explored the circumstances which after 1921 militated against the success of any revolutionary industrial strategy; and one may accept their broad analysis without embracing their suggestion that a better strategy would have been to avoid the vain pursuit of mass influence (and its attendant opportunist temptations) in order to consolidate a revolutionary cadre and preserve the immediate post-war theoretical achievement.[68] On the contrary, in the absence of revolutionary opportunity the Communist Party played a key role in stiffening the resistance of workers against repeated attacks on their living standards and shopfloor rights. The costs of defeat were severe but there is no evidence to suggest that the owners would have been more magnanimous to a docile workforce than they were to a pugnacious one. On the political field, similarly, the Party failed in its revolutionary objective but was nevertheless able to register certain limited achievements in those areas where it could overcome sectarian limitations. As to whether such activity should be considered 'revolutionary' or 'reformist' in its long-term implications, that is a question to which Marxists are still seeking an answer.

APPENDIX TO CHAPTER 8
Parliament – the debate among Marxists

The question of parliament is perennial to British Marxism and remains alive in present debate. Though the persistent failure of those outside the Labour Party to win elections might seem to render the whole question academic, its persistence is indicative of the grip of parliamentary democracy on the British political culture. All British Marxists have agreed that socialism cannot be achieved by parliamentary means alone – for the celebrated 'parliamentary road to socialism' is a myth and even such quasi-Marxists as Cole and Laski appreciated that a socialist government must be backed by something more than a parliamentary majority – and the real question is what part parliamentary activity should play in the total political strategy. For many years the B.S.P. (like the S.D.F. before it) and the S.L.P. had run candidates for parliament with a conspicuous lack of success. Their ostensible purpose was to utilise parliament for propaganda purposes only, since nothing more could be expected from an organ of the capitalist state. Yet both coquetted with a more substantial commitment. Though they would never admit it, the absence of alternative institutions of working-class power meant that parliament was a major arena of their political activity. Hence the S.L.P., for all its scepticism, held that parliament was the instrument 'specially fashioned to *destroy* Capitalism', though not to build socialism; thus it aimed at a parliamentary majority which could paralyse capitalist control of the machinery of the state and hand control over to working-class organs of power.[69] The B.S.P. did not look so far ahead but also made parliament the focus of its political activity. In this respect the dilemma of pre-war Marxists can be likened to that of the German Social Democrats; both were committed to a class analysis of the state and yet could find no other political expression than the state representative assembly.

The developments which changed British Marxism after 1917 simultaneously caused many activists to turn their backs on parliament. The pre-war influence of syndicalism was reinforced by an influential section of the shop stewards' movement led by Jack Tanner, which decided that the workers' objectives could be achieved only through direct industrial action.[70] The Russian Revolution was taken by many to demonstrate that parliamentary methods were obsolete, and it placed the issue at the forefront of the discussions which preceded the formation of the British Communist Party. Thus Sylvia Pankhurst, the best-known member of the anti-parliamentary Workers' Socialist Federation, appealed to Lenin thus: 'If you were here, I believe you would say: concentrate your forces upon revolutionary action; have nothing to do with the Parliamentary machine.'[71] And even J. R. Campbell initially interpreted Lenin's *State and Revolution* (British edition, 1919) as a complete and universal rejection of parliamentary activity – 'Lenin smashes Parliamentarianism', he entitled his review.[72] The growth of such anti-parliamentary feeling in Britain between 1917 and 1921 stemmed from a starry-eyed conviction that the revolution was at hand and therefore that the 'parliamentary machine' was as good as obsolete. In this light the running of candidates for parliament was seen as a 'sheer waste of time and energy', whose only effect was to 'bolster up a dying institution'.[73] Yet the anti-parliamentarians used other arguments which attributed an extraordinary potency to parliament: it was credited with sapping the revolutionary purity of workers' organisations. One foundation member of the Communist Party even asserted that 'men like Brace, Thomas and Clynes would probably have tended towards the revolutionary position had they not become members of the House of bombast and gas'.[74] In this manner parliament was blamed for subverting the fundamentally revolutionary disposition which these anti-parliamentarians detected in the mass of the British working class.

When Lenin took up the question of parliamentary activity in 1919 and 1920, he did so not simply because Pankhurst had appealed to him for support and he disagreed with her rejection of parliament, but because he believed more fundamental issues were at stake. He saw anti-parliamentarianism as a manifestation of 'ultra-leftism', that tendency to over-estimate revolutionary situations, exaggerate the revolutionary consciousness of the working class and advance unrealistic policies. He therefore devoted a chapter of his '*Left Wing' Communism – An Infantile Disorder* to the British ultra-leftists, distributed it to the British delegates at the Second Congress of the Communist International, and made sure that they published it in their various weeklies.[75] The wider import of this text was immediately recognised by British Communists, and their acceptance of the arguments it contained helped to dispel the pre-war tradition of inflexible revolutionary purity. The Leninist approach was debated and accepted at the foundation convention of the Communist Party and most dissidents accepted the outcome of that debate; by 1922 those elements who remained opposed to parliament were organised in Pankhurst's minuscule W.S.F. and Guy Aldred's even less substantial Anti-Parliamentary Communist Federation.[76] We can observe this reorientation of the majority perspective in their reception of Lenin's arguments.

His first argument was that the issue of parliamentary action could not be decided by the abstract proposition that parliament was a capitalist institution. The decision should be taken on the basis of an examination of the particular situation.[77] In certain circumstances it might be correct to boycott parliament if there was 'a possibility of an immediate transition to an armed fight for power', but 'Anti-parliamentarianism, on principle, in the sense of an absolute and categorical repudiation of participation in elections and revolutionary parliamentary work cannot. . .bear criticism, and is a naive childish doctrine. . .'[78] This approach was taken over by British Communists. Henceforth they insisted that even though 'it may be. . .necessary for the Communist Party to boycott elections and leave Parliament' if the class struggle grew more acute, in existing circumstances 'the revolutionary working class should use the parliamentary machine for all that it is worth'. The earlier debate whether parliament was a capitalist institution was superseded by the standpoint that 'We should be prepared to take every instrument of capitalism and use it to smash the capitalist system.'[79] Lenin's second argument was against the notion that parliament corrupted the workers who were elected to it and reinforced democratic illusions among the working class. He thought this objection was symptomatic of the isolation of the 'ultra-lefts' from the majority of workers and rebuked them thus: 'Don't attribute your doctrinairism to the masses!'[80] Here too he effected a change in outlook. British Marxists had previously clung to the view that the working class was fundamentally revolutionary and kept from expressing its real convictions only by the corrupt Labour leadership. This belief never disappeared altogether, but in the light of Lenin's strictures some British Communists came to accept that 'the majority of workers at present believe in parliament' and that 'to cure them of this illusion is impossible without a practical test'. Henceforth they accepted that parliamentary activity could be an effective way of exposing these 'parliamentary illusions'.[81] Finally, the Bolsheviks laid down a new method of parliamentary activity whereby Communist M.P.s were to act under the direct control of the Party and 'have no regard for Parliamentary form'. Besides exposing the 'fraudulent nature' of parliamentary democracy, they were to 'formulate demands on which the masses can unite for the struggle against capitalist rule'.[82] This was a more substantial function than the purely propagandist electoral mission of the B.S.P. and the S.L.P., and one directed more towards mobilising into action the rank and file of the working class. Communists were to integrate their parliamentary work into their general activities by entering Westminster 'not in order to delude the workers that they can achieve their emancipation by its means, but to use Parliament as a tribune whence to issue rallying calls and watchwords to the workers'. 'Above all, it is necessary that the centre of gravity of the struggle be outside Parliament, in strikes and other forms of mass struggles. . .'[83]

This new approach had little direct impact during the 1920s. There were never more than two Communist Members of Parliament at any one time, and neither Walton Newbold nor Shapurji Saklatvala, much less Colonel L'Estrange Malone, could be said to fulfil the model of a Bolshevik deputy. But although the significance of the controversy over parliament between 1917 and 1921 should not be exaggerated, it did usher in a new conception of politics: electoral and parliamentary activity became a consistent aspect of the Party's overall strategy. However unsuccessful it may have been in achieving its aims, this was an important difference between the Communist Party and the pre-war Marxist sects.

9. The problem of class consciousness

In the previous chapter we touched on an issue of crucial importance in the political discussion of the labour movement. Briefly stated, the problem lay in reconciling the class analysis of politics with the actual state of consciousness of the British working class. The working class constituted a majority of the population. To the left it seemed manifest that their interests lay in ending a social system which exploited them, and putting socialism in its place. Yet during the decade only a minority of British voters committed themselves to socialism, even at the minimal level of voting for the Labour Party. As Philip Snowden lamented, 'the very people for whom [the socialist] works and sacrifices are often indifferent, and seldom show any gratitude'.[1] Why did the British working class lack class consciousness?

Even though Labour preferred to use terms such as 'a new political and social mind' in place of the discordant phrase 'class consciousness', the question concerned even the most pragmatic members of the Labour Party.[2] All sections of the movement were agreed that the historical mission of the working class was to create 'the higher form of social organisation we call Socialism'.[3] Why then was the British worker so slow to apply himself to his mission? With the posing of this question at the end of the nineteenth century Labour Socialism was born, for the contradiction which gave rise to it lay at the very heart of the Labour Socialist mission. Back in 1893 Robert Blatchford had formulated the essential problem as clearly as any subsequent writer:

You never elect an employer as president of a Trades Council; or as a Chairman of the Trades Union Congress; or as a member of a Trade Union. You never ask an employer to lead you during a strike. But at election times, the whole body of Trade Union workers turn into blacklegs and fight for the Capitalist and against the workers.[4]

The question continued to perplex Labour and Communists alike between 1917 and 1933, and the question was sharpened for Labour by its increasing reliance on the parliamentary democratic methods of political change. Since it trusted 'no regeneration by trick or force', it had to consider those forces impeding its 'pilgrimage towards sweetness and light'.[5] The question of class consciousness assumed such importance in the first half of the 1920s precisely because the organised labour movement was then advancing to the stage at which it was looking for a majority. By the end of the decade it was apparent that Labour's success was not transitory, that it had indeed established itself as the second party of British politics. Moreover, by 1929 it was also clear that the Party leadership had warded off the challenges of Communists and other left critics.

It was commonly asserted by all shades of opinion in the labour movement that the capitalist class exercised overwhelming control over the instruments of public opinion. For the Communist it was 'perfectly natural that the class which owns the means of production. . .should strive to control every aspect of the life and thought of society, encouraging here, suppressing there, thus by direct and indirect means securing its privileged position'.[6] A prominent Labour propagandist put the same point in essentially the same terms: 'The class that owns the lands, mines, railways, ships, factories and workshops owns also the schools, churches, newspapers and cinemas. . .Capitalism does even more harm to our minds than it does to our bodies. . .Capitalism not only exploits the workers, it "fools" them also.'[7] Besides pointing to capitalists' control of public opinion by means of their ownership of opinion-forming institutions, many writers also drew attention to the mental process itself. For 'in order to control human actions, it is necessary to control the source from which all action proceeds – the mind'.[8] Once again, this attitude was shared by Labourists and Marxists alike. Inherent in this view was a belief that ideas bore a class character, that there was working-class ideology and bourgeois ideology, and that the purpose of the capitalist class was 'impregnating the minds of workers with its own views'. For 'so long as these ideas are swallowed by the worker, he is shackled to capitalism by chains stronger than those which of old bound the galley-slaves of Rome'.[9]

The use of such phrases as 'impregnating' minds and 'swallowing' ideas betrays an assumption that such ideas were alien to the working class and were imposed on it by the ruling class. The idea of a capitalist conspiracy was extremely popular in the 1920s and nowhere was it more widespread than in discussions of class consciousness. An extraordinary cohesion and far-sightedness was attributed to the capitalist class, which was credited in one Communist textbook with careful planning that 'the workers' brains should be completely enmeshed as if in a spider's web'.[10] Even the most moderate Labour writers used the same image of a capitalist plot to 'secure' the workers' minds and 'capture' their will.[11] However, the conspiracy thesis was taken to absurd lengths by Marxists, who believed that 'the capitalist class of this country is universally regarded as the most cunning and subtle of all the sections of the international bourgeoisie'; Palme Dutt once claimed that not only was there a conspiracy to suppress the writings of Marx, but the capitalists were even 'circulating through the university professorial ignoramuses still grosser stupider lies' about him.[12] Were there no depths to which they would not stoop? The striking weakness of this conspiratorial explanation of the suppression of consciousness was its inability to see that the prevailing ideology was genuinely popular among workers. The view that workers' interests, culture and ideas were *imposed* prevented British writers from recognising (as the Italian Marxist Gramsci did during the same period) how important these aspects were in their lives and how they were often generated spontaneously in workers' daily activities. Activists in the labour movement were therefore left with an explanation of the lack of class consciousness in the British working class that rested on a conception of ideology as empty and artificial. The inadequacy of this conception can be illustrated by examination of their descriptions of particular organs of public opinion.

The institution most frequently condemned was the press. 'The power of the press as a moulder of working-class opinion cannot be over-emphasised. The ideas and thoughts of most workers come from the capitalist controlled press.'[13] Newspapers received most attention, for during this period before the full development of radio and television they were the principal means of reaching a mass audience and exercised a singular influence on public opinion. This was also appreciated by the government, and Sir Basil Thompson, the Director of Intelligence, informed the Cabinet with some alarm in 1919 that 'My correspondents from the North report that the working man has ceased to believe any statements made in the "Capitalist" Press.'[14] It was often alleged that the press determined the outcome of parliamentary elections, and the episode of the Zinoviev letter was widely interpreted as a particularly blatant example of such control. The leaders of the Labour party reacted with striking unanimity to their electoral defeat in October 1924 – the Tories had won because of 'their possession of a huge press, able to broadcast their lies'. C. P. Trevelyan blamed the 'Plot Press'. Sir Patrick Hastings the newspaper 'bogy', J. R. Clynes the 'mercenary press'.[15]

The whole movement was united in condemnation of Fleet Street. And yet Marxists alleged that Labour did not properly understand the episode of the Zinoviev letter. Palme Dutt wrote that for Labour 'it is always an "accident" or "foul play" or "the power of the Press"...; but never what it is – the normal working of the machine of bourgeois dictatorship through the hypocritical forms of bourgeois democracy'.[16] There is some validity in this allegation. Although the Labour leadership mistrusted 'the Poison Gas of the Capitalist Press', and even regarded newspapers as 'an instrument used to pervert opinion',[17] they always interpreted episodes such as the Zinoviev letter as a misuse of the press attributable to individual newspaper magnates. The proper function of the press was to write the truth. But 'with great masses of the newspaper Press owned by businessmen who were not journalists', newspapers had been turned over to 'malignant slander'.[18] Rothermere and Beaverbrook in particular were thought to have turned the press into a servant of capitalist interests. Of course very many politicians regarded the press during this period with extreme disrespect, and when Marxists called it a 'kept harlot' they were merely using the same term that Stanley Baldwin chose later.[19] Where the Marxists parted company with Baldwin and the Labour front bench was in their insistence that newspaper bias transcended the political sympathies of individual owners. After all, the public B.B.C. was also 'a clever cunning conspiracy' to mislead the workers.[20] Therefore their attitude to the Zinoviev letter was that 'It is no use anyone in the Labour Party asserting that on this occasion they were beaten by a trick and that on the next occasion we will do better. On the next occasion the capitalist class will be able to avail themselves of another trick, and when tricks fail them – why, then force.'[21] While Labour regretted the debasement of the organs of public opinion, to the Marxist they were an integral part of the machinery of capitalist coercion.

A common feature of the Labour and Marxist attitudes to the media was a neglect of their commercial aspect. With the notable exception of Kingsley Martin, who analysed the press in a systematic fashion in *The British Public and the General Strike* (1926), it occurred to no one that newspapers were commercial enterprises, competing against each other for a mass circulation and therefore bearing a necessarily close relationship to the tastes of their readers. This is not to suggest that the press did not exercise a political influence, in most cases hostile to Labour; rather, that a paper's political sympathies were integral to its operation and not an extraneous or underlying real purpose. The conspiratorial view that there was 'absolute harmony regarding the need for a steady and united attack upon the demands of the workers' prevented the labour movement from recognising this.[22]

A similar conspiratorial view extended to all spheres of social activity – education, the arts, religion, and so on. It was applied particularly to forms of popular entertainment and recreation which were thought to distract the worker from his proper place in the struggle. Once again this was the deliberate intention of the capitalist class: 'Across the path of the underpaid, overworked toiler, there have been red herrings drawn. Sweepstakes, cup-ties, competitions, cross-word puzzles, the dazzling chance of winning someone else's money on one day to compensate for being defrauded of rightful earnings on every other day.' And in addition to diverting the worker, popular recreation insidiously filled his mind with competitive, anti-socialist attitudes. 'The organisation and the rule of sport', for example, were 'cunningly and carefully tinctured with capitalist principles and propaganda'.[23]

Kingsley Martin once remarked that you 'cannot propagate propaganda unless you have got the proper geese'.[24] This was a common reaction among activists to their inability to win general working-class support. In moments of disappointment they habitually placed responsibility for failure on the workers themselves. As Ramsay MacDonald put it, 'You cannot make a silk purse out of a sow's ear.' It was 'the fault of the minds of the people'.[25]

It might be argued that this attitude followed logically from the belief that the workers' minds were impregnated with capitalist indoctrination and hence that they were 'trained to be the recipients of orders which they obey from dumb inertia'.[26] But if this were the case, the victims could hardly be blamed for succumbing to a process over which they had no control. And the leaders of the Labour Party frequently expressed pique with the electorate in a startlingly bitter tone. MacDonald once said that 'the minds of masses of men (and still truer is this of women) are necessarily circumscribed' to such a degree that it seemed 'sheer folly and perversity to allow this mass to pass important political judgements'. The fault lay with the workers themselves, for if they 'would spend one-twentieth part of the money they now waste in drink and gambling on political and publicity organisation, the capitalist monopoly of the means of influencing public opinion would be quickly destroyed'. The trouble was that the populace 'desircs far more strongly to be narcotised' than to be free.[27] Such a view clearly reflects a lack of confidence in the ordinary man's intelligence that went far beyond the claim of capitalist indoctrination.

The Labour leaders' view of social consciousness was rooted in a positivist conception of human development. The positivist conception derived, for the most part unconsciously, from the evolutionary tradition of Herbert Spencer.[28] Society was progressing from primitive and superstitious origins towards the Socialist Commonwealth, guided and instructed by science and rational enlightenment; in this fashion the social organism 'eliminates the abnormal and diseased from the social body and gives the good, the true and the beautiful free play'.[29] At the level of social consciousness, the original mass mentality or mob passion had to be transformed into an educated democratic awareness. As Glasier put it, 'we are every one of us, in some degree the ancient savage and some degree the modern socialist man'.[30] Translated into political terms, the Labour Party had to overcome 'the marshalled opposition of mass habit'.[31] Because of Labour's attachment to parliamentary methods, the raising-up of public mentality was the regulator of its political progress. 'Gradualness is. . .inevitable because our people have not yet developed sufficient wisdom, knowledge and understanding to enable us to advance more speedily to our goal.' This was a lengthy and difficult process, for 'the masses retain the love of primitive man for gaudy ornament and sparkling plaything', and 'slowly, very slowly, do intelligence and reflection permeate the mass'. Furthermore, Labour was retarded by political opponents who sought to excite the residual primitive mentality and 'turn popular government into the rule of mob passion rather than that of the public will'.[32]

Such views were not exclusive to Labour. MacDonald himself cited Wilfred Trotter's *Instincts of the Herd in Peace and War* in support of his understanding of human nature.[33] Recognition of the irrational coupled with reaffirmation of the rational basis of the Great Society was a common theme during the period, finding its best-known expression in Graham Wallas's *Human Nature and Politics*. But in MacDonald's case the positivist vision served to heighten his contempt for present human frailty. 'Men are not sheep, but they have two of the dominating characteristics of sheep. They are gregarious and they are easily frightened.' This opinion also justified and reinforced the elitist tendency of Labour Party activists, for it set them apart from the gullible majority. 'We all know perfectly well', wrote MacDonald, 'that electoral majorities are composed of a small minority of active politically-minded people influencing a mass of people who have no fixed convictions or orientations.'[34] While seeking to educate this mass, Labour only grudgingly accepted its electoral judgements.

Thus Socialism was identified with rationality and conservatism with the 'non-rational and irresponsible' emotions of the masses.

Each social and political creed needs its own tactics for success. Conservatives depend upon the psychology of fear, Socialists upon responding to a half-realised longing for clean [sic], calm and sincere thinking.

A Socialist is a person, who, reading the signs of the times, undertakes the task of preparing Man for Civilisation. An anti-Socialist is a person whose mind, still in the semi-natural state, is unable to understand the message of the Socialist.[35]

From this perspective they interpreted every electoral rebuff as a victory for 'undiscriminating herd opinion'. When MacDonald was defeated in Leicester in 1918, he especially blamed 'the women – bloodthirsty, cursing their hate, issuing from the courts and alleys crowded with children, reeking with humanity – the sad flotsam and jetsam of wild emotion'. When Lady Astor won the Plymouth by-election that made her the first female Member of Parliament, it was because she had 'succeeded in turning over 50 per cent of the Plymouth voters into a mere mob'. When Morgan Philips Price failed to win his Gloucester constituency, it was because he 'had been sponged on and let down by the fickle mobs in Gloucester'. When Labour lost the Zinoviev letter election in October, 1924, it was the fault of 'the solid stupidity of many of our people', whose 'rabble formation leaves us too easy a prey to the Powers of Evil'.[36]

Such statements reveal something more than just frustration and loss of patience. They should be seen as the outcome in practice of Labour's positivist belief that altruism and rationality must ultimately triumph over selfishness and superstition. True, 'the great majority of mankind have not yet woken up to the facts'; but 'this awakening of the human race is all that remains to be done in order that the last remnants of the old system may be swept away'.[37] Such a voluntarist perspective also illuminates Labour's rejection of Marxism. While the Communists insisted that the working class must forcibly overcome vested class interests, the mainstream of the labour movement believed that political awareness alone would suffice. 'The thing that matters is the ripening of the thought and intelligence of the proletariat.' 'The workers have the numbers, the voices, and the votes, and ought to be politically supreme. Their actual power is not a tenth of their potential power...What they lack is knowledge.' Education was therefore the guarantor of mobilisation and political success. It would 'educate the electorate out of fear and panic', it would render impossible the old methods whereby the capitalist used to 'hoodwink and blind them to the truth'.[38]

It was because the Labour Party foresaw the development of political awareness in such optimistic terms that it was so frequently and so bitterly disappointed. Throughout the 1920s we can see Labour wavering between exaggerated confidence and bitter disillusionment. On the one hand:

[Labour] strives to transform through education, through raising the standards of mental and moral qualities, through the acceptance of programmes by reason of their justice, rationality and wisdom.[39]

On the other:

What men imagine is more important than what they think, or even than what they know. That is why our opponents have so successfully played upon their victims, the poor, the hungry, the enslaved and the recruit. They defeat our facts with their phantoms.[40]

Like MacDonald, the Labour publicists reluctantly acknowledged the potency of irrational factors and yet clung to a vestigial 'intellectualism', a belief that all human action was the product of a rational intellectual process.[41] The realisation that rationality alone would not convert workers into socialists was expressed most forcibly in the popular image of Henry Dubb.

Henry Dubb was created by the New York socialist paper, the *Call*. He was 'an archetypal figure created of late by Socialists in the U.S., he is the "good working man" of the capitalist imagination, one with no thought of his own rights, always willing to create surplus value for the exploiter, the unclassconscious proletarian'.[42] The original cartoon series of 'The Adventures of Henry Dubb' was reprinted in the Glasgow I.L.P. weekly, *Forward*, which after 1919 developed a native equivalent called John Willie. Henry Dubb cartoons also appeared from time to time in a number of other Labour newspapers, including the *Daily Herald*. Many other names were given to the conservative worker, such as the 'ragged trousered philanthropist', a term derived from Robert Tressell's book (first published 1914) which also passed into common currency; but Henry Dubb became an accepted stock figure in much the same way as Alf Garnett has done more recently. Besides the militants of *Forward* and the *Plebs*, he was cited by such authoritative figures as George Bernard Shaw, R. H. Tawney and Ben Tillett.[43] Even outside the Labour press he was invoked by correspondents who thought it unnecessary to explain his identity.[44] Tawney has even suggested that on one occasion a telegram addressed to 'Henry Dubb, Labour Party Conference' was duly delivered to the correct seaside resort. The statement that when the chairman invited the addressee to claim it four-fifths of the comrades sprang to their feet was, however, an exaggeration.

The uses made of Henry Dubb by various strands of opinion in the labour movement provide insight into their various attitudes to the recalcitrant worker. His creator, and the Scottish creator of John Willie, treated him as an incorrigible fool who would never stand up to the boss – he swallowed the red herrings of the capitalist press and was prey to every distracting vice, alcohol and sport in particular. Time after time the cartoon strip showed a neatly dressed socialist haranguing the slovenly Henry Dubb in terms of strictest orthodoxy. Henry invariably missed the point and more often than not was struck and abandoned by the frustrated propagandist. If Henry Dubb represented the apathetic masses whom Labour would never convert, he at least consoled the elect in their conviction that they were right and their audience manifestly dim-witted. A minority of socialists responded differently to Henry Dubb. R. H. Tawney, for example, embraced him as the 'common, courageous, good-hearted, patient, proletarian fool' with whom he thought the movement should be particularly concerned, and added that 'in the interminable case of *Dubb vs. Superior Persons & Co.*, whether Christians, Capitalists or Communists, I am an unrepentant Dubbite'.[45] Henry Dubb, the proletarian fool, was a highly ambiguous figure.

Marxists, too, frequently displayed contempt for the British working class. The frustration they felt for their conspicuous lack of success was often expressed in criticism not of the restraints operating on workers but of the workers themselves. One writer looked down his nose at 'the miserable and discontented people' who were 'too helpless to help themselves'. Marxists also accepted and made use of the image of Henry Dubb, the 'servile tool of capitalism'.[46] They invented dialogues with Henry Dubb which reveal with remarkable clarity their isolation from the mass of the working class. In one such dialogue the Marxist tried to interest Henry in Marx: 'If you had studied his theory of surplus value you would know that he is a sane and able writer who proves that capital tends to concentrate in fewer and fewer hands as industrial evolution proceeds, and hence – ' At which point Henry interrupted: 'I wish you would not talk so long-winded as all that. . .' And the Marxist returned with an obtuseness rivalling that of Henry himself: 'I am merely explaining the theories of Marx to you in his own language'.[47] Such attitudes towards the un-class-conscious worker had been extremely widespread before the war. Indeed they were specifically encouraged: the S.L.P. advised its members that 'should any "fakir, freak or fool" dare to cast ridicule on our Party or our principles, then the speaker should wade in and annihilate him as a street crowd always likes to see a "smart" chap get taken down'.[48] The reference to the street crowd is significant, for the conditions of open-air meetings imposed their own specific effects. T. A. Jackson is remembered as remarking that one reason for adopting an aggressive and even abusive stance before his audience was the need to win their respect. If control was lost the orator went in some danger of humiliation or even physical assault and 'you had to have methods for defending yourself'.[49] This likening of the soap-box orator to the lion-tamer, using his wits as his sole defence, can be picked up in other recollections. Tom Scollan, the veteran I.L.P. propagandist, recalled that 'you had to be on your toes all the time', as he deliberately set out to build an audience and establish his control over it with such provocative cries as 'Come and sharpen your wits on the whetstone of knowledge', and he could recall many close shaves.[50] Such sallies take us back to the pre-war socialist pioneers who operated in a more uniformly hostile environment and betrayed their fundamentally *external* relationship to the unregenerate masses. Take the example of an S.D.F. pitch in Walworth Road, London, where Harry Quelch 'called upon the people to come out of their bug-hutches and slums and fight for socialism. A man in the crowd, who looked as if he had come straight from a slum, rushed to knock him off the stool, shouting "You lying ——, call my —— home a slum and a bug-hutch!" '[51] This air of gloomy antagonism to the bone-headed working man was extremely prevalent among pre-war Marxists and emerges with particular clarity in Harry Quelch's own sub-Dickensian short stories about working-class life which were collected in his *Literary Remains* (1914). Indeed, *The Ragged Trousered Philanthropists* only elaborated and improved the literary quality of an established genre of such pessimistic proletarian fiction. Contempt for the unregenerate worker declined noticeably after the formation of the Communist Party, for it was obviously incompatible with the Leninist object of mobilising the whole of the working class on issues that directly affected them. Of course, many found it hard to discard their old habits and continued to speak and think in such elitist terms, yet there was a growing awareness of the changed orientation – and T. A. Jackson produced perhaps the most perceptive reflections on this new tack in his review of a new edition of *The Ragged Trousered Philanthropists* in 1927.[52]

Thus far Labour would seem to have much in common with the Marxists. Both shared a belief that capitalists manipulated organs of public opinion to control the workers' minds. Yet there was this vital difference. Where Labour viewed political mobilisation as an intellectual and spiritual process, imbuing the electorate with a higher ethos, Marxists advanced materialist explanations with an emphasis on action rather than education. Furthermore, the Communists needed a dual explanation of the political backwardness of British workers, for they had to account not merely for the failure of large sections of the working class to take part in the trade union and labour movement, but also for the refusal of nearly all those who did so to advance from Labourism to Communism. Hence they were dealing not just with apolitical Henry Dubbs but with 'Labour Henry Dubbs'.[53] In the remainder of this chapter we shall be concerned with three popular Marxist explanations and indicate their points of departure from the Labour approach.

The first and most established explanation was originally advanced by Engels. First in 1885, and again in the 1892 Preface to his *Condition of the Working Class in England*, he argued that

during the period of England's industrial monopoly the English working class have, to a certain extent, shared in the benefits of the monopoly. These benefits were very unequally parcelled out amongst them; the privileged minority pocketed most, but even the great mass had, at least, a temporary share now and then. And that is the reason why, since the dying out of Owenism, there has been no Socialism in England.

The privileged minority, in certain industries in which the labour of adult men predominated and was organised in unions, comprised a 'working class aristocracy'.[54] The idea that there was a conservative aristocracy of labour was not exclusive to Marxists, but Lenin subsequently generalised it into an international, rather than a purely British phenomenon, and developed it much further in his analysis of the British labour movement. Thus he argued in *Imperialism. The Highest Stage of Capitalism* that exploitation on a new scale had created 'the economic possibility of corrupting the upper strata of the proletariat' in all the monopoly capitalist countries. In the case of Britain, Lenin held adamantly that the labour aristocracy had been 'bribed out of imperialist superprofits and converted into watchdogs of capitalism, into corruptors of the labour movement'.[55]

British Marxists seized hold of the theory of the labour aristocracy to explain the quiescence of the workers. Its point of departure from Labour explanations was its materialist basis in place of Labour's concentration on knowledge and education. For Marxists, 'Class consciousness, as all consciousness, is determined by existence.' The argument in brief was that profits wrung from the economic empire made it 'possible for British imperialism to make concessions to the workers in Britain, foster illusions of never-ceasing prosperity, and imbue deeply a spirit of bourgeois liberalism'.[56] Two features of the British presentation of the theory stand out. First they repeatedly claimed that because British capitalism was losing its previously dominant position, the British working class would throw off its servile passivity. But they were never able to name the day of judgement. Secondly, British Marxists were unsure which sections of the working class comprised the labour aristocracy – whether it was workers in export trades, or better-paid workers, or some other group. Hence they displayed considerable uncertainty and imprecision in their use of the theory.

The reason given for the disappearance of the labour aristocracy was the drying-up of the fruits of empire. The economic development of Britain's former markets made them into competitors. 'The Empire, which was previously a source of limited advantage to a section of the working class, is now becoming a source of impoverishment and weakness to all sections, including the former aristocracy of Labour.' Thus 'to-day there are no surplus profits left and no hope of getting any. The whole working class is having to fight for its very existence.'[57] The political conclusions drawn from the demise of the labour aristocracy provide an instance of British Marxists' rigid materialist view that economic conditions directly determined political consciousness. The workers had been conservative because they were affluent: deprived of imperial spoils, they would now become radical.

There were a variety of interpretations of the identity of the labour aristocracy. The most usual term was the 'upper stratum' of the working class, but this too could mean many things. Sometimes it appeared that insofar as the whole of the British working class benefited from the fruits of monopoly capitalist exploitation, it should be regarded as representing the labour aristocracy *in toto*. This approach was taken by Theodore Rothstein in his book *From Chartism to Labourism* (1929), the most fully developed, if unorthodox, elaboration of the theory. Rothstein contended that 'the opportunist mentality and sentiments of the English proletariat' were caused not by the British industrial monopoly, for this had been undermined by the 1870s, but by a general cheapening of prices. This had increased the standard of living of the entire proletariat and replaced class consciousness with the conservative 'psychology of the consumer'.[58]

The view that all British workers were labour aristocrats disappeared later in the decade when it was established that the prosperity of the labour aristocracy contrasted with the deepening poverty of the 'broad working masses'.[59] But just who the labour aristocracy were remained unclear. Some suggested it consisted of those workers employed in export industries; others again during the Depression that the term should cover all those who remained in employment, however low their wage levels might be.[60] The common feature of these diverse understandings is that the labour aristocracy was regarded as a politically backward section of the working class, whose backwardness was linked to relative prosperity. Historians have debated this proposition, and Henry Pelling has argued that at the end of the nineteenth century 'militancy was much more likely to be found among the better off than among the poorer workers'.[61] In our period as well it seems that some relatively privileged sections of the working class were often among the most militant: the engineers are an obvious example. Yet the concept of labour aristocracy was sometimes used by contemporaries in a manner consistent with this fact. The Executive of the Communist International, for example, claimed that the labour aristocracy was created by capitalism 'endeavour[ing] to suppress the revolutionary strivings of the working masses by bribing the more developed and most intelligent sections of the proletariat'. And often during the 1920s native Marxists recognised that it was the 'organised and skilled' sections of the working class who responded best to their message.[62] From this viewpoint the labour aristocracy could be seen as a prosperous, organised section of the proletariat, whose political consciousness was by no means uniformly conservative and in many cases was highly developed. The crucial issue was then whether their political outlook was reformist or revolutionary, Marxist or Labourist. British Marxists frequently

attempted to understand why politically active workers retained a
Labour rather than a Marxist perspective, but failed to trace this
problem back to their theory of a labour aristocracy. For them it was
more a term of abuse than a tool of analysis.

For the same reason the doctrine found very little support outside the
Communist Party. There was a considerable body of anti-imperialist
feeling in the Labour Party, but it seldom saw a connexion between
the exploitation of underdeveloped countries, which it opposed, and
conservatism among the British working class. Most Labour opponents
of imperialism drew their ideas from the analysis provided by
J. A. Hobson and H. N. Brailsford, an analysis with some similarities
but important differences from the Marxist analysis. The Hobson–
Brailsford analysis was rooted in the economic theory of underconsumptionism, according to which there was insufficient demand in a
capitalist economy to purchase the total production. The workers
'cannot buy back all they produce; the rich do not care to buy all the
rest, and it is necessary to find markets in other countries'. From the
export of commodities capitalism had later turned to the export of
capital, which was able to find 'richer rewards' abroad.[63] But at this
point the Marxist and the follower of Hobson parted company.
Whereas the Marxist thought imperial exploitation enriched both the
capitalist and the worker in the metropolitan country, the Labour
critic believed imperialism benefited only the capitalist entrepreneur
and had a depressive effect on British wage levels. By establishing new
industries in the colonies with sweated labour, wrote Brailsford, imperialism 'has tended to depress the conditions of workers in the mother
country'.[64] The Labour Party adopted this view at its 1921 Conference,
where a resolution was passed declaring that imperialism tended 'to
perpetuate the reign of capitalism, not only by increasing the power of
wealth, but by neglecting the needs of the home market, and leaving
the natural resources of their own country undeveloped'.[65] And during
the 1920s there was an influential Labour Commonwealth Group
whose aim was to change the Empire from a 'boss-controlled Empire',
making use of cheap labour, to a 'Labour-controlled commonwealth,
in which we are the directors of policy'.[66] Labour's chief objection was
not to the Empire *per se* but to the use of native labour to undercut
British labour. Hence Labour never subscribed to the theory of a labour
aristocracy, though Marxists had a case for claiming that in this respect
they acted as one.

The second explanation advanced by Marxists for the non-revolu-

tionary character of the working class pinned the blame on the leaders
of the Labour Party and the trade unions. They stood between the discontented masses and a socialist consciousness, diverting discontent into
harmless reformist channels. Though it may seem that blaming the
leaders was the opposite response to blaming the workers, in fact the
two attitudes frequently went together. The leaders of the Labour
Party and trade unions were traitors to the working class: the working
class were fools because they allowed the leaders to pull the wool over
their eyes. This view was shared by militant sections of the Labour
Party and provided fertile ground for projects such as the Minority
Movement in the unions, the propaganda and educational activities
of the Plebs League, the Ginger Group organised by *Lansbury's Labour
Weekly*, the radical platform of the *Sunday Worker*, and the Cook–
Maxton campaign to radicalise the Labour Party. Like the Communist party, all these movements often blamed defective leadership
for Labour's shortcomings.

Unlike the Communists, however, they never went so far as to allege
that this was the essential purpose of the leadership. The Communist
Party asserted that 'Labour's political and industrial leaders were
"honoured" and paid by the capitalist class' specifically 'to prevent
any forward movement on the part of the workers'.[67] This belief was
inherited by the Party from its predecessors and specifically from the
followers of De Leon. Yet, although the Communist Party used similar
terms throughout the 1920s, they were not an essential part of its
political vocabulary until later in the decade. Individuals like Mac-
Donald, Clynes and Thomas were frequently accused of 'selling out'
their members, but Communists were noticeably reluctant to brand
the whole leadership of the labour movement as traitors. They recognised at this time that phrases such as 'agents of the bourgeoisie'
sounded insincere to British ears.[68] And after all, their own industrial
section was working alongside miiltant union officials such as A. J.
Cook, who after 1924 was secretary of Britain's largest union.

Only after the General Strike, and in response to the instructions of
the Communist International, was the antagonism towards the official
leadership translated into a fully fledged theory. The events of 1926
seemed to many workers a monumental demonstration that the principal concern of the General Council of the Trade Unions, and to an
even greater degree that of the Labour front bench, was to damp down
militancy. Basing their strategy on this widespread feeling of treachery
and betrayal, the Communists adopted the policy of 'Class Against

Class' in 1928 and became fully committed to the myopic belief that the principal factor holding back the rank and file from revolution was their reactionary leaders. Even Palme Dutt was rebuked by the Communist International for suggesting that the Labour Party still enjoyed the general support of British workers.[69] The corollary of this position was a claim that the Labour leaders were throwing off their cloak of loyalty to the workers and that the pressures of events compelled them to 'come out as open defenders of capitalism'. Because conditions were adjudged to be 'objectively revolutionary', the absence of any evidence of a leftward move was ascribed to the Machiavellian social fascist bureaucracy.[70] And in October 1931 the Communist Party announced that MacDonald, Snowden and Thomas had abandoned the Labour Party simply to maintain the charade, 'to divert all the kicks coming to the Labour Party'.[71]

This was too much for some British Marxists. One wrote to the *Daily Worker* that the incessant talk of treachery and cunning ascribed to the Labour leaders 'a degree of consciousness. . .that is very doubtful'. T. A. Jackson protested with his characteristic pungency that all this contrasting of 'leaders' and 'led', of 'officials' and 'rank and file', and of 'heads' and 'tails' was a poor substitute for real Marxist analysis and detrimental to the Party's work.[72] Similarly, in an area of local Communist strength like Mardy the Party was loth to accept such counter-productive instructions, and this was one element of the heresy of Hornerism. It seemed to many that in a number of cases the trade union and Labour Party leadership were pressing as hard as their weakened strength would allow, and Ernest Bevin embroidered this theme to great effect at the 1928 Trade Union Congress: 'It is all very well for people to talk as if the working class of Great Britain are cracking their shins for a fight and a revolution, and we are holding them back. Are they? There are not many of them as fast as we are ourselves.'[73] For all their talk of traitorous leaders, the Communists had eventually to recognise that 'The main thing that keeps the Right Wing leaders of Labour in their exalted place is the influence of capitalist ideas and "ideals" on the minds of the rank and file.'[74] The task facing British Marxists, therefore, was replacing capitalist ideas with Marxist ones, and this was a task that a simple theory of corrupt leaders could not perform.

The third and final explanation for the backwardness of the workers was simultaneously a guarantee that they would eventually advance.

During the 1920s Marxists expected that capitalist ideas would be vanquished, and Marxist ideas vindicated, on the field of action. 'The main thing', one Communist paraphrased Engels, 'is to get the workers into action as a class. That once accomplished, they cannot go very far wrong.'[75] Underlying this strategy was the expectation that experience rather than propaganda was the best teacher. Though they might be uninterested in socialist teaching, the 'every-day lessons are imposing the hard, irrefutable facts of Marxism upon the minds of the workers'. In the words of J. T. Walton Newbold, ' "Comrade History" has been a much better propagandist than any of us have.'[76]

The idea that as the result of its immediate experience the working class would spontaneously develop a revolutionary consciousness was subjected to criticism by Lenin in *What is to be Done?*, where he argued that revolutionary consciousness could only be created by a Marxist party and that left to themselves workers' organisations would only produce what he called an economist trade union consciousness. But *What is to be Done?* was not translated and Lenin's argument not incorporated into British Marxism until the end of the 1920s. Until then the C.P.G.B. exhibited a markedly economist attitude to the problem of class consciousness. The Party repeatedly claimed that experience alone would impel workers to revolutionary conclusions, that it would 'drum Socialism into the heads of even the most backward workers in spite of all the cunning, corruption and deceit of the bourgeoisie'.[17] The approach was used with particular reference to the Labour Party: many workers, it was acknowledged, believed that Labour stood for socialist policies and that a Labour government would satisfy their aspirations. According to the economist attitude, 'it would only be hard experience that would teach them otherwise'.[78] The expectation was that Labour's failure in office would impel the masses to Communism, that in initial defeat they would 'acquire a personal and collective experience which shows [their] errors and how to correct them'.[79] On similar grounds Palme Dutt interpreted the General Strike as 'the greatest mass-revolutionary lesson in British history' and assumed that it had dispelled at a stroke the reformist illusions that had previously retarded the working class.[80] The flaw in this argument was the failure to realise that workers might draw very different conclusions from defeat – instead of advancing to Marxism, they might be demoralised; instead of gaining strength from the failure of the Strike, they might retreat from militancy altogether. British Marxists allowed only one possible response to experience where in fact there were many.

This economist theory of class consciousness reached a climax during the debate on Party policy that took place during 1928 and 1929, and resulted in the policy of 'Class Against Class'. Though a similar change occurred throughout the Communist International, debate in Britain centred on the correct attitude to the Labour Party, and both sides enlisted the support of 'Comrade History'. According to the beleaguered majority of the Party executive, it was necessary to 'push' a new Labour government into office so as 'to help the workers by their own experience to convince themselves of the worthlessness of reformism'. The experience of the previous Labour administration had been 'too short and incomplete to convince the mass of the workers that the Communists were right'.[81] The critics of the executive, who would soon defeat it and impose the new policy, replied in kind. According to Palme Dutt, a leading spokesman for the new policy, the necessary 'exposure' of Labour had already occurred and 'in consequence the basis exists in the experience of the working class on which the Communist Party can drive home the lessons of experience'. It was the Party's responsibility 'not to determine policy by the level of understanding they [the workers] have reached', but to do so according to 'the true interests of the working class'.[82] Here was economism with a vengeance! Because conditions were pronounced 'objectively revolutionary' it was assumed that there must have been a leftward shift in the 'mood of the masses'; the Party could therefore initiate its sectarian policy of Class Against Class, aware that it lacked any significant support but comforted by the conviction that the policy accorded with the objective 'realities of the situation'.[83] Nothing could shake such logic.

Lenin's *What is to be Done?*, an essay written in 1902 in which he had set out the Bolshevik conception of political work, became available in Britain at the end of 1929 as a volume of the Collected Works, and soon reappeared in cheaper format as a volume in the Little Lenin Library. Its contents had been outlined before when the South African Communist D. Ivon Jones wrote from Moscow that the work contained 'much that is new and startling to the English reader', particularly its denial of 'the current impression that socialist consciousness comes to the workers inevitably from their own conflicts'. But such second-hand accounts had little impact and in some cases were extremely misleading, as with James MacDougall, who interpreted *What is to be Done?* in a leftist spirit so that 'we must always maintain our political activity at the heights of the historical task of the working class, and never allow it to be narrowed down to what is immediately acceptable or comprehensible to the working masses'.[84] So its translation at the end of the 1920s was particularly important in shaping a distinctively new approach to the problem of class consciousness.

The new approach was closely associated with implementing the strategy of Class Against Class. In adopting this strategy the Communist Party had shifted its emphasis from struggle against the capitalist class to struggle against what was now seen as capitalism's chief support, the 'Social Fascist' Labour Party and trade union leadership. The primary object became winning the workers away from Social Fascism, and it was to accomplish this task that the new approach to class consciousness was developed. The 'new line' was distinguished from two complementary errors that had vitiated Communist activity during the preceding decade. In the past the Party had either fought limited campaigns that misled the workers into believing that capitalism could satisfy their needs, or posed abstract revolutionary demands to which the workers had not responded. Now the working class was to be won by mobilising it on 'the smallest concrete issues', issues of immediate economic importance, while at the same time 'explaining the political meaning of these struggles' and driving home the revolutionary lessons inherent in them.[85]

The insights provided by Lenin undoubtedly enabled British Marxists to advance their understanding of the problem of class consciousness. They no longer had to think of the workers either as willing revolutionaries held back only by extraneous influences or as dupes blind to the truth. When Communists came to accept the need to approach workers on issues that immediately affected them and to communicate to them in their own language, the propensity to 'blame the worker for everything' was rejected.[86] Marxists were consequently prepared to examine their own shortcomings rather than to blame those of their audience. Yet like so much Communist theory between 1929 and 1931, this new approach was well-nigh impossible to translate into practice. By the end of 1930 membership had slumped to two and a half thousand, of whom fully half were out of work, so its attempts to mobilise workers on factory issues were in most cases doomed from the start. More fundamentally, the circumstances of the introduction of the 'new line' and the evasions and ambiguities involved in its implementation left this new doctrine open to major differences of interpretation. To resolve these differences and lay down consistent political directions required the Party's most Jesuitical logic.

THE PROBLEM OF CLASS CONSCIOUSNESS 217

The ambiguities can be illustrated by reference to one particular controversy. It began when Freda Utley used her review of *What is to be Done?* to accuse the British Party of continuing economist errors. She claimed that British Communists despised Marxist theory, were concerned only with economic demands, and 'bow[ed] down to the spontaneity of the masses'. 'The increasingly obvious oppression of the working class does not mean that the worker will "spontaneously" desire socialism', she asserted, and she appealed for a new method of work that would 'convince them by shedding the light of theory on their own experience'.[87] Utley's accusations called down the wrath of the Party: she had neglected 'the raising of concrete demands corresponding to the needs of the masses' and had relied instead on revolutionary propaganda alone to create revolutionary consciousness.[88] The outstanding feature of this debate was that all participants identified their position with *What is to be Done?* and used the critique of economism as the basis of their arguments, but used it in several different senses – economism sometimes meant a neglect of political for purely economic demands, sometimes a 'tailing' behind the demands of the masses, sometimes a simple contempt for theory. Because all participants thought the proper Communist method was to pose immediate demands with revolutionary significance, the argument was reduced to essentially verbal disagreement. Utley claimed the Party was subordinating revolutionary strategy to inadequate economic demands, while the Party claimed she was neglecting immediate demands for supposedly revolutionary theory. As Allen Hutt remarked of Walter Tapsell's contribution to the debate, they all had, 'apart from the usual selection of hackneyed phrases, nothing new to say, no contribution to make'.[89]

We can thus see that Marxists and spokesmen for the Labour Party advanced explanations for the backwardness of British workers that were similar in many respects. They differed more clearly over the strategies they advanced to overcome this backwardness. While Labour relied on the appeal of its message, Marxists had to effect a junction between theory and practice. Sometimes, like Labour, they concentrated on progagating their doctrine for social regeneration; more frequently in our period they looked to experience to revolutionise the working class. When the Leninist orthodoxy was assimilated into the British Communist Party, they glimpsed a method which might reconcile the two elements, but the circumstances of this assimilation were such as to vitiate that method's potentialities. In the early 1930s the political method laid down by Lenin was a platitude to which all Marxists formally subscribed and from which almost any conclusions could be drawn.

10. The Moscow Road

In the preceding chapters I have sought to specify the social basis of British Marxism and capture some of its doctrinal changes. Yet perhaps the most important change to befall British Marxism was not internal but external, concerning not who professed Marxism and how they professed it, but the sort of identity that the doctrine and its adherents possessed in the larger movement. For so far we have considered the arguments of Labour critics of Marxism in a piecemeal fashion: we have seen their objections to historical and dialectical materialism, to Marxist economics and the theories of class, state and politics; and though we have also considered their own views on these subjects, such a presentation of Labour Socialism does it less than justice by robbing it of its own structure and forcing upon it points of reference it never accepted. In actual confrontation the Labour critic seldom took his stand on the faults of the Marxist dialectic or the inadequacies of the labour theory of value. His criticisms were far more practical. They almost always arose in the context of debate about the respective merits of the Labour and Marxist methods of securing social change.

Before the First World War and even during the early 1920s no critic ever dismissed Marx absolutely. He was allotted a respectable niche in the Labour pantheon as one of the founding fathers, perhaps even 'the greatest name in the history of Socialism'.[1] His great achievement had been to replace utopian socialism with a more scientific approach which, for all its shortcomings, was at least based on the organised working class and grounded in a study of history. But Marx had 'explained Socialism in accordance with the thought of his own time', and Socialist theory had not stood still since his death. Socialism could not afford to become a static doctrine, for 'whilst the Socialist conception of Society remains fixed, its creeds and methods must never sink into infallible dogma, and its gospels become closed books. It is said of Marx that he was once overheard muttering to himself, "Thank God I am no Marxist." '[2] The chief faults of Marxism, it was thought,

lay not with Marx but with his disciples. British socialists before the
First World War were conscious of Marxism as an essentially continental phenomenon which had turned Marx's writings into liturgy and
which suffered from various dogmatic tendencies. Nevertheless, the
French, German and other Marxists were fellow socialists and part of a
common movement. The native Marxists of the B.S.P. and the S.L.P.
were in this sense regarded as atypical in that they were thought to be
fringe extremists quite out of touch with British realities.

The Russian Revolution and the subsequent consolidation of a Communist International were to transform this perception of Marxism as
an imperfect but far from useless doctrine and of Marxists as misguided
comrades in the cause. In its initial stages the Revolution attracted
widespread support, and this enthusiasm persisted in many sections of
the movement even after its Marxist character had become evident, so
that an influential local Labour paper could write that 'In Russia the
boldest, the most interesting and wonderful experiment in the world's
history is taking place before our eyes.'[3] And for several years after,
the *Daily Herald* championed the Russian Revolution. There were
some allegations of repression and despotism against the new regime,
but these were rendered less credible by the general campaign of
calumny and vilification conducted by the British government and
other untrustworthy sources – indeed, the absurd accusations carried
by Fleet Street in the early days of the Soviet regime (such as the
concoction of a decree in which the Bolsheviks were supposed to have
'nationalised' women) inoculated many working-class activists against
the more accurate allegations that emerged in the 1930s. The most
vociferous criticism from inside the Labour movement came from three
peripheral sources: first, certain trade union and Labour figures who
had been prominent supporters of the war and saw the Bolsheviks as
pacifists or worse; second, and largely for the same reason, the Marxists
of the re-established S.D.F. (initially the National Socialist Party), if
these embittered Hyndmanites can still be regarded as Marxists in any
significant sense; and third, the tiny S.P.G.B., who criticised the
Bolsheviks because they had taken a revolutionary short-cut past their
Marxist educational duty.[4] However, all critics were swimming against
a tide of interest in and support for this new working-class regime, and
while the Bolsheviks were fighting for survival, Labour spokesmen
mostly refrained from unqualified criticisms and supported the campaign against British intervention. Like the chairman of the I.L.P.,
many felt that 'until an honourable peace with Russia has been ratified

I do not propose to utter any criticism which could be misconstrued and made use of by the enemies of the Russian People'. And even those who did utter criticism nevertheless supported the new regime, feeling that 'There is no need to be in full sympathy with the policy and outlook of Russian Bolshevism in order to feel that the struggle of the Soviet Government against Capitalist reaction, both within and without, is of immense moment for the workers all the world over.'[5] In its campaign against the post-war upsurge of British Marxism, therefore, the Labour leadership was fighting with one hand tied, for it was constrained to give at least token support to the great achievement of Marxism, the Russian Revolution. Behind the Communists stood the 'prestige of experience'.[6] It would be some time before Labour moved on to the offensive and disputed that socialism had in fact been achieved in the Soviet Union: in the meantime their response was to accept the Revolution and emphasise its peculiarly Russian character. In effect they sought to throw a doctrinal *cordon sanitaire* around this dangerous new phenomenon.

The Russian Revolution, wrote MacDonald, 'is Russian. Its historical setting and parentage is Russian.'[7] And however reprehensible Bolshevik policies and methods might seem to British socialists, they were ultimately excused by this fact. MacDonald and Snowden in particular frequently drew attention to the extreme character of Russian Marxism and its departure from the spirit of the Second International. Snowden thought it a 'travesty of the teaching of Marx that he should be regarded today as the authority and support for the policy of violent revolutionary methods' pursued by the Communist International; and according to MacDonald, Communism was 'pre-Marxian' and 'pre-scientific' because it was guided by the same 'fanciful metaphysic and a barren logic' which 'Marx and Engels strove to eliminate from the Socialist movement and to supplant by scientific precision and objective accuracy'.[8] Nevertheless, 'if I were a Russian and lived in Russia, I would certainly be Bolshevist' was a commonplace of Labour literature in this period. This frequently involved the application of double standards – as in Laski's explanation of how 'what to the outsider seems savage cruelty' was justified in Russian circumstances[9] – but Labour Socialists were not bothered by such dual morality. Their point was that socialism could not be encompassed by a few abstract principles of universal validity: it must always reflect the particularities of its national context. 'Lenin and Trotsky had to face a Russian situation and not a British situation', MacDonald explained to an I.L.P.

audience; if they had a British Tsar and a disintegrating political order 'then they might go to Moscow for tips how to do it', but these conditions did not obtain. 'If we would only recognise this, nine-tenths of our troubles would disappear. Do not forget the old wise saying, "One man's meat is another man's poison."' [10] The great problem was that the Communists did not respect this relativism and sought to apply Russian methods to Britain: they had created an international movement which, said MacDonald at the 1920 Labour Party Conference, 'was a sort of mayfly created on the forcing ground of the Russian Revolution. It proposed to apply Russian conditions to international policy. Its whole justification was that Russian conditions could be and must be duplicated in France, in Italy and in England.' [11] The Communists had in fact jumped from the success of the Revolution in Russia to the 'ill-considered conclusion that Bolshevism ought to be adopted as a universal rule for Socialism'. They had made Moscow into a Socialist Vatican, 'issuing Bulls and Pronunciamentos on the Gospel according to St Lenin'. [12]

The chain of reasoning so far examined led to two distinct arguments whereby the Labour Socialists sought to turn the apparent disadvantage of Communist success abroad to its own advantage. The first was that Communism was peculiarly Russian and inapplicable to any other socialist movement. The second was that regardless of whether Communism applied to other countries than Russia, it certainly did not apply to Britain. The difference between the two arguments was never absolute, and books such as Norman Angell's *Must Britain Travel the Moscow Road?* (1926) used both, but the difference in emphasis is important. For while both arguments allowed the use of national stereotypes, the first more usually led to racial theories of the 'Asiatic mind', while the second was more conducive to discussion of the specific character of the British situation.

According to the first argument, Communism bore the indelible imprint of its Russian origins. This was sometimes argued within the context of the revived Second or Socialist International (in which the Labour leaders played a prominent role during the 1920s) and it was in this context that Kautsky's *Terrorism and Communism* (British edition, 1920) defined the grounds whereby Western socialism wedded itself to democratic principles. More frequently, the argument appealed to the popular image of Tsarist absolutism and its counterpart, small groups of bewhiskered and fanatical terrorists like Peter the Painter. Because it was 'evolved from Russian conditions, carried out by Russian

methods and adapted to the Russian psychology', Bolshevism was
tainted by the 'legacy of Tsardom'. 'Tsarism, the Black Hundred and
Siberia had bitten deep' into the 'souls and minds of the Bolsheviks';
'the violence, the more than occasional cruelty, the plotting, the
espionage, the suppression of free opinion, the indifference to truth –
these are Russian characteristics bred under despotism'. International
Communism was 'a product of Czarism and war mentality, and as
such we have nothing in common with it'.[13] The same prejudices could
also be dressed up in the pseudo-scientific garb of MacDonald's
positivist philosophy of social progress: thus democratic Britain had
advanced further along the path of progress than autocratic Russia,
and 'for a progressive movement here to try and copy Russian
methods, or create Russian conditions, is to go back upon our own
evolution'. Lenin could hardly be blamed for the backward state of his
society and MacDonald 'had never blamed him. But let them think of
the criminality of the men who came to ask them to create such a
condition of things in their own country.'[14] Finally, the argument also
lent itself to the use of crude racial stereotypes, as in Frank Hodges's
claim before the 1922 Labour Party Conference that Communism was
the product of 'the Asiatic mind'.[15]

The second argument, that Britain's particular circumstances were
unsuited to Marxism and Communism, was also susceptible to the
same crude appeal. 'Of all the Labour Movements of the world the
British was the best', boasted Frank Hodges in a not untypical piece of
Labour Podsnappery, for 'British democratic and working class forces
were making their contribution to world development when Russia was
in a hopeless stage of illiteracy and backwardness'.[16] Ironically, in their
own contemporary arguments with admirers of the Russian Revolution
the leaders of the German S.P.D. and of the French Socialist Party
made almost identical claims for the seniority of their own working
classes. Yet this argument was fundamentally a more serious one for
Marxists to answer. As Fenner Brockway reminded them, 'to model the
British Socialist Movement slavishly on the Russian pattern is a dis-
service both to Russia and Socialism. It is not Marxism to say that
Socialist tactics must in each country, whatever its historical circumstances and its present economic and political condition, follow the
same course.'[17] How then did Britain differ from Russia and other
centres of the international labour movement? What was it in Britain's
development that made Labour Socialism the appropriate ideology of
the movement here?

Labour gave a variety of answers to these questions. One common reply was that Britain was more advanced, both economically and politically. Britain was a mature capitalist society in which the working class constituted a majority of the population, and it was a constitutional democracy. There was 'no need to conquer political power. That the workers have already done.' 'In this country we have had our political revolution. . . .A Parliamentary election will give us all the power that Lenin had to get by a revolution.'[18] Thus it was contended that the Communist analysis of the capitalist state and its call for a dictatorship of the proletariat were not applicable here. Some critics of Communism even cited 'Marx's own conclusion that "England is the only country where the inevitable social revolution might be brought about entirely by peaceful means" '.[19] Underpinning such claims there was a general belief that socialism was the culmination of an orderly process of social progress, and thus that it would be achieved first in the country with the highest level of economic, political and cultural development. From such a perspective the very fact 'That a Marxist social revolution should have broken out in Russia at all was an anomaly',[20] which might have caused a reconsideration of Social Darwinist assumptions. But as an anomaly it did not induce Labour to reconsider its belief that Britain was leading the way to socialism.

Upon closer inspection most Labour arguments concerning the social and political character of Britain generally turned out to be not materialistic arguments but ones based on an abstract conception of the national character, a capitulation to the dominant images of the national identity. British workers had an ingrained attachment to constitutional methods; democracy was 'rooted in our national life by the tradition of seven centuries'. The great contrast between 'the English and Russian national characters' lay in the fact that revolution was 'alien to the British character'.[21] (Against such claims the populist tradition of Marxist history which was noted in chapter 5 is more readily intelligible.) One particular manifestation of this ill-defined national character was an aversion to theory, and Marxist theory especially – the same pragmatic temper that was so frequently attributed to William Morris to explain his alleged aversion to Marxism. G. D. H. Cole thought that 'The two things that most puzzle Continental Socialists about the British Labour Movement are its phlegmatic temperament and its seeming imperviousness to ideas', and this was generally accepted as a self-evident fact. The Labour Socialists might lament this 'British passion for inconsistency and lack of philosophy' which they encountered in their own missionary activities, but there it was.[22] The fact remained that Marxism made no appeal.

Many of these arguments were little more than chauvinism dressed up in respectable political clothing. Nevertheless, it is undeniable that men like Brailsford and Brockway were genuinely perplexed by the problem of Communism's applicability to Britain, and furthermore that the question is both real and significant. All British Marxists were extremely sensitive to the criticism described above, and so strongly did they feel on this issue that they devoted a considerable portion of their limited resources to the publication of explicit rejoinders: thus Harold Laski's *Communism* was answered by Ralph Fox's *In Defence of Communism*. This was a distinctly defensive posture for Marxists to adopt.

During the 1920s they used two main arguments. The first was that Lenin had developed Marxism not simply for Russian conditions but as a guide to the international labour movement: Leninism was the Marxism of the twentieth century. The second argument acknowledged the possibility that Britain might be different from Russia and sought to show how Leninism actually applied. Before examining these arguments, it should be noted that the unanimous acceptance of a Leninist Marxism in the 1920s constitutes a real watershed. Prior to 1917 British Marxism was a camp in which there were many tents, and in this it reflected the larger labour movement of which it was still an integral part. From 1918 this sense of plurality was lost both in the labour movement as a whole and in the Marxist fragment of it. An increasingly monolithic Labour Party thus confronted a Communist Party that took its lead, both organisationally and theoretically, from Moscow. There were a few individuals within the Marxist camp, as well as the minuscule S.P.G.B., who challenged the assumption that Leninism constituted a body of thought capable of guiding the British working class, but these dissidents were unable to develop any coherent alternative.[23] In the 1920s Marxism became identified with Communism and Communism with the Soviet Union, and these identities persist in the popular imagination to this day. Of course the situation changed in several respects in the next decade. A group of Trotskyists subjected the Soviet Union and the C.P.G.B. to a more systematic Marxist critique; John Middleton Murry and others began to develop a non-Leninist 'English Communism', whose chief characteristic was a humanist re-interpretation of historical materialism; scientists and philosophers such as John Macmurray, Hyman Levy and Joseph

Needham concurrently opened up a debate over dialectical materialism which also broke free of orthodox Soviet limitations; Marxism began to penetrate literature and other areas of the national culture; socialists such as Cole, Laski and Strachey adopted Marxism as a method of analysing class, state and politics. It is a striking fact that not one of the individuals named here had belonged to the Communist Party before 1930 and only two joined thereafter. In these and other hands Marxism was interpreted differently from the Leninist orthodoxy, but even then the inescapable fact of the Soviet Union and the attraction it exercised are of fundamental significance. The 1920s established that Leninism would be the point of Marxist reference.

It was suggested earlier that the impact of Leninism in Britain, while immediate and potent, was initially hampered by lack of information. The great majority of British Marxists certainly accepted that Lenin had provided 'the model for the builders of Socialism in other countries', and that 'The essence of Lenin's tactics. . .[is] applicable to every one of the modern capitalist–imperialist nations.'[24] Developing a sense of power and leading mass struggles towards a dictatorship of the proletariat were henceforth seen as the guiding objectives applicable to every workers' movement. But for several years Lenin was regarded as an innovator in tactics only: no one claimed for him any substantial theoretical originality, and insofar as his political tactics undercut the broader doctrinal assumptions of the Second International (including the B.S.P. and the S.L.P.) they were seen as purifying Marxism of unfortunate accretions rather than as original contributions in themselves. As late as 1923, therefore, J. T. Murphy could write that Lenin had merely restored 'the Marxism of Marx'. Marx's legacy had been 'crystallised and enriched by the experience and thought of the leaders of the Russian Revolution', but that was all. As Palme Dutt put it, Leninism was simply the 'realisation of Marxism' and neither departed from the master nor added to him. 'Leninism is social thinking in action. What Marx saw, Lenin achieved.'[25]

Leninism as a distinct theoretical corpus was thus born after the death of its founder in January 1924. His successors now insisted that he had done more than simply purify Marxism and apply it to the contemporary situation; he had established a new body of revolutionary doctrine – albeit one that lacked systematic structure because it was located in a large corpus of writings dealing with particular issues. The new claim was pitched highest by Stalin in his celebrated formula: 'Leninism is the Marxism of the epoch of imperialism and of the proletarian revolution. To be more precise: Leninism is the theory and the tactic of the proletarian revolution in general, and the theory and the tactic of the dictatorship of the proletariat in particular.' Stalin's formula became Communist orthodoxy within a few years, but essentially similar, if more moderate, elevations of the achievements of Lenin into the theoretical system of Leninism were produced during this period by Bukharin and other leading Bolsheviks. The earlier view that Lenin contributed a set of essentially tactical precepts and that Leninism was simply Marxism in action was now abandoned, and in 1925 the Communist International laid it down that 'the view that Marxism is only theory and Leninism is only practice is incorrect. Leninism is the theory and practice of Marxism in the period of imperialism, imperialist wars and proletarian revolutions. . .'[26]

The British Party immediately accepted the new formulation. Leninism, explained Andrew Rothstein at the end of 1924, 'is not *practical* Marxism, or *applied* Marxism'. For just as classical Marxism was the application of Marx's theory and practice to the problems of the second half of the nineteenth century, so 'Leninism is the application of Marxist theory and practice to the problems of the twentieth century'. Furthermore, it was 'not a Russian product, but the product of a whole generation of experience in the International Labour Movement' which Lenin had distilled.[27] The British Party was rebuked from time to time for its neglect and ignorance of the actual content of Leninism, but it could not be accused of failure to acknowledge his importance.

We can thus see that the Communist doctrine of Marxism–Leninism represented an *a priori* answer to Labour claims that the Moscow Road was irrelevant to Britain. It went roughly as follows: there is no genuine Marxism today which is not Leninism; Leninism is the Marxism of the current epoch of imperialism and proletarian revolution; therefore Leninism provides the blueprint for British socialists. Valentino Gerrantana has observed that the reduction of Lenin's thought to a systematic theory of such narrow dimensions involves a complete inversion of his own approach, since it obliterated the oscillations, approximations, mistakes and corrections essential to the development of his ideas, and celebrated the very qualities they so conspicuously lacked – consistency and universality.[28] Furthermore, this canonisation of Lenin's legacy lent itself to the struggle between his heirs, for it could be used as an infallible source of authority in the ensuing debates. Here too the creators of Leninism inverted Lenin's own practice. From 1917 to the second half of 1919 Lenin seemed to have expected Western European revolutionaries to win power and resume the international leadership which befitted their countries' more advanced development; and it was only after the reverses in Hungary, Germany and elsewhere that he became convinced of the need to provide a greater degree of guidance. In writings of this period such as *'Left Wing' Communism*, he explored this new belief that the Russian experience could be applied to the West. Yet even in his most hectoring moments, he retained a sense of caution and uncertainty: he was quite sure that certain aproaches were wrong but much less sure that his own recommendations were right, and this openness was apparent at the Second Congress of the Communist International in 1920. It was quite permissible to disagree with Lenin, and he went out of his way to welcome the disagreements of the Indian newcomer M. N. Roy and to rebuke his own acolytes who reacted with hostility to Roy.[29] In his dealings with the British delegates at the Congress, Lenin scrupulously avoided making use of his own authority and spent long hours in patient discussion – he thought it far more important to convince them of the efficacy of a style of Communist politics than to impose this or that decision upon them, for unless they shared an appreciation of the reasons for following a particular course of action, they would be incapable of implementing it properly. This is not to deny that the lessons were ill-digested, nor that they were *lessons*, with Lenin the teacher and Gallacher, Murphy and others the pupils; but it does contrast with subsequent relations between King Street and Moscow. By the second half of the 1920s it is increasingly clear that policies were being imposed on the British Party by the Executive of the Communist International, and that the British acceptance was premised on their prior acceptance of Leninism as an adaptable set of validating principles. And by 1930 there was an additional twist. Just as Lenin had developed and extended the work of Marx and Engels, so his 'unchallenged successor in the field of both theory and practice' was Stalin.[30]

It is hardly surprising that this *a priori* argument that Leninism was applicable to all countries in the imperialist epoch made little impression on the wider British labour movement, for it simply failed to address itself to the case made out by Labour spokesmen for the special character of Britain. It was therefore apparent that some more specific response to the Labour case was required – Marxists would have to say less about the architect of the Moscow Road and more about the native terrain over which it must pass.

In doing so they revealed their deep uncertainty. First, it remained unclear in contemporary British accounts whether Lenin himself meant Russian methods to apply to Britain. While the Executive of the Communist International, in its reply to the I.L.P., insisted that Britain was definitely suited to Communist methods, they also found it 'necessary to admit theoretically the possibility of variations of form' in future revolutions.[31] The question 'which Russian institutions and practices apply to Britain?' exercised all British socialists who visited Russia, but every visitor who spoke to Lenin brought back a different report. According to one, Lenin said that 'the Soviet system is the best, and that the English workers and agricultural labourers would accept it if they knew it'. On the other hand, Leslie Haden-Guest, the physician and Labour politician, reported him as saying, 'I am a pupil of English Socialism. It would be childish to say that all our institutions must be copied. The Left Communists in England are making blunders because they are too much copying the first forms of the revolution in Russia.' Lansbury described Lenin as more cautious, doubting that Britain would achieve a revolution without resort to Russian methods, but conceding that 'If in England you are able to do this, well and good.' Yet Bertrand Russell claimed that when he 'suggested that whatever is possible in England can be achieved without bloodshed', Lenin 'waved aside the suggestion as fantastic' (an unusual experience for Russell); and Arthur Ransome understood Lenin to say that the Soviets 'must be the instruments of revolution everywhere'. These early eye-witness reports clearly reflected ideological predispositions and shed little light on the problem – but they were widely read and much quoted in the immediate post-war years.[32]

The question of Lenin's understanding of British politics is a vexed one. He had of course lived in London for a brief period at the turn of the century and kept contact with some leading members of the B.S.P. (then, of course, the S.D.F.). He could read English and had translated the Webbs' history of trade unionism; he maintained the same level of interest in British affairs as he did in other vital centres of world politics; he read occasional British newspapers and eagerly sought out news from visitors amidst his onerous commitments; and he wrote sufficient material on Britain to make up a large volume. On the other hand there are numerous mistakes of detail and other lacunae in his knowledge, and after 1914 this fault was exacerbated by difficulties of communication at a time when many new developments occurred. It has been argued that his role in the formation of the British Communist Party was vitiated by the fact that he relied heavily on Theodore Rothstein and other members of the B.S.P., who were out of touch with these developments, and did not listen to leading militants such as John Maclean, Sylvia Pankhurst and the principal shop stewards.[33] But Lenin's writings during 1919 do not support this argument. Far from revealing an underestimation of the immediate revolutionary possibilities, they suggest that he overestimated the significance of Maclean, Pankhurst and the shop stewards, and exaggerated the radicalism of the working class in general. His intervention during 1920, when the Communist Party was finally formed, reflects a justified revision of his earlier optimism and an appreciation that the tide had already turned. Nor were his specific recommendations of momentous effect. His urging the formation of a new united revolutionary party did not require any detailed knowledge of the British left – merely an appreciation that the existing Marxist groups were small, sectarian and out of touch with the overwhelming majority of the working class (though valid criticism can be levelled at the survival of these sectarian antagonisms in the early leadership of the Party). His insistence that this new party should not abstain from parliamentary activity reflected the undeniable fact that parliamentary government showed no signs of disappearing and that it offered the left a potential platform they could not afford to ignore. And his counsel that the Communist Party should apply to affiliate to the Labour Party may have involved a misapprehension of the dominant trend of Labour development: yet this problem of Labour's increasing monopoly of working-class politics was inescapable and the Communist Party's prospects were in no sense jeopardised by their unsuccessful application.

Moscow gold and orders from the Communist International were of secondary importance in the establishment of the Communist Party of Great Britain and its reorientation of British Marxism. The debates of 1919 and 1920, which were conducted in the Marxist press, at the founding conferences of the Communist Party, and in local groups up and down the country, demonstrate that those concerned made up their own minds according to how they assessed the situation. The fact of the Russian Revolution and Lenin's consequent prestige were of fundamental significance in determining the new Party's development, but allow and it only afterwards turned into formal chains of command. this influence was far more natural than the critics of Communism

The initial transformation of British Marxism revolved around such intangibles as the new style and tone of political activity, dropping its preoccupation with education and propaganda for a much clearer sense of power and a commitment to constant and unremitting struggle. In that they were now playing for much higher stakes, this major re-orientation may indeed have served to isolate Marxists from other sections of the labour movement. More than any other factor, it was the Communists' premature attempt to construct a vanguard party by a short-cut, by the creation of 'fractions' and 'nuclei' designed to transform influence into control, that estranged Labour sympathisers. Lenin must share the blame for this, for he was singularly unappreciative of the British proletariat's deep attachment to national and democratic forms.

Underlying this new Communist struggle for leadership of the working class there was an unfortunate temptation to apply the Russian experience to the British situation, for the Moscow Road seemed particularly attractive in the period immediately following the Russian Revolution. Sometimes it appeared that Bolshevism applied to Britain because the differences from the Russian situation were so trivial that they could be ignored. Under the heading 'Learn to Speak Russian', the B.S.P. swept aside the argument that Britain was different because it possessed a democratic constitution: the constitution was a 'farce'; parliament consisted of '630 capitalists and their hangers-on out of 670 members'; the working class could only triumph by asserting its will 'in Russian accents'. Likewise Arthur MacManus scorned 'the foolishness of the idea that this country was different because it had a constitutional democracy behind it'; Communists took no regard of 'such capitalist symbols as the Union Jack'.[34] A more sophisticated version of the same approach allowed that there were British peculiarities, but subjected them to the universal laws of capitalism: 'The truth is, every country can claim exemption from the operation of social and historical forces on the plea of "peculiarities", since every country is "peculiar", but underlying all peculiarities are the same social factors – modern industry, capitalism, proletariat, and, now, world war – which are bound to produce the same effects.' Thus Communists insisted that 'there is no British Marxism'. 'There is no peculiar "British" way of avoiding the revolutionary struggle, there cannot be such a way.' The British working class must 'learn how to follow on the Moscow road to the conquest of power'.[35]

Such uncompromising insistence on the Moscow Road was far from universal. Marxists outside the Communist Party, and especially those associated with the Plebs League, thought that the lessons of the Russian Revolution had always to be translated 'into the terms of our own country's stage of development. It needs to be emphasised that not every word that proceeds out of the mouth of Lenin is hall-marked wisdom. One can appreciate his prophetic insight in general and yet maintain a critical attitude regarding details.'[36] And Communists could see that the British revolution would not be 'simply a recapitulation of the Russian Revolution' but would assume its own form. Mirsky and others reminded them that Lenin warned British readers of '*Left Wing*' *Communism* that 'it would be a mistake to deduce from the general applicability of Russian methods that Russia will always remain the model of Communist achievement'; and the Party stipulated that its own strategy arose 'from our close and careful analysis of the situation in Great Britain'.[37] Nor was this hollow rhetoric. Britain received the particular attention of a section of the Communist International, and the research section headed by Eugen Varga spent a considerable proportion of its time analysing changes in the British economy. There was also a keen native interest in the specific character of British capitalism, and contributions to the debate over the causes and tempo of its decline in the world economy demonstrated an impressive capacity for independent analysis. Nevertheless, this interest in British circumstances was always controlled by prior assumptions about the applicability of the system called Leninism.

What conclusions did Marxists reach about Britain? First, that it was an advanced, though declining, capitalist nation with a high degree of centralisation and trustification of industry and banking, and a large, organised proletariat. All these characteristics made it ripe for immediate 'socialist ownership and control'. Secondly, however, Britain had achieved a level of relative prosperity and had evolved a particularly tenacious political culture of bourgeois democracy, and these characteristics delayed the revolution, for they made Marxism seem irrelevant or unattractive to the working class.[38] To this extent British Marxists accepted the contention that Britain was peculiar – though they never paid the same degree of attention to Britain's peculiarity as did their American counterparts to 'American exceptionalism',[39] and they always identified the pecularities in terms of European stereotypes. As Trotsky wrote in *Where Is Britain Going?*, Marxists 'devoted great attention to the oddity of the British development. But we find the explanation of this oddity in objective conditions, in the structure of society and its changes.' Accordingly, they explained the non-revolutionary character as 'not something eternally British', but rooted in material reality.[40] However, the very terms of discussion prejudged British circumstances as abnormal historical accretions to be sloughed off so that the classical historical model could be followed.

Marxists devoted most attention to the British aversion to theory. This was thought to be a distinctly British obstacle to the acceptance of Marxism – or, rather, a distinctly English one, since the Celts were more receptive. As Marx and Engels had done before them, British Marxists sometimes represented this to be a national trait: it was 'the bluff common sense of a "nation of shopkeepers" to hold philosophies and broad generalisations in contempt'. Yet once again, English empiricism was not an inevitable and ineradicable defect, for it was engendered by the 'objective conditions' of prosperous security and progress. As the Scot Tom Bell put it, 'The excuse that we are not theoreticians has been insidiously spread abroad by "Little Englander" Socialists who are more bent on stifling Marxist thought.'[41] Further, because the objective conditions based on world supremacy which encouraged the disregard for theory were now disappearing, so it was repeatedly announced that Marxism would soon strike root in British soil.

This determinist conclusion has comforted successive generations that their labours will not always be in vain, and yet the Marxists of the 1920s were particularly aware of their own failings. They partly admitted the justice of the criticism that they had failed to keep their theory abreast of British conditions and adapt it to the British situation. British Marxism was derivative – 'Obsessed by the struggle for existence, battling against enormous obstacles, our Party has so far produced no original work'; instead it relied 'exclusively upon our classics, from Marx to Labriola, and, their brilliancy notwithstanding, they are insufficient for our present needs'. As a result, the British labour movement still derived its ideas from 'bourgeois sources' such as Keynes, Russell, Angell, Cole, Brailsford and Hobson, unlike continental movements which at least worked from an autonomous body of theory.[42] The same weakness was apparent in the universities. Maurice Dobb observed that Marxism had failed to stir 'the waters of academic discussion in Oxford, Cambridge, or London, as it did in Berlin, Vienna, Rome and Petersburg. It called forth no grand refutations, placed no appreciable imprint on intellectual thought, for the most part was noticed scarcely enough to be understood.' Hence the backward state of British socialism corresponded to the backwardness and insularity of the national culture, and could only be overcome by challenging the whole of that culture. 'We sorely need a real creative school of British Marxism – not a hole-in-the-corner affair, but a live body of critical, creative, first-rate minds who understand the present and are organically part of the active working-class movement.'[43] It is central to my interpretation of British Marxism in the 1920s that it was so cut off from the rest of society. Even today, when Marxism has struck root in the universities and other centres of intellectual life, Dobb's call for creative, critical first-rate minds with an organic relationship to the labour movement is still unrealised. Small wonder then that in the 1920s the handful of Marxists with real theoretical aptitude were occupied in more immediate tasks which left them little opportunity to spell out their doctrine, adapt it to national conditions and contest the cultural ramifications of the existing order.

Isolation cuts both ways. On the one hand, it hinders the efforts of the isolated party to make an impact on the majority; on the other hand, the isolated party is protected from forces which might otherwise swamp it – and it might well be the case in the 1920s that the benefits of cultural isolation temporarily outweighed the costs. But if Marxism is ever to fulfil its own objectives it must enter into everyday life, and in this country it still functions in intellectual circles as either a critique or an exegetical elaboration; only in rare instances is it practised in the full sense of the term. This self-conscious isolation of Marxism from the national mainstream remains a contemporary problem, and until it is solved there can be no real British Marxism.

Conclusion

The historian must work within certain restrictions and cannot soften their consequences. Hence while my chronological limits possess a limited validity in that they serve to mark off a distinct period in the history of Marxism in this country, it is undeniable that powerful trends run through my tidy divisions. In the long run such trends as the decline of industries such as mining, the transformation of others such as engineering, and the development of new industries altogether, or the consolidation of an increasingly monolithic Labour Party as the dominant form of working-class politics, exercised a far greater effect on Marxism than any decisions taken in King Street. Equally evident is the rhythm of national and local events which cut across my seventeen years – events such as the defeats inflicted on industrial militancy in 1921, the effects of 1926 on mining areas, or those of the debacle of 1931 on the labour movement as a whole. I am conscious also of themes which might have been woven into my account but which I have not been able to incorporate. The whole question of Marxist aesthetics and cultural attitudes before the much better-known developments of the 1930s is left untouched. An examination of Marxist analyses of sexual politics and of the closely related question of the position of women within the Marxist movement would repay attention. A preliminary investigation of British Marxists' understandings of imperialism had to be excluded also.[1]

The most important limitation concerns the mode of explanation employed within my study. Insofar as I am dealing with the history of ideas, it is difficult to resist the characteristics of that genre, which sees as its dynamics filiation, adaptation and change along internal lines of development. In addition, and like so many studies of Marxism, there is a persistent sense of orthodoxy against which the deviations can be measured and explained. I have tried to hold both these tendencies in check. But in so doing I am conscious of having sometimes gone to the other extreme, namely depicting the doctrines as the outcome of deep and intractable forces in British society. The problem with this extreme determinist position is that it explains both too much and too little: too much because it denies the actual human agency of the individuals concerned, too little because such explanation remains extremely schematic. The aspect of this study in greatest need of elaboration is that which holds together the important changes that occurred between 1917 and 1933 in the social, political and economic basis of British Marxism, and the specific ideological changes through which these changes were expressed. In short, something needs to be inserted between the first four chapters and the last six which can vitalise the doctrinal narratives.

This can be clarified by recapitulating my central argument. I have suggested that prior to 1917 Marxism in this country was preached by bands of enthusiasts who were largely isolated from the great mass of the British working class, and that this was manifested above all in the absence of a viable political strategy. Under the combined influence of the Russian Revolution and domestic events, these enthusiasts reconstructed their Marxism so that a distinct type of working-class Marxist came to enjoy a relationship with the rest of his class that was no longer an external one and in some instances can be regarded as organic. By 1921, however, the conditions that could support a sustained political initiative were eclipsed by the economic slump and the defeat of leading industrial militants. Thereafter the Marxists were constrained by the predominantly defensive posture of the organised labour movement and the increasing ideological grip of Labour Socialism. Furthermore, the initial transformation of British Marxism was incomplete since its broader theory lagged behind the political reorientation. Subsequent theoretical development occurred in less propitious circumstances and under the aegis of party discipline, so that even those changes which may be regarded as an improvement in terms of formal theory were often ill-digested and did not effect a commensurate advance in understanding. The weakness of the British Communist Party after the General Strike made it all the more vulnerable to the imposition of doctrine from above at a time when its political and industrial influence declined even further; and Marxism had only begun to recover from this decline in 1933. Finally, I have drawn attention to the decline of the working-class Marxist intellectuals, who lost their positions of ideological leadership of the Marxist movement and were increasingly marginalised in the labour movement at large.

One difficulty with this argument is that its different levels of explanation – ideology, politics and society – are too loosely assimilated. It relates the initial ideological advance to politics, and invokes the larger social process as well to explain the subsequent decline. What I have found particularly difficult to convey is that these elements were not random companions: they operated together throughout the period, for the development of British Marxism involved a constant interaction of circumstances and perceptions. Not even the most hard-headed of pragmatic trade unionists could escape his ideological preconceptions; and, equally, not even the most doctrinaire of Marxist purists ever made a decision on purely theoretical considerations. This point can be driven home by reference to the S.L.P.'s reception of Bolshevik doctrine and its attitude to the establishment of the Communist Party. As has been shown, the S.L.P. construed the Russian Revolution as a vindication of its own principles and was reluctant to merge itself into a united Communist Party, particularly one that applied for affiliation to the Labour Party. In previous writings on this subject, attention has been focused on the group of S.L.P. leaders who broke with their doctrinaire comrades, and discussion is largely taken up with the theoretical merits of their argument: Klugmann commends the national group who joined the Communist Party, Challinor and Kendall defend the validity of the 'first British Bolsheviks' who remained true to the S.L.P. Yet examination of a particular S.L.P. branch in the Vale of Leven reveals that the lengthy and complex national debate was mediated by a number of other factors. The issue was resolved principally along the lines of age and temperament. The older members are remembered by their younger colleagues as 'bitter as hell', 'dogmatic and sectarian' and 'never stuck for a virulent word', and their inflexible orthodoxy is suggested by public statements that the workers could achieve nothing before the final collapse of capitalism – this at a time when the Vale of Leven was in greater ferment than it had been since the decline of Chartism.[2] The younger members, on the other hand, had grown up in the war years and joined the S.L.P. simply because it was the only revolutionary organisation in the area. While the older members were considering the shortcomings of the new Communist Party, the younger ones simply pre-empted the decision and set up the Communist branch. Within two years they led the labour movement to victory in the local government elections. There were S.L.P. branches elsewhere where the outcome was quite different, but this is a good example of the way in which social and political circumstances interacted with doctrinal issues, and it should warn against any narrow treatment of ideology.

The weakest link in my argument is that which attempts to locate the long-term decline in the autodidact tradition. Even though the tradition did not cease abruptly, and continues to this day, it is indisputable that there was a contraction of the processes whereby home study and the labour colleges supported an intellectual culture quite distinct from that of the national intelligentsia. The diminution of interest in the rich collections of miners' institute libraries, their dismemberment, and the final conversion of their buildings to cinema and bingo were an all too typical chain of events. The problem is to explain this decline. The task may be divided into two parts, the first being the absolute decline in the ranks of the autodidacts, and the second being their loss of intellectual confidence coupled with their relative decline in the Marxist movement. The first aspect is related closely to the decline of other forms of cultural and intellectual activity, and I find it of some comfort that such acute commentators as Richard Hoggart and Raymond Williams have experienced similar difficulty in accounting for the general transformation. It is easy enough to point to indices of change – the changes in work processes which have largely obliterated that stratum of skilled workers who nourished their own forms of knowledge, the expansion of new media which erode autonomous forms of leisure, the creation of a national system of secondary education disseminating a syllabus consonant with the dominant national culture, and so on – but such factors beg as many questions as they answer. It would be a valuable project of research to take a group of working-class autodidacts at the turn of the century and study the impact of changes in the social and cultural environment over the ensuing half-century (for example, one might trace changes in their understanding of political economy brought about by a W.E.A. class in economics). In the absence of this sort of investigation which might confirm my highly tentative hypotheses, I have relied to a greater degree on the second aspect of the problem, namely the declining role of working-class intellectuals in Marxists ranks. It should be emphasised again that this was a matter of degree. There were working-class Marxists, both inside and outside the Communist Party, who remained active after 1933, and the Communist Party has maintained to this day a tradition of working-class leadership. What altered was the strategic importance of the working-class intellectuals in the pivotal theoretical debates. Bell, Campbell, Murphy and Paul had all been to the fore in the 1920s. By the 1930s there was an increasing demarcation of the role of the theorist from that of the organiser, and the principal theorists (notably

Palme Dutt) were those university-trained intellectuals who were fully conversant with Soviet Marxism. And in an analogous fashion, the working-class Marxists who were not Communists but who were active in the labour colleges and the Labour left were also marginalised in the Labour Party of the 1930s, yielding their places up to Sir Stafford Cripps and the patricians of the Socialist League. The fact that men and women who had grown up among the working class and learnt their Marxism from within that class were unable to provide theoretical leadership represents a considerable loss. It is a principal reason why Marxism lost its organic relation to some sections of the British labour movement, and came to be generally perceived as an implanted or alien doctrine.

Yet the process whereby the autodidacts were displaced from positions of theoretical authority was one of doctrinal rectification. In other words, the decline of working-class Marxism reflected an advance in Marxist doctrine. After 1917 the old working-class Marxist traditions of historical materialism, dialectics, economics and the understanding of politics alike were all superseded. Initially, until the favourable circumstances ended in the mid-1920s, this process of rectification can be regarded as one of self-criticism. Leninism was a goad to doctrinal revision, certainly, both as an example and as a doctrine; but the essential dynamic was the rapid advance of the British labour movement itself. After the General Strike the movement was in retreat and the changes were effected in much less favourable circumstances. The political authority of Moscow and its privileged position as the guardian of Marxist–Leninist orthodoxy were increasingly relied upon as a substitute for indigenous understanding and debate. This is the crucial paradox with which I have grappled, and the greater part of my attention has been devoted to investigating the significance of these doctrinal innovations. I hope that this investigation will not be construed as an end in itself, for it can be understood only in relation to the social and political circumstances I have endeavoured to identify.

Notes

ABBREVIATIONS

BSSLH *Bulletin of the Society for the Study of Labour History*

CHP Coalfield History Project: a collection of oral history under the auspices of the University College of Swansea and the Social Science Research Council, whose transcripts are held in the South Wales Miners' Library, Swansea

DLB *Dictionary of Labour Biography*, 4 vols. (London, 1972–)

MML Marx Memorial Library, 37a Clerkenwell Green

NCCL Records of the National Council of Labour Colleges: deposited by its Secretary, Mr J. P. M. Millar, in the National Library of Scotland, Edinburgh

SWML South Wales Miners' Library, 50 Sketty Road, Swansea

INTRODUCTION

1 Letter dated 21 May 1918, quoted by Kenneth O. Morgan, *Keir Hardie* (London, 1975), p. 40.

2 London, 1937; new edn East Ardsley, Yorkshire, 1972.

3 See the statistical table in Henry Pelling, *A History of British Trade Unionism*, 3rd edn (Harmondsworth, 1976), p. 294; B. R. Mitchell in collaboration with Phyllis Deane, *Abstract of British Historical Statistics* (Cambridge, 1962), p. 345.

4 Mitchell and Deane, p. 67; Sidney Pollard, *The Development of the British Economy 1914–1967* (London, 1969), p. 229.

5 Mitchell and Deane, pp. 116–17; Agatha Chapman assisted by Rose Knight, *Wages and Salaries in the United Kingdom 1920–1938* (Cambridge, 1953), p. 68.

6 Mitchell and Deane, pp. 180–3; Chapman, p. 99.

7 Pollard, p. 115.

8 Mitchell and Deane, pp. 132–3; Chapman, p. 98.

9 Mitchell and Deane, p. 117; Chapman, p. 98.

10 Mitchell and Deane, pp. 62–3; Chapman, p. 98.

11 Taken from E. H. Hunt, *Regional Wage Variations in Britain 1850–1914* (Oxford, 1973), pp. 150, 165, 171, 175.

12 The literature on the subject is listed and discussed in B. W. E. Alford, *Depression and Recovery? British Economic Growth 1918–1939* (London, 1972).

13 Sean Glynn and John Oxborrow, *Interwar Britain. A Social and Economic History* (London, 1976), p. 153. See C. H. Lee, *Regional Economic Growth in the United Kingdom since the 1880s* (London, 1971).

14 See the table in Sidney Webb and Beatrice Webb, *The History of Trade Unionism, 1666–1920* (London, 1920), pp. 741–3.

15 *Men Without Work. A Report Made to the Pilgrim Trust* (Cambridge, 1938).

16 For fuller accounts of the trade unions and the Labour Party during the period see Henry Pelling, *A History of British Trade Unionism* and *A Short History of the Labour Party*, 5th edn (London, 1976).

17 Mitchell and Deane, p. 345.

18 See Martin Jacques, 'Consequences of the General Strike' in Jeffrey Skelley (ed.), *The General Strike, 1926* (London, 1976), pp. 375–404. For contrary views see H. A. Clegg, 'Some Consequences of the General Strike', *Transactions of the Manchester Statistical Society* (1954), 1–29; and G. A. Phillips, *The General Strike: The Politics of Industrial Conflict* (London, 1976).

19 Jacques, p. 398.

CHAPTER 1. THE SOCIAL AND POLITICAL BASIS OF MARXISM

1 The chief accounts of these two organisations are Raymond Challinor, *The Origins of British Bolshevism* (London, 1977); D. M. Chewter, 'The History of the Socialist Labour Party of Great Britain from 1902–1921, with Special Reference to the Development of its Ideas', unpublished B.Litt. thesis (Oxford, 1965); Henry Collins, 'The Marxism of the Social Democratic Federation' in Asa Briggs and John Saville (eds.), *Essays in Labour History 1886–1923* (London, 1971), pp. 47–69; Walter Kendall, *The Revolutionary Movement in Britain 1900–1921. The Origins of British Communism* (London, 1969); Chushichi Tsuzuki, *H. M. Hyndman and British Socialism* (Oxford, 1961); Helen R. Vernon, 'The Socialist Labour Party and the Working Class Movement on the Clyde, 1903–1921', unpublished M.Phil. thesis (Leeds, 1967).

2 P. A. Watmough, 'The Membership of the Social Democratic Federation, 1885–1902', *BSSLH* 34 (Spring 1977), 35–40.

3 Leonard Hall in *B.S.P. Conference Report 1912*, p. 16.

4 *Further Reminiscences* (London, 1912), p. 459.

5 Collins, pp. 57–61. Jackson, manuscript autobiography, pp. 249–50. An incomplete version of the first part was published as *Solo Trumpet. Some Memories of Socialist Agitation and Propaganda* (London, 1953), and the full manuscript is in the possession of his daughter, Mrs Vivien Morton.

6 *Edinburgh Evening News*, 23 August 1904; quoted in Chewter, p. 45.

7 P. Henderson (ed.), *The Letters of William Morris to his Family and Friends* (London, 1950), pp. 348–9: quoted and discussed in Paul Thompson, *Socialists, Liberals and Labour. The Struggle for London 1885–1914* (London, 1967), pp. 124–5.

8 See Bob Holton, *British Syndicalism 1900–1914. Myths and Realities* (London, 1976).

9 Will McLaine in *B.S.P. Conference Report 1918*, p. 20. See also McLaine's *Trade Unionism at the Cross Roads* (London, 1917), pp. 14–15.

10 Fred Shaw in *B.S.P. Conference Report 1918*, p. 20.

11 James Hinton, *The First Shop Stewards' Movement* (London, 1973). Monds, 'Workers' Control and the Historians: A New Economism', *New Left Review* 97 (1977), 81–100; Hinton replies in the same issue.

12 The best accounts of these movements can be found in W. W. Craik, *The Central Labour College, 1909–1929. A Chapter in the History of Adult Working-Class Education* (London, 1964); S. T. Glass, *The Responsible Society. The Ideas of the English Guild Socialist* (London, 1966); Lucia Jones, 'Sylvia Pankhurst and the Workers' Socialist Federation – The Red Twilight; 1918–1924', unpublished M.A. thesis (Warwick, 1972); Kendall; and M. G. Woodhouse, 'Rank-and-File Movements Among the Miners of South Wales, 1910–26', unpublished D.Phil thesis (Oxford, 1970).

13 J. L. Williams, interviewed by David Egan, 24 April 1973: CHP.

14 Jackson manuscript, p. 262: quoted in Vivien Morton and John Saville, 'T. A. Jackson', *DLB*, vol. 4, p. 103.

15 Henry Pelling, *Popular Politics and Society in Late Victorian Britain* (London, 1968), pp. 1–18, 62–81.

16 See particularly J. T. Murphy, *The Workers' Committee. An Outline of its Principles and Structure* (Sheffield, 1917); W. Gallacher and J. R. Campbell, *Direct Action. An Outline of Workshop and Social Organisation* (Glasgow, 1919).

17 Hinton, p. 307.

18 *Plebs* IX, 219; Eden Paul and Cedar Paul, *Creative Revolution. A Study of Communist Ergatocracy* (London, 1920), p. 137.

19 Will McLaine, *The Evolution of Industry* (London, 1918), p. 30.

20 M. E. Quelch, *Call*, 14 February 1918.

21 Open letter to the Paisley branch of the S.L.P., published in *Forward* and *Worker*, 6 March 1920; *Communist Review* I (November 1921), 7.

22 Arthur MacManus, reported in *Labour Leader*, 1 September 1921. This exploration of the political reorientation of British Marxism is taken further in my 'Marxism in Britain, 1917–1933', unpublished Ph.D. thesis (Cambridge, 1975), pp. 10–24.

23 For a history of the S.P.G.B. see Robert Barltrop, *The Monument. The Story of the Socialist Party of Great Britain* (London, 1975).

24 The minutes of the S.D.F. executive are held in the National Library of Scotland, Acc. 5641 (2). See generally H. W. Lee and E. Archbold, *Social Democracy in Britain. Fifty Years of the Socialist Movement* (London, 1935), pp. 236 et seq.

25 This emerges from Reg Groves, *The Balham Group. How British Trotskyism Began* (London, 1974), and I commented accordingly in my review in the *Bulletin of the Conference of Socialist Economists* IV, 2 (June 1975).

26 The best accounts of the C.P.G.B. up to 1933 are James Hinton and Richard Hyman, *Trade Unions and Revolution: The Industrial Politics of the Early British Communist Party* (London, 1975); James Klugmann, *History of the Communist Party of Great Britain* (2 vols., London, 1968–9); L. J. Macfarlane, *The British Communist Party. Its Origin and Development until 1929*

(London, 1966); and Henry Pelling, *The British Communist Party: A Historical Profile* (London, 1958).

27 *Communist Papers. Documents Selected from Those Obtained on the Arrest of the Communist Leaders on the 14th and 21st October 1925*, Cmd. 2682 (London, 1926), pp. 70–1.

28 See William J. Fishman, *East End Jewish Radicals 1875–1914* (London, 1975) and E. Silberner, 'British Socialism and the Jews', *Historia Judaica* XIV (1952), 27–52.

29 After the 1930s see Kenneth Newton, *The Sociology of British Communism* (London, 1969).

30 *Communist Review*, n.s., III (September 1931), 378; IV (December 1932), 577–9.

31 This emerges from studies of individual industries in Roderick Martin, *Communism and the British Trade Unions 1924–1933. A Study of the National Minority Movement* (Oxford, 1969).

32 For Birmingham see John Strachey's letter to Palme Dutt, dated 24 December 1931, quoted in Hugh Thomas, *John Strachey* (London, 1973), p. 114. Mardy is discussed below.

33 For example, Paul Carter and Carol Carter, *Kilsyth Miners in the 1926 General Strike* (London, 1975), and John McLean, *The 1926 General Strike in Lanarkshire* (London, 1976), both produced by the History Group of the C.P.G.B.

34 F. W. S. Craig, *British Parliamentary Election Results, 1918–1968* (Glasgow, 1969).

35 For Sheffield I have relied on information from Bill Moore, a veteran Sheffield Communist, and Nellie Connole, *Leaven of Life: The Story of George Henry Fletcher* (London, 1961), esp. p. 163. For Maestag see Idris Cox in *Llafur* 2, 2 (1977), 18; and CHP. For earlier in the decade see Ross McKibbin, *The Evolution of the Labour Party 1910–1924* (Oxford, 1974), pp. 191–204.

36 There is an excellent life of Shaw in *DLB*, vol. 4.

37 John H. Goldthorpe, David Lockwood et al., *The Affluent Worker*, 3 vols. (Cambridge, 1968–9); David Lockwood, 'Sources of Variation in Working Class Images of Society', *Sociological Review*, n.s., 14 (1966), 249–67.

38 R. L. Davis and Jim Cousins, 'The "New Working Class" and the Old' in M. Bulmer (ed.), *Working Class Images of Society* (London, 1975), esp. pp. 198–202.

39 John Westergaard and Henrietta Resler, *Class in a Capitalist Society. A Study of Contemporary Britain* (Harmondsworth, 1975), pp. 394–5.

40 *The Classic Slum. Salford Life in the First Quarter of the Century* (Harmondsworth, 1973), p. 177.

41 *A Man's Life*, 2nd edn (London, 1944), p. 107.

42 I have drawn heavily on David Smith's account of Mardy in 'The Re-Building of the South Wales Miners' Federation, 1927–39: A Trade Union in its Society', unpublished Ph.D. thesis (Swansea, 1976), esp. pp. 141–85. Some other useful sources are E. D. Lewis, *The Rhondda Valleys* (London, 1959); *The Second Industrial Survey of South Wales*, prepared by H. A. Marquand and others (Cardiff, 1937); Arthur Horner, *Incorrigible Rebel* (London, 1960); the extensive transcribed interviews with residents of

Mardy which are part of the CHP; and the novels of Lewis Jones, *Cwmardy* (London, 1937) and *We Live* (London, 1939). The minutes of the Mardy Lodge are deposited in the SWML.

43 Illustrated and discussed by Philip N. Jones, *Colliery Settlement in the South Wales Coalfield 1850 to 1926* (Hull, 1969).

44 Will Picton, a leading Communist in Mardy between the wars: recorded at a Weekend School to commemorate the General Strike and published in *Llafur* 2, 2 (Spring 1977), 24.

45 The main sources for this account are Margaret S. Dilke and A. A. Templeton (eds.), *The County of Dumbarton*, Third Statistical Account of Scotland (Glasgow, 1959), pp. 189–200; Paul Carter, 'The West of Scotland' in Skelley, *The General Strike*, pp. 111–39; local government records; recorded interviews with residents held by John Foster, University of Strathclyde, and supplemented by my own interviews and correspondence. Some minutes of the Trades and Labour Council are held by Mrs Anne McGowan of Balloch.

46 *Lennox Herald*, 14 December 1918.

47 The description of Hugh McIntyre, who joined the S.L.P. in 1919 and was a foundation member of the Communist Party in the Vale: interviewed by John Foster, 22 November 1974.

CHAPTER 2. MARXISM AND LABOUR SOCIALISM

1 A Phase in the Social History of Socialism, c. 1885–1895', *BSSLH* 22 (Spring 1971), 7. See also Yeo, 'A New Life: The Religion of Socialism in Britain, 1883–1896', *History Workshop* 4 (Autumn 1977).

2 Quoted in 'The Labour Party and Books', an inquiry conducted by Wickham Stead in *Review of Reviews* XXXIII (June 1906), 570.

3 *From Radicalism to Socialism. Men and Ideas in the Formation of Fabian Socialist Doctrine, 1881–1889* (New Haven, Conn., 1975).

4 See generally Stanley Pierson, *Marxism and the Origins of British Socialism. The Struggle for a New Consciousness* (Ithaca, N.Y., and London, 1973).

5 Glasier, *William Morris and the Early Days of the Socialist Movement* (London, 1921); Arnot, *William Morris. A Vindication* (London, 1934). The wider debate is reviewed in my 'Marxism in Britain, 1917–1933', pp. 246–9.

6 Postscript to *William Morris. Romantic to Revolutionary*, 2nd edn (London, 1977), p. 807. This postscript contains very full references to the recent literature.

7 Percy Redfern, *Journey to Understanding* (London, 1946), p. 19.

8 Engels to Laura Lafargue, 13 September 1896, quoted in Thompson, *William Morris*, p. 471.

9 Such an interpretation is offered in Lucio Colletti's essay on the Marxism of the Second International in his *From Rousseau to Lenin. Studies in Ideology and Society* (London, 1972).

10 'Nordicus', 'The Mechanism Behind the Mind', *Plebs* XII (1920), 175; A. E. Cook, *The Socialism of Karl Marx* (Glasgow, 1918), pp. 14–15.

11 *The Letters and Journals of Katherine Mansfield*, ed. C. K. Stead (Harmondsworth, 1977), p. 81.

12 Murry, 'The Moral Basis of Revolution', *Adelphi*, n.s., III (March 1932),

363; Pat Sloan, 'The "Marxism" of Middleton Murry', *Adelphi*, n.s., V (March 1933), 445–6.

13 Quoted in Paul Thompson, *The Edwardians. The Remaking of British Society* (London, 1975), p. 214.

14 *The Meaning of Socialism*, p. 229.

15 *Labour Leader*, 30 March 1906, quoted in Morgan, *Keir Hardie*, p. 201.

16 Hannah Mitchell, *The Hard Way Up* (London, 1968), p. 116.

17 MacDonald, *The Socialist Movement* (London, n.d. [1911]), p. 90; and *Socialism: Critical and Constructive* (London, 1921), p. 135.

18 Herbert Tracey (ed.), *The Book of the Labour Party*, 3 vols. (London, 1925), vol. 1, p. 91.

19 MacDonald, *A Policy for the Labour Party* (London, 1920), p. 48.

20 Wyndham Albery, Clement Attlee, Michael Conway, E. D. Morel, Percy Redfern, Ben Turner, Jim Simmons in Dan Griffiths (ed.), *What is Socialism? A Symposium* (London, 1924), pp. 11, 15, 24, 54, 68, 78.

21 J. M. Hay, letter to *Plebs* XXV (1933), 94.

22 *In Place of Fear* (London, 1952), p. 18.

23 The best discussion of this subject is John Saville, 'The Ideology of Labourism' in Robert Benewick et al. (eds.), *Knowledge and Belief in Politics. The Problem of Ideology* (London, 1973), pp. 213–26.

24 See particularly R. E. Dowse's introduction to a one-volume reprint of Hardie's *From Serfdom to Socialism*; MacDonald's *Labour and the Empire*; and Snowden's *The Socialist's Budget* (Hassocks, Sussex, 1974); Bernard Barker, introduction to *Ramsay MacDonald's Political Writings* (London, 1972); and Rodney Barker, *Education and Politics 1900–1951. A Study of the Labour Party* (Oxford, 1972), chapter 1.

25 'The Progressive Movement in England', *Transactions of the Royal Historical Society*, 5th ser., 24 (1974), 171.

26 MacDonald, *A Policy for the Labour Party*, p. 107.

27 MacDonald, *Socialism: Critical and Constructive*, p. 12.

28 *Parliament and Revolution* (Manchester, 1919), p. 103.

29 *Socialism for Beginners* (London, 1929), pp. 17–18.

30 Welsh, *The King and the Miner. A Contrast* (London, n.d. [1924]), p. 6.

31 Dan Griffiths, *The Real Enemy, and Other Socialist Essays* (London, 1923), pp. 12–13.

32 See Pelling, *Popular Politics and Society*, pp. 1–36, 62–81.

33 MacDonald, *A Policy for the Labour Party*, p. 42.

34 C. T. Cramp, presidential address, *Labour Party Conference Report 1925*, p. 173 (his emphasis).

35 Reported in *Socialist*, 26 May 1921.

36 The constitution appears in *What is This Communist Party? A Plain Statement of a Plain Case* (London, 1921).

37 Marquand, *Ramsay MacDonald* (London, 1977), p. 92; Skidelsky, *Politicians and the Slump. The Labour Government of 1929–1931* (London, 1967).

38 Reported in *The Times*, 9 September 1924.

39 *Labour Party Conference Report 1918*, p. 140.

40 *Labour Party Conference Report 1925*, pp. 250–1. See also Alan Bullock, *The Life and Times of Ernest Bevin*, 2 vols. (London, 1960–7), vol. 1, pp. 243 et seq.

41 Thus 'Straight on Through the Wilderness'', *Labour Magazine* X (1931), 343–7.

42 For the Albert Hall see Basil Thompson's report to Cabinet, CAB 24/71 (2 December 1918). For Russia see L. J. Macfarlane, 'Hands Off Russia: British Labour and the Russo–Polish War, 1920', *Past and Present* 38 (1967), 126–52. The best general treatment of this neglected topic is E. Eldon Barry, *Nationalisation in British Politics* (London, 1965), pp. 226–300.

43 Arthur Henderson, reported in *Daily Herald*, 14 July 1919.

44 In this paragraph I have drawn on the argument of Martin Jacques, 'The Emergence of "Responsible" Trade Unionism, A Study of the "New Direction" in T.U.C. Policy, 1926–1935', unpublished Ph.D. thesis (Cambridge, 1976), esp. chapter 3.

45 A. J. Cook and James Maxton, *Our Case for a Socialist Revival* (London, n.d. [1928]), p. 2. The fullest examination of the provenance of the Cook–Maxton campaign is in Samuel Cooper, 'John Wheatley: A Study in Labour History', unpublished Ph.D. thesis (Glasgow, 1973), pp. 327–37.

CHAPTER 3. LITERATURE AND EDUCATION

1 *Counter Attack*, March 1932, p. 4.

2 See the S.L.P. catalogue of Kerr's list in N.C.L.C., Acc. 5120, Box 3, Folio 2; and Clunie's receipt in the Clunie papers, National Library of Scotland, Acc. 4334, Box 5.

3 Macintyre, 'Marxism in Britain, 1917–1933', pp. 336–46. The availability of Marxist literature in the nineteenth century is indicated in Dona Torr, *Tom Mann and His Times* (London, 1956), p. 326; for the situation by 1905 see Kendall, p. 69; see also Frank Jackson's article in *Marx Memorial Library Bulletin* 9 (January–March 1959), 2–3; and T. A. Jackson, 'We Don't Know How Lucky We Are. Selling Red Books Thirty Years Ago', *Daily Worker*, 7 February 1935.

4 *Counter Attack*, March 1933, p. 10.

5 *Pioneering Days* (London, 1941), p. 44.

6 See generally Richard D. Altick, *The English Common Reader: A Social History of the Mass Reading Public 1800–1900* (Chicago, 1957); J. F. C. Harrison, *Learning and Living 1790–1960. A Study in the History of the English Adult Education Movement* (London, 1961); Thomas Kelly, *A History of Adult Education in Great Britain*, 2nd edn (London, 1970); R. K. Webb, *The British Working Class Reader 1790–1848: Literacy and Social Tension* (London, 1955); and more recently Philip Corrigan and Val Gillespie, *Class Struggle, Social Literacy and Idle Time. The Provision of Public Libraries in England* (Brighton, 1978).

7 'The Atheist Mission, 1840–1900' in Robert Robson (ed.), *Ideas and Institutions of Victorian Britain* (London, 1967), pp. 205–35.

8 See Sims' letters to Winifred Horrabin in Winifred Horrabin Papers, University of Hull, Box 4; and her 'In Memoriam: G. F. Sims', *Plebs* XXXV (1943), 126.

9 Stella Davies, *North Country Bred* (London, 1963), p. 100.

10 *A Ragged Schooling* (Manchester, 1976), pp. 195–7.

11 See particularly 'Only – He was a Socialist', in Quelch, *Literary Remains*,

edited with a biographical introduction by Ernest Belfort Bax (London, 1914), pp. 30–7. Note the strong similarity to the realist fiction of Arthur Morrison.

12 James Kelly, Epilogue to Barclay, *Memories and Medleys. The Autobiography of a Bottle Washer* (Leicester, 1934), p. 137.

13 *Pioneering Days*, p. 57.

14 Interviewed by John Foster, University of Strathclyde, 19 June 1969.

15 Jackson manuscript, p. 364; Murphy, *New Horizons* (London, 1941), p. 216.

16 The best accounts of the labour college movement are Craik, *The Central Labour College*; Ruth Frow, 'Independent Working Class Education with Particular Reference to South Lancashire, 1909–1930', unpublished M.Ed. thesis (Manchester, 1964); Ian W. Hamilton, 'Education for Revolution: The Plebs League and the Labour College Movement, 1908–1921', unpublished M.A. thesis (Warwick, 1972); J. P. M. Millar, *The Labour College Movement* (London, 1978); Paul Yorke, *Education and the Working Class. Ruskin College 1889–1909* (Oxford, 1977).

17 Craik, p. 126; *Plebs* IX (December 1917), 258. See also John Thomas, 'The Economic Doctrines of Karl Marx and their Influence on the Industrial Areas of South Wales, particularly among Miners', a typescript dated 1922, held in SWML, p. 2.

18 Frow, pp. 26–30; Harry Pollitt, *Serving my Time: An Apprenticeship to Politics* (London, 1940), pp. 32–4.

19 T. Brennan, 'The White House', *Cambridge Journal* VII (1954), 243–8; James Griffiths, *Pages from Memory* (London, 1969), p. 20; and other recollections in CHP.

20 *From the Valleys I Came* (London, 1956), pp. 211–12. See also Albert Hall, 'Marxist Education Classes in 1904', *Marx Memorial Library Bulletin* 66 (April–June 1973), 10–11.

21 *Commission of Enquiry into Industrial Unrest. No. 7 Division. Report of the Commissioners for Wales, including Monmouthshire; No. 8 Division: Report of the Commissioners for Scotland*, Cmd. 8668–9 (London, 1917); CAB 24/26; G. T. 2073 (September 1917), quoted in Hamilton, 'Education for Revolution'.

22 Will McLaine, 'Scottish Labour Colleges', *Forward*, 14 February 1920; Millar, *The Labour College Movement*, pp. 21–2; N.C.L.C., Acc. 5120, Box 6, Folios 1 and 2.

23 Frow, p. 52.

24 N.C.L.C., Acc. 5120, Box 2, Folio 11.

25 N.C.L.C., Acc. 5120, Box 1, Folio 1.

26 Minutes of the London Divisional Council, N.C.L.C., Acc. 5120, Box 73, Folio 2; minutes of the National Committee of the Scottish Labour College, 1927–8 passim, N.C.L.C., Acc. 5120, Box 75, Folio 2.

27 Younie's charges were made in 1931–2 and investigated by a committee of the N.C.L.C.; see N.C.L.C., Acc. 5120, Additional deposit, Boxes 1 and 2.

28 Undated letter in the Younie file.

29 Millar, *The Labour College Movement*, p. 107.

30 Minutes of the Executive of the Plebs League, National Library of Scotland, Acc. 6889, item 10.

31 Arthur MacManus, 'Education Towards Communism', *Plebs* XII (1920),

163. See also his letter to Winifred Horrabin, dated 11 February 1921, in N.C.L.C., Acc. 5120, Box 1, Folio 1.

32 'The Constitution of the Plebs League', *Plebs* XVI (1924), 162.

33 *Fourth Congress of the Communist International. Abridged Report. . .* (London, 1923), p. 267.

34 The attack was launched publicly by Palme Dutt's scathing review of a Plebs textbook in *Labour Monthly* IV (1923), 124–8.

35 'Agreed Statement between the National Training Department and the Executive of the Plebs League', *Workers' Weekly*, 31 March 1923.

36 'Statement of the Executive of the C.P.G.B.', ibid.; 'Our Point of View', *Plebs* XV (1923), 244. See also MacManus, 'Working Class Education in Great Britain', *Communist International* 25 (1923), 51–6.

37 Winifred Horrabin's diaries for several years after 1923 also reveal continuing contact with leading Communists: Winifred Horrabin Papers, University of Hull.

38 For example, the Dundee branch: N.C.L.C., Acc. 5120, Box 8, Folio 4.

39 J. P. M. Millar, *The National Council of Labour Colleges: History, Report and Directory* (London, 1924), p. 59; *Education for Emancipation* (London, 1926); *Report of the Central Executive [of the C.P.G.B.] to the Seventh Congress* (London, 1925), p. 19.

40 Minutes of house meetings of students, 23 October 1919 to 10 November 1920, N.C.L.C., Acc. 5120, Box 70, Folio 3.

41 Minutes of Board of Governors, 25 November 1921, National Library of Scotland, Acc. 6889, Box 7. There is further material in N.C.L.C., Acc. 5120, Box 2, Folio 12.

42 Student manifesto to N.U.R. and S.W.M.F., 24 July 1923, N.C.L.C., Acc. 5120, Box 2, Folio 13.

43 Report of committee of enquiry, N.C.L.C., Acc. 5120, Box 2, Folio 13.

44 Interviewed by Hywel Francis, 9 June 1973: CHP.

45 Letter from seven students to the Governors, 13 July 1924, N.C.L.C., Acc. 5120, Box 2, Folio 14.

46 Minutes of Board of Governors, 3 September 1921, N.C.L.C., Acc. 6889, item 7; and Jackson's manuscript, p. 450.

47 N.C.L.C., Acc. 5120, Box 2, Folio 18; Box 5, Folio 2.

48 *Report of the Central Executive [of the C.P.G.B.] to the Sixth Congress* (London, 1924), p. 28: in MML.

49 Bob Davies, *Pages From a Worker's Life 1916–1926*, C.P.G.B. Our History series (London, 1961), p. 8.

50 Interviewed by David Egan and Hywel Francis, 20 September 1972: CHP.

51 Interviewed by Ian Hamilton, in Hamilton, 'Education for Revolution', pp. 86–7.

52 Propaganda Theses adopted at the Fifth Congress, in *Communist International*, 2nd ser., 7 (1924), 63–76.

53 See the report of the Agitprop Department of the C.P.G.B. in *Communist Papers*, Cmd. 2682, pp. 28–9.

54 *The Ninth Congress of the C.P.G.B.* (London, 1927), p. 29; D. R., 'The Present State of Party Education', *Communist Review*, n.s., III (1931), 25–9.

55 The quotation is from Murphy, *New Horizons*, p. 248. See also *Communist Papers*, pp. 21–4; *Report of the Seventh National Congress [of the C.P.G.B.]*

(London, 1925), pp. 124–9; J. T. Murphy, 'The First Year of the Lenin School', *Communist International*, 3rd ser., IV (1927), 267–9. There are interviews with British students at the Lenin School in the CHP.

56 'Party Training Notes', *Communist Review* VI (1925), 142–3; Party Training Committee, *Hints to Leaders of Training Groups* (London, n.d.).

57 'Party Training Notes', *Communist Review* VII (1927), 427.

58 The Ten Proletarian Maxims appear on the cover of pamphlets published by the Proletarian Schools; most are held by the National Library of Scotland. See Anderson's article in *Socialist*, 25 March 1920. Harry McShane recalls Anderson in his autobiography, *No Mean Fighter* (London, 1978), pp. 44–5.

59 For before the war see Thomas B. Stirling, *History of Vale of Leven Co-operative Society Limited 1862–1912* (Alexandria, Dumbartonshire, 1915); post-war meetings appear in the *Lennox Herald*.

60 I am drawing here on the unpublished research of John Attfield. Of course many Co-ops before the war engaged in Socialist activity.

61 Horace Morgan, interviewed by Hywel Francis, 9 January 1974; Will Paynter, interviewed by David Egan and Hywel Francis, 20 September 1972: CHP.

62 See Kelly, *History of Adult Education*, pp. 267–76; and Geoff Brown, 'The W.E.A. Between the Wars', a paper given at the Ruskin History Workshop, 2 May 1975.

63 Morgan interview; W. H. Gregory, interviewed by Richard Lewis and Hywel Francis, 23 November 1972: CHP.

64 W. H. Marwick, 'W.E.A.', *Journal of Scottish Labour History* 8 (1974), 35–6.

65 W. E. Williams and A. E. Heath, *Learn and Live. The Consumer's View of Adult Education* (London, 1936), p. 12.

66 See A. J. Corfield, *Epoch in Workers' Education. A History of the Workers' Educational Trade Union Committee* (London, 1969).

67 Quoted in J. Elfred Davies, 'Educational Settlements in South Wales with Special Reference to the Merthyr Tydfil Settlement', *Transactions of the Honorable Society of Cymmrodorion*, Session 1970, Part II, 188.

68 Harold Watkins, *Unusual Students* (Liverpool, 1947), pp. 10, 26. See also his *Life Has Kept Me Young* (London, 1951).

CHAPTER 4. MARXISM AS A CLASS CULTURE

1 This point is made by more than one contributor to Geoffrey Crossick (ed.), *The Lower Middle Class in Britain, 1870–1914* (London, 1977).

2 For Cole, Tawney and the Webbs see J. M. Winter, *Socialism and the Challenge of War. Ideas and politics in Britain 1912–1918* (London, 1974).

3 See Francis Meynell, *My Lives* (London, 1971); N. Barker, *Stanley Morison* (London, 1972); and 'Graham Pollard', *The Book Collector* 26 (Spring 1977), 7–28.

4 Marx's Place in Socialist Theory', *Plebs* XXV (1933), 65.

5 See Neal Wood, *Communism and British Intellectuals* (London, 1959).

6 *The Right Place – The Right Time* (Llandybie, 1972), p. 103.

7 *Martin Eden* (London, 1910), p. 109.

8 Winifred Horrabin Papers, University of Hull.

9 Examples of these wall-charts are discussed below in the appropriate

chapters. For samples see James Clunie, *First Principles of Working Class Education* (Glasgow, 1920).

10 Editorial in *Anvil* II, 3 (March 1926).

11 R. M. Fox, 'Dynamics of Social Change', *Communist Review* II (1922), 413. See also his autobiography, *Smoky Crusade* (London, 1937).

12 (London, 1920), p. 14.

13 Letter to *Worker's Life*, 2 November 1928.

14 Agitprop of the Communist International to the C.P.G.B., 24 February 1925: printed in *Communist Papers*, Cmd. 2682, p. 33. Agitprop of the Communist International, 'A Criticism of the Party Training Manual', *Communist* III (1929), 450–60. Hutt, 'The Revolutionary Role of the Theoretical Struggle', *Communist Review*, n.s., IV, 79.

15 Interviewed by David Egan and Hywel Francis, 11 October 1972: CHP.

16 G. A. N. Lowndes, *The Silent Social Revolution. An Account of the Expansion of Public Education in England and Wales 1895–1965*, 2nd edn (London, 1969), p. 81.

17 Watkins, *Life Has Kept Me Young*, p. 59.

18 'Scheme for a Labour College for South-West Lancashire and Cheshire', manuscript in N.C.L.C., Acc. 5120, Box 3, Folio 2.

19 Craik, pp. 173–4.

20 Besides letters to the *Plebs* in 1921 and 1922, see the editorial in *Anvil* II, 2 (1926).

21 N.C.L.C., Acc. 5120, Box 21, Folio 1.

22 N.C.L.C., Acc. 5120, Box 3. See the bitterly hostile articles by Harold Heslop, 'Raymond W. Postgate: A Memoir', and Henry Sara, 'Further Jottings on R. W. Postgate', *Communist* III (1928), 228–30, 290–6.

23 Meynell, pp. 127–8.

24 Gallacher, *Revolt on the Clyde. An Autobiography* (London, 1936), pp. 261–2; *Report on Organisation* (London, 1922).

25 Klugmann, vol. 1, p. 333, cites the minutes of the Political Bureau of 30 September 1924 for his departure, yet Postgate himself and contemporary evidence suggest a rift by 1923.

26 For election details see McKibbin, pp. 196–204. Newbold's papers are in the John Rylands Library, Manchester.

27 Jack Jones, *Unfinished Journey* (London, 1937), p. 292.

28 For the clothes see Bell, p. 263, and Jack and Bessie Braddock, *The Braddocks* (London, 1963), p. 10; for the manner see Gallacher, *Last Memoirs* (London, 1966), p. 190, and John McGovern, *Neither Fear Nor Favour* (London, 1960), p. 53; for the expenses see the minutes of the Manchester and District Plebs League, 1918, N.C.L.C., Acc. 5120, Box 80.

29 Jones, p. 201.

30 Gallacher, *Last Memoirs*, p. 190.

31 Jack and Bessie Braddock, p. 11.

32 See chapter 1, notes 5 and 14.

33 See Bell, *Pioneering Days*, p. 263.

34 *Communist*, 24 December 1921.

35 The chapter of his unpublished memoirs entitled 'The Art of Propaganda' is particularly illuminating in this respect.

36 *Solo Trumpet*, pp. 121–2.

37 See *Charles Dickens: The Progress of a Radical* (London, 1937).

38 *Sunday Worker*, 18 August 1929; and correspondence in possession of Mrs Vivien Morton.

39 Hans-Josef Steinberg, 'Workers' Libraries in Germany before 1914', trans. Nicholas Jacobs, *History Workshop* 1 (Spring 1976), 166–80; see also Dieter Langewiesche and Klaus Schönhoven, 'Arbeiterbibliotheken und Arbeiterlektüre im Wilhelminischen Deutschland', *Archiv für Sozialgeschichte* XVI (1976), 135–204.

CHAPTER 5. HISTORICAL MATERIALISM

1 For a general introduction to this area see J. W. Burrow, *Evolution and Society. A Study in Victorian Social Theory* (Cambridge, 1966).

2 Snowden, *An Autobiography*, 2 vols. (London, 1934), vol. 1, p. 72.

3 Interviewed by David Rubenstein, *BSSLH* 22 (1971), 28–9.

4 Kellogg Durland, *Among the Fife Miners* (London, 1912), p. 29.

5 Joseph McCabe, *Edward Clodd* (London, 1932), p. 29.

6 Susan Budd, 'The Loss of Faith. Reasons for Unbelief among Members of the Secular Movement in England, 1850–1950', *Past and Present* 36 (1967), 106–25. See also her *Varieties of Unbelief. Atheists and Agnostics in English Society 1850–1960* (London, 1977); and Edward Royle, *Radical Politics 1790–1900. Religion and Unbelief* (London, 1971).

7 *Clarion*, 23 January 1903; quoted in Logie Barrow, 'The Socialism of Robert Blatchford and the *Clarion*', unpublished Ph.D. thesis (London, 1975), p. 259.

8 F. J. Gould, *The Pioneers of Johnson's Court. A History of the Rationalist Press Association from 1899 Onwards* (London, 1935), p. 42.

9 *Two Pages from Roman History* (Edinburgh, 1908), p. 30.

10 Will Coldrick, interviewed by David Egan and Richard Lewis, 24 September 1973: CHP.

11 D. J. Davies, letter to *Daily Worker*, 16 February 1932.

12 *Solo Trumpet*, p. 59.

13 *Twenty Objections to Socialism* (London, 1920), p. 16.

14 George Warne in Griffiths (ed.) *What is Socialism?*, p. 79.

15 Marx to Weydemeyer, 5 March 1852, in Marx and Engels, *Correspondence 1846–1895* (London, 1934), p. 57. See also *Capital*, 3 vols. (London, 1954–72), vol. 1, pp. 184–5.

16 Cole, 'A Word to Max Beer', *Labour Monthly* III (1922), 314; see also 'Watery Beer', *Plebs* XIV (1922), 229–30.

17 'An Indispensable Book', Paul's review of Beer's *Social Struggles in Antiquity*, in *Communist Review* III (1922), 160–1.

18 'Historical Materialism', *Communist Review* VII (1926), 44–5.

19 Reprinted in F. H. Hayward and E. M. White, *The Last Years of a Great Educationalist* (Bungay, Suffolk, n.d. [1924]), p. 96.

20 Jackson manuscript, p. 251. The charts were published at the same time as the *Manual of Party Training* (London, n.d. [1924]).

21 (London, 1907), p. 103; and see W. W. Craik's notes of a course of lectures delivered by Hird at Ruskin, N.C.L.C., Acc. 5120, Box 37, Folio 3.

22 L. A. H., review of Haeckel, *Daily Herald*, 1 May 1929.

23 *Socialism and Society* (London, 1905), p. 104.

24 *Economics of Socialism* (London, 1896), p. 4.

25 *Plebs* XX (1928), 57.

26 W. Paul, *Communism and Society* (London, 1922), p. 142; for more criticism of MacDonald's biological socialism see Noah Ablett, *Easy Outlines of Economics* (Oxford, 1919), pp. 7–8; J. T. Murphy, 'The Political Mind of Ramsay MacDonald', *Communist Review* IV (1924), 475–8.

27 *Communist* II (1927), 234.

28 'What is Sovietism?', *Worker*, 10 July 1920; 'Are We Realists?', *Communist*, 5 November 1921; *Communism and Society*, pp. 16, 22 (his emphasis).

29 'Lenin on Materialism', *Plebs*, XX (1928), 117 (their emphasis).

30 Engels, *Herr Eugen Dühring's Revolution in Science* (London, 1935), p. 130.

31 D. Ivon Jones, 'Lenin's First Book', *Communist Review* LV (1924), 486; Zelda Kahan Coates, *Karl Marx: His Life and Teaching* (London, 1918), p. 25.

32 Eastman, p. 60. For his British links see his autobiography, *Love and Revolution. My Journey Through an Epoch* (New York, 1964), pp. 437–41; for British popularisation see Postgate, *Karl Marx* (London, 1933), p. 55.

33 Preface to *A Contribution to the Critique of Political Economy* (Moscow, 1970), p. 21.

34 *The Socialist Movement*, pp. 143–5; *Socialism: Critical and Constructive*, p. 12.

35 Laski, *Karl Marx: An Essay* (London, 1922), p. 33; Russell, *The Practice and Theory of Bolshevism* (London, 1920), p. 119; Wallas, *Our Social Heritage* (London, 1921), p. 247; Joad in *New Leader*, 16 January 1926.

36 Laski, *Karl Marx*, p. 34.

37 S. C. Sopote, 'Why Flatter Matter?', *Plebs* XXI (1929), 210.

38 Ibid.

39 'Karl Marx and Modern Materialism', *Labour Leader*, 9 May 1918.

40 J. Cochrane, 'Socialism and Materialism', *Forward*, 7 April 1923.

41 MacDonald, preface to 1924 edition of *Socialism: Critical and Constructive*, p. vi; G. N. Barnes et al., *Religion in the Labour Movement* (London, 1919).

42 For example A. E. Cook, 'Marx on Herron', *Plebs* IX (1917), 7; Maurice Dobb, 'Colonial and Imperial Expansion – A Marxist Analysis', *Plebs* XIII (1921), 263; Mark Starr, 'History and the Workers', *Plebs* XVIII (1920), 324.

43 R. M., 'Idealism and Economics', *Socialist*, 4 December 1919.

44 S. Mill, 'Educating Marxists', *Marxism Today* 13 (January 1969), 31.

45 *Plebs* XV (1923), 335.

46 H. Wynn-Cuthbert, 'The Materialist Conception of History', *Socialist*, September 1917, p. 96.

47 Paul, *The State: Its Origin and Functions* (Glasgow, 1917), p. 7; J. T. Walton Newbold, *Marx and Modern Capitalism* (London, 1918), p. 3.

48 Karl Marx, *Capital. A Critical Analysis of Capitalist Production*, trans. from the 3rd German edn by S. Moore and E. Aveling, ed. by F. Engels (London, 1901), pp. 382–3.

49 For example Russell, *Roads to Freedom. Socialism, Anarchism and Syndicalism* (London, 1918), p. 28; G. D. H. Cole, *What Marx Really Meant* (London, 1934), p. 94; Harold Laski, *Communism* (London, 1927), pp. 59–87 passim; C. Delisle Burns, *The Principles of Revolution* (London, 1920), p. 38.

50 Dutt, 'More British Marxism', *Labour Monthly* IV (1923), 126; Fox, letter to *Plebs* XIII (1921), 157; Clarke, *Marxism and History* (London, 1927), p. 10 (his emphasis).

51 (London, 1918), pp. 5–6.

52 'A New Book', *Call*, 14 February 1918.

53 Correspondence, *Call*, 28 February and 7 March 1918.

54 Joseph Stalin, *Leninism*, 2 vols. (London, 1928–33), vol. 1, p. 97.

55 Engels to Bloch, 21 September 1890, in *Correspondence, 1846–1895. A Selection with Commentary and Notes* (London, 1934), p. 475 (his emphasis). On vulgar Marxism see Hugo Rathbone in *Labour Monthly* XII (1930), 63. Jackson's comments in N.C.L.C., Acc. 5120, Box 28, Folio 2.

56 Louis Althusser subjects Engels's letter to this type of analysis in *For Marx* (London, 1965), pp. 117–28.

57 (London, 1932), pp. 14–15.

58 'Maurice Dobb's Distortions of Marxism', *Daily Worker*, 26 July 1932.

59 L. J. W., 'The Scope of Working Class Studies', *Socialist*, 3 February 1921.

60 *Marx, Lenin and the Science of Revolution*, pp. 51–2.

61 A. R., 'The Worker's Culture', *Plebs* XIV (1922), 38.

62 Eden Paul and Cedar Paul, *Proletcult (Proletarian Culture)* (London, 1921), pp. 11, 16, 23.

63 *Plebs* XVI (1924), 162; J. F. Horrabin and Winifred Horrabin, *Working-Class Education* (London, 1924), p. 9; J. F. Horrabin in *W.E.A. Education Year Book, 1918*, pp. 390–1; Eden Paul and Cedar Paul, 'Revolutionary Education', *Communist*, 7 May 1921.

64 W. W. Craik, 'The Labour College', *Labour Magazine* I (1922), 125; Morgan Philips Price, 'Independent Working Class Education in Britain', *Plebs* XVII (1925), 343.

65 'The S[cottish] L[abour] C[ollege] v. the W.E.A.', *Worker*, 11 October 1919.

66 *Leninism*, vol. 1, p. 94.

67 *Communist International*, n.s., VI (January 1930), 1151; reprinted in a different translation in *Leninism*, vol. 2, p. 253.

68 N. Bukharin et al., *Science at the Crossroads* (London, 1931, 2nd edn 1971).

69 T. Brennan, E. W. Cooney and H. Pollins, *Social Change in South-West Wales* (London, 1954), p. 154.

70 See Hywel Francis, 'The Anthracite Strike and the Disturbances of 1925', *Llafur* 2 (1973), 15–28.

71 E. T. Davies, *Religion in the Industrial Revolution in South Wales* (Cardiff, 1965), pp. 161–8; C. R. Williams, 'The Welsh Religious Revival, 1904–5', *British Journal of Sociology* III (1952), 242–59.

72 Robert Moore, *Pit-Men, Preachers and Politics. The Effects of Methodism in a Durham Mining Community* (Cambridge, 1974), esp. pp. 169–90.

73 For example, Tom Bell, *Pioneering Days*, pp. 26, 31–4; W. J. Brown, *So Far...* (London, 1943), pp. 117–27; Wil Jon Edwards, *From the Valleys I Came*; James Griffiths, *Pages From Memory*, pp. 18–19; J. T. Murphy, *New Horizons*, pp. 27–8, 33–6; John Paton, *Proletarian Pilgrimage* (London, 1935), p. 97; Emmanuel Shinwell, *Conflict Without Malice* (London, 1955), pp. 23–7.

74 Discussion in a W.E.A. Class, quoted in C. H. Armbruster, 'The Social

Determination of Ideologies. Being a Study of a Welsh Mining Community', unpublished Ph.D. thesis (London, 1940), p. 211.

75 J. Crispin, 'Education in the I.L.P.', *The International*, 3 July 1920. This was the short-lived weekly of the Communist faction of the I.L.P.

CHAPTER 6. THE DIALECTIC

1 For a forceful statement of this position see Perry Anderson, 'Components of the National Culture' in Alexander Cockburn and Robin Blackburn (eds.), *Student Power* (Harmondsworth, 1969), pp. 214–80.

2 Adam B. Ulam, *Philosophical Origins of English Socialism* (Cambridge, Massachusetts, 1951); Pierson, *Marxism and the Origins of British Socialism*.

3 Russell, *The Practice and Theory of Bolshevism*, pp. 119–21; John Lewis, 'Back to Materialism', *Forward*, 28 January 1922; A. L. Rowse, *Politics and the Younger Generation* (London, 1931), p. 244; Cole, *What Marx Really Meant*, p. 15.

4 Eden Paul and Cedar Paul, 'Lenin on Materialism', *Plebs* XX (1928), 117.

5 *Karl Marx*, p. 86.

6 Cole, *What Marx Really Meant*, pp. 10–11; Laski, *Karl Marx*, p. 4; Cole, *Some Relations Between Political and Economic Theories* (London, 1934), p. 69.

7 (Seattle, 1925), p. 178.

8 Beer, *Fifty Years of International Socialism* (London, 1935), p. 178.

9 Dorothy Emmet, 'Joseph Dietzgen, the Philosopher of Proletarian Logic', *Journal of Adult Education* III (1928), 26.

10 For biographical information see Lloyd D. Easton, 'Empiricism and Ethics in Dietzgen', *Journal of the History of Ideas* XIX (1958), 77–90; and the prefatory sketch by his son in Joseph Dietzgen, *Some of the Philosophical Essays on Socialism and Science, Religion, Ethics, Critique-of-Reason and the World-at-Large* (Chicago, 1907). Further references to Dietzgen's British readership are provided in my article 'Joseph Dietzgen and British Working-Class Education', *BSSLH* 29 (Autumn 1974), 50–4; and J. P. M. Millar of the Labour Colleges contributed his own recollections to *BSSLH* 31 (Autumn 1975) 14. For a generous account by an enthusiast see Adam Buick, 'Joseph Dietzgen', *Radical Philosophy* 10 (Spring 1975), 3–7.

11 Marz, *Letters to Dr. Kügelmann* (London, n.d. [1934]), p. 80; Engels, *Ludwig Feuerbach and the Outcome of Classical German Philosophy* (London, n.d. [1934]), p. 54.

12 *Philosophical Essays*, pp. 152, 190; *The Positive Outcome of Philosophy* (Chicago, 1906), p. 417.

13 Maclean to James Clunie, 24 July 1922, Clunie Papers, National Library of Scotland, Acc. 4334, Box 1. Letter from Dobb to myself, 12 June 1974; H. J. W. Edwards, *The Good Patch* (London, 1938), p. 170.

14 George Hardy, *Those Stormy Years* (London, 1956), p. 29; F. L. Rimington, letter to *Plebs* XVI (1924), 41.

15 James Clunie, *First Principles of Working Class Education* (Glasgow, 1920), p. 4.

16 Robert Holder, letter to *Plebs* XVI (1924), 40.

17 On Haeckel see Daniel Gasman, *The Scientific Origins of National Socialism. Social Darminism in Ernst Haeckel and the German Monist League* (New York, 1971); Niles R. Holt, 'Ernst Haeckel's Monistic Religion', *Journal of the History of Ideas* XXXII (1971), pp. 265–80.

18 H. Wynn-Cuthbert, 'Social Science Studies', *Socialist*, August 1917 (his emphasis).

19 I take these annotations at random from the copies of Dietzgen in the lodge libraries now held by the SWML. See also Michael Foot's reference to the 'much pored over' copy in the Tredegar Workmen's Institute: *Aneurin Bevan: A Biography*, 2 vols. (London, 1962–73), vol. 2, p. 620.

20 Dated 24 January 1873: *Capital*, vol. 1, p. 20.

21 Jackson, *Dialectics. The Logic of Marxism and its Critics – An Essay in Exploration* (London, 1936), pp. 490–1; H. Burke, 'Friedrich Engels', *Daily Worker*, 5 August 1930.

22 Engels, *Ludwig Feuerbach*, pp. 53–4.

23 L. Rudas, *Dialectical Materialism and Communism* (London, n.d. [1934]), p. 22.

24 G. A. Hutt, 'Militant Materialism', *Labour Monthly* XII (1930), 761; 'Marxism – The Science of the Proletariat', *Daily Worker*, 23 March 1933.

25 J. M. Hay, letter to *Plebs* XXV (1933), 94.

26 'Dialectical Materialism', in Hyman Levy et al., *Aspects of Dialectical Materialism* (London, 1934), p. 109. See also J. B. S. Haldane, *The Marxist Philosophy and the Natural Sciences* (London, 1937). Engels voiced the same complaint in *Dialectics of Nature*, pp. 33–4.

27 James Clunie, 'The Philosophy of Working Class Education', *Worker*, 17 May 1919.

28 Lenin, 'Joseph Dietzgen', *Labour Monthly* IX (1927), 117–18; in *Collected Works*, vol. 19, pp. 79–82.

29 Copy of letter from Eugene Dietzgen to Craik, 9 June 1926, in Casey file, N.C.L.C., Acc. 5120, Box 38, Folio 6. The new translation was published by Kerr in 1928.

30 Casey, letter to *Plebs* XVIII (1926), 415; 'Joseph Dietzgen 1828–1928', *Plebs* XX (1928), 269; 'The Marxism of Marx', *Plebs* XVIII, 226; *Method in Thinking. A Series of Popular Lectures* (Manchester, 1933), p. 194.

31 Casey, *Dietzgen's Logic. A Plain Introduction to 'The Positive Outcome of Philosophy' Written for the Plain Man* (Stockport, n.d. [1928]), p. 7.

32 Casey, 'Joseph Dietzgen', p. 269; roneoed and bound lecture notes entitled 'Science of Reasoning' in N.C.L.C., Acc. 5121, Box 38, Folio 3, p. 9.

33 *Method in Thinking*, pp. 38, 46; *Thinking*, pp. 182–4.

34 Casey, *Thinking*, p. 35; Jackson, *Dialectics*, p. 608.

35 Jackson, review in *Sunday Worker*, 2 October 1927.

36 N.C.L.C., Acc. 5120, Box 2, Folio 18.

37 Jackson manuscript, p. 370.

38 For the refusal to publish see a letter from J. P. M. Millar to Arthur Woodburn, 3 January 1928, misfiled in John S. Clarke papers, N.C.L.C., Acc. 5120, Box 28, Folio 1. For Casey's lectures at this time see the file of his notes, correspondence, etc. in N.C.L.C., Acc. 5120, Box 38.

39 D. R., 'Thinking. A Review', *Communist Review*, n.s., III (1931), 373 (his emphasis). Jackson manuscript, pp. 367–70, and *Dialectics*, pp. 560–625.

40 N.C.L.C., Acc. 5120, Box 38, Folio 2.

41 Jackson manuscript, quoted in *DLB*, vol. 4, p. 105.

42 The notebook is in N.C.L.C., Acc. 5120, Box 36.

43 Jackson manuscript, p. 259.

44 Dobb, letter to *Plebs* XV (1923), 517; Postgate, ibid., p. 566; 'Notes', *Anvil* 3, 2, p. 2

45 Pp. 24–7, 77, 169, 199. See John P. Diggins, 'Getting Hegel Out of History: Max Eastman's Quarrel with Marxism', *American Historical Review* LXXIX (1974), 38–71.

46 *Dialectics*, p. 36. The book was discussed by the Executive of the Plebs League in April 1926 and Horrabin was permitted to place a guaranteed order with Allen and Unwin, the publisher: Minutes of the Plebs League, National Library of Scotland, Acc. 6889, item 10. See also J. F. Horrabin to Winifred Horrabin, 20 May 1926, Winifred Horrabin Papers, University of Hull.

47 Horrabin, *Plebs* XIX (1927), 151; Postgate, 'Marx Shaved', *Lansbury's Labour Weekly*, 26 February 1927.

48 'Marxism. A Science or Religion', *New Leader*, 10 December 1926.

49 Macmurray, *The Philosophy of Communism* (London, 1933), pp. 64–7; Carritt, 'A Discussion of Dialectical Materialism', *Labour Monthly* XV (1933), 324–9, 383–91.

50 See Hilary Rose and Steven Rose, 'The Radicalisation of Science' in Ralph Miliband and John Saville (eds.), *The Socialist Register 1972* (London, 1972), pp. 105–32; and P. G. Werskey's introduction to Bukharin et al., *Science at the Crossroads* (London, 1931, 2nd edn 1971).

51 See David Joravsky, *Soviet Marxism and Natural Science 1917–1932* (London, 1961); Gustav A. Wetter, *Dialectical Materialism. A Historical and Sympathetic Survey of Philosophy in the Soviet Union* (London, 1958), pp. 128–81.

52 H. Wynn-Cuthbert, 'Social Science Studies', *Socialist*, July 1917, p. 77; Maurice Dobb, letter to *Plebs* XV (1923), 517.

53 'The Science of Society', *Workers' Weekly*, 16 April 1926.

54 'The Nature of Brain Processes', *Labour Monthly* IX (1927), 768.

55 *Collected Works*, vol. 13 (London, 1927), p. xxii.

56 'The Philosophical Discussion in the C.P.S.U. in 1930–31', *Labour Monthly* XIII (1931), 649–56.

57 I have investigated this problem further in 'Marxism in Britain 1917–1933', pp. 116–19.

58 (London, 1930), pp. 83, 90.

59 'Contemporary Philosophy in the Soviet Union', *Psyche* XII, 2 (1931), 2–18. Back in 1919 Hogben had praised Dietzgen for destroying metaphysics: *Plebs* XI, 53–4.

60 'The Hesitant Materialist', *Labour Monthly* XIV (1932), 651.

61 'Materialism and the Concept of Behaviour', *Labour Monthly* XV (1933), 44.

62 'Dialectical Materialism and Natural Science', *Labour Monthly* XV (1933), 84–95.

63 'Ex-Bourgeois', letter to *Daily Worker*, 19 February 1932.

64 John Lewis, letter to *Daily Worker*, 9 March 1932. Lewis later joined the C.P.G.B. but was at this stage a member of the I.L.P.

65 *Plebs* XXIV (1932), 190.

66 *Plebs* XII (1920), 61.
67 *Truth Will Out* (London, 1949), p. 305.

CHAPTER 7. ECONOMICS

1 *New Horizons*, p. 67.
2 See Robert Holder's voluminous notes, N.C.L.C., Acc. 5120, Box 37, Folio 4.
3 Ablett, *Easy Outlines of Economics* (Oxford, 1919), p. 13; Starr, *A Worker Looks at Economics* (London, 1925), p. 14; Paul, *Communism and Society*, p. 46.
4 'Principles of Communism Explained', *Workers' Life*, 20 September 1929.
5 A. E. Cook, *The Socialism of Karl Marx*, p. 21. Will McLaine, 'The Message of Marxism', *Call*, 2 May 1918.
6 Plebs League, *An Outline of Economics* (London, 1922), p. 21; Starr, *A Worker Looks at Economics*, p. 16; McLaine, 'Economics Without Headaches' (N.C.L.C., Acc. 5120, Box 29, Folio 1). See *Capital*, vol. 1, p. 38.
7 *A Worker Looks at Economics*, p. 18. These magical gold nuggets were first conjured up by Böhm-Bawerk.
8 Tom Scollan, interviewed by John Foster, 23 March 1970.
9 Paul, review of Bukharin's *Economic Theory of the Leisure Class* in *Sunday Worker*, 30 October 1927.
10 *Political Economy and Capitalism. Some Essays in Economic Tradition* (London, 1937), pp. 1–33.
11 Ablett, *Easy Outlines*, p. 60; James McDougall, 'The Economics of Capitalist Production', *Communist Review* VI (1925), 181; Emile Burns, *Imperialism. An Outline Course* (London, 1927), p. 5.
12 Will McLaine, 'The Message of Marxism'. Emile Burns, *What is the Communist Party?* (London, n.d. [1933]), pp. 3–4.
13 Burns, *Imperialism*, p. 5; W. Paul, 'For You Mr. Worker! Where Wages and Profits Come From', *Socialist*, April 1917.
14 Student manifesto in N.C.L.C., Acc. 5120, Box 2, Folio 13.
15 'More British Marxism', *Labour Monthly* IV (1923), 126.
16 *Karl Marx and the Close of His System* (London, 1898), p. 64.
17 F. R. Salter, *Karl Marx and Modern Socialism* (London, 1921), p. 94; J. A. Murray Macdonald, *Karl Marx and the Present Unrest* (London, n.d. [1922]), p. 23. See also H. W. B. Joseph, *The Labour Theory Of Value in Karl Marx* (London, 1923), and Laski, *Communism*, pp. 101–2.
18 'The Revival of Anti-Marxism', *Labour Monthly* I (1921) 425.
19 'Professor Laski in the Service of Capitalism', *Communist* I (1927), 260 (his emphasis). The point is repeated in Fox's *A Defence of Communism: in Reply to H. J. Laski* (London, 1927).
20 *Easy Outlines*, p. 93.
21 *An Introduction to Economics* (London, 1932), pp. 65–6. This booklet is reprinted in William Ross (ed.), *An Outline of Modern Knowledge* (London, 1931), pp. 595–623. And see Lecture XV of John Maclean's printed *Notes of Lectures in Economics Given by John Maclean* (Glasgow, n.d.).
22 Emile Burns, *Capitalism, Communism and the Transition* (London, 1933), p. 28.
23 *Communist Party Training* (London, 1926, 2nd edn 1927), p. 27.

258   NOTES TO PAGES 155–61

24 *The Bolshevik Theory*, p. 29. There is an interesting discussion of the economic fatalism of DeLeon in Carl Reeve, *The Life and Times of Daniel DeLeon* (New York, 1972), pp. 148–56.

25 For example Eden Paul, *Karl Marx and Modern Socialism* (Manchester, 1916), p. 2.

26 'Class Against Class – and Why', *Workers' Life*, 6 September 1929; Ralph Fox, *The Class Struggle in Britain in the Epoch of Imperialism*, 2 vols. (London, 1932), vol. 1, p. 56.

27 'Marxism Vulgarised', his review of Maurice Dobb's *On Marxism Today*, in *Communist Review*, n.s., IV (1932), 343–8.

28 *Marxist Study Course. Course 1. Political Economy. Lesson V. Wages and the Accumulation of Capital (part II)* (London, n.d. [1933]), pp. 14–15.

29 *Socialism and the Living Wage* (London, 1927), pp. 177–8 (his emphasis).

30 Maurice Dobb, *Wages* (London, 1928), pp. 73–6; A. E. Cook, *The Socialism of Karl Marx*, p. 22.

31 *The War after the War. In the Light of the Elements of Working Class Economics* (Glasgow, n.d. [1918]), p. 13.

32 *Evolutionary Socialism: A Criticism and Affirmation* (London, 1909).

33 For a summary of the breakdown controversy see Paul M. Sweezy, *The Theory of Capitalist Development. Principles of Marxian Political Economy* (New York, 1942), pp. 190–213.

34 Boudin, *The Theoretical System of Karl Marx. In the Light of Recent Criticism* (Chicago, 1907).

35 Newbold in *Labour Leader*, 20 February 1919; Amery St John Adcock, 'The Beginning of the End', *Call*, 12 September 1918.

36 W. Paul, *Communism and Society*, p. 16.

37 Herman Cahn, *The Collapse of Capitalism* (Chicago, 1919), p. 10.

38 'Will Capitalism Collapse?', *Call*, 28 August 1919; 'Is Capitalism Collapsing?', *Call*, 13 November 1919.

39 I. Lapidus and K. Ostrovityanov, *An Outline of Political Economy* (London, 1929), pp. 373–8; see also A. Bogdanoff, *A Short Course of Economic Science* (London, 1923), pp. 322–31.

40 M. Philips Price, 'The Religion of Catastrophe', *Socialist Review*, n.s., 9 (October 1926), 18–21.

41 Besides the article by Price just cited, see his 'Is the Revolution Coming? Capitalism's Change of Front', *Forward*, 10 April 1926; and Newbold, 'Is Socialism in Our Time Impossible?', *Socialist Review*, n.s., 3 (April 1926), 13–19; 'European Capitalism in Transition', ibid. 22 (November 1927), 32–41.

42 R. Palme Dutt, *Socialism and the Living Wage*, pp. 34–8.

43 It is discussed in my 'Marxism in Britain 1917–1933', pp. 142–4.

44 MacDonald, *Socialism: Critical and Constructive*, pp. 48, 51; Laski, *Communism*, pp. 23, 113–14; Hobson, *Free Thought in the Social Sciences* (London, 1926), p. 147; Webbs, *The Decay of Capitalist Civilization* (London, 1923), p. 166.

45 See Foxwell's Introduction to Anton Menger, *The Right to the Whole Produce of Labour* (London, 1899), pp. xxvi–xxvii, lxxi. Many later examples are noted in my 'Marxism in Britain 1917–1933', p. 154, n. 107.

46 For example, MacDonald, *Socialism: Critical and Constructive*, p. 51; Bertrand Russell, *Roads to Freedom*, pp. 29, 44.

47 'Political Principles in Practice', *Forward*, 22 January 1921.

48 (London, 1926), p. 36.

49 Frank Betts, 'The Clash of Ideas', *New Leader*, 5 June 1931. Betts edited the Bradford *Pioneer* and was the father of Barbara Castle.

50 This was the motion introduced by Snowden into the House of Commons, 161 H.C. Deb. col. 2472 (20 March 1923).

51 We may take as examples H. N. Brailsford, *Socialism for To-Day* (London, 1925), pp. 11–12; Charles Roden Buxton, *What is Socialism? A Plain Answer* (London, n.d. [1924]), p. 4; MacDonald, *Socialism: Critical and Constructive*, pp. 22–6; Snowden, *Labour and the New World* (London, 1921), p. 9; Sidney Webb and Beatrice Webb, *The Decay of Capitalist Civilisation* (London, 1923), p. 2.

52 Philip Snowden, *Wages and Prices* (London, 1920), pp. 6, 17; George Benson, *Socialism and Capitalism* (London, 1925), pp. 2–7.

53 'Karl Marx and the British Labour Movement' in *Revolutionaries. Contemporary Essays* (London, 1973), p. 104.

54 Seven members of the Labour Party, *The Labour Party's Aim. A Criticism and a Restatement* (London, 1923), p. 52.

55 151 H.C. Deb. col. 2475 (20 March 1923).

56 Michael Bleaney, *Underconsumption Theories. A History and Critical Analysis* (London, 1976).

57 Fred Henderson, *The Economic Consequences of Power Production* (London, 1931), pp. 184–5.

58 J. A. Hobson, 'Unemployment. The Root Cause', *New Leader*, 28 September 1923.

59 *Labour Party Conference Report 1925*, pp. 224–8; *1926*, pp. 259–61; *1927*, pp. 51–2, 216–21. The best account of Labour's cool reception is G. D. H. Cole, *A History of the Labour Party from 1914* (London, 1948), pp. 198–200.

60 Maurice Dobb, 'How Rationalisation Increases Unemployment', *Daily Worker*, 8 August 1930 (Dobb is summarising *Capital*, vol. 2, pp. 414–15); 'The Economics of Unemployment', *Plebs* XV (1923), 51–6.

61 Palme Dutt, *Socialism and the Living Wage*, pp. 145–6; Emile Burns, *The Only Way Out* (London, 1932), p. 47.

62 Minnie Pallister, 'Socialism Explained', *New Leader*, 5 February 1932.

63 MacDonald, *Socialism: Critical and Constructive*, p. 22.

64 Cole, *What Marx Really Meant*, p. 276; Snowden, *Socialism and Syndicalism* (London, 1913), pp. 73, 141.

65 In Arthur Henderson, *The Aims of Labour* (London, 1918), p. 105.

66 166 H.C. Deb. col. 1914 (16 July 1923); 'Organised Labour in Relation to Industrial Development' in Percy Alden et al., *Labour and Industry. A Series of Lectures* (Manchester, 1920), p. 250.

67 *A Policy for the Labour Party*, p. 38.

68 James J. Dodd, *If Labour Wins* (London, 1922), p. 50.

69 *Socialism for To-Day*, p. 13.

70 *The Decay of Capitalist Civilisation*, p. 67. Cf. *Capital*, vol. 1, pp. 158–61.

71 *Karl Marx's Capital*, pp. 56–7, 106. For a commentary on Lindsay see Ronald L. Meek, *Studies in the Labour Theory of Value* (London, 1956), pp. 215–20.

72 *Communism*, p. 121.

73 *Labour in the Commonwealth* (London, n.d. [1918]), p. 20; *The World of Labour* (London, 1913), p. 350. See also Cole's introduction to Eden and Cedar Paul's translation of *Capital* (London, 1930), p. xxix.

74 *The Common Sense of Socialism* (London, 1924), p. 24.

75 See A. M. McBriar, *Fabian Socialism and English Politics 1884–1918* (Cambridge, 1962), pp. 37–47; Maurice Dobb, 'Bernard Shaw and Economics' in *On Economic Theory and Socialism. Collected Papers* (London, 1955), pp. 205–14.

76 'The Principles of the Labour Party', *Herald*, 1 December 1917.

77 *Socialism for To-Day*, pp. 71–2.

78 'Labour Capturing the Heights', *Labour Magazine* I (1922), 3.

79 'With the Miners in the North', *Daily Herald*, 24 July 1920.

80 'Karl Marx and the British Labour Movement', p. 104.

81 His career is sketched by Eric Hobsbawm in C. H. Feinstein (ed.), *Socialism, Capitalism and Economic Growth. Essays Presented to Maurice Dobb* (Cambridge, 1967), pp. 1–9; see also the autobiographical notes in a memorial issue of the *Cambridge Journal of Economics* 2 (1978), 115–20.

82 *Capitalist Enterprise and Social Progress* (London, 1925), pp. 143, 397; 'The Entrepreneur Myth', *Economics* IV (1924), 78.

83 Starr, *A Worker Looks at Economics*, p. 11.

84 Letter to *Plebs* XVII (1925), 484.

85 'The Dynamics of Capitalism', *Economics* IV (1926), 35, 37.

86 *Workers' Life*, 7 June 1929.

87 *Political Economy and Capitalism*, esp. pp. 34–78, 130–87.

88 'The Sraffa System and Critique of the Neo-Classical Theory of Distribution', *De Economist* 118 (1970), 347–62.

89 For example Geoffrey Pilling, 'The Law of Value in Ricardo and Marx', *Economy and Society* I (1972), 281–307; Bob Rowthorn, 'Neo-Classicism, Neo-Ricardianism and Marxism', *New Left Review* 86 (July–August 1974), 63–85. They have been answered by John Eatwell, 'Controversies in the Theory of Surplus Value: Old and New', *Science and Society* XXXVIII (1974), 281–303.

CHAPTER 8. CLASS, STATE AND POLITICS

1 Palme Dutt, *Lenin* (London, 1933), p. 14.

2 For discussion of the census categories see A. M. Carr-Saunders and D. Caradog Jones, *A Survey of the Social Structure of England and Wales* (London, 1927), chapter six; and D. C. Marsh, *The Changing Social Structure of England and Wales 1871–1951* (London, 1958), chapter eight.

3 These statistics are taken from Westergaard and Resler, *Class in a Capitalist Society*, p. 112.

4 *What is the Labour Party? A Reply to Liberal Misrepresentation* (London, n.d. [1922]), unpaged.

5 MacDonald, *Parliament and Revolution*, p. 103.

6 Henderson, *The Aims of Labour*, p. 23.

7 Ibid.; Mary Agnes Hamilton, 'The Class War' in H. B. Lees-Smith (ed.),

Encyclopaedia of the Labour Movement, 3 vols. (London, 1928), vol. 1, p. 117.

8 MacDonald, *A Policy for the Labour Party*, p. 42; *Socialism for Business Men* (London, n.d. [1925]), p. 5.

9 *Syndicalism. A Critical Examination* (London, 1912), p. 50.

10 C. T. Cramp, presidential address, *Labour Party Conference Report 1925*, p. 173 (his emphasis); MacDonald, *The Socialist Movement*, p. 149.

11 See Bernard Waites, 'The Language and Imagery of "Class" in Early Twentieth Century England (c. 1900–1925)', *Literature and History* 4 (Autumn 1976), esp. 47–8.

12 (London, 1928), p. 5.

13 MacDonald, *Socialism and Government*, 2 vols. (London, 1909), vol. 1, p. 4; vol. 2, p. 113; Snowden, *Socialism and Syndicalism*, p. 175.

14 MacDonald, *Socialism and Society* (London, 1905), p. 149.

15 MacDonald, *Syndicalism*, p. 5; *Socialism and Society*, p. 151.

16 *The State: Its Origin and Functions*, p. 141.

17 *The Two Internationals* (London, 1920), p. 30.

18 Tom Bell, *The Capitalist State and the Way Out* (London, n.d. [1932]), p. 5; *Communist Party Training*, 2nd edn, p. 35; 'Principles of Communism Explained. The State', *Workers' Life*, 11 October 1929.

19 'The Capitalist State is Workers' Enemy. Cannot be Captured – Must Be Smashed', *Workers' Weekly*, 5 November 1926.

20 Emile Burns, *Capitalism, Communism and the Transition*, pp. 84–5.

21 Ralph Fox, *A Defence of Communism*, p. 22; Dan Richards, 'Parliament the Smoke-Screen for Finance Capital', *Daily Worker*, 3 September 1931.

22 R. Palme Dutt, 'Britain's First General Strike', *Communist International*, 2nd ser., 21 (1926), 19.

23 'Industrial Power', *Socialist Review* XV (1918), 327. Newbold's wall-charts are described in Jack and Bessie Braddock, *The Braddocks*, p. 11.

24 Paul Selver, *Orage and the New Age Circle* (London, 1959), p. 22.

25 Glass, *The Responsible Society* provides a history of the movement, which can be supplemented by Margaret Cole, 'Guild Socialism and the Labour Research Department' in Briggs and Saville (eds.), *Essays in Labour History 1886–1923*, pp. 260–83.

26 The best accounts of Cole's Guild Socialism are L. P. Carpenter, *G. D. H. Cole. An Intellectual Biography* (Cambridge, 1973), pp. 46–111; James Hinton, 'G.D.H. Cole in the Stage Army of the Good', *BSSLH* 28 (Spring 1974), 76–83; and Winter, *Socialism and the Challenge of War. Ideas and Politics in Britain 1912–1918*, pp. 121–49. There is no satisfactory study of Russell's early political thought, and Laski is also poorly served; see however Herbert A. Deane, *The Political Ideas of Harold J. Laski* (New York, 1955), pp. 13–74; and B. Zylstra, *From Pluralism to Collectivism. The Development of Harold J. Laski's Political Thought* (Assen, 1968). My discussion is developed at greater length in 'Marxism in Britain, 1917–1933', pp. 176–90.

27 *Social Theory* (London, 1920), pp. 145, 148; Cole and William Mellor, 'The World for the Workers', *Daily Herald*, 30 June 1914 (quoted in Winter, *Socialism and the Challenge of War*, p. 104); *Labour in the Commonwealth*, p. 185; 'National Guilds and the State', *Socialist Review* XVI (1919), 24.

28 *Roads to Freedom*, pp. 150–1; *Principles of Social Reconstruction* (London, 1916), p. 244; *The Practice and Theory of Bolshevism*, p. 136.

29 *Authority in the Modern State* (New Haven, 1919), pp. 81, 88 (quoted in Deane, *Political Ideas of Harold J. Laski*, p. 19).

30 *Labour in the Commonwealth*, p. 185.

31 *Roads to Freedom*, p. 144.

32 *The Next Ten Years in British Social and Economic Policy* (London, 1929), p. viii.

33 See particularly his entry for 'Socialism' in Lees-Smith (ed.), *Encyclopaedia of the Labour Movement*, vol. 3, p. 150.

34 Bertrand Russell in collaboration with Dora Russell, *The Prospects of Industrial Civilisation* (London, 1923), pp. 103, 134.

35 *The State in the New Social Order* (London, 1922), pp. 5–6, 11; see also *Communism*, pp. 168–80.

36 *The Next Ten Years*, p. 172.

37 Snowden, *Socialism Made Plain* (London, 1920), p. 10; see also MacDonald, *Parliament and Democracy* (London, 1920), p. 41; Henderson, 'The Outlook for Labour', *Contemporary Review* CXIII (1918), 126.

38 *New Clarion*, 17 September 1932 (quoted in Barry, *Nationalisation in British Politics*, p. 315). Barry unravels the complex history of this policy and can be supplemented by Robert A. Dahl, 'Workers' Control of Industry and the British Labour Party', *American Political Science Review* 41 (1947), 875–900, and G. N. Ostergaard, 'Labour and the Development of the Public Corporation', *Manchester School of Economic and Social Studies*, 22 (1954), 192–226.

39 Shaw, 'The Dictatorship of the Proletariat', *Labour Monthly* I (1921), 300; Brailsford, *Socialism for To-Day*, esp. p. 63.

40 'Socialism – Now and After the War', *Labour Leader*, 7 November 1918 (his emphasis).

41 Letter to *New Leader*, 11 September 1931.

42 The quotation is from 256 H.C. Deb. col. 1378 (21 September 1931); there is further discussion of Strachey's conversion in my 'John Strachey, 1901–1931: the Development of an English Marxist', unpublished M.A. thesis (Monash, Australia, 1971), pp. 206–18.

43 See Robert E. Dowse, *Left in the Centre. The I.L.P. 1893–1940* (London, 1966), pp. 168–84.

44 Constitution of the I.L.P. in A. Fenner Brockway, *Socialism at the Cross-Roads. Why the I.L.P. Left the Labour Party* (London, 1932), p. 14; Brailsford, 'Ourselves and the Labour Party', *New Leader*, 25 March 1932; Brockway, *The Coming Revolution* (London, n.d. [1932]), p. 5.

45 Brockway, *Socialism at the Cross-Roads*, p. 9.

46 *Can Socialism Come by Constitutional Methods?* (London, n.d. [1934]), p. 4.

47 *Modern Theories and Forms of Political Organisation* (London, 1932), p. 154; *Intelligent Man's Guide Through World Chaos* (London, 1932), p. 612; *What is This Socialism?* (London, 1933), p. 28.

48 *The Crisis and the Constitution: 1931 and After* (London, 1932), p. 49; *An Introduction to Politics* (London, 1931), p. 21; 'Some implications of the Crisis', *Political Quarterly* II (1931), 467; *Democracy in Crisis* (London, 1933), pp. 251–3.

49 'The Marxist and the Platonic Conceptions of the State', *Plebs* XXIV (1932), 132.

50 Snowden, *Labour and the New World*, p. 48.

51 *If Labour Rules* (London, 1923), pp. 8–9; for an almost identical statement see MacDonald in *Socialist Review* XVI (1919), 312.

52 *Labour Party Conference Report 1923*, p. 178; 'Fabianism' in Lees-Smith (ed.), *Encyclopaedia of the Labour Movement*, vol. 1, pp. 266–7.

53 Snowden, *Labour and the New World*, p. 45; editorial in *Daily Herald*, 31 October 1924.

54 'Draft Programme of the C.P.G.B. to the Comintern', *Communist Review* V (1924), 85; editorial in *Workers' Weekly*, 7 November 1924.

55 W. H. Gregory, interviewed by Richard Lewis and Hywel Francis, 23 November 1972: CHP.

56 James Wood, interviewed by Barry Stacey, May 1969: tape held by John Foster.

57 Wheatley, 'Why a Labour Party?' in Tracey (ed.), *The Book of the Labour Party*, vol. 1, p. 45; MacDonald, *Socialism: Critical and Constructive*, p. 229, and 'The Review Outlook', *Socialist Review* XVIII (1921), 8.

58 'Draft Programme of the C.P.G.B.', pp. 84, 85; *Communist Party Training*, 2nd edn, p. 40.

59 F. Borkenau, *The Communist International* (London, 1938), pp. 180–1.

60 Palme Dutt, 'Notes of the Month', *Labour Monthly* XIV (1932), 557.

61 For example, Laski, *Karl Marx*, p. 39; *Communism*, p. 170; C. E. M. Joad, 'Which Road to Socialism?', *New Clarion*, 25 February 1933; Snowden *Labour and the New World*, p. 53; Tom Johnston, 'If it Had Come to Revolution', *Forward*, 16 April 1921.

62 Fox, *A Defence of Communism*, p. 54; T. H. Wintringham, 'Modern Weapons and Revolution', *Labour Monthly* XV (1933), 46–52.

63 W. Rust, 'Communists and the Army', *Communist* III (1928), 335.

64 Eden and Cedar Paul, *Creative Revolution*, p. 36. The phrase 'justice, rationality and wisdom' echoes MacDonald, *Parliament and Revolution*, p. 203.

65 (London, October 1920), pp. 37, 77. A new translation was published in 1928: see *Collected Works*, vol. 31, pp. 53, 98.

66 Arthur MacManus, reported in transcript of meeting with Labour Party Executive, 29 December 1921: BSSLH 29 (Autumn 1974), 19; Constitution in *What is This Communist Party? A Plain Statement of a Plain Case* (London, n.d. [1921]), unpaged; W. Paul, *Communism and Society*, p. 171.

67 Klugmann, *History of the C.P.G.B.*, vol. 1, p. 200.

68 Hinton and Hyman, *Trade Unions and Revolution*, p. 73 and passim; and see my review in *Sociological Review* 25 (1977), 188–9.

69 W. Paul, *Scientific Socialism: Its Revolutionary Aims and Methods* (Glasgow, 1918), p. 20 (his emphasis). See also *The Development of Socialism in Great Britain* (Glasgow, n.d.), p. 29.

70 See Hinton, *The First Shop Stewards' Movement*, pp. 279–80; and James W. Hulse, *The Forming of the Second International* (Stanford, 1964), pp. 113–23.

71 *Communist International* 5 (September 1919), p. 51.

72 *Worker*, 22 November 1919.

73 Eden and Cedar Paul, 'The British Bolsheviks and the Parliamentary Election', *Workers' Dreadnought*, 7 December 1918; and *Creative Revolution*, p. 12; Ness Edwards, 'Some Thoughts on Tactics', *Workers' Dreadnought*, 24 July 1920.

74 J. R. Stead in *Communist Unity Convention (London, July 31st and August 1st 1920) Official Report* (London, 1920), p. 13.

75 See William Gallacher, *Revolt on the Clyde. An Autobiography* (London, 1936), pp. 251–4; E. Sylvia Pankhurst, *Soviet Russia as I Saw It* (London, 1921), p. 48; *M. N. Roy's Memoirs* (Bombay, 1964), pp. 317–18; 'Fortieth Birthday of an Outstanding Book', *Marx Memorial Library Bulletin* 15 (1960), 2–5.

76 See for example Sylvia Pankhurst, 'Gallacher's Revolution', *Workers' Dreadnought*, 31 December 1921; Guy Aldred, *Communism, Story of the Communist Party* (London, 1943), pp. 82–90.

77 *'Left Wing' Communism*, p. 21 (*Collected Works*, vol. 31, p. 35). The same point was made in an E.C.C.I. circular, 'Parliamentarism and the Struggle for Soviets', *Communist International* 5 (September 1919), 60–2.

78 *Parliamentarism. Trade Unionism and the Communist International* (London, 1920), pp. 5–6.

79 *Communist Party Policy and Electoral Programme* (London, 1922), pp. 4–5; W. Hill in *Communist Unity Convention*, p. 15.

80 *'Left Wing' Communism*, p. 69 (*Collected Works*, vol. 31, p. 89).

81 T. A. Jackson, 'Why Bother About Parliament?', *Communist*, 4 November 1922; 'Why Stand for Parliament?', *Workers' Life*, 8 March 1929.

82 Georgii Zinoviev, 'Parliament and the Struggle for Soviets', *Socialist Review* XVII (1920), 271; *Communist Party Training*, 2nd edn, p. 44.

83 *Speeches and Documents of the Sixth Congress of the C.P.G.B. 17–19 May 1924*, p. 32. *Communist Party Training*, loc. cit.

CHAPTER 9. THE PROBLEM OF CLASS CONSCIOUSNESS

1 *The Faith of a Democrat* (London, 1928), p. 3.

2 MacDonald, *A Policy for the Labour Party*, p. 181.

3 Snowden, *Twenty Objections to Socialism*, p. 16.

4 *Merrie England* (Manchester, 1893), p. 93.

5 MacDonald, *Parliament and Revolution*, p. 103; *A Policy for the Labour Party*, p. 183.

6 Emile Burns, *Capitalism, Communism and the Transition*, p. 81.

7 Dan Griffiths, *The Real Enemy, and Other Socialist Essays*, pp. 19, 21.

8 W. Paul, *Communism and Society*, p. 79.

9 Sylvia Pankhurst, 'A Reply to Philip Snowden', *Workers' Dreadnought*, 6 March 1920; J. P. M. Millar, 'Ten Minutes' Talks with New Students', *Plebs* XII (1920), 195.

10 Bukharin and Preobrazhensky, *The ABC of Communism*, trans. Eden Paul and Cedar Paul (London, 1922), p. 44.

11 Norman Angell, 'Capturing the Workers' Will', *New Leader*, 9 November 1923.

12 Thomas Bell, editorial in *Communist Review* IV (1924), 507; R. Palme Dutt, *Marxism After Fifty Years* (London, n.d. [1933]), p. 9.

13 W. Paul, *The State*, p. 187.

14 Directorate of Intelligence, Report of Revolutionary Organisations in the United Kingdom, 30 October 1919: CAB 24/92 (28).

15 Editorial, *Daily Herald*, 31 October 1924; ibid., 27, 28, 21 October 1924.

16 'Notes of the Month', *Labour Monthly* VI (1924), 714.

17 Advertisement for the *Herald* in *Labour Magazine* V (August 1926); MacDonald, *Parliament and Revolution*, p. 27.

18 MacDonald in *Daily Herald*, 25 October 1924.

19 William Paul, 'Race Riots and Revolution', *Socialist*, 10 July 1919.

20 'Broadcasting Babble Machine', *Labour Monthly* XIII (1931), 191.

21 *Workers' Weekly*, 26 December 1924.

22 William Paul, 'Capitalism, Labour and the Press', *Labour Monthly* VII (1925), 565.

23 Minnie Pallister, 'Labour Women Confer', *New Leader*, 5 June 1925; 'Workers' Sport', *Communist* III (1928), 461.

24 'The Press', in Lees-Smith (ed.), *Encyclopaedia of the Labour Movement*, vol. 3, p. 60.

25 *Parliament and Revolution*, p. 65; and reported at the 1921 Conference of the I.L.P. in *Labour Leader*, 31 March 1921.

26 Harold Laski, *Socialism and Freedom* (London, 1925), p. 5.

27 MacDonald, *Socialism: Critical and Constructive*, p. 234; Snowden, *Labour and the New World*, p. 51; F. H. Hayward and B. N. Langdon-Davies, *Democracy and the Press* (Manchester, n.d. [1919]), pp. 59–60.

28 The tradition is discussed with respect to MacDonald by Bernard Barker in his introduction to *Ramsay MacDonald's Political Writings* (London, 1972); and more generally by Rodney Barker, *Education and Politics 1900–1951*, chapter one.

29 'Socialism and Human Nature', *Socialist Review* XXIV (1924), 182.

30 *The Meaning of Socialism*, p. 7; quoted in Bernard Barker, 'The Politics of Propaganda: A Study in the Theory of Educational Socialism and its Role in the Development of a National Labour Party in London and the West Riding of Yorkshire, 1914–24', unpublished M.Phil. thesis (York, 1972), p. 42.

31 MacDonald, *Socialism: Critical and Constructive*, p. 283.

32 George Lansbury's presidential address, *Labour Party Conference Report 1928*, p. 150; MacDonald, *Socialism: Critical and Constructive*, p. 2, and *Parliament and Revolution*, p. 8; and his presidential address, *Labour Party Conference Report 1924*, p. 110.

33 *A Policy for the Labour Party*, p. 67.

34 'The Socialist Way', *Forward*, 10 September 1917; 'The Review Outlook', *Socialist Review* XVI (1919), 208.

35 MacDonald, *Parliament and Revolution*, p. 6; Clifford Allen, 'A Victory that Leads to Victory', *New Leader*, 7 November 1924; R. Neft in Griffiths (ed.), *What is Socialism?*, p. 57.

36 Arthur Ponsonby, 'Democracy and the Mob', *Socialist Review* XXII (1923), 60; MacDonald in *Forward*, 21 December 1918; MacDonald, 'The Review Outlook', *Socialist Review* XVII (1920), 9; Price, *My Three Revolutions* (London, 1969), p. 247; *Forward*, 8 November 1924; Michael Egan, 'A Race for Safety', *Socialist Review* XXIV (1924), 171.

37 Clifford Allen, *Socialism and the Next Labour Government* (London, 1925), p. 6.

38 John Scurr, 'The Dictatorship of the Proletariat', *Labour Leader*, 29 January 1920; Dan Griffiths, *The Real Enemy*, pp. 12–13; Ernest Bevin, 'Straight On Through the Wilderness', *Labour Magazine* X (1931), 347; George Lansbury's preface to Gerald Gould, *The Coming Revolution in Great Britain* (London, 1920), p. ix.

39 MacDonald, *Parliament and Revolution*, p. 103.

40 Clifford Allen, *Putting Socialism into Practice* (London, 1924), pp. 16–17.

41 Graham Wallas, *Human Nature in Politics* (London, 1908), p. 45.

42 Eden and Cedar Paul in *Labour Leader*, 17 January 1918.

43 Shaw, 'Are we Bolshevists?', *Labour Leader*, 24 April 1919; Tawney, 'Christianity and the Social Revolution' in *The Attack and Other Papers* (London, 1953), pp. 163–4; Tillett in *Daily Herald*, 31 October 1924.

44 For example in the Dumbarton *Lennox Herald*, 9 November 1918.

45 *The Attack*, p. 163. Ross Terrill explores Tawney's use of Henry Dubb in *R. H. Tawney and His Times. Socialism as Fellowship* (London, 1973), esp. pp. 178, 195–6.

46 James Gascoyne, 'The Coming Crash', *Communist* 12 August 1920; Eden and Cedar Paul, 'Socialist Education', *Workers' Dreadnought*, 10 August 1918.

47 L. A. Motler, 'Dubb Dialogues', *Workers' Dreadnought*, 16 and 23 August 1919.

48 *Socialist*, October 1904; quoted in Challinor, *Origins of British Bolshevism*, p. 37.

49 Recalled by Len Jeffreys, interviewed by David Egan and Hywel Francis, 20 September 1972: CHP. Jackson himself wrote an illuminating chapter on 'The Art of Propaganda' in the unpublished section of his memoirs.

50 Interviewed by John Foster, 12 March 1970.

51 George Lansbury, *My Life* (London, 1928), p. 111.

52 *Sunday Worker*, 18 September 1927.

53 *Socialist*, 24 December 1919.

54 (London, 1892), pp. xvii–xviii.

55 (London, 1926), chapter eight; and 'Imperialism and the Split in the Labour Movement' (1916) in *Lenin on Britain* (London, 1923), p. 142 (*Collected Works*, vol. 22, pp. 276–85; vol. 23, p. 110). See E. J. Hobsbawm's discussion of the theory in *Revolutionaries. Contemporary Essays*, pp.121–9.

56 Theodore Rothstein, *From Chartism to Labourism. Historical Sketches of the English Working Class Movement* (London, 1929), p. 266; J. Shields, 'The Struggle of the Indian Masses', *Communist Review*, n.s., IV (1932), 76.

57 R. Palme Dutt, *Modern India* (London, 1927), p. 172; Ralph Fox, 'A Communist Replies to Philips Price', *Socialist Review*, n.s., 8 (September 1926), 41.

58 Esp. pp. 255–66.

59 'Self-study Syllabus', *Communist* II (1927), 284.

60 Jack Leckie, 'Draft Programme of the C.P.G.B. to the Comintern Criticised', *Communist Review* V (1924), 185.

61 'The Concept of the Labour Aristocracy', *Popular Politics*, p. 61. For a contrary view see E. J. Hobsbawm, 'The Labour Aristocracy in Late

Victorian Britain' in *Labouring Men: Studies in the History of Labour*
(London, 1964), pp. 272–315. More recent contributions are listed in
H. F. Moorhouse, 'The Marxist Theory of the Labour Aristocracy', *Social
History* 3 (1978), 61–82.

62 *The I.L.P. and the Third International* (London, 1920), p. 17; M. Philips
Price, 'Impressions of the General Election', *Communist International* 24
(1923), 37.
63 Alfred Barton, *A World History for Workers* (London, 1922), p. 95;
Brailsford, *Socialism for To-Day*, p. 51.
64 'The Principle of Empire', *Olives of Endless Age* (New York, 1928), p. 283.
65 *Labour Party Conference Report 1921*, p. 207.
66 L. Haden-Guest, *The Labour Party and the Empire* (London, 1926), p. 7. For
discussion of this group see Partha Sarathi Gupta, *Imperialism and the
British Labour Movement 1914–1964* (London, 1974), pp. 64–5. The topic of
imperialism is discussed at greater length in my pamphlet *Imperialism and
the British Labour Movement in the 1920s* (London, 1975).
67 Tom Quelch, 'The Opposition to the Social Revolution in Britain',
Communist International III, 16–17 (1922), 99–100.
68 R. Palme Dutt, 'Notes of the Month', *Labour Monthly* VI (1924), 582–3.
69 G. Safarov, 'The Leeds Congress of the C.P.G.B.', *Communist International*,
n.s., VI (1930), 1162–9.
70 William Rust, 'The Moscow Road', *Communist Review*, n.s., IV (1932), 26;
R. P. Arnot, 'Tendencies in the British Party', *Communist International*, n.s.,
VI (1929), 103.
71 *Communist Review*, n.s., III, 423.
72 Letter to *Daily Worker*, 22 August 1932; Jackson, 'Self Criticism',
Communist Review, n.s., I (1929), 133.
73 Quoted in Bullock, *The Life and Times of Ernest Bevin*, vol. 1, p. 401.
74 *Communism is Commonsense* (London, 1926), p. 13. See also Allen Hutt's
perceptive comments in *The Post-War History of the British Working Class*,
p. 316.
75 Cowbrett, 'Immediate Demands', *Communist Review* V (1924), 255.
76 'Marxism', *Socialist*, 6 January 1921; Newbold, 'The I.L.P.: A Marxist
Study', *Socialist Review* XVII (1920), 86.
77 Editorial, *Communist Review* V (1924), 313.
78 'A Query and an Answer', *Communist Review* VII (1926), 339.
79 A. Bernard, 'Marxist–Leninist Education', *Communist Review* VII (1926),
378.
80 *Labour Monthly* VIII (1926), 323.
81 'The C.P.G.B. and the Labour Party: Thesis of the Central Committee',
Communist International, n.s., V (1928), 123, 125.
82 'The New Phase in Britain and the Communist Party', *Communist
International*, n.s., V (1928), 135, 142.
83 R. Page Arnot, 'Tendencies in the British Party', *Communist International*,
n.s., VI (1929), 103.
84 Jones, 'Lenin's First Newspaper', *Communist Review* V (1924), 64–72;
MacDougall, 'A Bible for the Bolsheviks', ibid. VI (1925), 329.
85 J. R. Campbell, 'The Outlook', *Communist Review*, n.s., I (1929), 624–6;
R. Palme Dutt, 'Notes of the Month', *Labour Monthly* XIV (1932), 70

86 Len Jefferies, 'Faith in the Working Class', *Communist Review*, n.s., IV (1932), 495.

87 'Economism Today', *Communist Review*, n.s., II (1930), 196–207; 'Raising the Theoretical Level of the Party', ibid., 432–41. See also Utley, *Lost Illusion* (London, 1949), pp. 33–4.

88 Political Bureau, 'The Theoretician of "Left" Sectarianism and Spontaneity', *Communist Review*, n.s., III (1931), 11–19. See also Walter Tapsell, 'Economism: A Reply to F. Utley', ibid. n.s., II (1930), 302–6, and 'The Opportunism of Comrade Utley', ibid. n.s., II (1930), 582–7.

89 'Fundamental Questions for Our Party', *Communist Review*, n.s., II (1930), 397.

CHAPTER 10. THE MOSCOW ROAD

1 Snowden, *Socialism and Syndicalism*, p. 65. See also MacDonald, *Socialism: Critical and Constructive*, pp. 48–50.

2 MacDonald, *The History of the I.L.P.* (London, 1922), p. 10; *Parliament and Revolution*, p. 97.

3 *Bradford Pioneer*, 6 February 1920; quoted in Carl F. Brand, *British Labour's Rise to Power* (Stanford, 1941), p. 208.

4 For the S.P.G.B. see Barltrop, *The Monument*, chapter seven.

5 R. C. Wallhead, 'The Present Crisis', *Labour Leader*, 12 August 1920; W. H. Hutchinson, presidential address in *Labour Party Conference Report 1920*, p. 113.

6 H. N. Brailsford, introduction to Trotsky, *Where is Britain Going?* (London, 1926), p. vi.

7 *Parliament and Revolution*, p. 98.

8 Snowden, *Labour and the New World*, p. 44; MacDonald, 'The Review Outlook', *Socialist Review* XVIII (1921), 77.

9 For example William Stewart, 'In Answer to a Question', *Forward*, 17 January 1920; Dan Griffiths, 'The Use and Abuse of Direct Action', *Labour Leader*, 7 August 1919; Laski, *Communism*, p. 47.

10 *I.L.P. Conference Report 1920*, p. 70; 'To a Doubting Internationalist', *Labour Leader*, 18 December 1919.

11 *Labour Party Conference Report 1920*, p. 173.

12 Letter to *Labour Leader*, 4 September 1919; P. M. Philips Price, 'A Lion at Bay', *Plebs* XVII (1925), 240.

13 Arthur Ponsonby, 'Labour and Bolshevism', *Labour Leader*, 23 September 1920; George Benson in *I.L.P. Conference Report 1921*, p. 114; Brailsford, editorial in *New Leader*, 21 November 1924; MacDonald in *Labour Party Conference Report 1924*, p. 109.

14 MacDonald, *Parliament and Revolution*, p. 93; *I.L.P. Conference Report 1921*, p. 122.

15 *Labour Party Conference Report 1922*, p. 198.

16 Hodges in *Labour Party Conference Report 1923*, p. 188; Robert Williams, 'The Gospel According to Trotsky', *Labour Magazine* IV (1926), 519.

17 'Why the I.L.P. Has Left the Labour Party', supplement to *New Leader*, 5 August 1932.

18 George Benson, 'Our Soviet Impossibilists', *Labour Leader*, 22 January 1920; MacDonald, *Parliament and Revolution*, p. 92.

19 Middleton Murry, 'Why I Joined the I.L.P.', *New Leader*, 1 January 1932.

20 Brailsford, *The Russian Workers' Republic* (London, 1921), p. 171.

21 George Benson, 'Our Soviet Impossibilists', *Labour Leader*, 22 January 1920; Brailsford, introduction to Trotsky, *Where is Britain Going?*, p. vii; Henderson, *The Aims of Labour*, p. 57.

22 Cole, *Labour in the Commonwealth*, p. 63; Bertrand Russell, 'Trotsky on our Sins', *New Leader*, 26 February 1926.

23 For two examples of this uncommon position see Postgate, 'Lenin's Record', *Lansbury's Labour Weekly*, 3 April 1926, and Walton Newbold in *Plebs* XVI (1924), 482–3.

24 B.S.P. Editorial Committee's foreword to Lenin, *Lessons of the Russian Revolution* (London, 1918), p. 3; William Paul, *Karl Liebknecht: His Work and Message* (Glasgow, n.d. [1919]), p. 17.

25 Murphy in *Plebs* XV (1923), 152–3; Dutt, 'Notes of the Month', *Labour Monthly* VI (1924), 135.

26 'Foundations of Leninism', in *Leninism*, vol. 1, p. 80; *Bolshevising the Communist International* (London, 1925), p. 150. The earlier appreciations of Bukharin and Trotsky were presented to a British audience in Bukharin, *Lenin as a Marxist* (London, 1925); Trotsky, 'The Tasks of Communist Education', *Communist Review* IV (1923), 324–7.

27 Rothstein, 'Leninism: A Subject for Plebs Studies', *Plebs* XVI (1924), 417 (his emphasis); 'Leninism', *Workers' Weekly*, 16 January 1925.

28 'Stalin, Lenin and "Leninism"', *New Left Review* 103 (May–June 1977), 59–71.

29 See *The Second Congress of the Communist International. Proceedings* (American Publishing Office of the Communist International, 1921), pp. 113–22; Lenin's response to Roy appears in *Collected Works*, vol. 31, pp. 240–5.

30 Allen Hutt, in *Communist Review*, n.s., VI (1933), 375.

31 *The I.L.P. and the Third International* (London, 1920), p. 44.

32 W. T. Goode, *Bolshevism at Work* (London, 1920), p. 22; Haden-Guest, *The Struggle for Power in Europe 1917–1921* (London, 1921), p. 46; Lansbury, *What I Saw in Russia* (London, 1920), p. 170; Russell, *Practice and Theory of Bolshevism*, p. 38; Ransome, *Six Weeks in Russia in 1919* (London, 1919), p. 80. See also Sylvia Pankhurst, *Soviet Russia as I Saw It*, pp. 45–52; Ben Turner, *About Myself 1863–1930* (London, 1930), pp. 220–1.

33 Challinor, *Origins of British Bolshevism*, chapter ten; Kendall, *Revolutionary Movement in Britain*, chapter thirteen.

34 'Learn to Speak Russian', *Call*, 14 February 1918; MacManus in *Manchester Guardian*, 25 April 1921.

35 John Bryan [Theodore Rothstein], 'What is our Position?', *Call*, 17 April 1919; Editorial, *Communist Review*, n.s., V (1933), 102; Andrew Rothstein, 'On Lenin's Method', *Communist* II (1927), 221.

36 George Sims, review of the Pauls' *Creative Revolution* in *Plebs* XI (1920), 136.

37 'The Russians Can Teach us Much', *Workers' Weekly*, 5 November 1926; Mirsky, *Lenin* (London, 1931), p. 165; J. R. Campbell, 'Tasks Before the Party Congress', *Communist Review* VII (1926), 178.

38 'Draft Programme of the C.P.G.B. to the Comintern', *Communist Review* V (1924), 92.
39 See Theodore Draper, *American Communism and Soviet Russia* (New York, 1960), chapter twelve.
40 Trotsky, *Where is Britain Going?*, p. 49; 'Are British a Peculiar People?', *Daily Worker*, 4 August 1932.
41 Dobb, *On Marxism To-Day*, p. 7; Editorial in *Communist Review* VI (1925), 54; Bell's review of *The Peasant War in Germany*, ibid. VIII (1927), 435.
42 Ralph Fox in *Communist* II (1927), 227; Fred Shaw in *Call*, 21 February 1918; Palme Dutt in *Labour Monthly* VI (1924), 133.
43 Dobb, *Russian Economic Development Since the Revolution*, p. 5; and his review of Ryanzanoff's *Karl Marx* in *Labour Monthly* IX (1927), 702.

CONCLUSION

1 Sheila Rowbotham's *A New World for Women* (London, 1977) is concerned with one outstanding individual, Stella Browne, but is restricted by insufficient consideration of the context. Sue Bruley is preparing a doctoral dissertation on Communist women during the period, which is to be submitted to London University. I discuss imperialism in chapter 9 of my 'Marxism in Britain'.
2 Hugh McIntyre and Bob Saunders, interviewed by John Foster. The Vale of Leven branch of the S.L.P. wrote letters to the local *Lennox Herald* during 1919 and 1920 explaining that nothing could be done to alleviate conditions.

Bibliography

No full-length compilation of sources on this subject has been assembled so far, and the bibliography in my doctoral thesis, which runs to over a thousand items, is little more than preliminary. The quantity and the largely ephemeral character of contemporary publications make it impossible to compile a satisfactory selection; however, I have omitted some items cited in the notes and included others of greater significance. There are no entries for works by Marx and Engels, for which see the Appendix to chapter 3.

1. UNPUBLISHED MATERIAL

Cabinet Papers. Reports on Revolutionary Organisations in the United Kingdom, 1917–21.

James Clunie Papers, National Library of Scotland.

Winifred Horrabin Papers, University of Hull.

T. A. Jackson, manuscript autobiography and papers in the possession of Mrs Vivien Morton.

Marx Memorial Library, documentary material mainly dealing with C.P.G.B.

National Council of Labour Colleges Papers, including the Plebs League, Central Labour College and several individual collections: National Library of Scotland.

J. T. Walton Newbold Papers, John Rylands Library, Manchester.

South Wales Miners' Library, interview transcripts of Coalfield History Project, and manuscript and documentary material mainly dealing with working-class education in South Wales.

2. PERIODICALS

Adelphi, n.s., 1930–3.
Anvil, 1925–8.
Call, 1917–20.
Communist (weekly), 1920–3.
Communist International, 1920–33.
Communist Review and *Communist* (monthly), 1921–33.
Counter Attack, 1932–3.
Herald and *Daily Herald*, 1917–33.
Daily Worker, 1930–3.
Forward, 1917–33.
Guildsman and *Guild Socialist*, 1916–23.
International Press Correspondence, 1921–33.
Labour Leader and *New Leader*, 1917–33.

Labour Magazine, 1922–33.
Labour Monthly, 1921–33.
Lansbury's Labour Weekly, 1925–7.
New Clarion, 1932–3.
Plebs, 1917–33.
Social Democrat, occasionally.
Socialist, 1916–24.
Socialist Review, 1917–29.
Socialist Standard, 1918–20.
Solidarity, 1917–21.
Sunday Worker, 1925–9.
Worker, 1917–21.
Workers' Dreadnought, 1917–24.
Workers' Life, 1927–9.
Workers' Weekly, 1923–7.

3. CONTEMPORARY PUBLICATIONS

Ablett, Noah. *Easy Outlines of Economics* (Oxford, 1919).

Alden, Percy, et al. *Labour and Industry. A Series of Lectures* (Manchester, 1920).

Allen, Clifford. *Putting Socialism into Practice* (London, 1924).

—— *Socialism and the Next Labour Government* (London, 1925).

[Anderson], Comrade Tom. *Comrade Josef Dietzgen. Proletarian School Lessons given...during August 1935* (Glasgow, 1935).

Angell, Norman. *Must Britain Travel the Moscow Road? With Special Reference to Leon Trotsky's Book, 'Where is Britain Going?'* (London, 1926).

Arnot, R. Page. *Trade Unionism: a New Model* (London, 1919).

—— *William Morris. A Vindication* (London, 1934).

Aveling, Edward. *The Student's Marx. An Introduction to the Study of Karl Marx's Capital* (London, 1892).

Barnes, G. N., et. al. *Religion in the Labour Movement* (London, 1919).

Barton, Alfred. *A World History for Workers* (London, 1922).

Beer, Max. *A History of British Socialism*, 2 vols. (London, 1920).

—— *The Life and Teaching of Karl Marx* (London, 1921).

—— *A Guide to the Study of Marx. An Introductory Course for Classes and Study Circles* (London, n.d. [1924]).

Bell, Thomas. *Nikolai Lenin. A Brief Biographical Sketch* (London, 1925).

—— *The Capitalist State and the Way Out* (London, n.d. [1932]).

Benson, George. *Socialism and Capitalism* (London, 1925).

Bernstein, Edward. *Evolutionary Socialism. A Criticism and Affirmation* (London, 1909).

Bevan, Aneurin. *In Place of Fear* (London, 1952).

Blatchford, Robert. *Merrie England* (Manchester, 1893).

—— *God and My Neighbour* (London, 1903).

Bogdanoff, A. *A Short Course of Economic Science* (London, 1923).

Böhm-Bawerk, E. von. *Karl Marx and the Close of His System* (London, 1898).

Boudin, Louis B. *The Theoretical System of Karl Marx. In the Light of Recent Criticism* (Chicago, 1907).

Brailsford, H. N. *The War of Steel and Gold. A Study of the Armed Peace* (London, 1914).

—— *The Russian Workers' Republic* (London, 1921).

—— *Socialism for To-Day* (London, 1925).

British Socialist Party. Conference Reports, 1912–20.

Brockway, A. Fenner. *Socialism at the Cross-Roads. Why the I.L.P. Left the Labour Party* (London, 1932).

—— *The Coming Revolution* (London, n.d. [1932]).

Bukharin, N. *Lenin as a Marxist* (London, 1925).

—— *Historical Materialism. A System of Sociology* (London, 1926).

—— and E. Preobrazhensky. *The ABC of Communism*, trans. P. Lavitch (Glasgow, 1921); trans. Eden and Cedar Paul (London, 1922).

Burns, Emile. *The Only Way Out* (London, 1932).

—— *What Is the Communist Party?* (London, n.d. [1933]).

—— *Capitalism, Communism and the Transition* (London, 1933).

Buxton, Charles Roden. *What Is Socialism? A Plain Answer* (London, n.d. [1924]).

Cahn, Herman. *The Collapse of Capitalism* (Chicago, 1919).

Campbell, J. R. *What is the Use of Parliament?* (London, 1924).

—— and W. Gallacher. *Direct Action. An Outline of Workshop and Social Organisation* (Glasgow, 1919).

Casey, Fred. *Thinking: An Introduction to its History and Science* (London, 1922).

—— *Chart of Ancient Philosophy* and *Chart of Medieval and Modern Philosophy* (London, 1922).

—— *Dietzgen's Logic. A Plain Introduction to 'The Positive Outcome of Philosophy' Written for the Plain Man* (Stockport, n.d. [1928]).

—— *Method in Thinking. A Series of Popular Lectures* (Manchester, 1933).

Clarke, John S. *Marxism and History* (London, 1927).

Clunie, James. *The Third (Communist) International: Its Aims and Methods* (Glasgow, 1920).

Coates, Zelda Kahan. *Karl Marx: His Life and Teaching* (London, 1918).

Cole, G. D. H. *The World of Labour* (London, 1913).

—— *Labour in the Commonwealth* (London, n.d. [1918]).

—— *Social Theory* (London, 1920).

—— *The Next Ten Years in British Social and Economic Policy* (London, 1929).

—— *What Marx Really Meant* (London, 1934).

Commission of Enquiry into Industrial Unrest. No. 7 Division: Report of the Commissioners for Wales, including Monmouthshire; No. 8 Division: Report of the Commissioners for Scotland, Cmd. 8668–9 (London, 1917).

Communism is Commonsense [C.P.G.B.] (London, 1926).

Communist International. Programmes, Reports and Congress Proceedings, 1918–33.

Communist Papers. Documents Selected from Those Obtained on the Arrest of the Communist Leaders on the 14th and 21st October 1925, Cmd 2682 (London, 1926).

Communist Party of Great Britain. Congress Reports and Proceedings, 1920–33.

Communist Party and the Labour Party, The. All the Facts and All the Correspondence [C.P.G.B.] (London, n.d. [1921]).

Communist Party Training [C.P.G.B.] (London, 1926, 2nd edn 1927).

Communist Political Education. A Manual for Workers' Study Groups [C.P.G.B.] (London, 1933).

Conzé, Edward. *An Introduction to Dialectical Materialism* (London, 1926).

—— *The Scientific Method of Thinking* (London, 1935).

Cook, A. E. *The Socialism of Karl Marx* (Glasgow, 1918).

Cook, A. J., and James Maxton. *Our Case for a Socialist Revival* (London, n.d. [1928]).

Cripps, Stafford. *Can Socialism Come by Constitutional Methods?* (London, n.d. [1934]).

De Leon, Daniel. *Two Pages from Roman History* (Edinburgh, 1908).

Dietzgen, Joseph. *The Positive Outcome of Philosophy*, trans. Ernest Untermann (Chicago, 1906); trans. W. W. Craik (Chicago, 1928).

—— *Some of the Philosophical Essays on Socialism and Science, Religion, Ethics, Critique-of-Reason and the World-at-Large* (Chicago, 1907).

Dobb, Maurice. *The Development of Modern Capitalism: an Outline Course for Classes and Study Circles* (London, 1922).

—— *Capitalist Enterprise and Social Progress* (London, 1925).

—— *Russian Economic Development since the Revolution* (London, 1928).

—— *On Marxism To-Day* (London, 1932).

—— *Political Economy and Capitalism. Some Essays in Economic Tradition* (London, 1937).

Dutt, Rajani Palme. *The Two Internationals* (London, 1920).

—— *Socialism and the Living Wage* (London, 1927).

—— *Lenin* (London, 1933).

—— *Marxism After Fifty Years* (London, n.d. [1933]).

Eastman, Max. *Since Lenin Died* (London, 1925).

—— *Marx, Lenin and the Science of Revolution* (London, 1926).

Education for Emancipation (London, 1926).

Elementary Course of Party Training, An [C.P.G.B.] (London, n.d. [1927]).

Fox, Ralph. *A Defence of Communism: in Reply to H. J. Laski* (London, 1927).

—— *The Class Struggle in Britain in the Epoch of Imperialism*, 2 vols. (London, 1932).

Glasier, J. Bruce. *The Meaning of Socialism* (Manchester, 1919).

—— *William Morris and the Early Days of the Socialist Movement* (London, 1921).

Glasier, Katharine Bruce. *Socialism for Beginners* (London, 1929).

Gould, Gerald. *The Coming Revolution in Great Britain* (London, 1920).

Griffiths, Dan. *The Real Enemy, and Other Socialist Essays* (London, 1923).

—— (ed.). *What is Socialism? A Symposium* (London, 1924).

Haeckel, Ernst. *The Riddle of the Universe* (London, 1900).

Hamilton, Mary Agnes. *The Principles of Socialism* (London, 1922).

Hay, W. F. *Education and the Working Class* (Liverpool, n.d. [1921?]).

Henderson, Arthur. *The Aims of Labour* (London, n.d. [1918]).

Hird, Dennis. *Easy Outline of Evolution* (London, 1907).

Hogben, Lancelot. *The Nature of Living Matter* (London, 1930).

—— 'Contemporary Philosophy in the Soviet Union', *Psyche* XII (1931), 2–18.

Horrabin, J. F. and Winifred Horrabin. *What Does Education Mean to the Workers?* (London, 1917).

—— *Working-Class Education* (London, 1924).

Hyndman, H. M. *Historic Basis of Socialism in England* (London, 1883).

—— *Economics of Socialism* (London, 1896).

—— *The Evolution of Revolution* (London, 1920).

I.L.P. and the Third International, The [I.L.P.] (London, 1920).

Independent Labour Party. Conference Reports, 1918–33.

Jackson, T. A. *Dialectics. The Logic of Marxism and its Critics – An Essay in Exploration* (London, 1936).

Joseph, H. W. B. *The Labour Theory of Value in Karl Marx* (London, 1923).

Kautsky, Karl. *The Economic Doctrines of Karl Marx* (London, 1925).

Labour and the Nation [Labour Party] (London, 1928).

Labour and the New Social Order [Labour Party] (London, 1918).

Labour Party. Conference Reports, 1917–33.

Lansbury, George. *What I Saw in Russia* (London, 1920).

Lapidus, I. and K. Ostrovityanov. *An Outline of Political Economy* (London, 1929).

Laski, H. J. *Karl Marx: An Essay* (London, 1922).

—— *Communism* (London, 1927).

—— *Democracy in Crisis* (London, 1933).

Lee, H. W. and E. Archbold. *Social Democracy in Britain. Fifty Years of the Socialist Movement* (London, 1935).

Lees-Smith, H. B. (ed.). *Encyclopaedia of the Labour Movement*, 3 vols. (London, 1928).

Lenin, V. I. *Lessons of the Russian Revolution* (London, 1918).

—— *The State and Revolution* (London, 1919).

—— *'Left Wing' Communism: An Infantile Disorder* (London, 1920).

—— *Materialism and Empirio-Criticism* (London, 1927).

—— *What Is To Be Done?* (London, 1929).

Levy, Hyman, et al. *Aspects of Dialectical Materialism* (London, 1934).

Lindsay, A. D. *Karl Marx's Capital. An Introductory Essay* (London, 1925).

London, Jack. *Martin Eden* (London, 1910).

MacDonald, J. Ramsay. *The Socialist Movement* (London, n.d. [1911]).

—— *Parliament and Revolution* (Manchester, 1919).

—— *A Policy for the Labour Party* (London, 1920).

—— *Socialism: Critical and Constructive* (London, 1921).

McLaine, W. *Trade Unionism at the Cross Roads* (London, 1917).

—— *The Evolution of Industry* (London, 1918).

Maclean, John. *A Plea for a Labour College for Scotland* (Glasgow, 1916).

—— *The War after the War. In the Light of the Elements of Working Class Economics* (Glasgow, n.d. [1918]).

—— *Notes of Lectures on Economics Given by John Maclean* (Glasgow, n.d.).

Manual of Party Training. Principles and Organisation [C.P.G.B.] (London, 1924).

Marxist Study Courses [C.P.G.B.]: a fortnightly series of pamphlets on Political Economy, Historical Materialism, etc. (London, 1932–3).

Mellor, William. *Direct Action* (London, 1920).

Millar, J. P. M. *The National Council of Labour Colleges: History, Report and Directory* (London, 1924).

Murphy, J. T. *The Workers' Committee. An Outline of its Principles and Structure* (Sheffield, 1917).

Newbold, J. T. Walton. *The Politics of Capitalism* (London, 1918).

—— *Marx and Modern Capitalism* (London, 1918).

Pankhurst, E. Sylvia. *Soviet Russia as I Saw It* (London, 1921).

Paul, Eden. *Karl Marx and Modern Socialism* (Manchester, 1916).

—— and Cedar Paul. *Independent Working Class Education* (London, 1918).

—— *Creative Revolution. A Study of Communist Ergatocracy* (London, 1920).

—— *Proletcult (Proletarian Culture)* (London, 1921).

Paul, William. *The State: Its Origin and Functions* (Glasgow, 1917).

—— *Scientific Socialism: Its Revolutionary Aims and Methods* (Glasgow, 1918).

—— *Communism and Society* (London, 1922).

Plebs League. *An Outline of Modern Imperialism* (London, 1922).

—— *An Outline of Economics* (London, 1922).

—— *How to Start a Social Science Class* (London. 1917).

—— *What Does Education Mean to the Workers?* (London, 1921).

—— *Do Your Own Thinking* (London, 1922).

—— *What To Read. A Guide for Worker Students* (London, 1923).

Pollitt, Harry. *Selected Articles and Speeches*, vol. 1 (London, 1953).

Portus, G. V. *Marx and Modern Thought* (Sydney, 1922).

Postgate, R. W. *The Bolshevik Theory* (London, 1920).

—— *Karl Marx* (London, 1933).

Price, M. Philips. *Socialism as a Science* (Gloucester, n.d. [1924]).

Quelch, Harry. *Literary Remains,* ed. with a biographical introduction by Ernest Belfort Bax (London, 1914).

Report of the British Labour Delegation to Russia [Labour Party] (London, 1920).

Rothstein, Theodore. *From Chartism to Labourism. Historical Sketches of the English Working Class Movement* (London, 1929).

Russell, Bertrand. *Roads to Freedom. Socialism, Anarchism and Syndicalism* (London, 1918).

—— *The Practice and Theory of Bolshevism* (London, 1920).

—— in collaboration with Dora Russell. *The Prospects of Industrial Civilisation* (London, 1923).

Salter, F. R. *Karl Marx and Modern Socialism* (London, 1921).

Snowden, Philip. *Socialism and Syndicalism* (London, 1913).

—— *Labour and the New World* (London, 1921).

Stalin, J. *Leninism,* 2 vols (London, 1928–33).

Starr, Mark. *A Worker Looks at History* (London, 1918).

—— *A Worker Looks at Economics* (London, 1925).

Tawney, R. H. *The Attack and Other Papers* (London, 1953).

Tracey, Herbert (ed.). *The Book of the Labour Party,* 3 vols. (London, 1925).

Tressell, Robert. *The Ragged Trousered Philanthropists* (London, 1914).

Trotsky, L. *Where is Britain Going?* (London, 1926).

Webb, Sidney, and Beatrice Webb. *The Decay of Capitalist Civilisation* (London, 1923).

—— *What Is This Communist Party? A Plain Statement of a Plain Case* [C.P.G.B.] (London, n.d. [1921]).

Williams, A. L. *What Is Marxism?* (London, 1933).

4. SECONDARY PUBLICATIONS

Arnot, R. P. *The Impact of the Russian Revolution in Britain* (London, 1967).

Barclay, Tom. *Memories and Medleys. The Autobiography of a Bottle Washer* (Leicester, 1934).

Barker, Bernard (ed.). *Ramsay MacDonald's Political Writings* (London, 1972).

Barker, Rodney. *Education and Politics 1900–1951. A Study of the Labour Party* (Oxford, 1972).

Barltrop, Robert. *The Monument: The Story of the Socialist Party of Great Britain* (London, 1975).

Beer, Max. *Fifty Years of International Socialism* (London, 1935).

Bell, Tom. *The British Communist Party: A Short History* (London, 1937).
—— *Pioneering Days* (London, 1941).
Braddock, Jack, and Bessie Braddock. *The Braddocks* (London, 1963).
Brennan, T., E. W. Cooney and H. Pollins. *Social Change in South-West Wales* (London, 1954).
Briggs, Asa, and John Saville (eds.). *Essays in Labour History 1886–1923* (London, 1971).
Buick, Adam. 'Joseph Dietzgen', *Radical Philosophy*, 10 (1975), 3–7.
Bulmer, M. (ed.). *Working Class Images of Society* (London, 1975).
Burrow, J. W. *Evolution and Society. A Study in Victorian Social Theory* (Cambridge, 1966).
Challinor, Raymond. *The Origins of British Bolshevism* (London, 1977).
Craig, F. W. S. *British Parliamentary Election Results 1918–1968*.
Chapman, Agatha, assisted by Rose Knight. *Wages and Salaries in United Kingdom 1920–1938* (Cambridge, 1953).
Clunie, James. *Labour is my Faith: The Autobiography of a House Painter* (Dunfermline, 1954).
Coates, David. *The Labour Party and the Struggle for Socialism* (Cambridge, 1975).
Cole, G. D. H. *A History of Socialist Thought*, vols. 4 and 5 (London, 1958 and 1960).
Connole, Nellie. *Leaven of Life: The Story of George Henry Fletcher* (London, 1961).
Corfield, A. J. *Epoch in Workers' Education. A History of the Workers' Educational Trade Union Committee* (London, 1969).
Craik, W. W. *The Central Labour College, 1900–1929. A Chapter in the History of Adult Working-Class Education* (London, 1964).
Davies, Bob. *Pages from a Worker's Life 1916–1926*, C.P.G.B. Our History series (London, 1961).
Davies, Stella. *North Country Bred* (London, 1963).
Davies, Walter Haydn. *The Right Place – The Right Time* (Llandybie, 1972).
Dictionary of Labour Biography (London, 1972–).
Diggins, John P. 'Getting Hegel Out of History: Max Eastman's Quarrel with Marxism', *American Historical Review* LXXIX (1974), 37–71.
Eastman, Max. *Love and Revolution. My Journey Through an Epoch* (New York, 1964).
Edwards, Wil Jon. *From the Valleys I Came* (London, 1956).
Emmet, Dorothy. 'Joseph Dietzgen, the Philosopher of Proletarian Logic', *Journal of Adult Education* III (1928), 26–35.
Foot, Michael. *Aneurin Bevan: A Biography*, 2 vols. (London, 1962–73).
Fox, R. M. *Smoky Crusade* (London, 1937).
Gallacher, William. *Revolt on the Clyde. An Autobiography* (London, 1936).
Glass, S. T. *The Responsible Society. The Ideas of the English Guild Socialist* (London, 1966).
Graubard, Stephen Richards. *British Labour and the Russian Revolution 1917–1924* (Cambridge, Mass., 1956).
Griffiths, James. *Pages From Memory* (London, 1969).
Groves, Reg. *The Balham Group. How British Trotskyism Began* (London, 1974).
Haldane, Charlotte. *Truth Will Out* (London, 1949).
Hardy, George. *Those Stormy Years* (London, 1956).

278 A PROLETARIAN SCIENCE

Hayward, F. H. and E. M. White. *The Last Years of a Great Educationalist* (Bungay, Suffolk, n.d. [1924]).

Hinton, James. *The Fir. t Shop Stewards' Movement* (London, 1973).

—— and Richard Hyman. *Trade Unions and Revolution: The Industrial Politics of the Early British Communist Party* (London, 1975).

Hobsbawm, E. J. 'Maurice Dobb', in C. H. Feinstein (ed.), *Socialism, Capitalism and Economic Growth. Essays Presented to Maurice Dobb* (Cambridge, 1967), pp. 1–9.

—— *Revolutionaries. Contemporary Essays* (London, 1973).

Hoggart, Richard. *The Uses of Literacy. Aspects of Working-Class Life with Special Reference to Publications and Entertainment* (London, 1957).

Holton, Bob. *British Syndicalism 1900–1914. Myths and Realities* (London, 1976).

Horner, Arthur. *Incorrigible Rebel* (London, 1960).

Hutt, Allen. *The Post-War History of the British Working Class* (London, 1937).

Jackson, T. A. *Solo Trumpet. Some Memories of Socialist Agitation and Propaganda* (London, 1953).

Jones, Jack. *Unfinished Journey* (London, 1937).

Joravsky, David. *The Evolution of Dialectical Materialism. A Philosophical and Sociological Analysis* (New York, 1967).

Kendall, Walter. *The Revolutionary Movement in Britain 1900–1921. The Origins of British Communism* (London, 1969).

Klugmann, James. *History of the Communist Party of Great Britain*, 2 vols. (London, 1968–9).

Lansbury, George. *My Life* (London, 1928).

Lawson, Jack. *A Man's Life*, 2nd edn (London, 1944).

McCarthy, Margaret. *Generation in Revolt* (London, 1953).

Macfarlane, L. J. *The British Communist Party. Its Origin and Development until 1929* (London, 1966).

Macintyre, Stuart. 'Joseph Dietzgen and British Working-Class Education', *Bulletin of the Society for the Study of Labour History* 29 (1974), 50–4.

—— *Imperialism and the British Labour Movement in the 1920s*, C.P.G.B. Our History series (London, 1975).

McKibbin, Ross. *The Evolution of the Labour Party 1910–1924* (Oxford, 1974).

McShane, Harry. *No Mean Fighter* (London, 1978).

Marquand, David. *Ramsay MacDonald* (London, 1977).

Martin, Roderick. *Communism and the British Trade Unions 1924–1933. A Study of the National Minority Movement* (Oxford, 1969).

Men Without Work. A Report Made to the Pilgrim Trust (Cambridge, 1938).

Meynell, Francis. *My Lives* (London, 1971).

Miliband, Ralph. *Parliamentary Socialism. A Study in the Politics of Labour* (London, 1961).

Millar, J. P. M. *The Labour College Movement* (London, 1978).

Milton, Nan. *John Maclean* (London, 1973).

Mitchell, B. R., in collaboration with Phyllis Deane. *Abstract of British Historical Statistics* (Cambridge, 1962).

Mitchell, Hannah. *The Hard Way Up* (London, 1968).

Moore, Robert. *Pit-men, Preachers and Politics. The Effects of Methodism in a Durham Mining Community* (Cambridge, 1974).

Murphy, J. T. *New Horizons* (London, 1941).

Newton, Kenneth. *The Sociology of British Communism* (London, 1969).

Pelling, Henry. *The British Communist Party: A Historical Profile* (London, 1958).

—— *Popular Politics and Society in Late Victorian Britain* (London, 1968).

—— *A History of British Trade Unionism*, 3rd edn (Harmondsworth, 1976).

—— *A Short History of the Labour Party*, 5th edn (London, 1976).

Pierson, Stanley. *Marxism and the Origins of British Socialism. The Struggle for a New Consciousness* (Ithaca, N.Y., and London, 1973).

Pollard, Sidney. *The Development of the British Economy 1914–1967* (London, 1969).

Pollitt, Harry. *Serving My Time: An Apprenticeship to Politics* (London, 1940).

Pribiçevic, *The Shop Stewards' Movement and Workers' Control. 1910–1922* (Oxford, 1959).

Price, M. Philips. *My Three Revolutions* (London, 1969).

Redfern, Percy. *Journey to Understanding* (London, 1946).

Roberts, Robert. *A Ragged Schooling* (Manchester, 1976).

Saville, John. 'The Ideology of Labourism' in Robert Benewick et al. (eds.), *Knowledge and Belief in Politics. The Problem of Ideology* (London, 1973, pp. 213–26.

Skelley, Jeffrey (ed.). *The General Strike, 1926* (London, 1976).

Skidelsky, Robert. *Politicians and the Slump. The Labour Government of 1929–1931* (London, 1967).

Snowden, Philip Viscount. *An Autobiography*, 2 vols. (London, 1934).

Stewart, Bob. *Breaking the Fetters. The Memoirs of Bob Stewart* (London, 1967).

Thompson, Edward. *William Morris. Romantic to Revolutionary*, 2nd edn (London, 1977).

Thompson, Paul. *Socialists, Liberals and Labour. The Struggle for London 1885–1914* (London, 1967).

Tsuzuki, Chushichi. *H. M. Hyndman and British Socialism* (Oxford, 1961).

Ulam, Adam B. *Philosophical Origins of British Socialism* (Cambridge, Mass., 1951).

Utley, Freda. *Lost Illusion* (London, 1949).

Watkins, Harold. *Unusual Students* (Liverpool, 1947).

Westergaard, John, and Henrietta Resler. *Class in a Capitalist Society. A Study of Contemporary Britain* (Harmondsworth, 1975).

Winter, J. M. *Socialism and the Challenge of War. Ideas and Politics in Britain 1912–1918* (London, 1974).

Wood, Neal. *Communism and British Intellectuals* (London, 1959).

Yeo, Stephen. 'A Phase in the Social History of Socialism, c.1885–1895', *Bulletin of the Society for the Study of Labour History* 22 (1971), 6–8.

—— 'A New Life: The Religion of Socialism in Britain, 1883–1896', *History Workshop*, 4 (Autumn 1977), 5–56.

Yorke, Paul. *Education and the Working Class. Ruskin College 1889–1909* (Oxford, 1977).

5. UNPUBLISHED THESES

Armbruster, G. H. 'The Social Determination of Ideologies. Being a Study of a Welsh Mining Community', Ph.D. thesis (London, 1940).

Barrow, L. J. W. 'The Socialism of Robert Blatchford and the *Clarion*, 1889–1918', Ph.D. thesis (London, 1975).

Chewter, D. M. 'The History of the Socialist Labour Party of Great Britain from 1902–1921, with Special Reference to the Development of its Ideas', B.Litt. thesis (Oxford, 1965).

Frow, Ruth. 'Independent Working Class Education with Particular Reference to South Lancashire, 1909–1930', M.Ed. thesis (Manchester, 1968).

Hamilton, Ian W. 'Education for Revolution: the Plebs League and Labour College Movement, 1908–1921', M.A. thesis (Warwick, 1972).

Jacques, Martin. 'The Emergence of "Responsible" Trade Unionism. A Study of the "New Direction" in T.U.C. Policy, 1926–1935', Ph.D. thesis (Cambridge, 1976).

Jones, Lucia. 'Sylvia Pankhurst and the Workers' Socialist Federation – the Red Twilight, 1918–1924', M.A. thesis (Warwick, 1972).

Macintyre, Stuart. 'Marxism in Britain, 1917–1933', Ph.D. thesis (Cambridge, 1975).

McLean, Iain. 'The Labour Movement in Clydeside Politics, 1914–1922', Ph.D. thesis (Oxford, 1971).

Smith, David. 'The Re-Building of the South Wales Miners' Federation, 1927–1939: A Trade Union in its Society', Ph.D. thesis (Swansea, 1976).

Vernon, Helen R. 'The Socialist Labour Party and the Working Class Movement on the Clyde, 1903–1921', M.Phil. thesis (Leeds, 1967).

Woodhouse, M. G. 'Rank-and-file Movements amongst the miners of South Wales, 1910–1926', D.Phil. thesis (Oxford, 1970).

Index

Ablett, Noah, 39, 74, 77, 81; on economics, 147–8, 150–1, 153
Aldred, Guy, 196
Anderson, Alex, 73
Anderson, Tom, 87–8
Angell, Norman, 64, 222
Anti-Parliamentary Communist Federation, 196
Arnot, Robin Page, 21, 51, 93, 183
Ashcroft, Thomas, 85
Attlee, Clement, 64
autodidacts, 38–9, 69–73, 94–105, 108–9, 125–6, 150–1; decline, 98–105, 137–8, 145, 238–9
Aveling, Edward, 105, 147

Backhouse, Jack, 86
Baritz, Moses, 73
Batten, Rex, 130
Bax, Ernest Belfort, 50, 111, 127
Bebel, August, 67, 105
Beer, Max, 68, 110, 128, 153
Bell, Thomas, 68, 233, 239; educational activities, 72–3, 86, 98; secularism, 108
Bernal, J. D., 94, 124, 133
Bernstein, Edward, 67, 115, 157
Bevan, Aneurin, 54
Bevin, Ernest, 14, 62, 213
Blatchford, Robert, 107–8, 167, 198
Bogdanov, A., 69, 151
Böhm-Bawert, E. von, 67, 152–4
Bolshevik theory, 33–4, 96–7, 114, 120, 132, 141–6, 158; see also Bukharin; Communist International; Lenin; Leninism; Russian Revolution; Soviet Union
Boudin, Louis, 68, 147, 153, 157
Braddock, Bessie, 36, 102
Braddock, Jack, 36
Brailsford, H. N., 64, 225; on economics, 163, 165, 167–8; on imperialism, 211; on the state, 180, 185
British Socialist Party, 17–20, 23–4, 192, 231; educational activities, 72–3;

Lenin's contact with, 229–30; on the state, 178, 194; see also Social Democratic Federation
Brockway, Fenner, 64, 180, 187, 223, 225
Building Trades Workers, National Union of: see under trade unions
Bukharin, Nikolai, 69, 141–3, 145, 148, 153, 227

Cahn, Herman, 158
Campbell, J. R., 29, 98, 195, 238
Carlyle, Thomas, 50, 71, 106
Carpenter, Edward, 50
Carritt, E. F., 140
Casey, Fred, 77, 134–8
Citrine, Walter, 14
Clark, Tom, 20
Clarke, John S., 100, 119
class consciousness, retardation of, 65–7; ignorance, 56–7; labour aristocracy, 208–11; by Labour Party, 211–13; by organs of public opinion, 121–2, 198–202; and theoretical practice, 213–17; workers' fault, 202–8
class, Marxist theory of, 172–4
Clay, Henry, 89–90
Clodd, Edward, 107
Clynes, J. R., 165, 201
Cole, G. D. H., on British labour movement, 2, 224; changes attitude to Marxism, 94; on dialectic, 128; on economics, 163, 166–7; on historical materialism, 110; on the state, 181–4, 186–7, 194
Communist International, 29–30, 33, 63, 155, 196, 210, 213, 232; and British conditions, 229–32; educational activities, 82, 86; theoretical authority, 95–6, 227–8; see also Bolshevik theory; Bukharin; Lenin, Russian Revolution; Soviet Union; Stalin
Communist Party of Great Britain; 'Class Against Class', 29–30, 213, 215–17; on dialectic, 132–4, 136–7, 144–6;